[signature]

Santiago IL.
Oct~ 1590

GLOBAL CASH MANAGEMENT

GLOBAL CASH MANAGEMENT

Louis J. Celi
Managing Director and Senior Vice President
Business International Corporation

Barry Rutizer
Vice President and Director
Global Financial Services
Business International Corporation

 HarperBusiness
A Division of HarperCollinsPublishers

Library of Congress Cataloging-in-Publication Data

Celi, Louis J.
    Global cash management / Louis J. Celi, Barry Rutizer.
      p. cm.
    ISBN 0–88730–468–0
    1. Cash management. 2. International business enterprises. I. Rutizer, Barry. II. Title.
HG4028.C45C45 1991
658.15′244—dc20   90–27091
                                                         CIP

International Standard Book Number: 0–88730–468–0

Library of Congress Catalog Card Number: 90–27091

Printed in the United States of America

90 91 92 93 CC/CW 9 8 7 6 5 4 3 2 1

Preface

This unique book is designed for international corporations seeking practical information on how to cut financial costs through improved intracountry and cross-border cash management. Written as a do-it-yourself guide, it will provide your company with an action plan for fine-tuning all aspects of your current cash management system, including cash reporting, domestic credit and collection, payables management, bank relations, short-term investment and borrowing, international collections and funds transfers, and cross-border cash management techniques and vehicles.

The book is a low-cost alternative to contracting with an outside consultant to conduct a cash management study of your firm's operations. Each chapter provides all you need to know to conduct your own internal cash management study, with step-by-step details on how to evaluate the effectiveness of your current cash management system and how to calculate the cost savings from applying the latest techniques. Most important, the book presents valuable recommendations on how to optimize internal funds and minimize financial costs, supported by numerous examples of successful cash management strategies and how-to checklists based on current corporate practices and consultants' advice.

This book is also valuable to companies that are trying to decide whether to contract with an outside consultant to review their cash management system. Its practical information will help you assess whether your company would actually benefit from a cash management review and gives you pointers on how to find and work with a qualified consultant. By reading the book, you will also be better able to identify the scope and problem areas that should be covered in the consulting study and thus make sure you get a study tailored to your company's needs. Finally, the book presents hundreds of innovative cash management ideas that you will want to discuss with your consultant or apply now on your own.

The book represents years of research conducted by Louis J. Celi, managing director of Business International (BI) Americas, and Barry Rutizer, vice president of global financial services at BI. The objective of the research was to identify the state of the art in international cash management and the most innovative and successful corporate strategies to manage in-country and cross-border cash flows. Its insights and practical know-how were gained through hundreds of on-site interviews, peer group interchanges, and questionnaire surveys conducted by BI cash management specialists in Europe, Latin America, the Asia/Pacific area, and North America.

As part of its massive research effort, BI studied multinational corporations at the parent, regional, and local levels; investigated the operation of international banks and local branches; and questioned acknowledged cash management experts from accounting firms, banks, computer service companies, and private consulting firms. BI also collected in-depth cash management audits and feasibility studies conducted by corporations, banks, and treasury consultants. Where possible, practical information was culled from these reports and incorporated into the how-to sections of the book.

The project team includes Louis J. Celi, project director and editor; Barry Rutizer, research manager and project contributor; Michael Williams and Bill Millar, project contributors and research associates; and I. James Czechowitz, Dan Armstrong, and Cathy Lazere, contributing editors.

We would also like to give special thanks to Andy Kerr, vice president, Citibank; Peter Warr, vice president, Chase Manhattan Bank; Hal Davis, consultant, Globecon; Robert Long, assistant vice president, and Stephanie T. Johnson, marketing officer, Philadelphia National Bank (especially for their substantial contributions to the chapter on export collections); and Joseph Saturnia and Henry Moyal, vice president and director, respectively, of cash management consulting, American Express Co. Without their kind support, this book would not have been possible.

Contents

4 Improving Export Collections   **145**

5 Paying Attention to Payables   **193**

Contents

GLOBAL CASH MANAGEMENT

1

Assessing Your Global Cash Management System

Over the past decade, massive corporate restructuring, new developments in financial information and technology, and intense banking competition have dramatically reshaped global cash management systems and strategies. In the 1990s, the profound structural changes taking place in the world's business and financial environments are certain to make cash management a top priority of all firms hoping to be competitive and profitable.

The growing importance of cash management to multinational corporations is the result of three key trends:

(1) **Globalization of business and financial markets.** Corporate business strategies now being implemented to meet the challenge of global competition—including mergers and acquisitions (M&A), cost controls, and new sourcing patterns—are forcing firms to redesign cash management systems throughout the world. At the same time, deregulation of trade and financial flows is making it easier than ever before to concentrate and manage cash effectively.

(2) **Rapid advances in computer and telecommunications technologies.** Companies are capitalizing on new computer hardware and software by installing integrated domestic and cross-border management information systems (MIS) that greatly simplify the task of managing cash on a global basis. These sophisticated corporate MIS systems are spurring banks to create a new breed of electronic services, from balance reporting and transaction initiation to electronic data interchange (EDI).

(3) **Significant changes within the international financial services industry.** The deregulation of global financial markets is causing fierce domestic and foreign competition, as well as thinner margins for banks and other providers of financial services. As a result, firms are better able than ever to obtain the services they need to manage cash efficiently—and at a very reasonable cost.

Boosting the Bottom Line

Companies that conduct thorough reviews of their cash management systems in specific country environments frequently meet with stunning success: One U.S. financial services company expects to save over US$7 million in Canada alone as a result of a recent evaluation of its cash management procedures in that country. A U.S. high-technology company, which conducts intracountry cash management studies around the world, estimates that it saves about 1 percent of each of its subsidiaries' sales. The company's European regional director elaborated: "It's a function of how poorly you were managing the cash before and of what kinds of markets and opportunities you have to manage cash better. As an example, we estimate that in Spain we will have a net savings of about $350,000 in a subsidiary that is probably in our bottom third in terms of size. It's not one of our big financial centers. Its sales are in the $40 to $50 million range."

The cost savings of introducing cross-border systems—such as multilateral netting centers, cash pooling operations, or reinvoicing companies—are equally impressive. One U.S. consumer goods company is now generating profits of $2 million each year, thanks to its new Geneva-based finance company, which pools the group's excess cash, makes intracompany loans, and handles currency management. The company also enjoys sizable benefits from concentrating its profits in Switzerland's low-tax environment. A U.S. high-tech firm is generating similar profits from its recently installed in-house factoring company in Geneva. According to its profit and loss (P&L) statement, the Swiss company showed net profits last year of $600,000 from factoring operations, $750,000 in reduced forex losses, $150,000 in lower funds-transfer costs, and $333,000 in decreased borrowing expenses.

But cutting costs is not the only reason to improve cash management. Many companies turn to the latest cash management tools as a way to improve managerial control and decision making. The deputy finance manager of a leading Italian firm describes his managerial problems before he established a cash management system: "We were split into forty subsidiaries and had forty different financial managers. Can you imagine the problems we had? Finance was not seen as an important function then, so the financial managers were really accountants given the responsibility of managing cash and bank relations. We realized we were throwing enormous amounts of money out the window from bad cash management." To remedy the situation, the firm established an offshore netting and reinvoicing operation. "We concentrated the whole of our exposure and liquidity in a central place, and we have the facilities and the trained people to manage the position. Before, we would have had to train cash managers in every location. This is much easier."

The treasurer of a Belgian chemicals company described more dramatically the managerial benefits of cash management: "We've learned that the subsidiaries don't know what they are doing. They're all running around on their own, destroying the natural equilibrium of the group as a whole." The firm is now trying to centralize cash and currency management at headquarters "so that we can manage things more efficiently."

In fact, some companies believe that discipline and control alone may sometimes justify the costs of using a new cash management tool. Said the treasurer of a major U.S. producer of consumer goods: "We have a netting system. It isn't justifiable on a strict cost/benefit analysis—it costs us more to maintain than the savings it generates. However, I wouldn't consider eliminating it. It has brought order and control into our intracompany trade. It also gives us a lot of information for our exposure management and reporting needs."

Look Before You Leap

Although new cash management systems offer a variety of advantages, they may also expose companies to unexpected problems:

· **Organizational disruptions.** Despite the cost and qualitative benefits for the company as a whole, parent and regional headquarters introducing a cash management system may meet with serious resistance from local financial managers. For example, a leading U.S. food and beverages company is currently postponing the development of a treasury vehicle because of subsidiaries' opposition. Lamented the assistant treasurer: "Our initial look indicates that we could generate large savings and improve efficiency in managing currency exposure by setting up some kind of centralized vehicle, such as a reinvoicing or factoring company in Europe. However, the subsidiary managers don't want it. Eventually we may go that way, but today the company just isn't ready. The operating managers are wary of any movements toward greater centralization."

Another company, a diversified German conglomerate, is in the process of establishing an international cash management system but is getting bogged down because of organizational problems. First, the group consists of subsidiaries in unrelated industries. "We have trading companies, manufacturing companies, and a bank all under one roof," said the spokesman. "It is nearly impossible to come up with a system that can tie all their requirements together." Second, the firm has followed a policy of total decentralization for over 100 years, leading to an organizational morass so complex that "it is confusing to us, too. It's hard to remember who reports to whom and where."

The firm is now trying to set up cash-pooling operations among the group's oil and chemical producers, coordinated by their trading companies in New York and London, and a domestic pooling center in Germany. It has met with only partial success. The subsidiaries, accustomed to independence, often ignore the system or send in cash too late. "If we knew that we needed money in London," the finance director complained, "or that we were short dollars in New York and long in Germany, we could just match the positions. But we can't. The information, the control, is just not there." Adding insult to injury, some subsidiaries simply refuse to give up their cash. "This morning, there was a German subsidiary that had Dm10 million in surplus. We needed the funds and offered to pay interest. But bank rates happened to be very high, and we could not match them, so it was a struggle to convince the sub. Eventually we compromised, but it shows how difficult it can be to keep money within the group."

· **Long developmental process.** Reviewing an existing cash management system and implementing changes can be very time-consuming—taking months, if not years, to complete. Not only will the mechanics of the system have to be assessed, but the company will have to familiarize itself with government restrictions and be prepared to negotiate with local authorities. As one treasurer said, "Our managerial resources are limited. We have to determine if we should invest their time in cash management or in some other area that may have a higher return. We certainly don't have the time to conduct a detailed study on our own. Even if we use outside consultants, a senior executive will have to work with them, and then we will be responsible for implementing their recommendations. All that takes time, and we're stretched thin as it is. We don't see it as a priority."

· **High start-up and administrative costs.** Conducting cash management studies can also be very costly; consultants can charge from $30,000 to over $100,000 for each review. Implementing sophisticated vehicles, such as reinvoicing and factoring companies, may be even more expensive: One company told BI that its offshore finance company cost $2 million to set up and run in its first year. If you are not confident that the benefits of a new cash management system will exceed the costs, you should think twice before conducting a major review.

Telltale Signs That Your System Is in Trouble

While it is impossible to identify all the indicators that reveal that a system is in trouble or needs improvement, companies should look for key signs. If you answer no to one or more of these questions, your company may be able to benefit from improving its cash management system.

(1) **Does your firm have a policy manual on cash management?** If so, have you reviewed it recently? Companies should have a policy manual that clearly defines cash management procedures and that can be adapted to local environments. The manual should be updated regularly to take into account changing financial conditions. As one cash management consultant suggested, a firm should ask itself four questions: When was the last time the policy manual was revised? When was the last time I looked at it? Have any of my subs ever looked at it? Should they look at it? Unfamiliarity with the company's policy manual may be one of the first warning signs that things are amiss. Manuals can be filled with absurd errors costing your firm thousands of dollars. For example, one company found that its policy manual was written in U.S. dollar terms but didn't have U.S. dollar signs. The manual was sent down to Brazil stating very clearly that any sale over 10,000 needs the approval of the general manager. A young treasurer who wanted to do the right thing requested approval on a sale involving over 10,000 cruzeiros—the equivalent of less than US$5. Said a cash management consultant, tongue in cheek: "If you want to be very cynical, take a ruler and measure the dust on top of the policy manual."

(2) **Does the finance staff work closely with other departments to solve cash management problems?** "When is the last time finance sat down with the marketing people and talked about sales incentives and their financial impact?" asked a cash management consultant. He added: "We have an interesting time when we work with companies in the collection area. Very often we'll question certain credit practices, and they'll say, 'We have to do it for marketing purposes.' And we'll say, 'Yes, but is that still the situation? Or is this something that's been allowed to linger?' As a warning sign, the fact that there is no coordination means that there have to be savings you can find."

All too often, companies also suffer from little interplay between finance and the purchasing department. For instance, finance should periodically review the discounts taken by purchasing for early payment to see if they are justified from a cash management point of view. Remarked one cash management consultant: " 'Two 10 net 30' is something every first-year accounting student learns. Now, the books were written in 1965; because they're great textbooks, they're still around, and they still say 'two 10 net 30.' But for a time between 1979 and 1982, 2 percent didn't mean a whole lot. It means a bit more now, but is it really appropriate? What is the cost of a 2 percent discount? If I pay ten days earlier, what is the cost of that? Has anyone calculated the cost to the company?"

(3) **Does your reporting system give you adequate detail on worldwide cash flows and the performance of local cash managers?** Do you sometimes feel like the CFO who remarked in frustration, "I don't know whether our international cash management system is any good. I wouldn't know where to start to look for problems. The reason is that we don't have a good reporting system—that's really my biggest problem. I just don't know what is going on."

Odds are that if your reporting is unreliable, so is your overall cash management system. Said a cash management consultant: "Most companies will say, 'We get telexes every month on balance sheet items.' You push them a bit, and they say, 'To be honest, we ask for the same information from everyone, but we don't get it.' " He adds, "We send out a questionnaire before we do a study for two reasons: one, to try to gather some information to help us focus our time when we're working on-site with a client; two, to see just what level of detail the company has. Will they fill out the whole questionnaire? If they can't because they don't have or can't find the information, it tells us that it's going to be a long study."

Equally important, does your tracking mechanism identify days sales outstanding, days payables outstanding, and other key cash management measures? Beyond that, do you know how your performance stacks up against industry and country standards?

(4) **Is your forecasting system accurate?** As the treasurer of one U.S. consumer goods producer said, "Cash forecasts are the most important tool for monitoring and

What Kinds of Companies Benefit Most from Improved Cash Management

Everybody knows that companies showing losses can prop up their bottom lines through better cash management. But curiously, profitable companies may gain the most from a refined cash management system. A cash management consultant explained: "A firm that's losing money has tried everything, legal and not so legal, to get the money in and delay the money going out. There are still big gains to be made, but if the company is profitable, its attitude will be, 'If it's not broken, don't fix it.' " The treasurer of a very successful computer company confirmed this assessment: "We probably aren't doing everything we should. But why should I spend my time looking for a possible savings of only a few hundred thousand dollars? It would make my job much more difficult, and top management wouldn't care. Perhaps if our profits drop, we'll look into some cash management reviews."

Decentralized companies—particularly those that have recently grown through acquisitions—are also good candidates for cash management studies. The reason: These companies can usually achieve significant savings by taking advantage of the synergies gained by borrowing, investing, trading currencies, and handling other cash

controlling corporate cash." Any foul-ups in cash forecasting will automatically lead to needless borrowings, dangerous currency exposures, surplus bank balances, missed investment opportunities, and a host of other cash flow snafus. To check the accuracy of your cash forecasts, you should compare them with your actual cash positions. If you find wide variances, then you probably will benefit from a cash management overhaul.

Be sure your cash management strategies take advantage of improved cash-forecasting procedures. A cash management consultant admonished: "A company might say, 'Our policy has always been to invest overnight, because we were never certain we could forecast. Now our forecasts have become better, so we can probably invest for seven to ten days. But we still invest overnight.' So you need to do little audits from time to time just to stay abreast of the times yourself."

(5) Do you know how many bank accounts you have and why you have them? "This is the first question you should ask because it can generate the largest savings," advised a cash management consultant. He added, "It's amazing how many times we work with clients and they say, 'Here's a list of fifty banks.'

" 'Do you work with all of them?' we ask.

" 'Well, not really, maybe twenty.'

" 'How do you deal with each one?'

" 'Well, a little of this, a little of that.'

management chores from a central point. The assistant treasurer of a U.K. natural resources firm drove this point home: "You need to centralize because there are so many economies of scale to be had. Take borrowings. You might have one subsidiary with excess cash and another out borrowing. Why not take it from one and give to the other? On top of that, the group can raise money more cheaply than any local operation by doing a swap or a Eurobond. When you look at a subsidiary that is borrowing above group rates, you realize that a lot of money is being lost."

Decentralized firms also lose money because of high currency and funds-transfer costs. For example, a decentralized Dutch firm has recently taken a close look at its worldwide exposure. According to the treasurer: "It's been an eye-opener to see exactly what's going on. I rang up Belgium to confirm that they had Bfr20 million in the bank. They called back later to say that only 10 million was in Belgian francs; the rest was in deutsche marks, dollars, etc. And meanwhile, some other subsidiary was buying those currencies. When you add it all up, we're wasting a lot of money on conversions and exposing ourselves needlessly."

A cash management consultant summed it up: "Any company that's really decentralized is probably going to benefit. The odds are that things are not going well."

"Bank relationships are usually developed from specific credit needs or specific transactions that have to be done. Or you develop a personal relationship with a banker—after three years of lunches, you'll open a small account and it sits there, and the balances sit there. We've worked with many major multinationals that say, 'We have 170 banks in the United States.' If they feel, for political or marketing reasons, that they need to have that many banks, fine. You can take that as almost a given. But it still begs the question: Which are your important banks? Why? What do you do with them? More important, how do you determine where you will direct certain business? If a company does not have a policy of reviewing its banking relationships once a year, there are probably gains to be made in doing so."

Should You Do It on Your Own or Use a Consultant?

Once a company decides to review its system, it must determine whether to do so on its own or to hire a consultant. To make this decision, you should ask yourself the following five questions:

(1) **Do you have the in-house expertise to conduct a cash management study?** A cash management study involves not only in-depth knowledge of the latest cash management strategies but also intimate familiarity with the environments under

Conducting In-House Cash Management Studies: Two Corporate Approaches

One company that has turned conducting internal cash management studies into a science is Company A, a well-known U.S. services company. Convinced of the value of good cash management, this firm employs an internal staff of several treasury specialists who work full time reviewing the company's cash management system in the United States and abroad. Said the firm's vice president of cash management: "Usually, I have it broken down into teams of two, and I go out with them the first time. We thought about tearing down the teams, but they are more effective—you can bounce ideas back and forth."

The vice president meets regularly with the research team to monitor their progress. "We will meet throughout the study," he said. "For instance, we're coming to the critical stage of a study now, and every day at 2:00 they go over their accomplishments with me and get my views and suggestions. I want to see the portion that is the current system. I want to see their proposed recommendations. I'm editing the write-ups, and I want to see the final write-up. I'll sign off on the final draft."

He calculates that his department can potentially save the firm "tens of millions of dollars." Better yet, by using internal staff familiar with the company rather than relying on outside consultants, the firm can save time and obtain more realistic and tailored recommendations. The group has been very successful. A recent full-scale study of its Canadian system, which took about six months to complete, is expected to save over $7 million per year.

Company B, a U.S. high-tech firm, has developed its own unique approach, which taps the expertise of in-house specialists located at regional headquarters in Switzerland and parent headquarters in the United States to conduct cash management

examination—including local banking systems and services, financial regulations, tax rules, and country-specific cash management techniques. This expertise is best gained through experience. As a cash management consultant said: "We deal with dozens of companies in over forty countries, and we have found in the process that a recommendation we made for an advertising company in Brazil can be used by a heavy equipment manufacturer in Australia. A company doing a review may not have access to that kind of broad information. The person undertaking the study must also know the procedures for reviewing a system. For example, if the company's records are inadequate, the auditor will have to know how to re-create them. He may have to send out a representative sample of checks and monitor their float. If the company does not have this expertise, it must turn to a consultant."

The European regional treasurer of a U.S. photographic equipment maker concurred: "It's nice to use your own staff as much as possible, but there is no question that consultants have advantages. We know—or we think we know—taxation and

studies. The European finance director explained the mechanics of his do-it-yourself approach:

"One of the services our treasury people in Geneva provide is performing cash management reviews. They have the experience of going into country organizations and looking at how they manage their cash. Because different vehicles are available in each country, they have to come up with a program to match the needs of the country."

The company conducts these studies periodically by country. The spokesman commented: "We operate in about sixteen countries, so we don't cover them all at one time because the studies do take quite a bit of time. We just recently finished one in Spain. These are full-blown studies. We go through everything—their investing, their cash, what kind of returns they're getting on it, how they're managing their intracompany accounts, and so forth. We do these on a one-time basis, and then probably in three or four years we'll be going back to the same country to do it again. But we also have treasury people in each of these country organizations; once the study is completed, they take over from there and implement its results. These studies probably involve one person for about six weeks to do all the research and to do the write-up."

Local managers generally are pleased with these in-house studies, since they have input into the findings. Said the finance director: "These things are worked up with their participation. They're involved in the process, so they don't have any surprises that show up on the study. I suspect that 90 to 95 percent of what is suggested is implemented." The treasury staff follows up on all the studies by meeting with local financial managers and reviewing the changes that were made based on the consulting report and the interest savings or income generated. In general, the firm calculates that it saves almost 1 percent of annual sales for each subsidiary review.

---

foreign exchange, but when it comes to cash management in several countries or across borders, they know more. They also have a better overview of what other companies are doing and what the banks have to offer us." A Swiss finance director adds that outside consultants offer fresh insights. "We of course are convinced we are doing the best thing, but we don't really know for sure. We are a bit isolated and need the latest ideas in cash management."

Companies looking to save money may want to bring in a consultant for the first study and then use what they have learned to handle follow-up reviews. The head of international cash management consulting at one bank elaborated: "The trend we see is to have our bank brought in to look at one or two big companies in big countries and to have a member of the corporate staff go with us and learn how to do it. We're training him to be a consultant." Added the finance director of a major Swedish firm: "We learned so much from our past studies that our level of expertise has increased tremendously. We just don't see the big problems that we had before, and we don't need new studies."

Fortunately for consultants, many companies cannot afford to hone their cash management skills in-house. As a cash management consultant explained, "Very often we find that they could do it, but they have head count constraints. They can't hire a junior assistant and say, 'We're going to fly you around the world for two years; study all this, and at the end of it you're going to be one great cash manager.' But they can always get a project approved and hire a consultant."

Companies may reap some benefits simply by taking the recommendations of one country study and distributing them to other subsidiaries. "From a company's standpoint, if I make a savings of $400,000 from one study, I may be better off sending my list of recommendations to other treasurers and asking if they'd looked at these areas. They will probably find the same problems in the same areas—credit and collection, discount terms, etc.," remarked one cash management consultant.

But some companies prefer to do it themselves, as the chief financial officer of a diversified French company pointed out: "Any company that keeps going to the banks for help will never know how to run its own treasury functions. If you don't understand how to solve problems and build systems, how can you hope to manage your cash effectively and to make improvements when new situations arise?" A U.K. treasurer echoed these sentiments: "My intention is for our staff to develop competence in cash management. Once we develop internal expertise, it is an ongoing thing that will improve the performance of the company for years to come." (See box on pp. 8–9 for detailed examples of how two companies use internal staff to conduct cash management studies.)

(2) **Do you have the time to spend on a cash management study?** A cash management review can be a tedious process. According to a seasoned cash management consultant, "A standard intracountry study for us would take three people who will spend ten days on-site averaging fourteen to eighteen hours per day, and an additional ten man-days back here refining the analysis. That includes the writing. So, if you're one person, you're talking up to three months of eight-hour days. If the company's records are in shambles, we work eighteen-hour days instead of twelve."

Of course, a cash management audit need not be so extensive. Many firms simply send a treasury manager for a quick review. Explained a cash manager of a leading consumer goods producer: "I fly in for a few days and look over what they are doing. I discuss their procedures with the local treasurer. I bring up approaches that have been used successfully in other countries and discuss the merits of using them in this country. It's not as thorough as what the banks might do, but I believe in the 80/20 rule [80 percent of the savings will result from 20 percent of the changes]. I'm sure that we capture most of the benefits from this brief review."

(3) **Do you want to incur the cost of a study by an outside consultant?** Proprietary cash management studies can be exorbitantly expensive—ranging from $30,000 for a small intracountry review to hundreds of thousands of dollars for a full-blown study of global operations. According to the finance director of a Belgian chemicals company, "We talked with the banks and other consulting companies that could give

us information, but it is always very expensive. So we thought, 'All right, for that price we can make it on our own.' " The finance director of a German chemicals firm drew the same conclusion after receiving bids on a consulting job: "I could not justify the cost. I couldn't find anything in the proposals to make it worthwhile to pay such high fees for just general advice."

To avoid paying out high fees for studies that may not provide concrete results, some firms are negotiating contracts with private consultants whereby fees are tied to the actual savings generated by the study. For instance, a Swedish capital goods producer used this pricing approach on several intracountry studies conducted by a U.S. bank. According to the firm's treasurer, "They charged us a small fee plus a certain percentage of the savings we made from implementing their recommendations. In the end, I think we wound up paying more money, but at least we knew we got good value."

(4) **Can you be objective in your assessment of subsidiary operations?** It can be difficult for the patient to cure himself. If in-house staff members are not objective, the study will reflect their bias. This is one argument in favor of using an outside consultant. As a consultant remarked, "We don't have any ax to grind; we're not on any witch hunt to find skeletons in the closet; we're not encumbered by 'This is the way it's always been done' or 'This is the standard practice in the industry.' We don't operate within that. We always say, 'I don't care, could you be doing something different?' "

Objectivity is the main reason a giant Swiss pharmaceuticals firm hires outside consultants for cash management studies: "It is very delicate when you, as a representative of the parent company, go to the subsidiaries and look into their books. They don't like it when you say, 'Here you made a mistake' and 'Here your duty is not fulfilled correctly.' When you go with an external expert, they more easily accept his advice and knowledge."

A Swedish finance director felt the same way: "The local managers would never go along with the idea of someone coming from the head office and trying to meddle in local affairs. They trust outside consultants more." And the treasurer of a U.S. consumer goods firm put it in more Machiavellian terms: "Our subsidiary managers would oppose any review coming from the parent. Most of our subsidiary managers are independent and powerful enough to veto any attempt for us to come in and study their fiefdom's cash management system. So we have to turn to outside consultants."

The use of outside consultants also may be more acceptable to the administrative staff. A cash management expert explained why: "There is the fear that you will be on a headhunt. It's not always easy for the internal auditor to say to the clerk, 'I want you to tell me how you process this piece of paper; it will not affect your relationship with your supervisor.' I don't care how many assurances you give him; he's wondering when he is going to lose his job."

How One Company Benefits from Using Outside Cash Management Consultants

The potential cost savings and organizational impact of intracountry studies were behind the decision of Company C, a U.S. electronics firm, to contract with a bank consultancy group for in-depth audits on subsidiaries in Belgium, France, Italy, Spain, and Portugal. The purpose of the studies was to evaluate the cash management practices of subsidiaries in those countries and to determine how the systems could be improved. According to the firm's director of international finance, some of the bank's recommendations were "so commonsensical that the local managers couldn't believe they weren't already doing them." And the benefits will be visible within a year. "Even if only 50 percent of the recommendations are implemented, the studies will pay for themselves in six to nine months."

One reason that the studies revealed such great savings opportunities is the firm's decentralized structure. Said the spokesman: "When you have multidivisional, fairly autonomous setups in each country, basic treasury work is being performed by the controllers of each division or business unit. The controllers have varying degrees of knowledge about the local environment." The studies, therefore, served a dual purpose: "First, they educated the local treasury people on how their cash management systems can be improved. Second, the studies educated the treasury people on the various systems their counterparts in other units use."

Once its cash management procedures have been fully documented and improved,

---

(5) **Do you have knowledge of your firm's operations that an outside consultant lacks?** Internal staff have one key advantage over external consultants: They understand the company. Consultants can spend a third of their time just learning about your business and the way you do things. Having someone in-house would eliminate this step. "We do it ourselves because no one knows the company as well as we do. We don't have to learn the basics," remarked the director of cash management of a leading financial services company.

In fact, some companies believe it is a sign of weakness to bring in an outside consultant. For instance, when asked whether his firm ever turned to outside consultants, a German treasurer became indignant: "Absolutely not. We have the experience and the specialized knowledge to take care of our own affairs without help. We have never paid a penny for financial advice to anyone."

How to Choose a Consultant

Once you have decided to employ an outside consultant to review your cash management system, you face the most important task of all: finding the right one. This is critical because the study is only as good as the consultant. The treasurer of a U.S.

Company C plans to come up with a treasury manual for each country. The country manuals will be as similar to one another as possible while leaving room for divergent local operating conditions. In addition, a standardized corporatewide cash-forecasting system will be integrated into the country manuals, permitting more effective coordination of European treasury activities.

How did the firm persuade local managers to go along with the studies? The director of international finance found that the most important point in selling local people is to convince them that corporate headquarters is not trying to "shove something down their throats." Sensitivity on the local level also made it critical that the cash management studies be conducted by an independent bank.

Only the study on Italy has been completed so far, and it is yet to be implemented, but the representative is optimistic that foreign subsidiaries will be receptive to the change. "Initially, there was some hesitation from the local people, because there was an audit connotation that came with a cash management study," he explained. "We got over that hurdle by convincing them that it was for their benefit and it was coming out of our budget. We also told them that although we would like them to heed the recommendations, if their marketing ability would be impaired, they did not have to implement the findings."

Follow-up is also important as a means of ensuring the long-term benefits of the study. Every six months, after an action plan has been agreed upon, a member of the treasury department in New York, along with a bank consultant, will visit the subsidiary and check on its implementation progress.

---

consumer goods company learned the hard way: "We wanted to set up a factoring company. We brought in a consultant to show us how to do it. They learned more from us than we did from them. We paid them $50,000 to pick our brains." To avoid this kind of pitfall, companies should carefully assess the qualifications of consultants they plan to use. Fortunately, firms have a wide range of qualified cash management consultants from which to choose: a consultant from a bank, an accounting company, or an independent company. Companies should weigh the following considerations to make the correct choice.

Objectivity

As discussed earlier, a key reason companies turn to outside consultants is to get an objective opinion. But you need to be careful if the consultant you plan to use works for an institution that may sell cash management and related services. Asked the assistant treasurer of a medium-sized capital goods company: "If I go to an outside agency, are they going to have a vested interest in what they do for me? In other words, are they, at the end of the day, going to shade their analysis to lead into products they want to market? Or will they, hand on heart, say, 'I demand a completely independent study'?"

This is one reason some companies prefer to use consultants from management accounting firms or private companies rather than from banks. "They do a study and then tell us we need their netting system or their treasury workstation. Some of their recommendations can be self-serving," remarked a treasurer of a leading multinational firm.

The treasurer of a Swiss firm is also leery of bank consultants: "We believe that a consultant should be from a neutral institution. That's why we use management accounting firms. If we were to use a bank, it could not have an important relationship to the group. If you ask your banks to analyze your forex management and they handle your forex deals, that's a problem. The banks would find it hard to be objective, and we don't want them to know everything."

However, many bank consultants are aware of these corporate concerns and go to great lengths to preserve their objectivity. "Our job is to improve their system," said one. "We try not to push our products. But if our product will do the job, we tell them. We have to fight very hard to promote ourselves as objective."

Another bank consultant argues that concerns about bank bias are exaggerated: "For instance, a bank does a study and says, 'Clearly, you need concentration accounts somewhere, and clearly, you need to control them from an offshore location. Therefore you need electronic banking facilities; therefore you need our system.' First of all, you can stop at some point and say that's a logical conclusion from the analysis of the information. But a company can decide for itself how far it wants to go with electronic systems. Second, if it says, 'Damn it, that is what we want,' then it's a very poor company that doesn't say, 'Wait a moment; if this bank is suggesting something like that, I'm sure some other bank might have a system worth looking at as well.' "

Reputation

Although some companies question banks' objectivity, most are convinced of their ability to handle cash management studies. As a U.S. treasurer said: "In the area of cash management—and treasury management in general—the banks have an edge. They know the business inside and out and have the most expertise." A Swedish treasurer who has used domestic and foreign bank consultants for years pointed to "the broad experience of banks. They are familiar with the problems of many companies and of course know banking. It is wise to use bankers for these studies."

However, a bank consultant may not be the best qualified for all countries, as the treasurer of a Dutch equipment manufacturer explained: "In this part of the world, most of the auditing companies have management consulting divisions. Banks have not specialized in this field." When conducting intracountry cash management studies—particularly in more exotic countries—companies should make sure that the consultants they plan to use have an intimate knowledge of the local banking services and cash management techniques.

The reputation of the institution is not enough: The bottom line is the qualification of the individual consultant who will work on your project. "Some consultants in a bank are better than others. You have to size up the individual," warned an assistant treasurer of a leading consumer goods company. This is where companies have to be careful. One private consultant cautioned: "The individual may be a salesman. He'll sell the concepts and sell the bank, and then someone else comes in and does the study."

Price

Consultants usually charge on a per diem basis—roughly $1,000 per day. While a number of banks and private consultants are involved in cash management consulting, they approach it from a different direction. In some banks, consulting is a profit center, and prices are set to make profits. Other banks see cash management consulting as a service and have the flexibility to set very competitive prices for favored customers. A cash management consultant in a leading U.S. bank said, "We did a study in Switzerland for a major company. It was ludicrously underpriced—$20,000—and led to savings of $500,000 a year. You could argue, 'But that was deliberately priced low, because you wanted to establish credibility in Switzerland and with that company.' Our bank doesn't make its profit from $20,000 for a study. It makes its profit by starting a long-term relationship—foreign exchange, bank accounts, whatever. We recognize that, and we can quantify that." Companies are in a strong negotiating position with such banks.

Quality of the Proposal

Companies should go to several consultants and get a written proposal. They should then examine the proposal not only on price but also on such key issues as methodology, time, and the individuals involved. A cash management consultant advised, "Look at the methodology. Does it suit your purposes? In many cases, the game they're selling is thorough, and they're able to do the number crunching. There's more of a promise to do that than to come up with any flashes of brilliance in terms of a whole new way to approach the situation. You look to see if they are competent and their methods sound. A good consultant does the most responsible job he can of figuring what the company wants. I think a good consultant is responsible in not prescribing something greater than what the company wants. An astute consultant might see a company and say, 'Let's give it to you in doses.' And those doses can go deeper into a country, from a simple overview to an in-depth test case."

Furthermore, a good consultant should be willing to tailor the study to your needs. In judging the proposal, make sure that the consultant has a full understanding of your concerns and has geared the project to suit your firm's unique situation. Also check to see if the proposal includes details on other relevant assignments handled by the consultant and an estimate of fees and expenses broken down by each project phase.

Confidentiality

Companies should be extremely careful that information provided to the consultant is kept confidential. For this reason, corporate treasurers are sometimes queasy about giving certain banks access to the information needed for a cash management review.

As one Dutch financial manager said: "With a bank, there is a natural reluctance to really open up our books to scrutiny. It would be difficult to be candid with them."

Of course, a major fear is that a bank consultant will give the data to lending officers. Interestingly, a bank consultant felt that this and other suspicions were at times justifiable: "It's not meant to happen. But the people selling products are often the same people that are the account officers. People say consultants don't pass on their findings, but it is pretty easy to get a report to the account officer." Many banks take steps to prevent this practice, as one consultant commented: "We have set up strict rules that this information remains confidential. We will not give the data to the account officer."

Willingness to Work Closely with You

The most successful reviews are those in which corporate financial staff are closely involved. As one cash management consultant advised: "If a company can free up an individual and get him out to the field, it will benefit internally, because all the knowledge is going to be in his head as well as in the report."

Many consultants encourage this approach. As one bank consultant said: "We prefer to have someone from your organization dedicated to the project team. We may uncover something very obvious that you can correct without waiting a year for our report. If we have one of your people there, we can pick something up and get it implemented while we continue with the routine audit. That's how you benefit. We benefit by having better interaction with the company."

Of course, a bank may have a problem with this approach: It may end up training someone in the company on how to do a cash management audit and thus lose follow-up business. But banks generally look at this issue philosophically: "We say it's fine because we have no choice. We're not in the business of doing studies to make money. We do these rather in the broad scheme of things." Said another cash management consultant: "We don't like it, but if we don't do it, someone else will. At least we'll get paid for the first study."

Compatibility

Finally, you have to "click" with your consultant. As one cash management consultant remarked, "It's people. You've got to feel comfortable. That's a difficult thing to put in a document. You can't write it down. It's similar to interviewing two or three people for a job. Two or three have very much the same résumé, but one really turned you on. You were comfortable with him."

How to Develop a Strategy for Auditing Your System

Step 1: **Decide where to start.** The first step in undertaking a review of your company's cash management system is to set the scope and terms of reference. This involves two issues.

First, determine which of the seven key areas of cash management need to be reviewed: (1) cash reporting, (2) credit and collection—including export receivables, (3) payables management, (4) banking relations, (5) short-term investment, (6) short-term borrowing, and (7) cross-border cash management. Are there any related areas, such as currency management, export financing, or automated systems, that should be included in the study?

Second, which countries and subsidiaries should be covered? Should the study examine only the parent company's domestic and cross-border cash flows, or should you review intracountry cash management systems developed by local subsidiaries?

Most companies will want to focus the study on areas that need improvement in order to keep the project to a manageable size. However, firms should be careful not to narrow the focus too much. Such a study may give an incomplete or even inaccurate picture. Warned one cash management consultant: "The areas tend to overlap. You can't just look at collections without looking at the banks that they're going into, the value dating, and the cost of those collections. Collections are dependent upon three things: your internal company practices, the host of payment systems around the world, and banking systems to process those payments. So, there are three areas where things can go awry. If my company's policies are a little fuzzy, then maybe my collection policies are a little fuzzy, so maybe I'm not doing a very good job of monitoring the bank collection policies, and my credits may be a few days late. If my internal policies are good and I'm a little lax in enforcing the collection terms, then that's out of sync."

When identifying the scope of a cash management study, companies should keep in mind the areas that usually lead to the biggest savings. A cash management consultant outlined those areas: "Based on our experience, the largest savings stem from reviews of bank balances. If a multinational corporation has overseas subs that engage in a great deal of intracompany trade, the next area to look at is intracompany payments or netting systems. Potential savings there are big; by big, I mean $200,000 to $1 million. The third area would be collections. These are the areas you have to approach in any cash management audit."

Once you have targeted the cash management functions to be reviewed, you must decide which countries and subsidiaries to include in the study. Since several factors will influence this decision, a cash management consultant suggests a matrix approach: "First, look at where your largest companies are located; then look at the countries where you're likely to derive the greatest savings because of inefficient systems—banking, postal, cost of funds. Along the top of the matrix, you'd have your largest subsidiaries, in descending order of sales volume. Along the side, you'd have the countries, from high potential to low potential—high being Italy, France, Brazil, Mexico, Argentina, Venezuela, the Philippines, Japan."

Companies should also assess considerations not captured in the matrix. For example, do internal politics prevent certain subsidiaries from being examined? Do political or regulatory conditions in a particular country undermine the usefulness of a cash management system? For instance, if you can improve the profitability of your Philippine operations through better cash management but cannot get dividends out, you might give that country low priority on your review list.

Step 2: **Gather all relevant internal company information.** Once the scope of the review is set, the next step is to collect information that will give you insight into your current cash management system and financial position. The simplest way to do this is to gather existing reports and information from subsidiaries and various departments at regional and parent headquarters. The director of cash management from a well-known U.S. services company described the process he follows for collecting information for an intracountry study:

"First, we ask for as much material as we can get. We collect it very quickly, in about two weeks. We brush over it just to get some background so we can talk about a game plan. We ask for bank analyses and statements; 10Ks; audit reports; information on banking networks; copies of daily cash position sheets; organizational charts—everything we can possibly lay our hands on.

"The financial reports can reveal much about the structure of the businesses and any legal and tax constraints. They also give an idea about their ascending curve: Are they making money? Should I add another 10 to 15 percent for projected collections each year?

"We also look at marketing's five-year plan, which we study very carefully, because anything we do has to be in tune with their objectives and philosophy. It helps us identify the network we want to build. Say they have 160 district sales offices. Are they going to continue with this, are they going to cut back, are they going to expand or go to a regional concept? This has a big effect on how we build a cash management system domestically. It helps us find out whether the banking network is going to expand or contract.

"We have all the internal cash management audit reports sent to us. These are very important because they go through a lot of departments we don't go into, so before we sit down with the treasurer, we know how people handle paper and how it flows through the system.

"The bank analysis reports are important to us. We also take a look at daily cash position sheets. We chart where the flow is coming in from, where it goes out to, and when it goes out. We get a flowchart of the whole banking network."

As this example shows, companies should request and examine the following information:

(1) Annual reports and financial statements

(2) 10Ks or equivalent

(3) Organizational charts of finance, marketing, and other divisions

(4) Procedure and policy manuals

(5) Cash flow or financial diagrams

(6) Recent consulting studies on related issues

(7) Internal accounting audit information

(8) Five-year plans and budgets

(9) Job descriptions and responsibilities

(10) All reports from the cash reporting system
  (a) Liquidity (daily bank balances, cash forecasts, etc.)
  (b) Credit and collection (aging, days sales outstanding, etc.)
  (c) Payables (aging, disbursements outstanding, etc.)
  (d) Bank relations (account analyses, bank activity, etc.)
  (e) Borrowings and investments

To reduce the time spent sifting through these reports—or if many of them are unavailable—you may want to request that the local cash managers fill out forms that ask for key pieces of information. The exhibit at the end of this chapter contains forms that cash management consultants at Chase Manhattan Bank used to gather information on a company prior to on-site visits. The information can help firms learn more about the company and identify potential trouble spots. A word to the wise: If key information is not readily available, it is a sign that the company may have serious cash management problems.

Step 3: **Obtain information on cash management practices, banking systems, financial regulations, and other background.** You must tailor your cash management strategies to local conditions. Banking services, payment practices, postal systems, exchange controls, and tax regulations are just some of the things that may vary sharply from country to country. One U.S. cash manager, sent to review his company's Canadian operations, said: "I had to learn about the banking system and legal ramifications there. I had to have that knowledge to be able to go and tell them more."

To get a good working knowledge of local environments and cash management techniques, cash managers should make a thorough review of cash management articles, reports, and surveys. They should also meet with local bankers, accountants, consultants, and corporate cash managers who have local experience. Although sometimes difficult to obtain, one of the best sources of information on specific countries is cash management studies conducted for other companies. By doing their homework, consultants will not only be able to come up with better recommendations but will gain the support of local people. Explained one corporate cash manager: "You have to gain the company's confidence and project some credibility. You have to know about banking systems. Call other companies; investigate what you can. Educate yourself before you make recommendations. In one country, we had about twelve pages of questions to ask; it has to be done."

Some corporate cash managers and consultants suggest that you spend several weeks to set the scope of the study and to review internal reports and secondary sources of cash management information—that is, to complete steps 1, 2, and 3.

Step 4: **Work out a game plan with the managers involved.** Once you have background information on internal and external cash management conditions, you are ready to meet with senior and local financial management to establish a game plan for the review. For your study to succeed, senior management—and especially local managers of the subsidiary under review—must agree with your goals and procedures. They should help you decide which departments and people to visit and what areas of cash management to explore. As one consultant said: "We try to let the treasurer set the tempo: What does he want to look at? What is he looking for? We then might nudge him toward things that we've found someplace else. We spend a day and a half with the treasurer hammering out a game plan. We explain what we want to accomplish at the site, and he sets up specific appointments for us over the next week or so. When we come out, our whole week is scheduled, and we get a lot done in a short time."

A key part of the game plan is examining the organizational chart and identifying each department you need to visit and which individuals you want to see. Remarked a corporate cash manager: "We said we want to take a look at every department in which a check or cash was handled—this was on the receiving side—in relation to incoming cash. But beyond that, we'd like to see every department that's involved in receiving payment. A lot of our subs are reluctant to have anyone tie up the individual who actually records the check in the computer, so you have to work out some arrangement."

Depending on the scope of the cash management study, here are the departments that may be useful to visit: treasury, accounting and control, financial planning, marketing, purchasing, credit and collection, payables, information management (EDP), international/export, and senior management.

It is important that you visit the staff as well as the managers. A cash management consultant cautioned: "You don't want just the supervisor, because many times he tells you just what you don't care to hear. You really have to go to the unit itself and see how the checks are brought in from the mailroom, when they are brought in, and what the clerk does with them."

Step 5: **Observe the existing system on-site.** Once the interviews and game plan have been set, the next step is to do an on-site visit. Said one seasoned corporate cash manager: "We go on-site and use an old technique to find out what is going on—talking to the people involved at each step." Although this process may be time-consuming—it can take up to several weeks—it is vital to the success of your study. Remarked one cash management consultant: "Consultants are routinely accused of wasting time asking how the system operates instead of how to improve it. But we must find out how things work, and the only way to do it is to talk with people and to watch. There is no substitute for on-site visits. We would sit down with someone and ask, 'How do you handle this?' and he would say, 'Here—this is how we've always handled this.' Then we would go and look, and we would find that in reality it's not that way at all."

During the course of on-site interviews, reviewers should try to maintain an objective stance by asking neutral questions. If local managers perceive your questions as critical, they may be less candid. One experienced cash manager elaborated: "On the whole, they are honest with us. But sometimes they detect from the question that they are doing something wrong, and they try to hide it. You have to be very careful not to point a finger at a particular supervisor or clerk."

A complete on-site investigation will examine the activities of those directly and indirectly involved in the cash cycle. For example, marketing people are frequently interviewed because they set the credit terms, policies, and prices, and make other credit and collection decisions that affect incoming cash flows. (For a list of departments that you may want to visit, please refer to step 4.) You also may want to meet with local banks, computer service companies, and others whose advice you may need in improving your local cash management system.

The on-site review will include the collection and analysis of data to evaluate current cash management procedures and to support recommendations for action. This activity will often include tracing the float at each stage of the cash cycle, thereby allowing cash managers to quantify the cost savings achieved by improving the system. For example, a cash manager may elect to monitor float on the collection cycle. As part of the investigation, he will calculate the time between the sale and the receipt of the order; between receipt of the order and receipt of the invoice; between receipt of the invoice and receipt of payment; between receipt of payment and the payment's deposit in the bank; and finally, between the deposit and credit to the company's account. Conducting a float analysis can be time-consuming. Invoices and records will have to be examined over a month or more. If records are inadequate—which is frequently the case—it may be necessary to conduct a controlled test, such as sending out a representative sample of invoices and tracking their float. Some cash managers cut down the time of such a review by applying the 80/20 rule and examining only the largest customers or largest payments.

Occasionally, companies will solve cash management problems during the course of the investigation. Said one corporate cash manager: "We had someone who received only dollar checks and held them for the whole month, because the executive at the bank to which he sent them to clear had said, 'Don't send me one check at a time.' He would sit on a $50,000 check, waiting until the end of the month. By the end of the month, he'd have $150,000 in checks. When I asked why he did that, he realized that he should have pursued it with the individual, perhaps to send checks every week. We encouraged him to do so; if you have meaningful volume, get rid of it every day. And if you're not succeeding with this individual, have your boss get in touch with his boss."

Reviewers should be good listeners. The best ideas are often generated by those closest to the system. Just as important, managers are more apt to introduce a change if they believe it is their idea. According to one corporate cash manager who has worked on numerous studies: "A clerk can offer suggestions as well. You can point out that there is an alternative, even if he doesn't have the answer. Give him an insight; let him grasp it and say, 'Hey—I can do this and this.' If he feels he participated in the idea, he may pursue it more aggressively. For example, we were getting checks from customers residing in the Caribbean, maintaining dollar accounts in Panama, and we were processing them through our New York bank and the bank was saying they were not collectible checks. We can't process them through the Fed. So we had to return items and re-present them. Which was taking between three and six days. In just brainstorming with the individual responsible for that unit, he said I ought to consider that instead of depositing them, we should just hand them over to the bank on a collection basis. This is a great idea. I said, 'I think we have a subsidiary in Panama. I'll bet you could work out a relationship with them to courier the checks directly to them. What is the bank in New York charging you?' 'Fifteen dollars per check.' It was a real good meeting that we had, and I left it. I didn't pursue it with him, because I knew I had planted a seed. Three months later I went to visit with him, and he showed me what he had done. He told me, 'I have an arrangement directly with a bank and I send them the checks. I intercept them from the outset; I don't deposit them. I send them directly; it costs me $2. It is cleared within a week, and I have reduced the cost of the check.'"

Step 6: **Document the existing system.** Once the interviews are completed, the system must be documented. You should clearly describe the cash management procedures as you understand them and draw up flowcharts and organizational charts. A cash management consultant explained: "A study has to document what's there. Go into a system and find out exactly what they're doing, and go back to the treasurer and say, this is what you thought was being done, but this is what is actually being done. The hardest part is documentation of what's happening today. It's going to be the most tedious job, the most frustrating, and it's probably going to be the longest part of the study."

After you have documented how the system works, you should have the various departments involved verify the accuracy of your report. In the words of one corporate cash manager: "We flowchart essentially everything. We send it back out and ask them to verify it. We ask them, 'Is this what you really do?' Every write-up, along with the schematic, is sent back out, asking for verification from the very person we sat down with. Did we understand your job correctly? Each piece we send out, they mark it in red and send it back, and then we change it. Then you've got the verification."

Step 7: **Compare your cash management practices with local standards.** Once the documentation has been verified, the procedures should be reviewed and assessed in light of sound cash management practices and standards in the country or countries under investigation. For example, if you see it takes twelve days to process a sales order, the first thing you should ask is whether twelve days is appropriate. To answer that question, you will need to dig deeper. A cash management consultant explains: "That's when you look at your customers. I'll look at the ten largest customers and see their sales order float and invoice creation float; that will probably be dependent upon the processing of the paper. If the big customers are processed in six days and the company norm is twelve days, then the small customers are rightfully being shoved to the side to expedite the big ones. Should they accelerate? All depends. If it means I have to hire people to expedite by one day, can you do it? Will it pay?"

To improve the system, it is necessary to identify specific procedures that are out of line with local standards. A cash management consultant illustrates: "If it only takes eight days from the time the invoice goes out to the time the payment comes back, don't even worry. If it's taking fifty days, then you've got a problem. Then we look at the date of the check. If that is close to the date that it's received in the office, then you know that the delay happened before that—or you have a very shrewd treasurer who postdates his checks. If the date is two weeks before you receive it, then you've got mailroom problems or the postal system may not be the most expeditious way to go about collecting from customers. Once you get the payment in, look at how long it takes to process it and make a deposit. Then we look at the time it's deposited and the time it's credited to the account."

Current practices should be checked against standards in the country. This information is often available from local finance or industry organizations, cash management research firms (like Business International or Phoenix Hecht), banks, accounting firms, and various other institutions. If the data you seek is difficult to find, you may want to take the following advice offered by a well-known cash management consultant: "Call a fellow treasurer in a competing company and ask how long it takes over there. He may or may not answer, and the answer may or may not be right, but at least it gives you a check. Or go to a bureau that amasses statistics and compare." And if all else fails, run your own mail survey or cash management test.

Step 8: **Develop new, more effective, cash management procedures.** Once the existing system has been assessed and its weak points identified, the next step is to come up with innovative ways to improve the system. Because of the time and effort it takes to change existing procedures, the recommended modifications should lead to a significant cash savings. As one cash management consultant remarked: "We're not going to make a change just for the sake of making a change. We will change it for a number of reasons: one, to increase efficiency; two, to increase cost effectiveness; and three, to generate some cash gains for the company. We would like to change the system as little as possible."

The new procedures should be carefully considered and quantified. One cash management consultant elaborated: "We quantify the savings by doing collection models, by checking out salaries, by getting the budgets for each department that we're looking at, and so on. We bring up the dollar figure, because it will make them consider the ramifications in light of the dollars saved." Indications that there are large dollar savings may lead to follow-up studies to explore other facets of the system.

Make sure that the alternatives are feasible; do not suggest changes that make conceptual sense but are too difficult to implement. Discuss your ideas with local staff, bankers, accountants, and other knowledgeable parties to determine the viability of your new approach. Equally important, carefully consider the ramifications of recommended changes. For example, what banks will need to be added or cut? Can a system be purchased, or must it be created in-house? Will more or less manpower be needed?

Step 9: **Write up your findings and recommendations.** After you have weighed the alternatives, you should write them up and present them to senior and local financial management. A cash management consultant from a leading U.S. bank described how he does it: "We put the whole package together in a draft, send it out to the treasurer, and say, look at this; feel free to edit it and make comments. We then take his changes, incorporate them, and send the package back for a final okay."

Many companies underestimate the time it takes to write up the findings and recommendations. The process may take several weeks to several months, depending on the depth of the study. But the document must be thorough and clear if the recommendations are to be successfully implemented. Said a corporate cash manager about his experience with writing cash management reports: "One-third of your time is going to be spent looking at the current system, one-third is going to be spent developing alternate systems, and one-third of the time is spent writing up and documenting. That's where we really fell into a trap on the first study we did. I said to myself, I thought identifying the current system was going to be long, and it sure was. I thought developing alternative systems was going to be long, but I thought we'd write it up in a minute. No way! We had writes and rewrites, and it goes on and on and on—count on a third of the time putting that baby to bed. It took us six months—it's 248 pages."

Since most senior executives do not have the time to read a lengthy document, it may be necessary to give them an oral presentation of the findings. A cash management consultant describes the process: "It takes about two hours. We always have an executive summary as a talking document when we make the presentation. Everybody has a copy of the entire study. We don't go down to too deep a level. We let them talk to the people involved in the study."

Step 10: **Implement the recommendations.** This is the most important step. The best recommendations are useless if they are not implemented. Although these statements may seem obvious, a common complaint voiced by companies conducting cash management studies is that the recommended changes were never made. For example, one well-known electronics firm contracted with a U.S. bank to conduct an intracountry study of its Venezuelan subsidiary's cash management system, but none of the bank's recommendations were implemented because the local staff felt they were impractical.

Another gripe of companies that have gone outside for cash management studies is that they are given a list of recommendations and then are abandoned by the consultants. This is indeed unfortunate, since having access to cash management expertise can be of great help during the implementation stage. Said one corporate manager who handles cash management studies in-house for his firm: "Meeting with banks and other institutions is useful when you're formulating your recommendations and you don't know whether your ideas are feasible or not. So, what we did was to call up a lot of banks in that country and said, come on down and spend a day with us—we want to talk about some alternatives. Are you able to do this sort of thing? And sure enough, we were able to determine if our alternatives could be implemented. We'll meet with couriers, look at the postal system. We do more. We implement the recommendations. We recommended to the division that they hire a cash management specialist, who does nothing more than look at cash management for that division. I was instrumental in evaluating all the résumés, giving them leads and people to look at. He is now on board. He'll go out and negotiate with the banks. We would tell them what banking services are available. Essentially we tell them what banks to talk to if they want to do it on their own. I've got one man on my staff at the call of the treasurer. This gentleman went out there and helped them implement a brand new bank analysis system. We taught an employee how to do it on a day-to-day basis. That's how we differ from many outside consultants."

Banks can be particularly helpful when implementing a new cross-border cash management system. For instance, to ease the transition to reinvoicing, one leading multinational turned to the U.S. bank that was running its multilateral netting system. Said the treasurer: "They worked with us day and night, writing procedure manuals and helping us adjust our internal reporting system to reflect how the subsidiaries were receiving benefits or suffering disadvantages from the system."

Experienced cash managers often implement changes during the on-site investigation. A cash management consultant gave an example: "The first week we were out there, we took a glance at some of the bank analyses and we looked at internal wire transfers. We found that the banks were charging an exorbitant amount of money. So we got on the phone and said we'd like to see a cash management officer, called him over, checked it with him, and said, 'You've got to be kidding.' They changed the price, lowered it by 75 percent. This is on the spot, quick. These are things we are doing all the time. We fix a lot of things on the spot because of our experience."

Exhibit

In order to review a cash management system companies need to have pertinent information. The following forms are used by cash management consultants at Chase Manhattan bank to gather basic information as the first step in conducting a cash management study. This data can help you spot areas that may benefit from a closer view.

Subject Company for Cash Management Study:
    Name: Location:

Financial Data for Most Recent Financial Year:
    Financial Year: Interest Expense:
    Gross Sales: Interest Income:
    Cost of Goods Sold:

State all figures in thousands of local currency.

If there is not enough space in various sections please submit an extra sheet of paper.

1. SALES DATA

a. *Annual Sales Volume and Number of Collections per Collection Instrument*

	Cheque		Bank Giro		BACS		Direct Debit	
	Volume	No.	Volume	No.	Volume	No.	Volume	No.
DOMESTIC								
- Intercompany	. . . . .	. . .	. . . . .	. . .	. . . . .	. . .	. . . . .	. . .
- Third Party	. . . . .	. . .	. . . . .	. . .	. . . . .	. . .	. . . . .	. . .

	Cash		Postal Giro		Other		Total Domestic Volume
	Volume	No.	Volume	No.	Volume	No.	Volume
- Intercompany	. . . . .	. . .	. . . . .	. . .	. . . . .	. . .	. . . . .
- Third Party	. . . . .	. . .	. . . . .	. . .	. . . . .	. . .	. . . . .

EXPORTS per		Cheque		Bankers Draft		Telex Transfer (Swift)		Mail Transfer		Total Volume
Country	Curr	Volume	No.	Volume	No.	Volume	No.	Volume	No.	Volume
Intercompany										
. . . . . .	. . . .	. . . . .	. . .	. . . . .	. . .	. . . . .	. . .	. . . . .	. . .	. . . . .
. . . . . .	. . . .	. . . . .	. . .	. . . . .	. . .	. . . . .	. . .	. . . . .	. . .	. . . . .
. . . . . .	. . . .	. . . . .	. . .	. . . . .	. . .	. . . . .	. . .	. . . . .	. . .	. . . . .
. . . . . .	. . . .	. . . . .	. . .	. . . . .	. . .	. . . . .	. . .	. . . . .	. . .	. . . . .
. . . . . .	. . . .	. . . . .	. . .	. . . . .	. . .	. . . . .	. . .	. . . . .	. . .	. . . . .
. . . . . .	. . . .	. . . . .	. . .	. . . . .	. . .	. . . . .	. . .	. . . . .	. . .	. . . . .
. . . . . .	. . . .	. . . . .	. . .	. . . . .	. . .	. . . . .	. . .	. . . . .	. . .	. . . . .
. . . . . .	. . . .	. . . . .	. . .	. . . . .	. . .	. . . . .	. . .	. . . . .	. . .	. . . . .
. . . . . .	. . . .	. . . . .	. . .	. . . . .	. . .	. . . . .	. . .	. . . . .	. . .	. . . . .
. . . . . .	. . . .	. . . . .	. . .	. . . . .	. . .	. . . . .	. . .	. . . . .	. . .	. . . . .
. . . . . .	. . . .	. . . . .	. . .	. . . . .	. . .	. . . . .	. . .	. . . . .	. . .	. . . . .
Third Party										
. . . . . .	. . . .	. . . . .	. . .	. . . . .	. . .	. . . . .	. . .	. . . . .	. . .	. . . . .
. . . . . .	. . . .	. . . . .	. . .	. . . . .	. . .	. . . . .	. . .	. . . . .	. . .	. . . . .
. . . . . .	. . . .	. . . . .	. . .	. . . . .	. . .	. . . . .	. . .	. . . . .	. . .	. . . . .
. . . . . .	. . . .	. . . . .	. . .	. . . . .	. . .	. . . . .	. . .	. . . . .	. . .	. . . . .
. . . . . .	. . . .	. . . . .	. . .	. . . . .	. . .	. . . . .	. . .	. . . . .	. . .	. . . . .
. . . . . .	. . . .	. . . . .	. . .	. . . . .	. . .	. . . . .	. . .	. . . . .	. . .	. . . . .
. . . . . .	. . . .	. . . . .	. . .	. . . . .	. . .	. . . . .	. . .	. . . . .	. . .	. . . . .
. . . . . .	. . . .	. . . . .	. . .	. . . . .	. . .	. . . . .	. . .	. . . . .	. . .	. . . . .
. . . . . .	. . . .	. . . . .	. . .	. . . . .	. . .	. . . . .	. . .	. . . . .	. . .	. . . . .

b. *Sales collections per bank*

Banks Used	Approximate Annual Volume
Domestic—Sales	
. . . .	. . . .
. . . .	. . . .
. . . .	. . . .
. . . .	. . . .
Export—Sales	
. . . .	. . . .
. . . .	. . . .
. . . .	. . . .
. . . .	. . . .

c. Please classify your customers as large, medium, and small, according to your sales to them, and state number of customers and total sales per group. (Large = above 5% of your sales to one single customer. Medium = 1–5%. Small = less than 1% of sales.)

	Large		Medium		Small		
	No.	Sales	No.	Sales	No.	Sales	
Domestic	. . .	. . . . .	. . .	. . . . .	. . .	. . . . .	
Foreign	. . .	. . . . .	. . .	. . . . .	. . .	. . . . .	

2. *ORDER PROCESSING SYSTEM*

Please give a brief description of how orders are received and processed, invoices prepared and
sent out, means of communication used, etc. For example:

Day 1: Salesman receives order
Day 2: Order is mailed to office
Day 4: Office instructs warehouse to ship
Day 5: Goods shipped
Day 6: Warehouse informs office that shipment is made.
Day 8: Invoice prepared and sent out

3. *CREDIT CONTROL*

a. Please list normal sales terms, number of days due, discounts, letter of credit, etc.
(if any) and please supply a copy of each different type of invoice that you use.
   Domestic:

   Foreign:

b. Please describe follow-up procedure for accounts receivable *not* paid on time.

- How soon do you remind after due date?

- How frequently?

- How are customers rated for creditworthiness?

- Please supply a reasonable aging schedule of receivables.

4. *DISBURSEMENT DATA*
a. *Annual Supplier Disbursement Volume and Number of Payments per Payment Instrument*

	Cheque		Bank Giro		BACS		Direct Debit	
	Volume	No.	Volume	No.	Volume	No.	Volume	No.
DOMESTIC								
- Intercompany	. . . . . .	. . .	. . . . . .	. . .	. . . . . .	. . .	. . . . . .	. . .
- Third Party	. . . . . .	. . .	. . . . . .	. . .	. . . . . .	. . .	. . . . . .	. . .

	Cash		Postal Giro		Other		Total Domestic Volume
	Volume	No.	Volume	No.	Volume	No.	
- Intercompany	. . . . . .	. . .	. . . . . .	. . .	. . . . . .	. . .	. . . .
- Third Party	. . . . . .	. . .	. . . . . .	. . .	. . . . . .	. . .	. . . .

IMPORTS per		Cheque		Bankers Draft		Telex Transfer (Swift)		Mail Transfer		Total Imports
Country	Curr	Volume	No.	Volume	No.	Volume	No.	Volume	No.	
Intercompany										
. . . .	. . . .	. . . .	. . .	. . . . . .	. . .	. . . .	. . .	. . . .	. . .	. . . . . .
. . . .	. . . .	. . . .	. . .	. . . . . .	. . .	. . . .	. . .	. . . .	. . .	. . . . . .
. . . .	. . . .	. . . .	. . .	. . . . . .	. . .	. . . .	. . .	. . . .	. . .	. . . . . .
. . . .	. . . .	. . . .	. . .	. . . . . .	. . .	. . . .	. . .	. . . .	. . .	. . . . . .
. . . .	. . . .	. . . .	. . .	. . . . . .	. . .	. . . .	. . .	. . . .	. . .	. . . . . .
Third Party										
. . . .	. . . .	. . . .	. . .	. . . . . .	. . .	. . . .	. . .	. . . .	. . .	. . . . . .
. . . .	. . . .	. . . .	. . .	. . . . . .	. . .	. . . .	. . .	. . . .	. . .	. . . . . .
. . . .	. . . .	. . . .	. . .	. . . . . .	. . .	. . . .	. . .	. . . .	. . .	. . . . . .
. . . .	. . . .	. . . .	. . .	. . . . . .	. . .	. . . .	. . .	. . . .	. . .	. . . . . .
. . . .	. . . .	. . . .	. . .	. . . . . .	. . .	. . . .	. . .	. . . .	. . .	. . . . . .

b. Please classify your suppliers into large, medium, and small, according to your purchases, and state number of suppliers and total disbursements per group. (Large = above 5% of your total purchases from each supplier. Medium = 1–5%. Small = below 1%.)

	Large		Medium		Small	
	No.	Amount	No.	Amount	No.	Amount
Domestic	. . .	. . . . .	. . .	. . . . .	. . .	. . . . .
Foreign	. . .	. . . . .	. . .	. . . . .	. . .	. . . . .

c. *General Expenses*

	Annual Volume	Frequency of Payment	Payment Instrument	Payment Day
Wages	. . . . . .	. . . .	. . . .	. . . .
Salaries	. . . . . .	. . . .	. . . .	. . . .
Paye + NI	. . . . . .	. . . .	. . . .	. . . .
VAT	. . . . . .	. . . .	. . . .	. . . .
Corporation Tax	. . . . . .	. . . .	. . . .	. . . .
Rent	. . . . . .	. . . .	. . . .	. . . .
Other	. . . . . .	. . . .	. . . .	. . . .
	. . . . . .	. . . .	. . . .	. . . .
	. . . . . .	. . . .	. . . .	. . . .

d. Subsidiaries and/or other collecting and disbursing entities subject to the cash management study (e.g., plants, sales offices, branches, etc.). Figures should include both sales and suppliers as well as general expenses.

		% of Receipts	% of Disbursements
Name:	Location:	. . . .	. . . .
Name:	Location:	. . . .	. . . .
Name:	Location:	. . . .	. . . .
Name:	Location:	. . . .	. . . .
Name:	Location:	. . . .	. . . .

e. *Disbursements per Bank*

Banks Used	Approximate Annual Volume
Domestic Disbursements	
. . . .	. . . .
. . . .	. . . .
. . . .	. . . .
. . . .	. . . .
Foreign Disbursements	
. . . .	. . . .
. . . .	. . . .
. . . .	. . . .
. . . .	. . . .

5. BANK ACCOUNT MANAGEMENT

a. Please list all bank accounts and short-term bank facilities per bank. Please state purpose and size of account or facility, e.g., check account, deposit account, overdraft, short-term loan, FX line, etc. Include postal giros.

Bank	Purpose of Account or Facility	Size
. . . .	. . . .	. . . .
. . . .	. . . .	. . . .
. . . .	. . . .	. . . .
. . . .	. . . .	. . . .
. . . .	. . . .	. . . .
. . . .	. . . .	. . . .
. . . .	. . . .	. . . .
. . . .	. . . .	. . . .

b. For each current account and short-term loan account, please give an estimate of the average daily value dated debit or credit balances (both debit and credit if the account fluctuates) *per quarter* of last financial year. This information is most conveniently available from monthly or quarterly summary statements used by the banks for interest calculations. Add all daily credit balances per quarter and divide by 90. Add all debit balances per quarter and divide by 90.

Bank Account	Debit Balances per Quarter				Credit Balances per Quarter			
	1st	2nd	3rd	4th	1st	2nd	3rd	4th
. . . .	. . . .	. . . .	. . . .	. . . .	. . . .	. . . .	. . . .	. . . .
. . . .	. . . .	. . . .	. . . .	. . . .	. . . .	. . . .	. . . .	. . . .
. . . .	. . . .	. . . .	. . . .	. . . .	. . . .	. . . .	. . . .	. . . .
. . . .	. . . .	. . . .	. . . .	. . . .	. . . .	. . . .	. . . .	. . . .
. . . .	. . . .	. . . .	. . . .	. . . .	. . . .	. . . .	. . . .	. . . .
. . . .	. . . .	. . . .	. . . .	. . . .	. . . .	. . . .	. . . .	. . . .

6. VALUE DATING AND BANK CHARGES

a. What value do you receive on items (cheques, drafts, wire transfers, foreign transfers) deposited in your accounts (e.g., for cheques deposited today, when do you receive good value)?

Bank	Type of Item	Value Dating Terms
. . . .	. . . .	. . . .
. . . .	. . . .	. . . .
. . . .	. . . .	. . . .
. . . .	. . . .	. . . .
. . . .	. . . .	. . . .
. . . .	. . . .	. . . .
. . . .	. . . .	
- FX transactions	buy	. . . .
- FX transactions	sell	. . . .

b. What fees or charges do you pay for day-to-day operation of your accounts?

	% of Transaction Value	and/or	Amount
- account turnover charge:	. . .		. . . .
- Per item charge:	. . .		. . . .
- Postage and statement charge:	. . .		. . . .
- FX transaction charge:	. . .		. . . .
- Transfer charge:	. . .		. . . .
- Other (list)	. . .		. . . .
	. . .		. . . .
	. . .		. . . .
	. . .		. . . .
	. . .		. . . .

c. Please list banks that do and do not provide written confirmation of bank charges.

Written Confirmation Provided Please Enclose Photocopy	Written Confirmation Not Provided
. . . .	. . . .
. . . .	. . . .
. . . .	. . . .
. . . .	. . . .
. . . .	. . . .

d. Interest earned on current account credit balances.

Bank Account	%
. . . .	. . .
. . . .	. . .
. . . .	. . .
. . . .	. . .

7. *SHORT-TERM FINANCING AND INVESTMENT ALTERNATIVES*
a. How are your short-term financing requirements met?
   Average total balance of short-term financing in last financial year: . . . .

	Avg. Share of Total S-T Financing %	Interest Pricing* Structure	Current Cost %	Fees and Charges
- Overdrafts	. . . .	. . . .	. . . .	. . . .
- Short-Term Advances	. . . .	. . . .	. . . .	. . . .
- Acceptances	. . . .	. . . .	. . . .	. . . .
- Supplier Credits	. . . .	. . . .	. . . .	. . . .
- Other (Describe)	. . . .	. . . .	. . . .	. . . .

*e.g., LIBOR + spread, base + discount rate + etc.

b. *How are cash balances used?*

	Share of Total Excess Cash %	Current Yield %
- Left in current account	. . . .	. . . .
- Interest-bearing bank account credit balances:	. . . .	. . . .
- Short-term time deposits:	. . . .	. . . .
- Other (Describe):	. . . .	. . . .
	. . . .	. . . .
	. . . .	. . . .
	. . . .	. . . .

8. ORGANIZATION OF FINANCIAL DEPARTMENT
Please submit an organization chart, and describe briefly each function and the number of staff involved.

9. Please give any information not covered by this questionnaire that you feel is important.

2

Establishing an Effective Cash Monitoring System

The road to successful global cash management starts with effective cash monitoring and forecasting. Timely, accurate, and detailed cash flow data helps firms avoid idle bank balances, bloated inventories, overdue accounts receivable, inefficient payables practices, needless borrowings, missed investment opportunities, and dangerous currency exposures. Equally important, adept reporting allows both parent and regional headquarters to assess the performance of local cash managers and to upgrade managerial control.

The treasurer of a major U.K. manufacturing company summed up the importance of good reporting this way: "The prime tool of any corporate treasurer is cash monitoring and forecasting. Unless you know where your cash is and where it is going, you might as well give up. If you can't anticipate your cash flows, you can't manage your foreign exchange risk. If you don't know when you are to receive or disburse payments, it is impossible to know what your borrowing needs are. You just cannot do anything without good reporting and forecasting."

A top-notch reporting system is a sine qua non in countries with extravagant rates of inflation, tight credit conditions, or high interest rates. Unfortunately, many companies learn this lesson the hard way. As the finance manager of a paper manufacturer in Italy pointed out: "You can't afford to relax your cash monitoring even for a day. If you have surplus money lying around without knowing it, the banks will pay maybe 5 percent on it—if you are lucky. And if you have an unnecessary overdraft, you pay 13 to 14 percent for it, so considering that spread, that's costly money. You have to have good information to help you minimize idle funds and optimize your whole cash management system."

To help international firms refine their cash monitoring, this chapter offers guidelines for developing good internal reporting systems at the local as well as the cross-border level. It reviews how companies can analyze their subsidiaries' systems and determine local and headquarter information needs. Special emphasis is placed on how to purchase electronic banking services and resolve common problems such as consolidating information from two or more banks. The chapter concludes with an analysis of how companies can enhance the quality of their cash reporting with computer systems and software packages.

Analyzing Subsidiaries' Reporting Systems

The first step toward improved cash monitoring is a systematic review of subsidiary reporting. You may discover that some of your operating units rely on woefully inadequate cash monitoring systems established years ago, perhaps without headquarters' guidance. New technologies may have made them obsolete, or the local company's sales and cash flows may have grown so much that a more elaborate reporting structure is necessary. The system may have been set up by local controllers with little understanding of cash management trends. For instance, said one company spokesman of his Korean operations: "It's disgraceful to say this, but some of our companies do not know what their foreign exchange position is, to be honest. About six months ago when we tried to get the monthly foreign exchange report, we failed."

Such problems are not confined to less developed countries (LDCs). A U.S. computer manufacturer recently conducted a cash management review of its Italian subsidiary only to find an antiquated cash reporting system that cost the firm an estimated $87,000 p.a. The problem: The Italian firm would telephone its bankers every day to find out what its ledger balances were on the accounts, and it would adjust these balances by known debits and anticipated credits. But the process was sadly lacking in accuracy: The subsidiary had idle daily balances of nearly $800,000, some of it earning a mere 0.5 percent. To remedy the situation, the consulting team made the following recommendations:

· **Subsidiary management should carefully track and adjust balances for bank float.** It should compare forecasts with actual balances shown on quarterly statements and try to account for variations to allow more accurate calculation of float. In this way, the firm could set optimal balance targets.
· **The subsidiary should err on the side of too large an overdraft rather than allow idle balances.** The cost of borrowing on overdraft vs. investing over the short term was 2 percent (based on an overdraft rate of 14 percent and an investment rate of 13 percent), while the opportunity cost of idle balances was effectively 13.5 percent (if the funds were used to reduce loans at 14 percent instead of earning 0.5 percent on credit balances).

These stories are not unusual: Because of poor bank balance reporting services in many countries and a lack of emphasis on good cash management, many subsidiaries monitor cash flows poorly. Often, parent companies find that local cash managers, lacking an outside perspective, may not even realize the inadequacies of their reporting system. As one consultant remarked, "Overseas treasury staffs are often so thin, it is all they can do just to keep up with the day-to-day work load; they just don't have the time to analyze their systems." To ensure that expanding information needs are being met by subsidiary reporting systems, companies should start by answering the following questions:

(1) **What cash management information is available on the system?** Is data on daily cash positions, customer credit histories, days sales outstanding (DSO), cash disbursements outstanding (CDO), aging of receivables and disbursements, investment and debt positions, and cash forecasts readily accessible? Is any vital information missing? "Look at the physical reports and the information that you have," a consultant from a major U.S. accounting firm advised. "Then compare it to what you need."

(2) **Which reports are used for each cash management function (e.g., accounts receivable, investment management), and how timely, detailed, and frequent are they?** Which functions need summary reports, and which require more detailed information? The same consultant recommends that firms "look at the sources of information and see if there is another alternative; maybe another department could get it to you two days faster or with more details."

(3) **Is there coordination between the various users of reports?** A lack of communication between internal departments often results in one area missing out on details that are being generated elsewhere. Remarked a bank consultant, "Different people may devise reports and never talk to each other. The accountants do this and treasury does that, and if one makes a change, they throw the other's form out of whack." Another consultant warned, "I've seen companies where the treasurer put information into his format and sent it on to accounting, and they rewrite it into their form and send it on, and so forth. The same bit of information has moved and been transformed x times."

(4) **Do available reports support proactive cash management, or do they simply provide reactive, historical data?** Some companies do not generate cash management information per se and simply send reports designed by accounting over to treasury.

(5) **How is cash management data gathered from local operating units?** Is the reporting system manual or automated? Are telephone, telex, and telecommunications facilities adequate in this country? Can local communications be used more effectively to speed up information flows without increasing costs significantly?

(6) **How is bank balance data obtained (over the phone, through the mail)?** Are automated services available, and if so, is it cost-effective to use them? How timely, accurate, and detailed are your current bank reports? Do your bank reports give you today's or yesterday's balances? Are you getting actual balances (i.e., adjusted for float or value dates), so that you have a clear idea of the amounts being left idle in your accounts?

(7) **Have you negotiated with your banks for more timely or detailed information or a change in the delivery mechanism?** Are you using banks that provide the best reporting services in the country? Can you shift additional balances to banks that are providing you with good reporting services? Are you using concentration accounts, zero-balance accounts, and other cash management tools that simplify balance monitoring? Are you using the most efficient means to consolidate information from different banks?

(8) **How sophisticated and accurate are the cash forecasts?** Is variance analysis conducted to measure, explain, and reduce discrepancies between actual and forecasted cash positions? Does the format of the forecast report facilitate trend analysis? What data is used to create forecasts? How often are forecasts issued and updated, who uses them, and for what purposes?

(9) **How is cash management data stored and organized?** Is a computer system used? If so, is it a mainframe, a mini- or a microcomputer? Is a stand-alone computer or an integrated micro-mainframe system used? Are the needs of the cash manager given a back seat to those of the controller? Does information exist in the central data base that can be used for cash management purposes? Has a cost/benefit analysis been conducted to measure the benefits of upgrading the computer system? How much does the system cost to operate? What are the initial and ongoing charges for hardware and software, data transmission, and clerical and managerial time?

(10) **Does the cash manager have sufficient influence over the design and maintenance of the data base?** What organizational or cost barriers stand in the way of the cash manager and hinder necessary improvements in the cash management data base? Be forewarned: Many consultants find that their corporate clients put the cart before the horse by tackling such technical issues before deciding what information they really need. "Too many treasurers look at the 'how' before they look at the 'what' and 'why,'" remarked one consultant.

Improving Local Information and Reports

A cash management review team must first look closely at existing cash management reports to understand a subsidiary's cash flows and how well they are being managed. In fact, a bad reporting system is often the root cause of cash management problems— as illustrated by the case of a giant Italian manufacturer that several years ago brought in a new chief financial officer (CFO) with experience in cash management. With the firm facing sagging profits and a heavy debt burden, the CFO turned his attention to the company's cash management system and was horrified by what he saw. "We had nothing," he said. "No idea of what our cash flows were or what would happen next. This was intolerable." A rigorous analysis of the reporting system, therefore, is an integral part of the review of the subsidiary's overall cash management system.

A German food producer was able to make a dramatic improvement in its overall cash management following a detailed review of its reporting system. In conjunction with a consulting team from a major U.S. bank, the firm conducted a thorough audit of its cash management system. As a result, the firm learned that it was experiencing significant delays during the collection process, that its banks were not living up to value-dating agreements, and that it was consistently in overdraft at one bank while piling up surplus funds earning low rates at another. "The costs to the company in terms of reduced profitability and managerial time devoted to collecting overdue accounts of funds delayed in the banking system are considerable," concluded the consultants. The culprit was the cash reporting system. "An effective information system that can *plan for* rather than *react to* problems will improve both the decision-making process and the profitability of the company."

To achieve these goals and to avoid costly mistakes, the bank consultants recommended installing a computerized daily cash management reporting system, supported by sales and customer account ledgers and by direct coordination with the company's banks. The new system contains an extensive data base and produces timely reports on daily cash position, daily investments and borrowings outstanding, interest rates on credit and debit positions by bank and currency, and forecasts of expected receipts against planned disbursements. Now, by 10 A.M. each day, the firm's finance department receives the previous day's ending balance and details of all incoming receipts in excess of Dm50,000. The book balance is then reconciled with the bank balance, including unrecorded disbursements and anticipated receipts. The finance director is thereby apprised of all required disbursements and maturities of short-term debt, and investment strategies can be developed to use the expected receipts most effectively and to roll over short-term debt and investment portfolios.

Companies eager to follow the example of the above firm should emulate these procedures:

· **Review the information the local staff receives to manage cash and ask to see copies of their reports.** Ask local cash managers (and even clerks and bookkeepers) what information they would like to receive, but presently do not; sometimes the information is already available but simply is not reaching the right people. Perhaps they are getting too much or too little detail, or receiving monthly reports where daily or weekly reports are required.
· **Examine the reports for level of detail and completeness, keeping in mind not only local concerns but also headquarters' needs.** For example, while the local operating unit probably needs detailed DSO data so that it can monitor personnel and customer performance, the parent may only need special summary figures on DSOs to monitor subsidiary performance.
· **Tailor reporting formats to your own cash flows and organizational structure.** There is no ideal reporting system. But subsidiaries should strive for a well-rounded system that provides information to help them manage the key areas of cash management: credit and collection, disbursement control, bank relations, and bank account management.

To assess the completeness of subsidiaries' reporting systems, parents should compare local systems with the checklist of cash management reports on p. 40 to see if subsidiaries are overlooking key pieces of information. Of course, only essential reports should be used. Too many reports are just as bad as too few, as the treasurer of a major U.K. electronics firm pointed out: "You can get overwhelmed with information and find that you're just sorting through reams of data. Unless you're going to do something with information to make a profit, why bother?" A bank consultant agreed: "Overkill can be a big problem with some reporting systems, because too many reports that people just can't look at can be almost as bad as not enough reports." (For more detailed descriptions of each report and its use, see the chapter covering that functional area.)

Evaluating Local Data Delivery Systems

After reviewing the information gathered at the subsidiary level and determining what additional data should be reported, companies must examine how the information is transmitted and stored. Even if the subsidiary is tracking the right information, a poorly designed delivery system will result in untimely or infrequent updates, incorrect balance figures, forecasting errors, and other problems. If an automated system is used, be sure that the local cash manager understands the issues involved with transmitting and organizing data and improves communication with EDP personnel. Keep in mind that systems issues will have a strong impact on any cost/benefit analysis of plans to upgrade cash management information.

Although many cash managers in the United States and other industrial countries take electronic systems for granted, the majority of foreign subsidiaries—especially in developing nations—continue to rely on the traditional data transmission methods of telex, telephone, mail, and messenger. If a nation suffers from inadequate telecommunications and computer facilities and poor bank reporting services, cash managers will need to rely on these traditional reporting methods, although they too may be plagued with difficulties. In Venezuela, for example, telephone service is maddeningly unreliable, the telex system is fair at best, and the postal system is hardly a system at all; mail can take two to three weeks to travel from rural areas to cities. As a result, firms must rely on courier services to speed vital data to local headquarters. One indigenous firm has actually set up its own private telephone network.

A particularly challenging environment for building good local reporting systems is the Philippines. Making telephone calls is a frustrating experience even in major cities, and local calls outside of urban areas often take several hours to complete. The mail is even worse; documents sent through the postal system may take a week and a half to arrive from rural areas and nearly a week between cities. Longer delays are not uncommon, and many companies complain that mail is frequently lost. Even telex facilities are below par: They are currently stretched to capacity, sometimes resulting in garbled messages, and do not exist in many areas of the country. According to a local banker, "Maybe the problem is oversubscription of the available lines. You can have all the modern telex hardware, but if your line itself is defective, there is nothing you can do." Finally, the telephone company has a monopoly over the lines needed for computerized reporting, and it has not yet granted sufficient access to companies for on-line systems.

Companies should press their local financial managers to find innovative solutions to their telecommunications problems. They must tailor their local reporting systems to the environment of the country in which they operate, making the best of what is available. For example, a Philippine beer company depends on cars, trucks, jeepneys, and even canoes to gather information from its massive local operations, which include over 120 sales offices and 17 regional headquarters scattered throughout the country. To facilitate data transmission, the company is attempting "to tie all our area offices together by citizens band radio because there aren't telecommunications everywhere. We would have to lay our own lines to use the telephone, and then you may as well go into the communications business."

In many countries, of course, conditions are better: Telephones work, and the mail

Key Cash Management Reports: A Checklist

(1) **Credit and collection reports** are used by local receivables clerks, credit managers, and finance managers to monitor credit and collection performance and to maintain day-to-day control of customer accounts. In many companies, invoice listings and customer status reports are updated continuously on a computer data base and accessed via terminal rather than printed out every day. The accounts receivable data base should include full details on the credit terms, rating, and history of each customer, as well as detailed entries for each transaction. Ideally, this data can be pulled by transaction or by customer to review details or accessed in the aggregate to monitor DSOs and the overall aging of receivables. A variety of overlapping reports can be generated from this data base, but key forms include the following:

· **Invoice listings** compile all invoices generated, outstanding, or paid during a period. Entries include invoice amount and reference number, currency of payment, due date, special terms, date paid, and so on. These listings are used by receivables clerks to process receipts and customer statements, solve problems, and reconcile accounts.
· **Detailed customer status reports** are essentially credit histories of each customer. Credit managers use them to track customer credit limits and exposures and payment performance. Important credit data includes credit terms, credit rating, the use of discounts and penalty fees, outstanding amounts, name of account representative, and volume of purchases to date.
· **Major accounts outstanding reports** record credit histories and amounts overdue on key delinquent accounts to support the dunning process. As one cash manager put it, "You need some sort of summary analysis to draw your attention to problems with customer creditworthiness." An aging analysis and a column for recording actions taken to collect outstanding sums can be included on the form. Instead of recording delinquent accounts, some companies use special forms to monitor "accounts that are important from a marketing and sales point of view, whether delinquent or not, because they always need special processing or attention."
· **Accounts receivable reports** are monthly summary analyses used by credit and finance managers to evaluate the credit and collection function's performance. Key

may take only one or two days between major cities. Companies operating in these countries can rely on the national communications infrastructure for their reporting. For example, the subsidiary of a U.S. manufacturer of food products in Australia has constructed a successful cash monitoring system based on traditional transmission methods. Every morning, over thirty units send in reports to Melbourne headquarters via telephone, telex, or messenger detailing bank balances and anticipated receipts and disbursements. Headquarters treasury staff consolidates the data and identifies the company's overall net cash position.

Even if a subsidiary's telex- or telephone-based system seems to be operating

items generally included are **total sums collected; DSOs** (average number of days that sales are outstanding), which can be broken down by sales unit, sales manager, and sales region; **days overdue,** which subtracts credit terms from DSOs to generate a more precise measure of late payments; **aging of receivables,** which identifies the percentage of sales that are past due, usually broken down in thirty-day increments; and **bad-debt expense,** which can be recorded by number and percentage of customers and total billings. Bad-debt expense not only helps to monitor performance but, as a U.S. cash manager pointed out, "you need it to fund and reconcile your reserve accounts for uncollected invoices."

· **Anticipated receipts** should be determined to support the cash position and cash forecasting reports (see below).

(2) **Payables reports** help local managers analyze their disbursement management and track outflows of funds. Many cash managers receive disbursement information informally. As the assistant treasurer for a major U.S. chemicals manufacturer explained, "We don't have formalized payables reports. Our payables department is on-line and generates computer runs now and then. But normally, they just pull up data on the terminal and read it to you over the phone." However, formal payables reports can bring enormous savings to the cash manager. Companies should therefore consider taking a more rigorous approach to this commonly underappreciated area. The accounts payable data base should be able to generate the following key reports:

· **Actual disbursements** should be broken out by supplier and by day. Important entries are invoice due date, the date payment is actually remitted, and the date the disbursement account is debited. These reports can be used by payables clerks to process payments, resolve disputes, track lost checks, develop float forecasts, track bank performance, and so on.
· **Disbursement summary reports** are used to measure the performance of the payables department. Managers should use them to monitor **CDOs** (the average number of days cash disbursements are outstanding) and to analyze the **aging of payables** to show the percentage of payments that are made in, say, fifteen- to thirty-day increments broken down by payment instrument, bank, region of payee, etc. These

▶

smoothly, however, companies should conduct a cost/benefit analysis to determine if it is time to switch to computer links. According to the treasurer of a major German metals manufacturer, "Without an automated system, you cannot have the up-to-date information you need to perform good cash management. Everything takes too long, and there are too many errors. The old ways just aren't good enough. Everything suffers: Collections are slow, payments are missed, bank reconciliation is messy." Information can be transmitted electronically via telecommunications networks operated by service companies or through proprietary systems run on leased lines from the national telephone network.

reports can be used to monitor the impact of disbursement timing on supplier relations and to measure the impact of discounts and penalty fees on liquidity.

· **Anticipated disbursements** should be determined to support the cash position and cash forecasting reports (see below).

(3) **Bank relations reports** are used to control compensation paid to banks in the form of fees, compensating balances, and extra business, and to monitor the value and cost of each bank relationship. Two of the most important bank relations reports are the following:

· **Account analyses** should be issued by banks, although this is not the case in most countries. As described by one cash manager, these reports "are like a bill, an invoice of services rendered." The analysis should show the activity in each account and review charges during the period broken down for each service, such as check processing, lockboxes, concentration and controlled-disbursement accounts, and so on. Fees, balances, and costs per item should be clearly indicated. Unfortunately, in the United States, "one of the biggest issues we have in the cash management world today is the lack of uniformity in bank account analyses," the cash manager commented. "They don't have the same service descriptions or categories, some banks bundle their services so you can't distinguish costs for individual services, and so on. It's a real headache."

· **Bank activity reports** are created in-house to show volumes of investments, borrowings, letter-of-credit business, concentration-account activity, etc. "They are more strategic and political than account analyses," remarked another U.S. cash manager. "They are used to measure the overall importance of each bank relationship." These reports track historical levels of total business and rates and quality of account service by bank. They are typically issued monthly or quarterly to senior personnel for negotiating with the banks and to cash managers for reviewing the accuracy of the banks' account analyses. Some companies have developed specialized reports to track particular activities, such as foreign exchange bids, to facilitate comparison of banks' services.

(4) **Liquidity and bank account management reports** allow cash managers to maximize their internal use of funds by closely tracking daily balances and cash inflows

---

One company that regularly evaluates its local data delivery system is a mid-sized U.S. consumer goods manufacturer. In the assistant treasurer's words, "Years ago we went from a mail-based system to telex, and now to telecommunications. We use telecommunications because it is quicker, and we need reports by the seventh working day of each month. Our most recent study showed that our time-sharing charges

and identifying future cash disbursement needs. The essential reports are listed below.

- **Balance reports** are generated by banks to show account positions and transaction details for the day. Figures should reflect ledger, collected and available balances, and value-dated transactions. Optimally, they should represent current balances, rather than those from the previous day, to enable cash managers to fine-tune their account management. In countries where bank reports are not available or timely, companies should retrieve balance information over the phone and construct their own reports.
- **Consolidated reports of all bank account balances** show the overall cash position of the company. These reports can be calculated manually from the balance reports described above or generated by an outside service or an in-house microcomputer software package. "Consolidated reports are essential to help you control your overall position," explained one banking relations manager. "But you still need the individual bank reports to respond to your position and take action; you have to shift funds around, target certain accounts, and keep checks from bouncing."
- **Investment and borrowing reports** list all nonbank portfolio activity, including commercial paper, government bonds, bankers acceptances from banks the firm does not have a regular relationship with, and so on. The form should indicate the principal amount, the maturity schedule, and the rate.
- **Daily cash position reports** show the day's starting bank balance position (from the balance report or consolidated balance report) adjusted for the anticipated cash flows (from the collections and payable departments) for that day. The cash flow information should include all incoming funds, such as receipts from sales, investment earnings, loan proceeds, and infusions of cash from the parent company, as well as debit items like payroll, taxes, supplier payments, interest and debt payments, and disbursements to the parent. It may be useful to include an entry for the target balance and a column for bank float to reflect deposited or disbursed checks that are still in the clearing process.
- **Cash forecast reports** anticipate the impact of future disbursements and collections on the cash position. Similar to a cash position report, the forecast takes a starting cash position, adds inflows and subtracts outflows (many taken from the anticipated collections and payables reports), and computes an ending cash position. The time frame, however, can be weekly, monthly, or longer, and the figures should be periodically revised based on a variance analysis comparing forecasts with actuals.

were really getting pretty steep. So now we're just taking raw data through the wires and reformatting everything here to keep transmission costs down."

In addition to choosing a delivery mechanism for gathering data from units, subsidiaries must establish an internal data base to store and organize the information. Most parent companies in developed countries have long since computerized their accounting, if not their cash management, data base, but many foreign subsidiaries still lag behind in computerization. Some cash managers are scared away from electronic systems by their large start-up costs (often in the millions of dollars) and maintenance fees. Other problems—especially in LDCs—include staffing and working with an in-house EDP department. Furthermore, electronic systems are impossible to establish in some countries and may not be cost-effective for small operating units.

Fortunately, there are options available to help companies take advantage of computers without making a massive investment. For example, if a companywide mainframe is not cost-effective, it may be possible to put cash management data on an inexpensive microcomputer or to use a time-sharing service. Or companies may want to follow the lead of one Korean company, whose accounting and finance staff calculates financial reports with abacuses. Quipped the corporate spokesman, "The accounting manager just recently asked me for two more. I said, 'Why don't you buy electronic calculators?' He replied, 'No, they are not fast enough.'"

Domestic Reporting: Two Case Examples

Before resigning themselves to accepting mediocre reporting systems at the subsidiary level, parent companies should familiarize themselves with some success stories. One such story is that of the Brazilian subsidiary of a giant U.S. oil corporation with three operating divisions in the country: for chemicals, oil exploration, and petroleum products. The firm's retail and industrial sales volume is enormous—over $3 billion per year, or about $10 million a day—and the collections are spread over the entire country. At the same time, the bulk of its payables go to Petrobras, the state oil agency located in Rio. To facilitate its tremendous cash-gathering task, the company has a sophisticated, tightly controlled cash management system.

To keep track of the huge volume of funds, the company has installed an elaborate reporting, forecasting, and review network at its Rio headquarters. Every day the plants send computer disks to headquarters containing accounting documentation, sales receipts, and deposit slips. These disks are fed into the main computer, which uses the data, along with other information supplied by the headquarters staff, to produce a consolidated daily cash report for the treasurer. The report details receipts, disbursements, borrowing positions, foreign exchange transactions, and a forecast for the next day.

But this is just the first step. According to a company spokesman, forecasting is crucial in his business. "We have to place orders with Petrobras as much as five months in advance and can adjust them by only 7 percent either way. Since we're really locked in, it's a delicate balancing act to ensure that we have adequate inventories to meet sales requirements and adequate cash to finance those inventories."

To determine its future cash position, the firm's treasurer prepares a monthly report estimating receipts, disbursements, financial transactions, and portfolio levels for the following six months. This report is submitted to the board of directors, which also receives a report that forecasts the following for one year out: cash flow, dividend payments, DSOs, aging of receivables, interest income, expenses, and other financial parameters. At this time, the board assesses the performance of the marketing department, which is responsible to management for meeting certain credit levels and DSOs. New targets for the following year are also set. Finally, the board receives a five-year outlook that includes an update on the annual forecast.

The firm monitors all deposits to make certain that banks receive collections quickly and that funds are cleared to the main account in Rio accurately and rapidly. The firm has an extensive telephone network at its Rio headquarters with direct links to its major banks to obtain daily bank balance information. But the company does not rely solely on its banks. Once a month, the corporate treasury department analyzes the deposit information sent in by its plants and compares this data with the monthly bank statements. "We need to have a good monitoring system to pinpoint when the banks are not clearing," said the company spokesman. "Otherwise, they'd just sit on the money."

A blueprint for a successful reporting system tailored to the Japanese environment is provided by the subsidiary of a U.S. pharmaceuticals firm. To track its domestic operations, the firm has established on-line hookups between its three largest sales offices and a central computer in Tokyo; the other seven offices are connected by facsimile machines. Every day, all ten offices report their sales and collections. The headquarters computer then transmits relevant invoice information via a direct hookup with the company's warehouse.

In addition to accelerating invoicing and shipping, this mechanized system provides headquarters staff with full information on inventory movements, plus the credit and collection histories of all customers. The firm uses the computer to check credit limits and produce aging and DSO reports. Also, the firm inputs other data on its cash flows, including payables, taxes, borrowings, investments, and bank balances. The computer is thus able to generate a monthly cash forecast projecting the cash position by day for the next month, plus a six-month forecast twice a year. The treasury staff updates the forecasts each day, comparing their actual cash positions with the forecasts.

Although the system cost $3.5 million to implement, the firm's spokesman believes it is worth every penny. "The real saving can't be quantified. We know exactly what everything is now. We can make borrowing and investment decisions much more accurately. We can control our cash management."

Getting the Best Bank Reporting Services

In addition to the challenges of transmitting and organizing internal cash flow information, many subsidiaries encounter enormous problems with reporting services from their banks. Up-to-the-minute balance information is essential for daily funds management and forecasting, for tracking actual inflows and outflows, and for account analysis and bank relations management. In the words of the CFO of a diversified French manufacturing firm, "Bank information is the missing piece of the puzzle. I can get a lot of information internally, but not the actual balances or the transfers between banks that we don't know anything about. We need the banks for that."

To determine if a subsidiary is adequately tracking bank balances, examine how it receives bank information from each active account. Banks report via messenger, telephone, telex, or through a telecommunications link or computer disk. In some countries, many banks issue timely reports throughout the day (intraday or real-time reports); in others, reports on the previous day's balances may not arrive until the afternoon, and may be incomplete or inaccurate. Companies should find out if personnel who must rely on these reports for forecasting, investing, and making other decisions encounter specific problems with the quality of bank information they receive. Critical factors to look at are the frequency, accuracy, detail, timeliness, and cost of bank reports. The quality of bank data must be compared with what is available in that particular country. The following are some of the key problems—and possible solutions—companies face in getting bank balance reporting:

· **Absence of high-quality services.** The primary reason for poor balance monitoring is that a large number of banks—especially in developing countries—simply do not provide timely information to their corporate customers. Local banks do not offer automated balance reporting services in many developing countries, and these services are just starting to be developed in some industrial nations, such as Italy and Spain. Even when local banks report balances, they do not usually distinguish clearly between ledger and collected balances (i.e., posted totals vs. immediately available funds), and some even make numerous errors. Deposited checks rarely represent immediately available funds because of float lost to the clearing process and the common practice of value dating.

To minimize these problems, subsidiaries should regularly review the services of all major banks in the country. New banks regularly join the ranks of those that offer automated reporting services. Since such banks often offer other high-quality services, such as competitive investment rates, funds availability, and so on, a firm may want to pool accounts with one of these banks to simplify its reporting and cash management system. In those countries where timely reporting services are not available, companies may prefer to negotiate with their banks for special offset, zero-balance, or automatic-investment accounts, since these services minimize the need for information to manage accounts.

· **Lax corporate habits.** Relying on shoddy bank reports may reflect a generally lazy attitude toward cash management on the part of subsidiary personnel. For example, when asked why he did not get detailed daily balance reports from his bank, the spokesman for an Australian transportation firm replied, "I know more or less what our position is, and anyway, I've got the overdraft to back me up. To look at it any more closely would just be playing with the rats and mice." But because of the steep cost of money in Australia, deficit balances carry a sizable interest expense, and credit balances result in large opportunity losses. Daily bank reporting is available in Australia; the problem is with the company's attitude toward managing its accounts. A disregard for balance reporting—and misunderstanding of the bene-

Worksheet for Estimating Closing Collected Balance

Opening balance—bank ledger		$500
Add:		
Wire transfers—in	XXX	
Investments maturing today	XXX	
Other immediate credits	XXX	
Subtotal	XXX	
Subtract:		
Wire transfers—out	XXX	
Other immediate debits	XXX	
Checks picked up by messenger yesterday	XXX	
Checks mailed—three working days prior[1]	XXX	
Loans repaid	XXX	
Investments made	XXX	
Subtotal	XXX	
Net additions (withdrawals)[2]		(200)
Estimated closing collected balance		$300
Plus: Current-day deposits[3]		100
Estimated closing **ledger** balance		$400

[1]Estimation of mail float (number of days will vary by country); can be obtained from the payables department.

[2]Net of two subtotals.

[3]Based on next-day availability (availability will vary by country).

fits of cash management—was reflected in the words of a Korean financial manager: "When we pay, we don't mind whether the vendor deposits the money or not. We think of it as drawn. Even though it is in our bank, we don't use it." In cases such as these, headquarters must intervene to instill a more disciplined approach to cash management.

Calculating Balances in Countries with Poor Bank Reporting

Despite these obstacles, subsidiaries should establish effective balance-monitoring systems that provide vital information promptly, even in problem countries. Parents should pay particular attention to the balance reports of subsidiaries in countries such as Mexico and Italy, where electronic reporting services are not yet offered by many local banks, or where reports arrive late in the day and are incomplete. In many countries, banks only provide ledger balances, which show merely the amount of funds deposited—not the portion of the balance figure still in the clearing process.

It is not enough to rely on book balances, even in countries with efficient funds transfer systems and immediate credit availability. "Oh, I know what they say," commented the international treasury manager of a U.S. chemicals company with operations in Korea. " 'Book balance always equals bank balance in Korea.' And it's largely true. But it's just good managerial practice to check up daily, and they do find discrepancies. Times are tough there already; why make it harder on yourself?"

Rather than passively accepting and working with sloppy bank reports, subsidiaries can use a worksheet (which is easily adaptable to a computerized spreadsheet) for estimating closing collected balances at each local bank (see box on p. 47). (It should be noted that this worksheet may result in occasional overdrawn *book,* or accounting, balances as kept by the corporate accounting office; but if disbursement-float estimates are conservative, actual bank overdrafts should not occur.)

Subsidiaries should instruct their local banks to provide daily information on their *opening* ledger balance. Midday balances are not useful to the cash manager, since they may not include all debits and credits for the current day and often do not specify which—if any—are missing. Furthermore, banks in some regions do not commonly report on a collected-balance basis. In these cases, collected balances should be estimated by determining that a certain percentage of deposits tends to clear in one business day, a certain percentage in two business days, and so on, based on experience and discussions with local bankers.

The Pros and Cons of Electronic Banking Services

Fortunately, automated bank reporting is now available in a growing number of countries. There are three key reasons why subsidiaries should examine the availability of electronic services in their home country if they have not already done so:

- **Improved quality and timeliness of information.** Electronic bank reporting provides the foundation upon which cash managers can base quick decisions. As the treasurer of a Swiss manufacturer put it, "Electronic bank reporting provides me with better information more rapidly from the banks. And that translates into better cash management."
- **Cost savings.** Companies are looking to their banks for electronic services that will cut idle balances and float. According to the treasurer of a U.S. firm that slashed its balances by 80 percent via electronic reporting, "The main benefit is getting rid of all those idle funds you never knew anything about before. We're saving a lot of money."
- **Reduced administrative work loads.** By tapping electronic bank reporting services, firms can cut their manpower needs and boost efficiency. "Writing telexes, sending letters, and manual reconciliation are time-consuming and error-prone procedures," said the senior financial officer of a Belgian chemicals company. "We're looking for less manpower and more time at this office. Bank reporting will give it to us."

It should not be assumed, however, that every subsidiary that is not using electronic services in countries where they are available is derelict in its duties. For smaller units, or those with very regular cash flows or automatic investment services, electronic reporting may be overkill. As the assistant treasurer of a major U.K. consumer products firm said, "We get such good personalized service over the telephone that the improvement from terminal systems would be marginal. Besides, the telephone is free."

Limited availability in many countries can also reduce the value of electronic services. For example, one consultant remarked that because only a handful of local banks offer electronic banking in Brazil, companies there will inevitably have so many accounts at other banks that only a partial picture of their cash position can be obtained electronically. Furthermore, automated balance reporting services offered by banks headquartered outside a subsidiary's country of operation are of little use because those banks usually lack the extensive local branch networks needed for collection and disbursement accounts.

Another drawback to electronic systems in many countries is that consolidated, multibank reports are sometimes expensive or even impossible to obtain. Thus, companies may be forced to total their balances manually, which defeats the whole purpose. The inability of banks to provide information to one another results in part from technological problems. For example, one German banker was reluctant to provide data because of "all the different formats in the bank systems, which produce increased paperwork from the sending bank. We don't want to set up several terminal systems here just to get information to other banks the way they want to collect it." But the remarks of another German banker came closer to the crux of the problem: "If we report to the system of another bank, we will lose business."

Selecting the Right Electronic Reporting Service

If electronic bank reporting services are chosen for a local unit, the decision should be made very carefully, with parent involvement. Not only can an unprepared shopper end up with a service that doesn't meet his cash management requirements, but the decision can have a strong impact on both subsidiary and parent banking relations. Companies will want to go first to the banks with which they do a lot of account business to avoid upsetting their present relationships. After weighing these concerns, cash managers can use the following checklist to do some comparison shopping:

· **Emphasize system dependability.** Banks try to impress customers with the bells and whistles of their electronic systems. As a result, companies sometimes forget to find out how dependable a system is. The case of the U.S. subsidiary of a U.K. financial services company shows just how severe the consequences of this oversight can be. To monitor its European activities, the company relies heavily upon its concentration bank's reporting system. The daily reports are used by a variety of departments, including accounts receivable, accounts payable, treasury and investment, and bank reconciliation. Combined, over fifty clerical and supervisory staffers spend the bulk of their time working with the electronic bank reports.

Cutting Costs and Errors Through Automatic Reconciliation

One of the most important reporting services a company can obtain from its banks is automatic account reconciliation. Without it, large clerical staffs must spend hours—even days—poring over dozens of bank statements, comparing them with bank debit and credit advices. After a statement has been reconciled, numerous entries must be made to a subledger system and then keyed into a firm's data base. This manual, multistep process is slow, costly, and decidedly vulnerable to human error.

With automatic reconciliation, firms can reduce this process to just a few hours a month with a handful of staffers. Moreover, because the bank information is computerized, the accuracy of the reconciliations is vastly improved through reduced human involvement. For example, a French manufacturing firm has been using an automatic reconciliation service provided by one of its banks for the past several years. According to a spokesman, "We have been able to reduce our reconciliation staff to three people. We used to have nine people in that unit. The savings are good, and the efficiency is even better."

To maximize these benefits, companies should look for the most sophisticated methods to reconcile accounts. Computer tapes are currently very popular because most banks and companies do not yet have the technological sophistication to allow a direct flow of information between their computers. However, in anticipation of improved technological capabilities over the next several years, the use of direct access—or computer-to-computer—hookups will start to replace tapes. As one U.K. treasurer who is contemplating an automatic reconciliation service put it, "The worst solution is to have the bank throw a tape in a taxi and run it over to our offices, and we then take the tape and put it into our computer. In the future, we'll be able to

---

After the bank system had been used for about a year, problems started to develop. Instead of being available at 8 A.M. as promised, access was often delayed until midafternoon. Then, with increasing frequency, the bank reports were not available at all. The bank had a list of excuses that ranged from transmission problems between the bank and the information network to internal malfunctions. Although the bank had a five-day-history function built into the system, the detailed data was often lost, which was critical to the company, since the accounts reconciliation unit of the firm required detailed invoice data.

According to the firm's cash manager, the problem reached epidemic proportions. "We were without our daily electronic reports for four or five days each month," he said. "Although that may not seem like a lot on the surface, when you're missing this information four days out of twenty-two business days each month, you've got real problems. I had dozens of clerks and supervisors sitting out there with nothing to do each day. This came to $9,000 in idle workers' salaries we were paying each month. Naturally, I took a lot of heat from senior management for that. And I put that same heat on our bank."

cut out all those steps. Direct computer links are a lot faster, with fewer people involved."

A good example of how sophisticated companies can use automatic reconciliation is provided by a Swedish auto maker. The firm has developed a package to reconcile a broad range of banking activities that runs on an IBM mainframe. According to a company spokesman, "We've tried to create a system that would link our bookkeeping department with the banks and allow us to keep track of our exact positions. The bank information comes over a special network, which is designed for computer data transmission. All the bank information is transmitted into our bank terminal here and is then manually entered into a file on our computer. When we get the various bank debit, credit, and other paper advices, we also manually enter the information into our internal system. Then we run the two files against one another and get a reconciliation."

To eliminate these extra steps, the firm originally had some of its banks deliver the reconciliation data via computer tapes. "It saved us a lot of manual labor to have the tapes read directly into our system. The problem was that we wanted to have this process completely automated." For this reason, the firm is arranging direct computer-to-computer links with its banks. According to the spokesman, "The banks use the same network we're now using, but instead of the information going to our bank terminal and then into our computer, it feeds straight in."

The company is reaping major benefits from the system. "We've speeded up reconciliation tremendously. Today, it is the best part of our internal systems—where we save the most money. Previously, it was a big problem, because it took a long time to complete a reconciliation. And as we were completing a statement, other things would come through the pipeline, which could have significantly influenced the true picture of our reconciled position, especially at year-end."

A good way to prevent the problems that this subsidiary suffered is to talk to present users. Some banks will provide names of users as references to potential customers. It is a good idea to ask for these references and follow up with phone calls to find out about the frequency of system downtime or lost and scrambled data.

· **Ask for test runs.** Before buying a system, companies should insist on having the bank conduct test runs on a portable system. These test runs should demonstrate the different screen and printout formats that are available with the reporting system. Some banks will even put in actual company information for the test and will make alterations to accommodate a company's needs. Firms should also learn the sign-on procedures for accessing the data. This is particularly important for companies that use electronic reporting systems from a number of banks, since systems that have lengthy sign-on requirements can be unnecessarily time-consuming.

- **Have access to bank support staff.** Make sure you are given access to the electronic reporting operations staff at your bank. If the system is down, for example, a staff member should be able to identify the problem and tell the user when the system will be running again. Data can also show up on the screen or printer in a garbled state. A staffer should be able to identify the problem, correct it, and let the user know when the data can be accessed. As one corporate cash manager said, "The big concern for us is that we can rely on the bank if a problem occurs. We know that we have people we can talk to who are responsive to our needs."
- **Select appropriate data frequency.** The transmission capabilities of electronic reporting systems range from real-time data to intraday updates to previous-day information. The importance of speedy data transmission was expressed emphatically by the finance director of a major Dutch firm: "I will never buy a system that isn't real-time. I want to be able to take action quickly, without the risk that information will be communicated too late. That is what electronic banking is all about."

Some companies find that without real-time capabilities, electronic services are inferior to what they are already getting from their banks. According to the finance department head of a German metals manufacturer, "Quite frankly, we're not interested in electronic bank reporting right now. All they're giving us is day-old information. That means we can get this information over a printer early the following morning. That's no better than what we have now. It only costs more."

Not all companies, however, want or need real-time information. And since banks charge more for speedier information, companies should make sure that the data availability meets their needs. If their daily routines do not require intraday or real-time updates, they shouldn't be paying for them. For most companies, however, the previous day's data is next to useless for proactive cash management.

A word of caution: Companies should be aware that banks' definitions of system features vary; what some banks advertise as real-time access, for example, is often just a series of intraday updates. In fact, only a few banks have true real-time capabilities. It is important for a company that thinks it is buying a real-time system to make sure it's not getting a speedy batch-processing system.

- **Use a smart terminal.** Smart terminals, or micros, can be better integrated with internal automated systems to save clerical time and cut costs. In the words of a U.K. finance manager, "It was very time-consuming to have to wait for a full printout on our dumb terminal just to get one piece of information I needed from the end of the report. With a smart terminal, you can go right to the information you need."

The assistant treasurer of a large U.S. chemicals concern agreed: "We can save a few hours out of a person's day by using smart terminals. First of all, the smart terminal can call up each of the individual bank reporting systems. This way, we don't need someone watching over a dumb terminal waiting for one bank report to finish so he can call up the next bank report. Second, the smart terminal can be programmed to automatically manipulate the data into the formats that we need. This adds up to a tremendous time savings."

- **Get the right amount of detail.** Many companies find that they need a service that provides a wealth of detail, rather than simple summary information. This is important because bank information is often needed by departments other than corporate treasury, which is mainly interested in simple balance information. For example, the deputy treasurer of a huge U.K. chemicals concern stated, "My group and I care about the balances and nothing else. We're involved in investment, and we just need to see the overview. But my colleagues in the credit control department need a lot of detail. They want to know if an Italian customer paid, the name, references, and the invoices paid." Thus, companies investigating electronic reporting systems should bear in mind the requirements of their full cash management function, as well as the needs of marketing and other departments.

Some electronic bank reporting systems provide a broad array of data in addition to account balances and transfers: foreign exchange contracts, loan contracts, maturity dates, and lines of credit, for example. The additional reports usually cost money, of course, so a company that has no need for them shouldn't be paying for them, especially if it is getting this information elsewhere. "You have to look at what you need from your bank's system," said one executive. "We use Reuters for forex and interest rates, so we didn't need the same thing from our bank system."

- **Ensure sufficient fields for reference information.** Companies should find out how many reference details and storage characters the system can accommodate. If a company has to know which remitter is depositing funds and which bank they came through, it needs a system with a large character field. Additionally, if a firm needs specific descriptive data, it should ask the bank if it can transmit that information as well.
- **Select a sufficient data-history option.** To meet specific needs, companies may require a system that stores old information. Normally, companies should demand a system with a history feature of at least three to five days. Some systems have the capability of providing up to sixty days of system history.
- **Seek gross and available balance/value dating.** Insist that the reporting system break account balances into gross and available figures and that individual collections and disbursements be value-dated. Some non-U.S. banks are leery about this, but enough banks are offering it to allow companies to ask for this feature. A Dutch bank offers a service that allows the company to insert back-value days itself, because the bank is the last to know about disbursements being made today that affect yesterday's balances.

Negotiate the cost. Keeping down service costs is always a prime consideration. "Our decision is based solely on cost," the CFO of a huge German metals manufacturer emphasized. "These systems are very expensive." Banks have significantly different pricing policies on electronic reporting systems, and companies have a good deal of latitude for negotiating. Some banks charge companies nothing at all or only time-sharing costs; others impose monthly or per-module fees, as well as additional charges based on the frequency of data access or the number of lines of data. As a general rule, however, banks will cut rates for their important customers to prevent business from moving to banks with better systems.

Coping with Multibank Reporting

Most cash managers must consolidate reports from different banks to arrive at a picture of their total cash position. A common problem with electronic bank services is that, without an automated system to consolidate information, cash managers get stuck with one terminal reporting from each bank. As the treasurer of a French engineering firm put it, "We deal with about ten or fifteen banks, all of which have their own systems. But I can't have ten or fifteen terminals sitting around my office. I am not a pianist." On the other hand, companies do not want to be trapped into using just one bank's system. As the treasurer of a Swiss consumer products firm put it, "To get the full advantage of one of these systems, I would have to move all our business to one bank, and I'm not going to do that." The finance director of a German chemicals firm put it more bluntly: "We won't sell our soul to one bank."

Companies can use one of two different methods to consolidate electronic bank information. These methods differ in cost, efficiency, and availability from country to country. Some banks, especially U.S. money center institutions, offer customers **multibank reporting services** that incorporate data from their own records as well as those of other banks. For example, a prominent U.S. bank recently introduced a service at its European locations that permits customers to access any bank's reporting system via a personal computer. According to the bank's London-based spokesman, "All the customer has to do is comply with the other banks' password controls and formats. He still has to pay the other banks for the service. We offer it because we want it to be our terminal sitting there."

Multibank reporting received a boost early on in the United States from work done by the Bank Administration Institute on standardizing reporting formats. Unfortunately, it is not so easy in other parts of the world. In Europe, for example, multibank reporting systems have not caught on because of a lack of cooperation between banks, as well as corporate concern over poisoning bank relationships by favoring one bank over the others through using its system only. The regional treasurer of a U.S. capital goods producer explained, "The banks here just aren't cooperating with one another in providing consolidated information to their customers the way they do in the United States. The European banks are delaying because they're competing with one another and because they do not want to make it easier for companies to reduce their own use of idle funds and the float."

Many companies, however, are taking an aggressive stance in their quest for consolidated bank data. For instance, the Amsterdam-based regional headquarters of a U.S. manufacturer was having difficulty convincing a major Dutch bank to report information into a U.S. bank's electronic system. According to a company spokesman, "We laid it on the line. We told them that if they didn't do it, we would go over to the American bank with our accounts."

The second alternative—and probably the more promising one in the long term—is to access each bank separately and use an **in-house program** or **treasury workstation** with a bank consolidation module to translate the banks' data to create a consolidated report. The finance director of the French subsidiary of a U.S. electronics firm is using a program on his personal computer to consolidate reports from ten different banks. Despite the differences in their computer systems, he uses the same package for each bank, explaining that "the service firm we go through formatted a common reference table and equivalences, so the coding is standardized. It is one table: On the left you have all the microcomputer software codes; then you have the codes for each bank that relate to your code. These codes all mean exactly the same thing. The bank just needs [to be able to provide] electronic transmission. It's not expensive for them; we pay for it."

The Geneva regional headquarters of a U.S. electronics firm developed a particularly sophisticated program that provides an integrated, real-time, consolidated bank information system. The firm has always been a leader in reporting systems: For over a decade, its European subsidiaries have relied on an automated internal reporting system for treasury management. The system functions as a pipeline for all internal systems, including sales, cash management, and accounting. Through the regional headquarters, every subsidiary is hooked up to the system via lease lines or dial-up lines. Each subsidiary also has its own automated system for tracking forex contracts and credit and collections. However, consolidated bank balance information from each unit's multiple accounts is calculated manually.

According to the firm's director of financial services, the absence of a direct interface with its banks was the most serious drawback to the company's highly automated network, preventing real-time assessment of each operating unit's bank accounts. With the consolidation package, the company will be able to interface with the banks' reporting systems and gain access to bank information—including value dates—concerning its own accounts. "We'll just hook up and dial into the banks' computers," commented the spokesman. "The treasurer in a country can then take that information and quickly reinvest idle funds before the end of the day."

Utilizing data from the banks and from selected internal systems (accounts payable, accounts receivable, and forex), the package will issue confirmation letters and telexes, accounting reports, decision-support data, and a series of cash position reports. These reports will provide information by account, bank, currency, entity, and type of funds. With these reports, the subsidiary treasurers will be able to detect cash management opportunities at a glance. In time, the program will also be able to issue reports with sophisticated graphics attached, which will aid trend analysis and provide formatting for "what-if" scenarios.

Among the reports the firm's software system will generate are the following:

- An **audit report** will present daily details of all transactions from all accounts. The information will include amounts, reference numbers, source of transfers, etc.
- **Value-dated balances,** in both detailed and summary form, will clarify exactly how much cash is available at any given moment and thus prevent errors. Treasurers will then be better able to monitor float and bank clearing times. Value dating is extremely critical for managing cash—especially in Europe, where dating is negotiable—because of its influence on real banking costs.
- **Deposit, borrowing, and forex positions** will be presented according to maturity dates, daily position, and amounts outstanding by bank and by borrower. This will alert staff to pending due dates on time deposits and loans, and it will track currency requirements for forward forex contracts. Treasurers need this information to determine accurately their borrowing and investment needs.
- A **weekly cash position report** will present the cash position by entity and country and will compare actual positions to previous forecasts, leading to better forecasts in the future.
- **Accruals, interest, and commissions** will be detailed to reconcile internal records with bank fees and interest payments on deposits and loans. Banks in Europe do not generally provide detailed account analyses of charges and interest payments, which makes it difficult to detect errors.
- A **bank activity statistics report** will indicate daily receipts and payments by account, by bank, and by total. It will present average balance and activity volume, will list interest and commissions, and will report on the status of credit lines. This will help treasurers detect idle balances and unnecessary credit lines. It will also assist in evaluating the utility of each account.

According to the firm's spokesman, the system will allow the firm's European treasurers to manage their cash more effectively and efficiently. Specifically, the package will result in "better forecasting, fewer emergency loans, better balancing of overdrafts with credit balances, and better control of bank costs." As a result of these benefits, the director of financial services insists, "there isn't a bank system around that will do all the things our package does."

Mastering the Art of Cash Forecasting

By using data generated by internal systems and banks, cash managers are able to develop what is in many ways the central cash management report—the cash forecast. Forecasts enable cash managers to manage bank balances, anticipate financing requirements for daily operations and future activities, make investment decisions, and match anticipated inflows and outflows. As the treasurer of a U.S. consumer goods producer's Venezuelan subsidiary pointed out, "Cash forecasts are the most important tool for monitoring and controlling corporate cash. Without them, good cash management is simply impossible."

To discover if a subsidiary's forecasting is inadequate for its needs, look for these telltale signs:

· Funds regularly lie idle in low- or non-interest-bearing bank accounts, the treasury regularly under- or overshoots its target balances, or the subsidiary relies too much on overdrafts.
· Investment maturity schedules are not matched with predicted funding requirements. This can lead not only to liquidity bottlenecks but also to lost revenue as internal cash is invested at rates lower than those for borrowing (the higher the differential between debt and investment rates, the greater the damage).
· Actual cash balances, fund flows, and float times are consistently different from the original forecasts, and there is no regular review and correction of discrepancies between actuals and forecasts.

The equation for forecasting cash flows can be expressed as follows:

Starting balance + cash inflows − cash outflows = ending balance.

Companies should organize their forecasting on a multiple-period, rolling basis so that unanticipated events can be factored in. Forecasts must be updated quickly; even if the cash manager obtains bank balance reports early in the morning, it will be difficult to borrow and invest if a forecast of the day's ending balances is not available until late in the day. Forecasts can be either short-term (daily, weekly, or monthly) or long-term (semiannual, annual, or longer). The methodologies underlying these two types of forecasts vary greatly. Long-term outlooks are often based on net-income forecasting, including estimates of net income, depreciation benefits, and other items, and resemble sources-and-uses-of-funds statements. Short-term forecasts, on the other hand, are generally simpler calculations of straightforward receipts and disbursements to project future cash flows. They combine the cash flow forecasts of disbursements and collections with bank account positions. Cash managers should consider establishing a continuously updated profile of their corporate financial positions using the following schedule:

· **Daily:** Exact treasury position for that day, with a rolling (i.e., updated) forecast for the next five to fourteen working days, revised daily on the basis of the daily cash report and a variance analysis comparing forecasts with actuals.
· **Weekly:** Rolling forecast for the next four weeks.
· **Monthly:** Rolling forecast for the following four quarters.
· **Annually:** Rolling forecast for the next year, presented by month or quarter.

Forecasts can be fine-tuned by separating the overall cash flow into discrete parts (see the form on page 58). Projecting the timing for certain cash flows is straightforward (the disbursement of payroll or the maturity of an investment or borrowing),

Cash Forecast

Unit/division, etc: _____

Period: _____   Date: _____

	Week 1	Week 2	Week 3	Week 4	Total
Beginning Bank Balance					
Receipts					
Collections					
Unit A					
Unit B					
Unit C					
Intracompany					
Other (interest earnings, etc.)					
Other (loans)					
Total Receipts					
Disbursements					
Vendors/suppliers					
Payroll					
Working fund					
Taxes					
Debt service					
Intracompany					
Other (pensions, etc.)					
Total Disbursements					
Total Net Flows					
Ending Balance					

whereas for more irregular flows (customer payments or variable production costs) it must be predicted as accurately as possible based on experience and intuition, or on analytic techniques such as float forecasting, historical trending, and multivariate time series analyses.

Specific cash flow items will vary widely among different companies, but the following are some of the most common:

Cash inflows

- Major customer payments made traditionally at a consistent time from the invoice
- Irregular customer payments
- Proceeds from a local or foreign borrowing

- Maturing investments with fixed tenors
- Infusions of cash from the parent company
- Dividends, royalties, licensing fees, and other incoming profits

Cash outflows

- Payroll and union contributions
- Major suppliers with consistent payables (e.g., utilities)
- Irregular payments to suppliers
- Tax, bank, and insurance payments
- Interest and principal payments on loans
- Investments
- Dividends, royalties, licensing fees, and other ongoing payments

In addition to financial information, forecasters must consider nonfinancial information, such as production and price trends, to estimate future cash flows. For example, to forecast properly for the copper mining industry, a financial officer at a Brazilian metals firm must consider "government requirements, restrictions, foreign exchange, and both internal and external factors." The firm built a computer model to enable the finance staff to conduct sensitivity analyses of a variety of factors, including copper prices, refining costs, foreign exchange movements, inflation, and interest rates. According to a company spokesman, "We feed all this data in, and then I can play with the computer. I can say, what if for the next ten years prices are such and such, or every two years it's good, then every two years it's down, it's up, down, up, and so on." For its forecasts of the cruzeiro, the firm depends primarily on inflation rate differentials. "If the inflation rate here is so much, and the U.S. dollar is getting stronger by a given percentage, then we try to calculate how much the cruzeiro will depreciate." Once the finance staff has chosen the scenarios that seem most probable, the computer generates a full forecast for the following year.

To forecast their cash needs, cash managers should start by isolating and identifying financial inflows and outflows. They can then use a variety of statistical or nonstatistical methods for predicting actual disbursements and receipts. Intuition and experience are also helpful in estimating customer payment patterns and seasonal trends, as are various modeling techniques. But incorrect assumptions can easily creep in here and undermine the entire forecast. For example, although it should be obvious, many firms record entries on a date-due basis and fail to factor clearing float and other delays into their cash forecasts. As a result, cash flows based on actual funds availability will be mismatched, resulting in idle funds and unnecessary loans. Any discrepancies between forecasts and actual figures should be analyzed regularly so that the reasons for such deviations can be pinpointed and corrected.

A commonly overlooked aspect of cash forecasting is variance analysis. A consultant from a major cash management bank explained, "One of the things we're trying to get companies to do is to have columns for actuals and percent variance of the forecast. Week two is dependent on week one's accuracy, week three on week two, and so on. If you're way off the mark in the beginning, then the rest of your forecast doesn't stand a chance. What we usually say is that if variance is more than, say, 5 to 10 percent, you should explain why you are that far off. Maybe you're 15 percent over on collections because one huge sale came through; you need to note that so people don't think that's going to happen every week. Or you may find yourself with two bank holidays on the same week, so your disbursements are unusually low. This helps you to fine-tune your forecasting and not get confused by one-time events."

To prepare their forecasts, companies can use methods that range from informal, manual systems to highly sophisticated software packages. How the forecast is generated can determine its timeliness and accuracy. If a company using a manual system is getting to the market late or producing crude summary forecasts, it may be necessary to upgrade the system with a microcomputer package. The treasury manager at a mid-sized manufacturer investing in the New York markets did just that and found that "by having what you need to know by 9:30 instead of 10:30, you can enter the markets and get better rates because, as the morning goes on, there is that much less out there and they can lower the rates." On the other hand, many large firms find that highly sophisticated forecasts are too detailed (and therefore an unnecessary expense) for their daily funds management. Remarked the funds manager of a U.S. media giant, "We're so large and have so many receipts and disbursements that minor swings are simply inconsequential; all I need to see is the broad brush strokes and the daily cash position."

Manual forecasting, which uses only a piece of paper and the cash manager's intuitive judgment, is the simplest method of tracking cash flows. Under such systems, firms prepare a cash budget each week or month that shows the exact date and amount of repetitive items, such as payrolls, taxes, loan interest and principal, payments to major suppliers, and receipts from long-standing customers. To determine the resulting cash balances, they must then rely on a worksheet. One consultant advises companies to simply use a calendar: "If a company can't use a computer, I draw a calendar out for them and tell them to put in the big items—mortgages, payrolls, and other repetitive payments. If you put that down you have probably 50 to 70 percent of the forecast done." For example, if a company knows a tax payment of $70,500 is due on the tenth of the month and a $100,000 short-term investment is also maturing on that date, it can enter both amounts on the calendar. The cash manager now knows that at least $29,500 will be available to cover disbursements.

Simple electronic spreadsheets provide an attractive alternative to manual methods. The cash manager simply plugs in aggregate receivables, payables, and balance-position figures off the general ledger data base and the program updates the forecast. As the international treasurer of an Italian manufacturer pointed out, "If you use something like VisiCalc [a popular program], it's very simple. You just change the numbers in the different places, and in a fraction of a second you have a new forecast. I program it myself on my personal computer; it is very user-friendly." Similarly, a Canadian treasurer uses "a spreadsheet that we update. It has rolling forward numbers, which change every time I update information. If I deposit $200,000 today, it rolls my position forward for the next forty-five business days and pinpoints the next spot where I really need my money. It also keeps a rolling record of real and anticipated receipts in both U.S. and Canadian dollars."

Firms with more complex cash flows may prefer to fine-tune cash forecasting through computer models that chart historical trends and explore alternative financial scenarios. For example, a Belgian chemicals manufacturer has built a computerized data base for tracking receivables and payables patterns at various times during the year. The firm uses this information to adjust its forecasts for seasonal trends. In addition, the company inputs various currency and interest rate forecasts for "what-if" analyses. Thus, the firm "is able to play with the data and see what would happen if conditions change by such an amount," said the treasurer. "It's a very useful tool."

For the most sophisticated cash managers, the ultimate goal is to link the company's entire data base to the forecasting model. As one U.K. finance director remarked, "I've got a forecasting system that is not terribly good. What you need for a cash forecast is the whole hog: the accounting data base, all the receivables and payables, and so on. But not just that. You have to begin with your sales and production forecasts. Right now I have to physically extract this from other reports. What I want to do is take our computerized data base and have my cash forecasting subsystem look outside the treasury subsystems and find the next month of sales or production in the United Kingdom and convert this into revenues, which will feed right into my cash forecast so that the whole thing will be mechanized."

One firm that has already attained this level of sophistication is a Swedish automobile manufacturer. The company has created a cash forecasting module that uses data generated by the sales, production, and accounting functions. The firm's mainframe stores information on the company's borrowings, investments, all incoming and outgoing payments, projected sales, and production targets. The treasury staff then taps into this data base via the computer terminal to produce four-week rolling forecasts of the company's liquidity requirements.

Which of the above approaches should be adopted? If a subsidiary's present system is producing good, timely forecasts, then clearly there may be no reason to change. The required level of forecasting will depend on the country's environment and the subsidiary's particular needs. As part of their review, therefore, companies should keep in mind whether the unit's funding and investing options are very limited or highly complex, or if its cash position remains predictable or fluctuates wildly.

Cross-Border Reporting to Parent or Headquarters

In addition to developing reports to satisfy local needs, subsidiaries must transmit cash management data to their regional headquarters or parent. Firms should closely review their cross-border reporting systems to determine the frequency, accuracy, completeness, and usefulness of current information. It is helpful to talk with decision makers and staff at headquarters to see if any critical reports are missing or if any superfluous data can be cut.

To monitor subsidiary performance, parents must be able to monitor trends in bank balances and costs, bad-debt expense, DSOs, CDOs, borrowings and investments, and forecasts compared with actuals and variance. To facilitate trend analysis, information can be presented according to the following categories: yearly averages for the two previous years; year to date; averages for two previous months; this month's closing; original forecast for this month; difference between forecast and actual; and next month's forecast. Examples of trends that could be uncovered this way include a steady shift toward lengthened CDOs or an increase in idle bank balances accompanied by growing borrowings. Local forecasts should be carefully compared with actual results, and discrepancies should be explained and, if possible, corrected.

Parents and regional headquarters should give subsidiaries as much feedback on their operations as possible to reinforce the habit of communication. Just knowing that somebody else is looking at their results will encourage many local cash managers to conduct their work more conscientiously. Said the treasurer of a U.S. entertainment company with numerous foreign subsidiaries, "Even if we throw the report away, it forces our management out there to take a look at their balances. So there's a value in simply having the report. But we don't throw it away."

Headquarters can also use the reports to set clear objectives for subsidiary management, as pointed out by the Hong Kong regional treasurer of a Canadian natural resources firm. "When companies start getting out of line, we just slam an MBO [management by objective] on the local managing director and chief financial officer." For example, the firm's Indonesian subsidiary recently let its DSOs slip from sixty days to eighty-five. "So they've been given an MBO that by September their DSOs must be back down to sixty days. If they're not, then when the CFO is evaluated for his salary increase and his bonus comes up—well, he didn't meet his objective: Too bad. If they don't know how to bring down their DSOs, then they shouldn't be managing the company. It's that simple."

Good cash management information not only helps headquarter personnel evaluate subsidiary performance, it makes it possible to catch problems early. For example, the Hong Kong regional headquarters of a well-known U.S. chemicals manufacturer relies on a monthly reporting system that includes forecasts of cash positions, financial expenses, and currency exposures, as well as a credit report that includes DSO levels and an aging analysis broken down by product. The reports, which are sent in by mail or telex, are used essentially to evaluate the performance of local cash managers. Said the regional treasurer: "We're looking for untoward things that prompt you to ask why. That's our job here: to dig and to keep breaking our nationalistic tendencies. People working in Australia may be doing things that are great for Australia, but they don't have the overall picture for the corporation."

The regional treasurer in Hong Kong representing the Canadian natural resources firm has created a reporting system that gives him tight control over subsidiaries. Every month, local financial managers send "flash reports" to Hong Kong detailing twenty key items, including borrowings, investments, payables, receivables, DSOs, aging, bank balances, foreign exchange exposure, and a cash forecast for the next month. Local cash managers are also required to prepare a forecast each quarter for three years out, with the first eighteen months broken down by quarter. Reports are always telexed because "the mail just takes too long. Indonesia to here is ten days, Thailand to here is anywhere from eight days to a month, so don't bother with a letter, please."

In addition, local cash managers must supplement reports with frequent telephone calls. Said the regional treasurer, "I work a very simple system with my people in the field. If you've got a problem—I don't care whether it's covered by a report or not—I want to know about it when you know about it. If you happen to find out at three o'clock in the morning, then I want to know at three o'clock. The system is very simple. If you don't tell me and I find out, your life expectancy is very, very short."

Strict reporting requirements are especially important for subsidiaries in hyperinflationary and other difficult environments where cash management can mean the difference between survival and failure. For instance, a U.S. pharmaceuticals manufacturer requires specific information relating to the cash positions of its Mexican units. The reason: Because of the financial risks of operating in Mexico, the parent prefers its Mexican companies—which often experience large buildups of excess cash—to make as many remittances as possible. Local financial managers send detailed forecasts of projected receipts for the next quarter, along with a breakdown of their excess cash investment portfolios and information on inventory and receivables turnover, via telex each month to corporate headquarters. As part of the budgetary process, the Mexican cash manager analyzes the variances between actual performance and targets and telexes this information to the firm's Latin American regional headquarters in Florida. The parent and regional headquarters motivate local managers to meet targets by providing incentive compensation and continual feedback.

Another U.S. chemicals concern with Latin American regional headquarters in Florida reacted to the crisis there by installing computerized cash management systems at each of its Latin American subsidiaries for daily monitoring and forecasting of receivables, payables, borrowings, and investments at the local level. In Brazil and Argentina, local units have also automated bank balance reporting, permitting daily tracking of cash needs and surplus funds and continuous reconciliation of bank statements. Moreover, regional headquarters is now contemplating upgrading local computer capabilities from the IBM System 3 batch mode to the more sophisticated on-line IBM System 34.

This tight reporting at the local level lets subsidiaries provides a wealth of information to both regional and parent headquarters for monitoring purposes. On the sixth working day of each month, local units report full balance sheet and P&L statements plus complete breakdowns of DSO levels, aging of receivables, and credit terms, along with explanations of the differences between forecast and actual levels. These reports are transmitted via telex to both parent headquarters—where they are fed directly into the corporate computer—and regional headquarters. The region uses the reports to analyze subsidiary cash management for the parent, comparing predictions with actual results, and submits a report to the parent with comments on problems between individual subsidiaries and updates on devaluation rates and interest costs in every country. The parent's computer consolidates subsidiaries' income statements and balance sheets and produces an estimate of the region's profits.

Overcoming Common Barriers to Cross-Border Reporting

Getting subsidiaries to provide regular cash management information is not as easy as it might seem. Here are four common problems that parent headquarters often encounter—with practical advice on how your firm can avoid them:

(1) **Language difficulties.** Language differences often cause communications barriers between the parent and its subsidiaries, particularly those in Asia, in Latin America, and in European countries such as Spain and Italy. To facilitate subsidiary-to-parent communications, a U.S. pharmaceuticals giant instituted programs at its Japanese offices to develop increased fluency in English among local staff. According to a spokesman, "Good communications with headquarters is considered important. Although most of our staff can read and write English from studying it in school, only limited numbers can conduct business in English." For similar reasons, the parent has transferred several members of an Australian subsidiary's financial staff to Tokyo headquarters. Said the spokesman, "This is working quite well. Our young expatriates from Australia have greatly lessened our language problems."

(2) **Local resistance.** A good example of this problem comes from another firm, whose cash manager said, "One time, the parent tried to stick its nose in our operations. There were so many questions by telex, by telephone. We got sick and tired of it and gradually stopped sending the information." In fact, it was the spokesman's pride that was offended by the requests for regular reporting of data: "We had to convince them that we are not a sloppy company, that we are not a lousy company." When upgrading reporting systems, parents should take steps to ensure the support of subsidiaries in order to avoid appearing to undermine their authority.

(3) **Technical problems.** Subsidiary-to-parent reporting systems are often hampered by many of the same communications problems that local systems encounter. In countries such as the Philippines, international telex transmissions are frequently interrupted by brownouts, and direct international telephone dialing is unavailable, often requiring hours to make an international connection. In some nations, international telecommunications lines are extremely undeveloped. Remarked the assistant treasurer at a U.S. consumer goods conglomerate, "In countries without good telecommunications, such as Uruguay, we just use telex with automated input into our system. It takes a little more time and is more error-prone, but it's just a few countries so it's okay."

Even in more advanced countries, however, companies sometimes encounter frustrating technical problems. One firm, for example, found that it could not get a coherent signal for transmissions from its U.K. office. After months of effort, the company is considering relying on a special program at headquarters to pinpoint errors while trying to find an alternate network for telecommunicating.

(4) **Government regulations.** Governments sometimes place restrictions on cross-border data flows. The most sensitive areas are instructions relating to transaction initiation and forex purchases. Some governments insist on seeing all the data that goes out. Another typical concern is payroll information, which can be considered confidential. On balance, however, restrictions on data transfer have not become the major problem some analysts once feared, although it is impossible to predict what the future holds.

In addition to restrictions on content, governments sometimes complicate corporate plans for cross-border systems through their control of the national communications system. Some governments restrict the use of private lines and insist that reporting be done over state-owned lease-lines, which may limit the way data is formatted. These monopolies often cause inordinate delays as well, as one firm found when it took six months to obtain a special line and modem from the Belgian telecommunications authorities.

Companies should plan ahead for such delays and restrictions to minimize problems. Said the assistant treasurer of a major U.S. electronics firm, "We've had problems in a number of countries, such as Malaysia, but we've always been able to negotiate with local governments on the right type of telecommunications equipment. You just have to be a little flexible and you can always work it out."

Decentralized Reporting Systems: Case Examples

The type of local information required by headquarters will depend in part upon the group's organizational and ownership structure. Generally speaking, decentralized firms require less cash management information than centralized companies. Unfortunately, some decentralized firms carry this trend to an extreme and ask for little more than standard accounting reports. These reports leave the parent in the dark as to how well subsidiaries are managing cash and do little to motivate local managers to make savings through better cash management.

The lax reporting practices of many decentralized companies are exemplified by a major electronics firm based in the United Kingdom with operations throughout Europe, North America, and the Asia/Pacific region. The firm takes a completely hands-off approach to monitoring its overseas operating units: "We don't get in their hair; we just don't have the time." As a result, the company has made little effort to construct an efficient cross-border reporting system. Parent headquarters receives monthly reports from subsidiaries on the third week of the following month, "but they are primarily on balance sheet items." Cash forecasts are sent in only quarterly, and the firm never asks for reports on currency exposures, collections, disbursements, DSOs, and other key cash management data. The company's reporting system relies mainly on the mail and telephone, which, said the treasurer, "is somewhat ironic; we make computers, but we do not use them for our monitoring and cash management."

The firm's spokesman was aware of the deficiencies of his reporting system—which are more a result of his firm's lack of concern for cash management than of its organizational structure: "We're certainly not sophisticated. We see ourselves as a manufacturing business, not a bank, so we haven't yet made the effort to control our cash positions. But who knows what the future will hold?"

A company that carries decentralization one step further is one of Japan's fastest-growing electronics firms. This well-known corporation has over forty sales offices and manufacturing subsidiaries in the United States, Europe, Australia, Hong Kong, Malaysia, the Philippines, Singapore, Taiwan, and Thailand.

Despite its vast international operations, the company follows a policy of total decentralization. As the manager of international finance remarked: "We do not control local subsidiaries. I cannot use that word. They can decide on their own initiative. They are responsible for their own financial matters. It is impossible to control from Japan; I have no television to watch them."

One of the firm's objectives is to integrate subsidiaries into their local environments so that they appear not to be manipulated by the parent. As the spokesman put it, "Each subsidiary should seem to be that country's company." To make sure that corporate policies are followed, senior financial management at each subsidiary is made up of expatriates with years of training at parent headquarters. More important, the firm has a deep-rooted commitment to decentralization: "If we control from our side 100 percent, I think they will depend on us 100 percent. I can give you no other explanation." As a result, the company does not employ any of the cross-border techniques that are standard in the West, including cash pooling, netting, and reinvoicing. In fact, the spokesman was not even able to evaluate the performance of local cash managers. When asked how he could tell whether subsidiary management was doing a good job, he replied, "That is a very good question. But I am not in charge of such matters, I am a finance person."

These decentralized companies should not tolerate such laxness: They should strive for reporting systems that allow the parent to review how well subsidiaries are managing cash but leave the day-to-day control over cash management decisions up to local managers. One decentralized company that has come up with a model reporting format is a U.S. consumer goods manufacturer. The parent's treasury department receives a detailed cash management report from overseas subsidiaries every month. The subsidiaries input the data into microcomputers that transmit balance sheet and P&L data via a time-sharing network to the parent. The parent's computer then generates a report for treasury with the following information:

- Total disbursements and receipts for the month, previous month, year to date, previous year, and forecast for next month.
- DSOs, CDOs, bad-debt expense, and aging of receivables for the month.
- Total debt and investment broken down by short-term, long-term, and intracompany figures.

According to the company's spokesman, "We compare the information we get with published material, we talk to accountants and bankers and some of our internal people with foreign experience, and try to get as good a feel as we can for what the standard operating practice is in those countries. We don't monitor their daily cash, but we like to keep on top of things."

Another decentralized firm, a major U.S. industrial manufacturer, is able to ensure that local management adheres to corporate policies through a good reporting system. According to the firm's manager for corporate finance, "Even though we're very decentralized, with higher-level management just receiving reviews of local operations monthly, a Japanese manager just does not do his own thing for three months and report on it casually. We're more disciplined than most other companies; we really work at it. We want to know what's going on, we want to know fast, and we do not want to be surprised."

To meet its information needs, the company set up a worldwide state-of-the-art reporting system in the mid-1960s for large subsidiaries in Australia, Japan, and the Philippines and sourcing operations in Hong Kong, Malaysia, and Singapore. All the units are fully computerized and transmit monthly reports via the firm's own time-sharing network either to corporate headquarters (in the case of subsidiaries) or to individual product divisions (in the case of the sourcing operations). According to the firm's spokesman, the company has encountered no government restrictions on cross-border data transmissions anywhere in Asia. To avoid any possibility of government constraint, the Asian units process all the data locally. In addition to full financial statements for accounting purposes, local units provide information on balances, currency exposures, borrowings, investments, DSOs, and aging of receivables.

Once the processed data is received in the United States and consolidated, the parent's treasury staff can retrieve a variety of reports from the computer, including cash flow and working capital analyses and projections. The firm also carefully scrutinizes the data to ensure that subsidiaries are following corporate guidelines. For example, the spokesman explained that borrowing limits have been set for each unit, "and if our group in the Philippines is getting near the top of the band, we're sure as hell going to find out why. We set targets and goals on all these cash management items, and we monitor them very, very closely."

In Search of Data: Centralized Reporting Systems

While all MNCs must have good cash management reports from overseas subsidiaries to monitor the performance of local cash managers, centralized companies have particularly rigorous needs because the parent must make global cash management decisions (i.e., currency hedging and netting). Companies trying to establish cross-border systems for cash pooling, netting, reinvoicing, in-house factoring, or financing require highly detailed and frequent reports to centralize control over widespread foreign currency positions and cash flows.

To support its cross-border reinvoicing/in-house factoring system, a U.K. manufacturer of consumer products designed a fully automated internal reporting system to track its subsidiaries' cash flows and positions throughout Europe, North America, Latin America, and the Far East. The computer program was built in-house rather than purchased from a vendor because, in the words of the company's group treasurer, "If we went out and bought the package, the cost would have been around $5 million. We found out that nobody had such a package anyway. It would have to have been tailor-made for us, and we'd have ended up paying consultants vast sums of money to come up with a specific package."

The company's internal reporting system operates with three separate subsystems, all linked to support the centralized treasury. The three perform synergistic functions.

Subsystem One

· **Contains all reports on all customer accounts.** "If they like, the operating companies working through the factoring company have no need to keep ledgers of their own," the treasurer said. The data base, for instance, maintains over 800 specific customer ledgers for the United Kingdom alone. According to the treasurer, this cuts down on costs. "They can access at any time their complete ledger, or subsets of that ledger split into any market they can devise a code for." The operating companies can break down any information by settlement, country, quantity, or any combination of these variables. "And if at the end of the year they want to see the whole damned lot, they can access that too," the treasurer added.

· **Stores information on invoices, payment instructions, and third-party transactions and assists in reconciling intracompany trades.** The system consolidates all account information and prints confirmations. The subsidiaries are then able to access their accounts and can pull off whatever status reports they require. European firms access and update the system on a daily basis; systems that interface with foreign divisions such as those in the Far East, Canada, and Australia are still being developed.

· **Creates strategic reports.** This particular capability was a key selling point to top management. "This is a tremendous aid to our planning processes—especially hedging and forex," the treasurer pointed out. Based on the information that can be retrieved from the document files, the system can create detailed reports of anticipated cash flows and signal potential surpluses and shortages of specific currencies. This system is also used to provide twelve-month exposure forecasts.

Subsystem Two

· **Monitors external financial activities.** According to the treasurer, this subsystem "does reporting balances on the various accounts we've got—the instruments we've entered into." The subsystem lists bank investments, borrowings, and forward contracts. "This lets us keep track of maturity schedules and other time periods so we know where we are with these people."

· **Provides the tactical transition forecast (TTF).** This lets the treasurer "pull out absolutely everything that's contractually on the system." The TTF enables him to see forecasts of his companywide cash position for each day up to a six-month horizon—a particularly valuable tool for liquidity management. In the treasurer's words, "It provides us with a total company account balance position."

Subsystem Three

· **Generates internal accounting reports and required published reports.** This is the administrative internal bookkeeping program. It functions as a bridge, assimilating data from the other subsystems into necessary accounting reports. This has allowed the company to "cut down enormously on administrative costs, paper, and the head count."

The firm's computerized cash management system is by no means fully evolved. "What I'm working on at the moment is developing some goodies that can be bolted on at the end," the treasurer noted. This includes "some modeling techniques. We'd like it to apply our actual exposure profile and come up with an optimization of the existing portfolio—given certain interest rates and other variables, like the use of options and futures." The next stage, to be developed in about a year, is "a direct interface with the banks for information and automatic reconciliation."

Another good example of a centralized reporting system is that of a cash-rich airline domiciled in Singapore. The firm's far-flung operations encompass all major continents and virtually every country in the Asia/Pacific region. To keep tabs on its worldwide operations, the company has instituted a weekly reporting cycle. Each Friday, all subsidiaries telex to Singapore headquarters a report that includes sales, cash inflows and outflows, surplus funds, and a forecast of the following week's cash position. "Cash cows"—the big money makers—are required to report in every two or three days. These reports are supplemented by a monthly cash summary that details total cash inflows and outflows, collections, payables, remittances, and the end-month cash balance. According to the company spokesman, "We use the monthly summary as a countercheck against the weekly reports to make sure that what they're reporting is accurate." All data is fed into a computer, which generates a variety of reports, including aging, DSOs, and currency exposures.

This tight monitoring system enables the firm to maintain a highly centralized cash management operation. Headquarters staff makes all investment and foreign exchange decisions and implements financial policies wherever possible. The only exceptions are countries with stringent exchange controls. Even in those cases, the spokesman noted, "we make up our minds here, and we just get our offices to carry out the policy at their end."

For example, the company has set up an advanced pooling system. After receiving the weekly report, treasury staff instructs subsidiaries to remit funds either in Singapore dollars to corporate headquarters or to a U.S. dollar hold account in New York. Headquarters arranges the necessary spot contracts in Singapore on behalf of its subsidiaries. However, the firm must modify its system for several countries. Said the firm's treasury manager: "In some countries we can wait maybe three weeks or a month before getting approval to remit. They quibble on every item, and that jams up your money." As a result, the firm monitors these subsidiaries closely and instructs them to invest surplus funds locally, earning interest until approval for remittance is received.

To tighten its control over corporate cash resources, the company is contemplating adopting the automated balance reporting system of a major U.S. money center bank. According to the firm's spokesman, the bank is "linking up the money centers of the world, and we could just sit here in Singapore and see what our bank balances are all over. We could also key in payment instructions." Thus, the headquarters staff could initiate funds transfers directly wherever exchange controls permit. Yet, the firm is hesitant to subscribe to the service—despite its seductive advantages—because the airline already uses the balance reporting system offered by another U.S. bank. Like other Asian companies, it tries to avoid disrupting traditional banking relations: "This is a very serious matter. Such an action would have to be approved by the managing director and the chairman of the board, and it will be a very difficult decision. This is a long-standing relationship."

When to Use Cross-Border Electronic Bank Reporting

Although bank reporting is normally a local affair, some parents have established cross-border electronic links with banks in foreign countries to monitor especially important accounts. These can include the major accounts of the largest subsidiaries or problem-plagued operations and key hold accounts of the parent company. The most important reasons for acquiring cross-border electronic banking capability are the following:

· **To upgrade monitoring of subsidiary cash positions at parent headquarters.** Companies that want to emphasize and enforce improved global cash management may prefer to obtain timely and detailed information on subsidiary banking activities directly from the banks. A Dutch capital goods producer is one firm that plans an ambitious overhaul of its cash management operations. According to the assistant treasurer, "If this plan is to succeed, we must have improved control over our foreign units through electronic balance reporting."

· **To monitor foreign currency accounts of the parent.** Some hold accounts are so large or volatile that they are worth the expense and trouble of monitoring from abroad on a daily or intraday basis. For example, the Swiss subsidiary of a U.S. MNC uses the electronic reporting service of a New York bank to monitor its CHIPS account, which represents its most active foreign currency account, on a daily basis.

· **To help run cross-border cash management vehicles.** For firms with netting centers or reinvoicing, in-house factoring, or finance companies, electronic reporting services are a critical component of sophisticated systems designed to manage cross-border cash flows. In the words of the assistant treasurer of a U.K. reinvoicing company, "I wouldn't even consider putting in a reinvoicing center if I didn't have access to a support mechanism like the reports the banks can give us. We wouldn't be able to exercise control over the operation."

Computerizing Cash Reporting Systems

Companies around the world are taking major strides toward automation of their cash reporting systems: According to a recent Business International (BI) survey, four out of five international cash managers will be using computer systems over the next three years. Although cash managers can apply computers in a variety of ways, there are three chief benefits from automating a cash reporting system:

(1) **Reduced administrative costs and managerial time.** Computers slash manpower needs and improve productivity by eliminating tedious hours of filing and other administrative chores. When treasurers compare the cost of implementing and maintaining automated systems with the expense of employing a large clerical staff, the computer usually wins. Computers also minimize nonproductive use of manage-

rial time and help motivate financial staff, since many mundane and unpleasant tasks are handled automatically.

For example, the Brussels regional headquarters of a U.S. chemicals firm installed a fully automated reporting system. According to the company's treasurer, "The first and main benefit is that it will reduce the accounting staff by four or five people. We won't need people to prepare the payables by matching them with invoices or to enter information from bank statements to reconcile our accounts. So we are saving a lot of time, and that means saving people." The treasurer of a major Swiss pharmaceuticals firm found even greater labor savings in his computerized operation: "I tell you, if we had no computer here, I would need another ten people to run this operation. But even that wouldn't be sufficient; they are not as quick as the computer."

(2) **Instant data retrieval.** Computers enable firms to respond swiftly to a broad range of cash management problems. In the words of the assistant treasurer of a highly automated U.S. consumer goods producer, "It's all there at the push of a button—credit limits on customers, borrowings, our investment portfolio. We even have interest rates and currency rates in our data base, which we update every day, so I know what's going on."

Computer speed is an invaluable aid to companies attempting to stay on top of sudden changes in currency and money markets. One French treasurer recalled how the computer helped his firm avoid a major currency loss: "Two banks called us and said the Bundesbank was intervening and selling the dollar. We immediately figured out our position on the computer and realized we had an excess of $12 million, and immediately we sold it. We were able to know our exact position instantly, and there is no manual system that can do that."

(3) **Improved decision making.** Companies with automated systems can store enormous amounts of cash management data that can be clearly and easily organized into concise reports and graphs. "As our data output became greater," the finance director of a Swedish oil firm recalled, "we were burying ourselves in facts and figures. We couldn't forecast well because it was too hard to get a complete picture of our activities. We moved to automation primarily to increase the quality of our decision making, to manipulate all this information in a simple format."

Equally important, by reducing administrative work, computers give cash managers more time for complex problem solving. For example, a major Swedish car manufacturer uses an automated system to record 25,000 foreign exchange transactions per year, for a total value of Skr35 billion, and to generate bank confirmation letters. The firm's money desk manager summed up the result: "The new system will give us more time to do what we are hired to do—treasury management."

The type of computer used, of course, will have a great impact on how effective a company is in achieving these benefits. Firms can choose from among a wide range of computer systems, but essentially they come down to four major options: time-sharing services, mainframe systems, stand-alone microcomputers, and integrated systems where two or more computers are linked together. Each of these options is described below, with illuminating examples of how companies have successfully applied them to improve cash reporting systems.

Time-Sharing Systems: An Inexpensive Alternative

The simplest way to computerize a cash reporting system is to use a time-sharing system, which allows you to rent storage space in a service company's computer and access its programs from an in-house terminal. Time-sharing systems are popular among companies leery of making an expensive commitment to computerization by purchasing their own computers. One such firm is the Swiss subsidiary of a U.S. telecommunications giant, which uses a smart terminal to access a time-sharing system on which it maintains a proprietary data base. Information is removed from the data base and downloaded into a software package on the micro, allowing staffers to manipulate it in-house.

The subsidiary's treasurer explained how the interface works: "We do not have any access to the [time-sharing] computer during the day, because this connection is pretty expensive. But by using a micro we can do more work locally, which saves a lot on time-sharing costs. If we wanted to do this ourselves [on our own mainframe], it would be much more expensive."

Of course, when it comes to computerization, companies are in the game for the long haul, which may make it wise to instruct subsidiaries to move away from time-sharing. Many firms have found that rising time-sharing fees and falling hardware prices are changing the entire cost equation. Because time-sharing costs go up as the work load increases, more and more companies are purchasing in-house computers to accommodate anticipated growth in data processing needs.

Using Mainframes for Greater Horsepower

The advantages of mainframes are that they have enormous processing power and can store huge amounts of information. A good example of how a mainframe can be used to develop a top-notch reporting system is that of a large Paris-based chemicals and textiles manufacturer. The company has built a computerized reporting system based on an IBM mainframe that facilitates a panoply of cash management responsibilities—from pooling cash and selecting the best investment and borrowing instruments to preparing forex reports for the central bank and monitoring bank compensation. According to the firm's assistant treasurer, "Our goal is to computerize almost every aspect of our cash management."

The company first began automating its sales and credit and collection functions ten years ago, when it implemented a sales order entry system on its mainframe. The system monitors daily sales orders generated by the group's subsidiaries and agents, both inside and outside France. Daily sales orders are input in one of three ways, depending on the subsidiary's size. In countries with high commercial volume— Germany, the Netherlands, the United Kingdom, and Belgium—orders are sent via on-line hookups between subsidiaries and the mainframe in Paris. For lower-volume countries—Switzerland, Greece, and Italy—a cheaper system is used under which telexed information is automatically input into the mainframe without manual intervention. In very-low-volume countries such as Ireland, sales reports are sent by telex and input manually into the computer.

According to the firm's spokesman, the system was originally established "to give us precise data on every new order in every part of the world. The information was used for inventory and production management, for our purchases of raw materials, and to solve shipping problems." But the finance department quickly realized that the data had applications for credit management: "A little while after the order entry system began, we started using it to check customer credit limits and, combined with receivables information, to produce collection reports."

For its domestic cash management, the company has purchased sophisticated software that operates on the IBM mainframe. According to the assistant treasurer, "It's a full treasury system, giving us everything we need to manage our cash in France. It calculates cash positions, lets us do 'what-if' analysis, the whole thing." The basic package was obtained from a French computer service company and modified by the finance staff and the software house manager to meet the company's specific requirements. "It was a good program, but we had to link it to our administrative structure, reporting systems, bank accounts, and so on."

The company uses the mainframe in conjunction with an automated balance reporting service offered by another French computer company to run a cash-pooling scheme among the firm's twenty-four domestic subsidiaries. The balance reporting system, which is linked directly to the firm's computer, monitors its forty-plus domestic bank accounts, consolidating data from eight different French banks for input into the mainframe. The software program then identifies "the cash position of each company at all their banks. If we find that a company is long in one account and short in another, the computer will produce funds-transfer instructions to pool the net amount in a single location." Excess funds from the various companies within the group are first moved into one of seven divisional concentration accounts and then consolidated in a central account managed by headquarters staff. "We keep the divisional accounts separate because we want the industrial units of the group identified very clearly, to keep their own identities. But we can move the funds around as easily as if they all came into one account."

The firm also uses the computer system to calculate its operating units' upcoming borrowing requirements and to conduct analyses that compare the various funding and investment alternatives, based on cash and interest rate forecasts. Information on the full range of available borrowing and investment vehicles is stored in the mainframe, and interest rates are updated daily. According to the assistant treasurer, this helps "us compare borrowing options very quickly—for example, foreign vs. domestic ones. Or U.S.-dollar bankers acceptances, where interest has to be paid in advance; the computer takes this into account. It also tells us which are the highest-yielding money market instruments when we have surplus funds."

A key advantage of a mainframe system is that it is possible to take advantage of synergies between accounting and cash management information. An excellent example of a company that obtains good cash management reports by drawing cash data directly off the accounting data base on the mainframe is the Brussels-based European regional headquarters of a U.S. chemicals concern. Until recently, the treasury staff, like that at many other firms, faced enormous difficulties in tapping into the accounting system. The key problem was that the system had been developed to create historical data for the controller before the years when cash management became a critical concern; as a result, information was not integrated properly for use by the treasurer, and cash management reports had to be assembled manually.

In the mid-1970s, the company embarked on a multistep program to overhaul its existing system and turn it into an integrated, on-line accounting and cash management system. It hoped to improve both the accounting and the cash and currency management functions. The company's first step was to establish on-line order and billing capabilities. Video terminals were installed in each sales location so that customer orders were electronically reported to the order and billing department in Brussels and to the manufacturing plants. This allowed the company to devise five-week cash forecasts based on due dates or on customers' historical habits. In addition, billing is now automatically generated by the release of a shipment.

The second step was to integrate accounts receivable with the general ledger and to put them on-line. Order and billing, accounts receivable, and the general ledger modules are now interactive and can share the same terminals and computer. The third step, near completion, is to put the accounts payable ledger on-line. According to the assistant treasurer, "Once you have your on-line receivable system and your on-line payable system, it is easy to turn it all into an on-line reporting system."

Information received by the reporting system is sent to the U.S. parent and is also used for a variety of cash management functions, from monitoring credit terms and forecasting cash positions to analyzing short-term borrowing scenarios. According to the spokesman, the recent improvements mean that "we can look at any accounts receivables in Europe or Africa. When we look at the account of a customer in Finland, we get on the screen here the same information that they get in Finland."

The accounts receivable module contains the daily sales information for each European sales office, which is vital to credit management. With this system, the individual sales offices can access the data base to get a real-time statement for every customer: the overall balance outstanding, the amount overdue, the aging of accounts, the amount invoiced to date, and payments received to date. The regional headquarters can do the same from its centralized computer terminal, monitoring the region's $200 million in customer exposure.

The accounts payable module monitors due dates of payments to suppliers. And by consolidating the accounts receivable and accounts payable modules, the accounting system is able to generate daily cash-balance reports, by currency and by bank. In short, the reporting system helped the treasury staff to improve credit and collection, the timing of disbursements, and cash reporting and forecasting.

Although the system was costly to develop, the savings have been impressive. "If I had to make an assessment," said the assistant treasurer, "our savings on both the accounting and the cash management modules were between $300,000 and $500,000 from a systems-development standpoint, let alone in terms of operational savings. The main benefit will be to reduce accounting staff. Because everything is done automatically, our accounting staff spends less time preparing entries or reconciling them when they receive invoices. And in treasury, we will be able to process payments in a much more accurate and efficient way."

The Stand-Alone-Micro Option

Although microcomputers have been around only since the late 1970s, they have made a powerful impact on corporate treasuries. Typically, a company may keep its massive accounting data base on a mainframe while establishing a separate cash management data base on a microcomputer. The advantages of the PC include low cost, flexibility, and enhanced treasury control over systems. However, there are potential drawbacks to a PC package as well: It cannot handle the level of detail and amount of historical data that a mainframe can, data from the mainframe of other sources must often be retyped into the program, and the cash manager's numerous duties are increased by the tasks of systems management.

Packages for microcomputers can range from simple spreadsheets to highly sophisticated treasury workstations. Spreadsheets enable the cash manager to write his own program that automatically updates the cash position as new data is keyed in. Treasury workstations are comprehensive packages built by computer service companies and banks to handle all of a treasurer's needs at just one terminal, with modules for bank monitoring, cast forecasting, currency management, borrowing, and investment analysis, and "what-if" modeling. (The term "treasury workstation" is applied to a broad array of packages; for example, some banks offer treasury workstations whose sole function is to consolidate balance information from numerous banks.)

Before rushing out to buy an expensive PC software package, companies must carefully evaluate their needs and resources. The assistant treasurer of a U.S. automotive firm is in the process of upgrading his system from a simple but effective spreadsheet to a workstation package purchased from a computer service company. "What we want to do," he argued, "is bring in a very small system, play with it for a while, and see what we really need. We decided, let's crawl, walk, and then run. Until you have it to play with, you can go to all the demonstrations you want, but you can't really tell. So this is a small learning investment." Indeed, this executive found that all the bells and whistles on the more sophisticated treasury workstations that he sampled seemed to impede easy control of information, and he preferred a spreadsheet that he wrote himself.

But for companies that want a more versatile computer system, a treasury workstation may be the answer. This was the approach taken by a large U.K. natural resources company and a small U.K. glassware manufacturer. According to both firms, the package, designed by a computer service company and marketed by a U.S. bank, is compatible with three popular microcomputer models and will soon be adaptable to others. The program consists of two floppy disks and a hard disk with a large memory capacity; when run on the preferred hardware, the data base can store several thousand transactions. The system can hold information from hundreds of banks and subsidiaries on a wide range of currencies.

The primary purpose of this particular package is to help users manage their liquidity. The package allows treasurers to perform analyses to determine how their cash positions would change based on projected swings in exchange and interest rates. The workstation also includes a bank reporting function that electronically provides updated information on balances and account activity.

The package is designed to permit interfaces with other external data bases as well.

For example, the glassware company has electronic access through the system to a currency rate and forecasting service offered by another bank. The firm's treasurer explained the benefits of this interface: "If we are trying to work the Australian dollar vs. sterling, for example, we've got to calculate them against the U.S. dollar exchange rate. But when you start working with various forward rates, you get lost in a pile of calculations. If the system can accept exchange rates automatically, the process is speeded up a lot."

Both firms emphasize the comprehensiveness of the workstation. According to the spokesman for the natural resources firm, the treasury workstation "gives us a clear picture of our complete position, and it makes our job easier. We use it to monitor the interbank market, our money deposits, our forex exposures, and the short-term money market. It helps us monitor all our positions better." The product's major attraction, said the treasurer of the glassware company, is that "it is a time-saving device that imposes discipline on you. It forces you to do things in an orderly manner." This treasurer spends less than an hour a day at the screen monitoring and analyzing his positions. Although he does not use all the available modules, he is satisfied with the package. "What I pay for and what I really use is the data base. But I've still got a lot to learn. I feel there is more room for me to improve than for the machine."

Although both firms want more customized features—especially interfaces with their accounting systems—they realize that they are getting a lot of computer punch for their money. One spokesman remarked, "We looked at a number of systems before selecting this one. This package is designed for companies like ours. We would like to see an accounting link, and we need more sophistication, but [with a price tag of less than $10,000] a system like this workstation is so cheap that it could be disposed of in two years and still be cost-effective."

As these examples show, cash managers use the microcomputer not just for reporting but also for "what-if" analysis and decision-support functions. Treasury workstations or software systems with decision-support capabilities simplify the analysis of manipulation of cash management information. These packages allow corporate treasurers to make timely decisions about working capital management and help them take advantage of currency and money market fluctuations. One CFO described how he uses his package to answer questions about conditions in these important markets: "What does borrowing lire or deutsche marks cost on the Euromarket? What does it cost in Italy? We input all this information on an Apple computer. Then we have several options: forward cover, borrow, deposit, lead and lag, or do nothing. The computer tells us which option is the cheapest, and then we go ahead and execute."

Decision-support packages are particularly useful for tracking the foreign exchange exposures of an MNC. For example, a U.S.-based insurance company runs a sophisticated foreign exchange exposure management program on an Apple PC. The microcomputer contains data on the company's total exposure, broken down by currency, subsidiary, and due date for all commercial, financial, intracompany, and third-party transactions. "The machine produces a currency aging analysis," said the firm's treasurer. "For deutsche marks [the model shows] what your exposure would be next month and the month after. We know the actuals, and we have an actual gains-and-losses report by currency, by company, and consolidated."

Developing an Integrated Reporting System

An integrated system allows many microcomputers to operate independently while sharing a central data base. It permits users to transfer data electronically between computers without having to keypunch data twice. Rekeying is time-consuming and risks introducing new errors into the data. Integrated systems can even be used cross-border, allowing subsidiaries to input data directly into the corporate data base and to withdraw information at will.

A Canadian natural resources firm with extensive international operations relies on an integrated system. According to the company's treasurer, the firm's EDP department has built an interface between the mainframe and the finance unit's micro, permitting easy access to detailed information on "all our billing procedures and our accounts payable." This data is the "key to our whole cash management exercise. We can go back and retrieve the last six months of production of an oil field, and a full list of all their customers and how much they owe, so that we can do our forecasts. We use an IBM PC to retrieve data from the mainframe and interpret it any way we want."

The firm has even more ambitious projects in the pipeline. "The long-term plan is to utilize more efficiently our information-retrieval pools. For example, one of the things we want is all the information on check clearings. Now, when we take out this information from the mainframe, we have to punch it back in again. The problem with our system is that it doesn't automatically re-create certain information fields, such as what day the money cleared and how many mailing days it took. Someone has to sit there and put those information fields back in. And while that's happening, we can't determine what our float is. It's not uncommon to have half a million dollars out and not have a clue when it's going to clear."

One of the most sophisticated cross-border reporting systems used today is that of the French-based European regional headquarters of a U.S. computer manufacturer. Originally conceived in the mid-1970s to support a European multilateral netting scheme, the firm's internal system has evolved into a highly integrated network serving a broad array of both intracountry and cross-border reporting needs. Both the local treasury and the regional staff rely heavily on the computerized operation.

The reporting system runs on a proprietary network of telephone lines connecting the central mainframe to an extensive network of personal computers as well as mainframes. It is on-line and interactive, permitting both local and regional treasury access to the data bank twenty-four hours a day. Subsidiaries in Europe report full balance sheet and P&L information monthly and supply details on collections and disbursements, as well as a cash flow forecast. Data is also collected on operating units' bank accounts, overdraft charges, loans, and investment yields. Subsidiaries receive daily statements from their banks through their PCs; these data are then fed into their mainframe. While the information is centralized only monthly, the local treasury staff utilizes daily information before consolidating it for the regional treasury at the end of the month.

The data base generates numerous reports, from the regional office's balance sheet and P&L statement to the subsidiaries' daily cash forecasts. As the treasury manager

Buying a Treasury Workstation

Buying a treasury workstation is a complex decision, demanding careful analysis and deliberation. A U.S. foods manufacturer purchased a treasury workstation following an extremely rigorous analysis of the options available on the market. Lacking sufficient internal expertise, the firm hired a software consultant who worked with a special in-house committee composed of members of the treasury, credit, and EDP staffs. The entire review process took several months, but the firm was very confident of the end results.

The committee's first step in the purchasing process was to compile formally a list of features they needed. Based on this, it composed a questionnaire with detailed feature matrices to be sent to selected vendors. After researching the vendor and product surveys produced in various periodicals and by industry groups, the committee and the consultant agreed on nine target vendors. Each vendor received a copy of the questionnaire, a detailed description of the firm's needs, existing systems and treasury organization, and a request for copies of their annual reports and promotional literature.

After a close review of the questionnaire's responses, the committee used an intricate scoring system to narrow the field down to three vendors, who were invited to make on-site presentations. The vendors were informed that the company was particularly concerned with training, data storage, and several other issues, and that the presentation format should include an hour of discussion and two to three hours of software demonstration. The demonstrations covered all major areas of cash management that the package would be used for. They were scheduled several days apart to enable the staff to absorb and debate the experience. To ensure an objective evaluation, the demonstrations were attended by staff from different areas who could ask the vendors a wide variety of questions, especially difficult technical ones. Finally, using a checklist format, the staff evaluated the presentations and graded each vendor in a variety of categories.

---

explained, "The system produces two sorts of data—one for the local people and one for me at the regional level." The local reports include detailed transaction information and assign invoice numbers to receivables, as well as internal reference numbers and disbursement dates to payables. Checks are indexed by number so they can be reconciled in the subsidiaries' general ledgers. The company's local treasurers forecast out thirty days, using a spreadsheet program on the personal computer, and are penalized for missing their target cash balances.

The local reports, including forecasts and transaction reports, are incorporated directly into the balance sheet of the regional treasury, where everything is reviewed as part of a checks-and-balances strategy. "We'll do a walk-through just to make sure the numbers are all correct," said the regional treasurer. The regional report is a summary,

After references were checked, the package deemed most appropriate for the firm's treasury needs was chosen.

Companies can use the following checklist to make sure they don't overlook any important points in their search for the best package:

Software Features

- Every personal computer is different, and software must be designed specifically to operate on particular models. Is the workstation *fully* compatible with your hardware?
- Are you paying for modules and capabilities that you do not need? Are there too many bells and whistles? Is it possible to buy only the modules you need?
- Are any essential modules missing? The key functions include daily bank activity report, cash position worksheet, debt and investment portfolio, bank relations management, transaction initiation, and data storage. Are there any unique additional modules such as a spreadsheet interface, graphics, word processing, report writer, communications, "what-if" analysis capability, or accounts reconciliation?
- Is the system user-friendly? Can you switch easily from menu to menu? Are the menu codes easy to remember and interpret?
- How large is the data storage base? Is it too small, or even too big (and therefore an unnecessary expense)? Does each module provide sufficient detail? Keep in mind that companies often underestimate the data storage capacity they need, especially two or three years down the road.
- Are security safeguards adequate to control access to sensitive information? Are there backup facilities to protect the user in the event of computer failure or natural disaster?
- Are there links with the general ledger or other data bases (e.g., an exchange rate data base)? Can you upload and download?   ▶

---

although it includes daily balances for each bank account. "We are kind of a paradox in cash management," said the treasury manager. "On a month-by-month basis, our balance sheet is centralized, but on a daily basis, we are decentralized. The local guy here in France is responsible for seeing that the cash is managed daily."

The regional treasurer conducts his cash management with a variety of software programs, which are written in-house for the microcomputer. "The unique thing," he noted, "is that we can do horizontal or vertical consolidation of our spreadsheet in just seconds—and that includes forecasts going way out." This enables the finance department to analyze the information it receives by product division, by subsidiary, by group, and so on. All the reports are then relayed from France to corporate headquarters in the United States via satellite.

- How many banks and accounts can be accessed for balance and transaction information? How much does it cost for additions?
- How quickly is data processed? Can more than one operation be performed at a time?
- Does the system alert you to target balances, maturing investments, and debts?

Service and Support Features

- Is the vendor vulnerable to an industry shakeout so that it might become unavailable to service its software? Has another institution (i.e., a bank) made arrangements to take over servicing commitments if the vendor collapses? Who has the source code? Does the vendor have full rights to the package or is it a licensee?
- How extensive is your support agreement? Could future servicing cost a lot of money? How expensive is regular maintenance, and are monthly fees mandatory or optional?
- Is the vendor's support staff knowledgeable, helpful, and committed?
- Is customer service available when you need it, either over the phone or through on-site visits? Does the vendor have a strong commitment to and the resources for future service?
- New modules and features are constantly being added and improved. As a client, are you eligible to receive future enhancements and modifications for free or at a minimal cost?
- Will the vendor customize the package if necessary? How much will this cost, and how long will it take?
- Is there an active user group you can join to trade ideas and solve common problems?

In-House Development or Outside Vendors?

When companies automate their cash reporting systems, one of the biggest questions facing them is whether to use internal EDP staff to develop tailored systems or to purchase packages offered by computer service companies, banks, accounting firms, and other providers. To decide what approach your firm should take, you should review the following six issues:

(1) **Speed of implementation.** The fastest way to get a software program up and running is to purchase a standardized, mass-produced spreadsheet or workstation package from a vendor. However, for those who want the convenience of computer-to-computer interfaces and larger, more complex, integrated systems—such as cash forecasting programs that generate reports by bank, currency, subsidiary, and

- Is the user manual complete, detailed, and up to date without being overly voluminous and obscurely written?
- Are there software installation and training charges? How many days of training are offered? What are the arrangements for future training of new personnel?

The Selection Process

- Have you looked at enough packages? As a rule, companies should examine five to ten different models before making a decision to buy.
- What was the quality of the vendor's proposal and presentation? Was it sufficiently detailed? Did you receive satisfactory answers to hard questions that went beyond the buzzwords (e.g., what does "flexible" really mean)? Did you advise the vendor of your particular needs and provide company-specific data to use in the demonstration?
- Can special pricing arrangements be made, such as a discount or payment through balances (if the vendor is a bank)?
- What is the payback time frame for the system? (First, calculate the costs of hardware and software, monthly fees, and other anticipated service charges; then determine the savings from reduced time-sharing and dumb-terminal costs, improved interest and investment earnings, and lowered labor costs.)
- Did you get input from all appropriate parties before making the purchasing decision? Relevant staff could come from treasury, cash management, EDP, accounting, and credit departments.
- Should you use an outside consultant to help you with your purchasing decision?
- Did you construct charts or checklists to track differences between packages and record the responses of staff and consultants to the vendor's presentations?
- How well did the vendor's references check out?

source—internal development may be the best option. As one financial officer put it, "The main advantage to buying packages is that you can be operational immediately—but this is impossible if you have to make your own modifications to the package, which take time to work out."

(2) **Customization.** Software customization is an important factor for the majority of cash managers, and many believe that their in-house EDP staff is best suited for this task. Many vendors, of course, will customize their programs, but the inefficiencies in reworking a program that was expensive to design in the first place may reduce the cost effectiveness of this approach. The treasurer of a large French chemicals firm explained the importance of customization: "The problem is that each system must be suited to the specific company. I don't think that one company's system could be taken by another company. Even our own subsidiaries must adapt [the parent's] system to their own needs."

Shopping for a New System? How to Build an RFP Your Banker Can Use

No matter what cash management system your company decides it needs, a critical step is to build effective communication with potential system providers. Too often, corporate managers miscommunicate with suppliers and create suboptimal systems at presumably higher cost. In general, companies need to remedy the problem by (1) evaluating their own needs and (2) translating those needs into a more effective request for proposal (RFP).

The Providers' Lament

According to system providers, their corporate clients make the process of system selection more difficult than it should be. "Frankly, 99 percent of the [RFPs] we receive aren't helpful in telling us what the customer wants," says Citibank London Vice President Terry Fitt, an expert in European cash-management systems. Since the provider is unable to determine his customer's real needs, he cannot suggest a specific system, and therefore a reliable price quote cannot be offered. This means the customer will have no tangible basis of comparison stemming from his RFPs, "presumably the reason he submits to several [providers] in the first place," asserts Fitt.

The most common RFP submitted is a simple shopping list, which asks a bank (or software house) what services are available and at what cost. "We get them all the time," says Fitt. "They just want us to check the boxes and name a price."

RFPs That Work

To get the most from a systems search, it is best to try and work with providers in a manner they *can* respond to. Company managers should strive to take the following steps to provide as much useful information as possible:

(1) **Don't confuse an RFP with an RFI.** An RFP should be an invitation to bid on a specific system. An RFI, one cash manager's acronym for "request for information," is only a preliminary step in sending out an effective RFP.

At the RFI stage, it is appropriate to ask for a provider's literature, which will outline the features that are available. For example: Does the system offer real-time reporting? What balance history is shown? How flexible is the screen formatting? What control features are there?

This is also the time to sit down with the provider's analysts and listen critically to their recommendations. This will not only improve a company's own knowledge and decision making, but will offer an early glimpse of the provider's expertise and willingness to help.

(2) **Determine specific needs: Who will manage . . . ?** The best RFP—that is, the one that will be most helpful in gathering comparative data for decision making—is one that gives a provider the specific basis for his offer. The two most critical questions to be answered are: (1) Which locations will manage? and (2) Which ones will monitor? These two concepts should be the basis for building any system.

For example, if your firm wants to place a Cayman Islands manager in charge of European investing, this should be stated in the RFP. Specifically, the Cayman Islands cash manager should be able to access each European subsidiary's available balances and insert payment instructions for each account. Alternatively, this capability could easily be created in a London location or even a U.S. site. But it must be decided and stated.

(3) **Who will monitor?** Some locations will not be initiating transactions, and therefore need only a data feed. However, they may still need the same information. For example, noted one cash manager, "our London office does the trading, but the system feeds the general ledger both [in London] and Chicago [the headquarters]." In this case, the functions of the two locations were vastly different, but the details needed were similar. The firm opted for intraday updates in London and end-day detail in Chicago.

(4) **Decide on the frequency of updates.** An active trading room may indeed need an on-line, interactive system. However, the more rapidly updatable a system becomes, the more expensive it is. Companies will need to decide just how critical it is to have real-time data, or whether intraday or end-day updates would suffice.

(5) **Decide on the level of detail.** The more information accessible, the higher the cost. To help a provider build the lowest-cost system for your needs, it is important to show what data is needed where. For example, a trading room might need external-account numbers; an accounting location might need both external- and internal-account numbers.

In general, the more a firm can tell a bank or other provider about its needs, the better that provider will be able to quote an offer, forecast installation time, etc. In the end, by doing its homework on the RFI and RFP, a corporation will build a far better system at lower cost—both up front and ongoing.

(3) **Compatibility with existing systems.** Because companies do not usually start automating from scratch, the idiosyncracies—even the inefficiencies—of their existing systems need to be accommodated. Standardized packages are not likely to do this. According to a Swedish credit manager, "It's easier for our own EDP people to build new systems interactive with what we already have."

Many treasurers felt that the complexities of the technical problems involved with reworking systems are best left to those intimately familiar with a program's history and design. New cash reporting programs are often written as add-ons or modifications to old packages.

(4) **Debugging.** One advantage of buying a ready-made package is that presumably the bugs have all been worked out. The treasurer at the French subsidiary of a U.S. electronics firm explained the long-term advantages: "When you buy an outside package you get releases for any [future] improvements that the vendor will make, and you belong in fact to a community of users that gives feedback and improves the system."

(5) **Lack of in-house EDP capabilities.** Companies that have not staffed up on computer programming personnel may find it impossible to pursue the option of building cash management software in-house. According to the president of a Swiss subsidiary of a major Japanese firm, "Lots of people within our company request EDP support, but we don't have much EDP staff. This is true all over the world: It is very difficult to employ capable EDP people. If we try to get something from the EDP department we have to wait—half a year, one year, two years. They will say, 'This is not so important, your job is low priority.' " And a European treasurer who prefers in-house development remarked, "We would still consider buying from outside because, basically, we can't do everything."

(6) **Software costs.** Most treasurers—especially those with highly experienced EDP departments—believe that it is less expensive to build packages in-house than to purchase them. An executive at a Canadian firm has not approached vendors for software because he believes the cost of using one would be "horrendous. And we have systems people who should be doing that anyway," he added.

The expense of adapting store-bought packages to internal systems must be added to the equation of software costs. "We have found that when we buy an external system the cost of adapting it to our own is very high," said the Swedish credit manager. "The cost of buying a new one outside and adapting it to our in-house systems is the same as starting from scratch inside."

Not all corporate executives agree that building in-house is the cheapest route. The French treasurer cited above saves money by buying packages off the shelf. "We buy standard packages, with modifications," he explained. "Normally these are pretty good and complete, so you don't need a lot of changes. The changes are always minute. Internal development costs too much, and you don't necessarily have that expertise."

Global Cash Management

3

Minimizing Collection Delays and Credit Risks

The need to maximize internal cash flow is forcing companies the world over to pay more attention to receivables management. Unfortunately, credit managers must overcome many obstacles on the road to a more efficient collection cycle. Collections are often a tug of war between suppliers and customers: While creditors struggle to accelerate receipts, many debtors do everything possible to avoid prompt payment. What's more, suppliers around the world must often work with inefficient mail and bank systems and outmoded internal administrative techniques that can add days or even weeks to the cash collection cycle.

What encourages cash managers to tackle these challenges are the enormous rewards that improved credit and collection management can bring. As the treasurer of a U.K. subsidiary of a U.S. electronics giant said, "Credit and collection is crucial. We tell our people, 'Look, if you can't get payment, there's no cash to manage, and then there's no business at all.' We put great emphasis on receivables management; it's one of the principal areas to which we devote our time."

This equation shows the huge cash savings that streamlined receivables management can generate:

$$\text{Annual savings} = \frac{\text{annual sales} \times \text{days saved}}{365} \times \text{local cost of money}.$$

For example, assume a firm operating in the United Kingdom has annual sales of $500 million, a DSO of sixty-five, and financing costs of 16 percent p.a. If the company were to tighten up its collection of accounts receivable by ten days to a DSO level of fifty-five, its annual cash savings would be over $2.1 million:

$$\$2,191,781 = \frac{(\$500 \text{ million} \times 10 \text{ days})}{365} \times 16\%.$$

Conducting a Credit and Collections Review

To pinpoint opportunities for improved cash management savings, companies should periodically review each subsidiary's credit and collection system. Because the collections cycle is only as strong as its weakest link, a receivables study must examine every possible feature of the system that might contribute to poor performance. As one consultant put it, "How do you know why things go awry? It could be that your policies are a little fuzzy, or you're not doing a good job of monitoring your banks' clearing times, or you're lax in enforcing collection terms. It's like a subway ride: Just one bad connection and you don't get home on time." Following a brief synopsis of how to conduct an accounts receivable study, this chapter will provide detailed guidelines to help companies review their subsidiaries' credit management and collections cycles.

The first step in a receivables study is to gather all internal reports and other background data on the firm's customers, organization, and credit procedures. Key materials to collect include the following items:

- Background data on the company's product line and customer base. How many customers are there? Where are they located? Does the 80/20 rule apply? (This rule says that for most companies the customer base is distributed so that only 20 percent of the clients account for 80 percent of sales. This enables companies to save time and money by basing the credit and collection review on that key customer segment.) What is the value of receipts by location and currency? How many bank accounts are used for receivables? Where are they located?
- Organizational charts describing reporting relationships and job descriptions of officers and clerks responsible for the credit and collection function.
- Procedure manuals and policy statements.
- All internal credit and collection reports that are used by local managers, including DSOs and bad-debt expense.
- Background data on the local cash management environment, including reports from banks and consultants on intercity mail times, the national clearing system(s), and typical credit terms.

After gathering all available information, the next step in a receivables review is to construct a flowchart of the company's collection cycle. As one bank consultant explained it, "The first thing you do is trace through the process, then draw a flowchart. The purpose is to isolate the sources of float in the cycle. There is float between the sale and receipt of an order, between the receipt of the order and the creation of an invoice, between the invoice mailing and the receipt of payment from the customer—and then the banking float in clearing funds into the account, and so on. What you do is go back through a sample of randomly selected invoices from a reasonable time period and check all the dates to find out what the typical pattern is."

Companies conducting an in-house review should interview clerks and managers, follow a number of specific billings through the entire system, and count the days

How to Educate Your Staff on Improving Credit and Collections

The best-laid plans mean nothing if no one understands them. Therefore, it is essential to set clear policies, goals, and strategies for operating units around the world and to communicate them to local personnel.

A good first step is to write an international credit and collection manual. Since no manual can cover the diverse local customs and practices of dozens of countries, the author of the manual should not try to spell out exact credit and collection procedures to be followed worldwide. Instead, the manual should recommend general practices that will lead to increased control in all key areas. Ideas can be drawn from the subsidiaries with the best receivables performance, as well as from secondary sources. Local managers of each subsidiary can then determine the specifics within these broad outlines for themselves. After its procedures and the resulting yearly goals are approved by corporate management, the performance of each subsidiary can be more fairly and usefully reviewed.

For example, to ensure consistency in his regional credit and collection report for Asia, the Hong Kong-based credit manager of a well-known U.S. chemical producer put together a manual on sales, credit terms, and DSO targets known as "The Bible" among his cash managers. Permissible levels are negotiated with local management and vary sharply from country to country in conformity with local norms. Local financial managers are free to use their own cash management styles and strategies as long as receivables stay within the specified limits. "You have to set your authority limits sensibly, so there's a right amount of work given to the local guy, so he has freedom to act. But then the exceptions should be bounced out in each country up here."

A credit and collection manual alone is not enough. Firms should also consider implementing educational programs that either send cash managers from the parent to train local staff or bring local employees to corporate headquarters to learn the most advanced techniques. Such programs can pay off handsomely. For example, a large U.S. steel company has been running training seminars at the local and regional levels in Latin America over the past few years. As a result, DSO levels dropped from ninety-six days to sixty-two, while sales more than doubled.

(and fractions thereof) between the receipt of the customer order and the collection of good funds. It is essential that the collection cycle of each instrument (check, draft, transfer, direct debit, and so on) received by the subsidiary be examined separately. An exhaustive review can be a very time-consuming and tedious task, sometimes taking several weeks of very long days.

As a final step, companies should interview local personnel on their policies and techniques for accelerating receipts. This could involve a standardized questionnaire, an informal discussion, or both, on how they use dunning, lockboxes, and messengers. In-house consultants should use these sessions to informally stimulate thought and awareness of effective techniques ("to plant a seed," as one consultant put it) in the minds of local cash managers. For example, companies can review methods used at other units or in other countries for accelerating collections and debate how they might be adapted to the present environment.

Organizing Credit and Collection for Better Control

In order to understand a subsidiary's credit and collection process, the parent should start by analyzing the organization of the function. Key questions are: Who is responsible for credit decisions? Who is responsible for setting terms? Who determines pricing? Who approves discounts and penalty fees? Who establishes and monitors collection accounts with banks? Who purchases lockboxes and other cash management services? Who has overall responsibility for the operations (invoicing systems and so on)? To whom does the head of marketing report? What is the relationship between finance and marketing?

How the credit and collection function is organized and how the marketing staff interacts with it either facilitate or undermine the collection process. Unfortunately, receivables is a classic source of conflict between the finance and marketing departments. And, as one consultant remarked, "The best warning sign that there is trouble is when there is no coordination between finance and marketing. In these situations, we almost always find savings."

Most cash managers would like to see credit and collection under the direction of the finance department because the extension of credit and the collection of remittances have a direct impact on working capital; marketing departments, of course, prefer to maintain control because of the impact of credit terms, collection practices, and other elements of receivables management on customer relationships and sales.

As the treasurer of a U.S. MNC put it: "Say you want to reduce credit terms because of inflation. We tell people you've got to do this, and the marketing guy sits there and says, 'I can't do it, because we'll lose sales.' The marketing people are as far apart from me on this as you can ever get. You know, it's almost like they're saying, 'Come out of your ivory tower.' "

"On the one hand," the Latin American treasurer of a U.S. electronics giant added, "we'd like to keep credit terms as short as possible. On the other hand, our operating management may have an objective of market penetration, say 10 percent more market share by the end of the year. So they're going to go out and lengthen terms. And instead of thirty days, we're going to go for sixty or ninety."

Both higher sales and accelerated receipts enhance the bottom line: A balance must be found. A successful review will help to tear down the fence between finance and marketing and result in procedures that coordinate the two departments' activities and goals. After determining the reporting responsibilities and the informal relationship between the marketing and finance managers (do they talk to each other or have meetings?), companies can proceed to restructure the credit and collection function to redress any imbalance.

Once considered the sole purview of marketing, the extension of credit should be a joint decision between marketing and the financial officer because of the impact on cash flows. Even decisions on sales incentives, such as offering a discount, should be evaluated by the financial manager. For example, while 100 widgets sold for $1 will generate $100 in sales, discounting the widgets to 75 cents to produce 120 sales will generate only $90 in receipts. A cash management consultant illustrated how the financial impact of credit decisions can damage the bottom line when there is no coordination between sales and treasury: "Let's say that for competitive reasons marketing decides to discount the price of a product. The cost accountants will go along if they feel that the additional volume will lead to lower cost per unit and a higher profit margin. But do they realize the impact that will have on treasury? If they are offering a price discount or volume discount, that means that there may be less money coming into treasury. That means the treasury may have to go into the market and borrow funds. Is the cost of borrowing worked into the marginal cost of the product?"

One way to prevent oversights is to have the treasurer or cash manager sit on a pricing committee so that he can raise these issues and explain the financial impact of credit decisions. Other problems of coordination between marketing and finance can be resolved by educating the sales force on the impact of credit and collection on the bottom line. As the treasurer of a U.S. oil company said, "We try to make them more than just salesmen. We make them more aware of the impact of their activities on the business as a whole and get them to appreciate that it's not just selling accounts that's important, it's also getting paid for it."

However, as long as sales personnel are not held responsible for the payment performance of their accounts, they have little incentive to address the credit manager's problems. They may be easily tempted to overlook credit terms by, for example, offering unofficial discounts to keep their customers happy. For instance, at an Asian subsidiary of a well-known German pharmaceuticals firm, salesmen undermined a discount scheme the company initiated to speed up payments. Under the system, customers were to receive a 15 percent discount for payment within sixty days and 10 percent within ninety days. But according to a spokesman for the firm, "The salespeople have a very lenient attitude toward these terms. A certain customer agrees to the discount and then he doesn't pay until sixty-five days, and he still gets a 15 percent discount. And they're trying like this all the time, one day, two days. It's getting worse all the time, and then you have customers that don't pay at all and after a certain period—I don't know, 200 or 250 days—they make a claim and that's it. We forget everything and just call it a discount and start over. All not to lose the customers." The firm has never even considered imposing penalty fees because "the salesmen would have to go to the customer and try to collect the fee, which would be impossible."

To motivate salespeople, companies should devise a system of collection targets and incentives. For example, for years the Brazilian branch of a U.S. pharmaceuticals corporation has set a collection quota for its salesmen that is a prerequisite for monthly sales bonuses. The quota is based on two targets: one for current debts to be collected during the month, the other for amounts to be collected on accounts more than ninety days past due. Said the firm's treasurer: "The way you set these quotas gives you a lot of control over the salesmen both for their selling and the collections. We have always operated with the idea that collections must be made." Salesmen can also be invited to finance meetings to encourage an awareness of the importance of the time value of money.

Perhaps the best way to improve control is to create a separate credit and collection department. This will enhance administrative control over credit data and increase coordination between marketing and cash management concerns. One chemicals firm, for example, has approximately 15,000 customers and adds over 1,000 new customers every year. According to the company's treasurer, keeping track of that much information requires a dedicated collections staff. The department also helps police marketing personnel, who naturally tend to be more concerned with generating sales than with receiving funds.

The case of a German consumer products firm offers useful insights into the benefits of establishing a separate credit and collection department. A bank consulting team conducted a thorough review of the company's credit and collection procedures, opening a Pandora's box of receivables mistakes: lengthy order- and invoice-processing times, widely varying credit terms, bloated DSO levels, and inappropriate discounts and rebates. Making matters worse, there was no coordination between credit and marketing personnel. As a result, salesmen continued to book new orders from late-paying customers even after the credit manager had sent out four dunning letters to the account.

To cure these credit and collection ills, the consultants recommended that the firm set up a new department to establish credit policies and monitor overdue accounts. The department would be responsible for regularly reviewing the credit status of existing and prospective customers and for coordinating collection strategies with marketing staff. To ensure an independent appraisal of credit and collection procedures, the department would be under the direction of the finance staff. The reason: The study found that when collection procedures required tightening, the greatest resistance came from the sales staff, which was more concerned with meeting sales targets than with analyzing credit risk or following up on slow-paying accounts.

The company established a credit department under the following rules:

- The responsibility for credit approval rests with the general credit manager. It is a staff function that may be delegated only with the written approval of the finance director.

- All orders are approved or rejected by the general credit manager or his designee. In the event of disagreement on a credit decision, the matter is referred to the finance director for resolution.

- Exceptions to the standard payment terms may be granted only with the written approval of the general credit manager or his designee.

- The general credit manager monitors the entire accounts receivable and debtor statements and provides counseling and collection assistance.

- Collection objectives and responsibilities are established by the managing director, based upon the recommendations of the general credit manager and line management. Assigned collection objectives are a component of the performance objectives of operating units.

- The general credit manager establishes overall corporate procedures for administering collection activities.

The new credit department serves as the liaison between the finance and marketing groups and prepares the following reports:

(1) Evaluations and approvals of credit transactions above individual customer limits;

(2) Determinations regarding the invoice status of new transactions;

(3) Notification of collections of payment to marketing; and

(4) The status of outstanding transactions.

Monitoring Performance Through Internal Reporting

The best way to monitor a subsidiary's performance is to study its internal credit and collection reports. If these reports do not clearly describe the state of the receivables function, then not only are they inadequate for the parent's review, but they are clearly a source of trouble for the day-to-day collections function. Without good reports, local personnel will not be able to monitor trends and identify problems in the collection cycle.

For the parent, the key entries in the accounts receivable report are DSOs, aging of receivables, and bad-debt expense. These figures should be compared to the subsidiary's historical performance and to those of other companies where possible. It is important, however, to acknowledge the impact of local billing and customer payment practices, which vary sharply from country to country. It would be unfair to impose the same corporatewide standards for subsidiaries domiciled in, say, the notoriously slow-paying countries of Italy and Venezuela and those in prompt-paying Germany and Japan. As the regional treasurer of a U.S. chemicals firm put it: "DSOs are one of our key monitoring tools. When they start to balloon, it's one of the earliest and best signs that things are amiss and we have to move in quickly. But you have to set individual targets for each country and each product. Agricultural chemicals, for example, always have higher DSOs, because the terms are longer; you have to give the farmer time to get his crops in. And you have to take into account the country factors. One country, even with the same targets, may traditionally have fifteen to thirty days' higher DSOs than another, not because of bad management but because that's just the way things are there."

Because DSOs do not reflect credit terms, they should be augmented by the aging figures, which state how many days past due payments are. DSOs should be reviewed in local-currency terms, especially in hyperinflationary countries. As a financial executive at a U.S. subsidiary in Brazil explained, "Although the periodic maxidevaluations in Brazil inevitably make us miss our dollar profit targets, they have a positive effect on our DSOs, which the parent wants us to calculate in dollars. The DSOs will improve simply because the dollar value of the cruzeiro receivables will be much less due to the devaluation. This distorts the true picture."

To support their review of the receivables function, then, and to ensure that local personnel are not hobbled by poor reporting, parents should carefully review the accuracy, detail, timeliness, and completeness of their subsidiaries' credit and collec-

FORM A
Major Delinquent Accounts

Unit/Division: _____ Date: _____

Account No./Name	Internal Credit Rating	Invoices More Than 30 Days Overdue	Due Date and Terms	Total Account Sales (Last 12 Months)

Action taken

Comments

tion reports. The report above and that on p. 94 have been culled from companies with successful receivables systems; companies may want to adapt these forms for their own special needs and organizational structures.

· **Customer status reports,** most commonly compiled on a weekly or monthly basis, record customer credit limits, monitor credit exposure, and track specific delinquent invoices. The payment performance of each customer account is reported in detail, and cross-referencing identifies combined exposures to affiliated companies. These reports typically include the following data on each customer: credit terms, the use of discounts and penalty fees, invoice and due dates, and adherence to terms by individual transaction, as well as average performance.
· A list of **major accounts outstanding** records credit histories and amounts overdue to help focus efforts on the larger delinquent sums. It can also be used to monitor the performance of the sales and the credit and collection staffs and to adjust customer credit ratings.

Remarked one bank consultant, "You probably have ten major accounts that are half your business, so we recommend that companies do a separate analysis of those big customers. That way they can figure out if the problem is with the many small accounts or just one or two big ones."

It is especially useful to include a column to record actions taken to resolve outstanding sums. These reports should be issued frequently, especially if credit terms are short or problematic, although many firms rely on monthly reports (see Form A).

- **Accounts receivables reports** help companies control and accelerate collections by monitoring **total receipts** and monthly **DSOs** (the average number of days that sales are outstanding). Many companies measure **days overdue** (credit terms subtracted from DSOs) instead of DSOs to remove the bias generated by varying lengths of credit terms (see Forms B and C).

  Like any statistic, DSO figures must be handled carefully. Separate figures should be compiled for different groups of customers to prevent specific problems from being masked by an average figure, and the use of discounts must be factored into the DSO analysis. Furthermore, managers should realize that fluctuating sales or terms from period to period can distort DSO levels without representing any change in receivables management performance.

  The standard formula for calculating DSOs is the following:

$$DSO = \text{receivables at end of period} \times \frac{\text{days in period}}{\text{sales in period}} .$$

  To pinpoint specific problems, identify weak points in the collections cycle, and develop float forecasts, collection managers may want to break down receivables information by collection instrument and clearing bank used. Because some of this information may take time to retrieve, a separate report for float analysis may be advisable.

  Armed with this data, the subsidiaries can quickly spot developing trends in collections and devise new strategies to speed up receivables. As the treasury manager at a major U.S. automotive company remarked, "The key to using receivables reports is to look for trends, improvements, and deteriorations over the past year. Then we review trends by sales region, distributors, and so on."

- An **aging-of-receivables analysis** is important to identify the percentage of sales that are past due, broken down in thirty-day increments, for example. Aging reports are often used to track the performance of customers, sales managers, product divisions, and so on, depending on how the data is compiled and detailed. Cash managers can monitor trends by glancing down the column representing, say, past due over ninety days to see if seriously delinquent accounts are swelling month by month. Advised one consultant, "You need an aging report because the parent is going to ask just how old things are to monitor your performance; they'll want to see that sixty days and over column. It also helps you to analyze your customers' creditworthiness; if they've been paying on time for years and suddenly they pay later and later, it could be a sign of trouble." The cash manager at a midsized U.S. corporation agreed: "You look at the over ninety days due column and your problems just leap out."
- **Bad-debt expense** should also be highlighted and broken out by number and percentage of customers and total billings. This data can be further analyzed by sales region or other categories. The overall use of discounts and penalty fees should also be monitored (possibly on a separate form) to determine their impact on cash flows and customer payment practices.

Minimizing Collection Delays and Credit Risks

FORM B
Accounts Receivable Report

Unit/Division: _____   Date: _____

Period: _____

Credit Term Breakdown:

Percentage Breakdown

Credit Term[1]	By Number	By Value	Actual Average[2]
Delay			

Bad-Debt Expense

Number of customers _____   Percentage of total customers

_____

Cash amount _____   Percentage of total billings[3]

_____

Discounts/Penalties	Discounts	Penalties
Amount given/charged		
Number of times taken/applied		
Percentage of total invoices		

---

[1]Standard industry credit terms should be marked with an asterisk.

[2]By value.

[3]Total billings should be for the period when the bad debts were originally billed.

In addition to this data, parents should review more detailed reports on the day-to-day operation of the collection cycle. For example, commonly overlooked data that should be reported on a separate form is the dates the shipment and the invoice went

FORM C
Accounts Receivable Report

Unit/Division: _____   Date: _____

Period: _____

Collections	This Month	Last Month	Year to Date	Last Year
Beginning balance				
Invoiced				
Collected				
Corrections/adjustments				
End balance				
DSOs				
Average Credit Terms				
Average Days Overdue				
Bad-Debt Expense				
Comments				

out. According to one consultant, "People tend to focus on how long it takes from the receipt of the check to when it is deposited in the bank and credited, but if they can invoice two days faster they'll accelerate all their inflows by two days over the year." Only by carefully monitoring and reporting key dates in the *entire* collection cycle can float time be identified and shortened.

Analyzing Customer Credit Risk

Now that background data, organizational information, and internal credit and collection reports have been gathered and reviewed, it is time to take a look at the first step in the collections cycle: assessing customer credit risk. By weeding out poor credit risks, firms can prevent costly slowdowns and defaults in later stages of the credit and collection cycle. It is therefore essential that subsidiaries be effective in evaluating the creditworthiness of new customers and monitoring exposure to old customers.

To determine the adequacy of a subsidiary's credit-assessment procedures, parents can start by looking at reports on bad-debt expense. These figures should be compared with historical performance and with the results other companies in the same environment and industry are realizing. Next, ask credit managers the following questions:

- Are you looking beyond the financial condition of the customer to examine the health of the industry and the general economic conditions in the country? Industry and national economic conditions will have a sharp impact on the ability of customers to pay for purchases—which is why credit standards should vary from country to country to reflect these different circumstances.
- What steps are you taking to improve credit analysis and to reduce bad-debt expenses?
- Are you meeting with marketing personnel to discuss acceptable levels of customer risk and to measure its impact on the bottom line? A willingness to incur greater credit risks to improve market penetration may be justified.
- How do you store and retrieve credit data? Is it efficient? Have you considered computerizing your data base?
- Is the level of customer risk factored into credit terms?
- What sources of information are you tapping to measure the creditworthiness of potential customers? Are you using credit agencies and bureaus, bank and supplier references, and personal visits to customer facilities?

Finding the Best Sources of Credit Information

The quality of information sources for analyzing credit risk varies widely from country to country. In Japan, the United Kingdom, and the United States, **financial statements** are reliable and easily accessible. In other countries, however, analysis is hampered by the paucity and unreliability of published credit data.

In Latin America, for example, firms often keep several sets of financial statements for presentation to stockholders, the government, and banks, as well as internal reports. The reports available for external consumption naturally paint a rosier picture of the company's financial condition than do the internal accounts. In Germany, credit analysis is hampered by regulations relieving many firms of the obligation to publish their financial results.

A number of **credit rating services** specialize in the investigation of credit records for a fee, including Dun & Bradstreet, the most prominent worldwide (see table on p. 97). Suppliers can purchase reports showing customers' balance sheets and payment records, as well as general background and history. Dun & Bradstreet offers an on-line service to its clients. The growing data base currently includes companies from the United States, the United Kingdom, and the Netherlands. For a higher fee, the on-line system will supply the same data as the usual paper-based reports. This service is available worldwide.

The usefulness of credit rating services varies widely from country to country.

Selected Customer Credit Risk Analysis Services*

Country	Service
Australia	Association of Central Credit Unions State Credit Rating Agencies
Brazil	Chemical Producers Association Federation of Industries of Sao Paulo Journal do Comercio Service do Protecao ao Consumidor
Canada	Creditel
France	Andre Piguet Association Francaise de Tresoriers d'Enterprise Pouey International SCRL
Germany	Berger Kreditreform
Italy	Centrale del Rischi
Japan	Teikoku Koshinjo (Imperial Data Bank) Tokyo Stock Exchange Industry-specific sources
United Kingdom	Extel Statistical Services
United States	NACM/FCIB

*Dun & Bradstreet offers services worldwide.

Many firms report that Latin American rating services are inadequate, for example; according to the spokesman for a U.S. chemicals company with operations in the region, the services "basically report what the companies tell them—which is often wildly inaccurate." An experienced credit manager for a French electronics firm advised, "There is no substitute for doing it yourself. I have a feeling that a lot of the credit-checking agencies work with the banks, and if a company is not in very good shape, the banks don't want you to know that: You might not sell to it, and then the banks can't get their loans repaid. They have a vested interest in not giving you the right information."

Despite this problem, direct contact with **bankers** is a popular source of credit advice. According to the cash manager of an oil and construction service firm, the banks "just give you broad information; they have to be cautious about breaking confidentiality with their clients. However, if you read between the lines you can get a good sense of it. The banks are good for answering questions like 'Should we give a customer a $100,000 credit line?' Banks do not charge a fee for the service if you have very good contacts with them."

To supplement credit information, especially in countries with scarce credit-information resources, companies sometimes look to **government agencies** for assistance.

Keeping Credit Analysis Friendly

Some firms have managed to turn the potentially confrontational task of monitoring customer creditworthiness into an exercise in customer relations. For example, the Japanese subsidiary of a large U.S. oil firm has established a department of ten credit analysts. These "credit counselors," as they are called, oversee nearly 1,000 end customers and independent sales agents. According to the company's treasurer, "They try to spot problems and work closely with our customers. The agents perceive the counselors as trying to help them do better for us."

The counselors give customers advice on how to improve their own sales and collections. But at the same time, they conduct detailed financial analyses and produce reports on customers' DSOs, overdue accounts, and over-limit accounts. The treasury staff uses this information to determine whether credit limits should be modified or credit terms should be secured by some form of collateral (a common practice in Japan). Problem customers are graded as "cautionary" or "dangerous" accounts and are closely monitored: "Depending on how bad the account is, we might have to control deliveries, maybe do cash on delivery or eliminate credit terms."

Similarly, the Japanese subsidiary of a U.S. pharmaceuticals firm has organized an association of its 400 wholesale distributors. The firm set up a special department of "wholesaler coordinators," who look after the group and organize regular meetings and trips. According to the firm's manager of finance, in this way the wholesalers "know each other and us better. We are trying to make our relations much closer and deeper."

But the coordinators also keep tabs on the financial health of the wholesalers. "If they feel someone is doubtful or dangerous, they report it to us, and we investigate immediately." The firm has established a fully automated credit system; all credit histories and limits are stored on a computer, which generates detailed DSO and aging reports by customer. The company is now working on a system to code each wholesaler by its credit limit. Said the spokesman: "If an order exceeds their limits, the computer will show warning signs and we won't ship."

Some **industry groups** also produce reports to help members analyze common customers. A good source of data in many countries is the **record of legal proceedings** (protests) initiated against delinquent customers published in newspapers and elsewhere. In Brazil, for example, the *Journal do Comercio* is highly respected for its complete listing of protests.

If a subsidiary seems to be relying on incomplete or suspect credit information, it should be advised to sharpen its use of internal resources. The most telling insights into old accounts come from the customer's past payment performance. The Venezuelan subsidiary of a U.S. pharmaceuticals company, for example, calls up the last six purchases and payment schedule of the customer from the computer every time an order arrives. If the customer is paying poorly, the firm may shorten the credit terms or limit or deny credit.

For both old and new accounts, companies should utilize **on-site visits** to customers to inspect their operations. A U.S. subsidiary, for example, has its salesmen gather annual reports and other pertinent documents from customers and actually tour their offices and manufacturing facilities to see firsthand that the operations are in good shape. "The salesmen are invaluable; they are out there every day in the field and know exactly what is going on. They can check up quickly when a rumor is going around about a company. They have the contacts and know whether the company is really in trouble or not," a spokesman related.

Internal credit analysts should also make **informal contacts** outside the company to check on their customers. According to the credit manager of a German pharmaceuticals firm, "From time to time we ask other companies familiar with the customer what they think of it. We speak with local credit managers and associations; they know each other, and we ask them what they think of the risk." The treasurer of a German chemicals company uses a deceptively simple technique to get free credit advice from insurance companies: "When an insurance agency approaches us, we show them our customer list and ask if they would insure such companies. If they will, we know we have done our work and have a list of creditworthy customers."

Establishing and Monitoring Credit Limits

Setting appropriate credit limits—and then carefully monitoring them—is a seller's main defense against loss of payment. Often firms set limits by rule of thumb, basing decisions on past sales or a simple formula like 10 percent of net worth or 5 percent of turnover. If a subsidiary's bad-debt expense is unacceptably high, it may be because it uses a seat-of-the-pants approach that results in sloppy analysis. No matter how good the credit information is, it is useless if it is not used intelligently. Answers to the following questions may reveal serious shortcomings:

- Does the procedure for credit analysis incorporate all available information? Does it take into account that many factors can influence a company's ability to pay short-term debts?

- Are exceptions to established credit limits being regularly granted? Who has the authority to do this?

- Are records and credit limits being updated to reflect changes in customers' financial health or payment performance?

- Are orders being shipped to customers who have exceeded their credit line or are seriously in arrears on previous billings?

- How are limits monitored? If the credit-analysis system is not already computerized, should it be?

The first step, then, is to make certain that credit information is used to establish precise credit limits based on consistent standards. A good example of such a system comes from a Canadian rubber and plastics manufacturer, whose information sources include financial data obtained from annual reports, trade and bank references, and visits by sales representatives to the customer.

Playing It Safe with Risky Customers

Even the best monitoring of customers cannot completely eliminate the risk of customer default. For extremely risky customers, companies can take advantage of several risk-reducing mechanisms.

- A **bank guarantee** requires a bank to assume the credit risk in the event of a default. For example, a German electronics firm obtains bank guarantees for all but its most secure and well-known customers. The treasurer generally asks for a guarantee on 60 or 70 percent of the total transaction, which is approximately the cost of producing the product. "In case this customer goes bankrupt, we want to recover at least our cost," explained the spokesman. "This method has really helped us avoid trouble," another cash manager reported. "Out of six customers with bank guarantees, two have gone bankrupt!" When dealing with the subsidiary of a major MNC, firms can also consider requesting a parent company guarantee.
- A **factoring company** can reduce the risk to a firm by assuming the risk and administrative expenses of collection. The client gives the factor a copy of an invoice and receives the face value of the invoice, less a reserve for returns and cash deductions. Factors either purchase receivables in full or, for a fee, simply assume the risks and administrative expenses of collection. If they buy receivables outright, they cannot ask the borrower to participate in an eventual loss.

The company's credit department uses the information to calculate these indicators: profitability ratios (net return on capital, total assets, and turnover); liquidity ratios (cash, quick and current ratios, DSOs, and stock turnover); financial or solvency ratios (debt/equity); fixed asset cover; reserves; and past payment performance. The firm then assigns numerical values to each of these categories with the following maximum point totals:

Liquidity	25
Fixed-asset cover	20
Profitability	20
Payment experience	15
Solvency	10
Reserves	10

It then uses the point total to develop credit limits in combination with a further calculation of net worth and turnover. The firm takes the sum of 10 percent of net worth and 3 percent of sales turnover, and divides it by 2 to arrive at a base. For a firm with sales of $20 million and a net worth of $10 million, assume that its point total equals 85. The base figure is then calculated as follows:

For example, in France a typical factoring transaction works like this: The factor pays out 80–90 percent of the value of the invoice immediately. The client pays interest (several percentage points above the prevailing prime rate) on the funds used from the time they are drawn until the customer pays the invoice to the factor. In addition, the client pays a 0.5–1.5 percent commission, depending on the work and risk involved. Among the items considered before a final rate is agreed upon are the client's sales volume, number of customers, maturity of invoices, percentage return of faulty goods, and normal percentage of canceled orders. Factors' fees are usually 1–2 percent of turnover.

· **Credit insurance.** For a fee, an insurance company will promise to refund a supplier for losses due to bad trade debts. According to the finance director of a German chemicals concern, "We use insurance companies because we deal with so many small firms that it takes too long to run internal credit checks on each one. We build the cost of the insurance into the product's price." Firms that cannot simply pass on the cost of insurance in this way, however, must carefully weigh the charges against expected losses on defaulted receivables. An Italian paper manufacturer had this experience in the area of credit insurance: "We used to insure ourselves in the past, but statistically we had a big loss every three or four years. The premiums paid on insurance were higher than the periodic losses."

$$\frac{(\$20 \text{ million} \times 3\%) + (\$10 \text{ million} \times 10\%)}{2} = \$800,000.$$

It then applies the following formula:

$$\text{Base figure} + \frac{\text{base figure} \times \text{point total}}{100} = \text{credit limit}.$$

So the firm's credit limit is determined to be

$$\$800,000 + \frac{\$800,000 \times 85}{100} = \$1,480,000.$$

This information is fed into the firm's computer, which is used to check a customer's credit limit whenever a new order comes in. All data on customer credit limits is updated every year.

Of course, all of this computational effort will go to waste if sloppy monitoring enables the customer to exceed the prescribed credit limit. Subsidiaries that have not already developed a computerized data base should be encouraged to do so to keep track of their customers' credit limits. For example, one U.S. manufacturing company stores customer credit limits in the central data base of an IBM mainframe computer, along with all invoice and payment information on its customers. The computer program prevents oversights by flagging overdue accounts as well as orders that exceed the predetermined credit limits.

Evaluating Your Subsidiaries' Credit Terms

Because credit terms set the pace for the collection cycle, companies should reevaluate them regularly. Credit terms that are too long will overextend the collection cycle and increase DSOs, while terms that are too short will undermine a company's competitiveness. A good way to review a subsidiary's terms is to start with the following questions:

- What are the current credit terms for each product line? Have they lengthened or shortened in recent years?
- Is there synergy between credit and pricing decisions? Is there good communication between the finance and marketing departments on the influence of credit terms on both pricing and cash flows?
- Are discounts and penalty fees recalculated regularly to reflect the impact of fluctuating interest and inflation rates on the time value of money? What about their impact on cash flows and sales?
- Has the finance staff researched the credit terms of other companies in the industry, either through personal investigation or the use of credit agencies and reports?
- Is any effort being made to negotiate shorter terms with customers?
- Do current terms accurately reflect the firm's market position, as well as industry standards and country practices?

When evaluating credit terms, financial managers at the parent or regional headquarters must understand the differences in payment practices by industry and country (see the table on pp. 103–105). If the subsidiary's terms are tighter than local standards, customers will resist paying promptly, and the company may even lose market share. Companies are much better off setting credit terms that their customers will accept and then strictly enforcing the rules.

In some countries, such as the United States and Germany, credit terms are short—typically net thirty days—and customers are expected to heed them. In other countries, such as Italy and Japan, terms are much longer. As the spokesman for a Japanese pharmaceuticals firm put it, "Everyone gives long terms in Japan. Everyone depends on everyone else here. We are financing each other through what is called 'credit among industry.' This is one way of financing ourselves without going to the banks."

Along with formal credit terms, parents must consider how the corporate culture in each country influences the observation of those terms. In the United Kingdom and Australia, for example, credit terms that are officially thirty days net in practice are much longer, thanks to the common practice of paying from the end of the month of billing. A customer billed on thirty-day terms on January 2 would not be expected to pay until the end of February. So thirty-day terms may, in effect, extend to as much as sixty days, costing suppliers up to thirty days extra on their receivables.

"Our credit terms are officially net thirty days from date of invoice," complained the CFO of a diversified firm. "But nobody in this country takes any notice. They wait until they receive the invoice and then pay thirty days from the end of that month. That means they get an average of forty-five days' credit." To counter such problems, subsidiaries should be encouraged to buck the trend and insist on receiving payments thirty days from the invoice date.

Another common problem is that customers grab a few extra days by willfully misunderstanding their credit terms. For example, some companies choose to interpret the terms of sale as being based on *receipt* of invoice rather than the *date* of invoice. A German electronics firm with standard terms of thirty days net found that, because it takes up to a week to receive the invoice, some customers effectively gain seven days' extra credit by quietly applying their own interpretation to the terms and paying from receipt of invoice. To prevent such abuses, companies should highlight the terms on the invoice, aggressively phone customers that pay late, and slap on penalty charges on the basis of the intended terms.

Customers may also bend the rules by taking cash discounts or ignoring penalty charges even when they pay late. Many suppliers are naturally willing to give more leeway to valued clients. As the finance director of a food producer said, "In principle, we try to stick to our rules, but you can imagine that if somebody has 15 percent or 20 percent of your business he might get one, two, or even three extra days on payments." Nevertheless, the practice of offering discounts and charging penalties can become self-defeating if inconsistently enforced.

Speeding Collections Through Tighter Credit Terms

Without ignoring country practices, the best way to speed up customer payments is to shorten the terms. For example, the treasurer of an Italian chemicals firm finds that "it's almost impossible to get anyone to pay on time in this country. To reduce DSOs, you have to give shorter terms." The company recently cut its terms from ninety days to seventy-five: "You will never keep DSOs under 100 days with 90-day terms. Never." Another Italian manufacturer discovered that its customers were paying, on average, six days after the maturity date of *ricevute* because of the time its bank took to request payment. The firm reduced invoice terms by six days to compensate for the bank's slow bureaucratic methods.

Subsidiaries must be discouraged from taking an overly passive approach to credit terms. Instead, local managers should adopt the policy of a leading Japanese steelmaker. Said a spokesman for the company: "We always try to reduce our terms by discussing our situation with customers." The firm points out the cost of credit it is

Typical Credit Terms

Country	Industry	Terms (Days)	Discounts	Penalties	Observance
Australia	Pharmaceuticals	40	2/10 discount often offered but usually ignored by customers.	Rarely effective, even when imposed by the largest suppliers.	Days past due range from a low of 4 for service firms to a high of over 60 for the chemicals industry. Late payment is compounded by the common practice of paying from the end of the month of billing.
	Machinery	26			
	Metals and mining	45			
	Services	36			
Brazil	Pharmaceuticals	30–60	Discounts range from 2% to 7% for payments before 30 days.	Charges competitive with financing costs are becoming more popular.	Collections are often a problem, especially with government agencies.
	Capital equipment/ industrial components	30			
	Industrial chemicals	30–60			
	Health care	30			
Canada	Office equipment	30	Typical discount is 2/20–30, but few customers take advantage of it.	Very effective; penalty rate charged is normally set close to prime rate, but can be over 25%.	Credit terms have shortened in recent years. Suppliers do not hesitate to stop shipment, sometimes as a first recourse, when days past due exceeds 25
	Metals	30			
	Textiles	30			
	Pharmaceuticals	45–60			
France	Air conditioners	45	Offered, but customers do not usually take advantage of them.	Imposed but usually ignored.	Tight credit condtions encourage customers to delay payments for long periods, resulting in days overdue of 30 or more.
	Agricultural equipment	90			
	Metals and mining	30–90			
	Office machinery	45			

104 Global Cash Management

Country	Industry	Terms (Days)	Discounts	Penalties	Observance
Germany	Food	30	Discounts are typically 2/10 and are very popular.	Imposed but usually not collected.	Payment delays are unusual in Germany because of the role reputation plays in developing and maintaining good relationships with suppliers
	Capital equipment	30			
	Steel	15th of month following billing			
	Oil services	30			
	Oil services.	30			
Italy	Consumer nondurables	30–60	Rarely effective; customers prefer to rely on supplier credit rather than take discount.	Companies experience mixed results. Penalties tied to short-term bank rate.	Due to customer resistance, poor postal services, and long clearing times DSOs in Italy often run 20–25 days higher than in other European countries.
	Manufacturing tools	90			
	Industrial chemicals	75			
	Food	60–90			
Japan	Pharmaceuticals	75	Offered at 1–2% above prime rate.	Effective and very popular.	Payment delays can ruin supplier relationships, so number of days overdue rarely exceeds 20. However, payment terms in many industries do not begin until the end of the month in which delivery was made, adding more than 30 days to DSOs.
	Electronics	48			
	Metals and mining	30			
	Services	35–40			▶

Typical Credit Terms (Continued)

Country	Industry	Terms (Days)	Discounts	Penalties	Observance
United Kingdom	Pharmaceuticals	30	2/30 is commonly offered and often effective.	Rarely imposed because ineffective.	Common practice is to pay from the end of the month of billing, which can extend DSOs up to 30 days.
	Electronics	30			
	Chemicals	20th day of month following month of invoice	2/30 is commonly offered and often effective.	Rarely imposed because ineffective.	Common practice is to pay from the end of the month of billing, which can extend DSOs up to 30 days.
	Services	30			
United States	Pharmaceuticals	30	1–2/30 offered for certain industries; others, like automotive and energy, have industrywide payment terms precluding discounts.	Some states impose restrictions on rates charged.	Days past due should not exceed 15. To delay payments while keeping within terms, customers use remote-disbursement banks to add 1–3 days' float to payments.
	Capital goods	35			
	Metals	30			
	Services	30			

Note: 2/10 refers to a 2% discount for payment within 10 days; 2/20 to a discount for payment within 20 days; etc.

granting, and if the customer will not agree to shorter terms, the firm attempts to build its costs into the price.

One way to negotiate better terms is to take a tough stance with customers, who often exaggerate the terms offered by competitors. For example, the Korean subsidiary of a Swiss food producer was told by its distributors that its competitors granted terms of more than ninety days. The firm's spokesman stated that "we checked around and found out that wasn't true. So, we told them that our policy was to sell only on a cash basis. They wanted ninety days, so we just split the difference—which was still better than our competitors."

Of course, negotiations won't always be successful. This is especially true for companies in highly competitive markets, where credit managers often have to yield

Global Cash Management

to marketing considerations. For example, the credit manager of a French steel producer complained, "Although we have thirty- or sixty-day terms for most of our customers, our two biggest clients insist on ninety days or more. They represent a large part of our sales, and they can impose their conditions on us. We try to negotiate, but they need the credit, and they are just too strong."

Economic recessions also boost competition—and hence the push toward more generous terms—but also increase the damage done by longer DSOs as suppliers are forced into expensive credit markets while waiting for payment. In hyperinflationary environments, companies suffer double damage as the value of their receipts erodes day by day. Even under highly competitive conditions, therefore, it may be best to resist the trend to longer terms. Said one French treasurer, "When times were better, we let the sales department give out the terms. But we're a lot less cash rich now, and we have a much more aggressive credit policy. Now the credit department makes the final decision. The credit people can override the salesmen when they think the terms are getting out of hand."

When all else fails, subsidiaries should simply factor the opportunity cost of longer terms into product prices using the following formula:

$$\text{Money market rate} \times \frac{1}{360} \times \text{number of days extra credit} \times \text{invoice amount} = \text{amount of price increase.}$$

For example, a Korean MNC routinely integrates anticipated customer requests for longer terms into its pricing. According to the firm's director of finance, "When we consider a price, we consider what the expected terms are, and when the customer makes the period long, then we negotiate and impose price increases. First we calculate our production costs and profits. Then the customer's situation is taken into account—whether they are expected to pay beyond normal terms. Then some interest must be considered." To encourage faster payment and a recognition of the time value of money, many companies inform their customers of these calculations.

Enhancing Terms Through Discounts and Penalties

An important point to review with subsidiaries is the use of discounts and penalties to accelerate the collection cycle. The potential effectiveness of discounts is demonstrated by the experience of a German chemicals company. Standard payment terms in its industry are thirty days net from date of invoice, but by offering a 2 percent cash discount for payments received within fourteen days, the firm has kept its DSOs down to twenty-five days. "Today," the spokesman claimed, "50 percent of our customers pay within fourteen days and get the discount." The technique must be applied cautiously, however: "Many of our customers consider the 2 percent discount part of the price. So we have a strict campaign to weed out those who take the discount but pay in twenty-four to twenty-five days. We send out nasty letters, and we've convinced most of them that they must pay within fourteen days if they want the discount."

Discounts that work are competitive with the rates customers can get on investing short-term cash. At the same time, they are counterproductive if they exceed the supplier's borrowing costs. Therefore, firms should position the discount between their own financing costs and the rate their customers make on short-term investments. "If the customer has excess cash, he might get 10 percent at his bank," said the treasurer of a Brazilian consumer goods firm. "If I'm borrowing from the bank I might get 11 percent. So I go to the customer and arrange for him to pay at a discount of 10.5 percent. I get that much less on my borrowing charges and he gets more on his cash, and everybody is happy—except the bank."

To determine the annual interest cost of offering discounts to an account with continuous sales, companies should use the following formula:

$$\frac{(1 + \text{discount})}{1 - \text{discount}}^{365/\text{acceleration}} - 1 = \text{annual equivalent cost.}$$

Acceleration can be calculated as credit terms minus discount terms (if a discount is offered for payment in ten days on terms of thirty days, acceleration is thirty minus ten equals twenty days) or, more accurately, the historical DSO for the customer (terms plus delay) minus the discount terms. For one-time sales, a simpler formula can be used:

$$\text{Discount} \times \frac{1 + \text{discount}}{1 - \text{discount}} \times \frac{365}{\text{acceleration}} = \text{annual equivalent cost.}$$

The effectiveness of offering discounts to encourage speedy customer payments varies widely from country to country. For example, discounts are not very effective in Italy because many customers have limited access to bank funds and must use supplier credit to fund themselves, whatever the consequences. On the other hand, discounts for early payment are popular in Japan and the United Kingdom. Perhaps the least favorable environments for offering discounts are hyperinflationary countries where companies must continuously revise terms. For example, a firm giving a 1 percent discount for payment within ten days, net amount due in thirty days, is offering its customers an effective annual saving of 18 percent. Obviously, in countries with triple-digit (or above) inflation and interest rates, such a discount would be unappealing. Thus cash managers are forced to raise discount rates regularly to meet climbing interest costs—a practice equally unattractive to suppliers. As an Argentine treasurer who gave up on offering discounts put it, "We just can't compete with inflation."

The flip side of a discount for early payment is a penalty fee for late payment. Especially in hyperinflationary and credit-poor countries, firms must strive to make these fees higher than bank financing rates. Even if late fees are properly structured, however, many companies that charge them complain that customers simply ignore them. The treasurer of a French steel producer explained, "We have an automatic system for the penalty fees. The computer emits a debit note to late-paying customers and calculates the fees. We charge the cost of our overdraft plus a small administrative charge. But we don't even bother to book the fees into our accounting system because generally the customers refuse to pay. Maybe we are not tough enough about it."

This treasurer's attitude is unacceptable, and parents should come down hard on subsidiaries that take a soft approach to enforcing penalties. Local personnel should emulate the French capital goods manufacturer that has taken a hard line in collecting penalty fees, set at rates at least 3 percent above its opportunity cost of funds, for delayed payments. In fact, the firm insists that customers make certain that payments arrive in its account on a specified value date—rather than on the due date—to avoid the interest charge. According to a spokesman, the tactic has forced most customers to pay on time, and there has been no problem collecting the fees from those who do not.

Subsidiaries may argue that interest fees on overdue accounts are difficult to collect and tend to alienate customers, but an aggressive stance pays off more often than not. In the Philippines, where most companies claim that penalties do not work, the subsidiary of a U.S. paper products firm sets penalty charges at slightly above prevailing borrowing costs (about 2 percent a month). The spokesman boasted that interest income averages about P1.75 million per year and flatly stated that "penalties do not hurt sales. But you can't play favorites; you weaken your position if you do. All you have to do is give the example of the big company paying interest. For the volume they are giving me, I could easily condone it, but I don't."

Tightening the Collection Cycle

Once credit policies and terms have been assessed, the next step is to examine the collection cycle. The following sections will look at each of the three phases of the cycle: (1) generating the invoice and delivering the bill to the customer; (2) obtaining the payment instrument from the customer and transporting it to the bank; and (3) clearing funds through the bank for good funds in a collection account. The precise steps will vary somewhat from company to company, but the general sequence might run like this:

(1) Customer order received;
(2) Credit limit and terms checked;
(3) Order processed and shipped by warehouse;
(4) Shipment data entered into system;
(5) Invoice generated and delivered to customer;
(6) Payment received from customer and deposited in bank;
(7) Good funds available in supplier's account; and
(8) Delinquent customers dunned.

To pinpoint sources of float, each step in the collections cycle must be timed. To do this, in-house consultants should speak with local personnel about the procedures they use and the problems they encounter. Interviews can be conducted with the financial managers who oversee the operations, salesmen who bring in the sales orders, billing clerks who process the invoices, warehouse staff who ship the goods and the invoices, bank relations officers who monitor customers' funds as they clear through the banking system, and so on. Consultants often find that clerks, because they are generally closest to the nitty-gritty of the collections process, provide some of the best insights into the strengths and weaknesses of current procedures.

Next, take a sample of sales orders and follow them manually through the entire cycle to track how long each step takes. Record dates and hours, labor time for each segment, stamps on envelopes and checks, and so on. One consultant explained the importance of a manual review of the cycle this way: "You have to analyze each step in the collection cycle for each instrument, using a representative sample of customers over a period of time, such as four weeks. This is important because it quantifies delays in the cycle, and the savings to be made from improvements can also be quantified."

With this information, companies can identify float delays and work with local personnel to minimize them. The following sections will review each phase in more detail and offer suggestions on how firms can tighten each step in the collection cycle.

Phase One: Refining Internal Billing Procedures

The collections cycle starts with the receipt of the customer's order. After the order has been approved for delivery on the basis of agreed-upon credit terms and a review of the customer's credit standing, the billing process starts. During this segment of the cycle, the order is processed and shipped, generally by the warehouse (or, in the case of a service company, service is initiated or rendered), the shipment data is entered into the internal information system, and an invoice is generated and delivered to the customer. Because billing is the one stage that is completely under the company's control, billing delays are self-inflicted injuries. Fortunately, internal processing can be upgraded easily through refined procedures or increased automation.

Much of the time spent on the manual examination of the collection process will be devoted to this segment because most of the rest of the cycle occurs at the customer's location and the bank and is not as accessible. "Trace the flow of the sales order," advised a bank consultant. "How many desks does it hit, how long does it take to process? Ask your collections manager, 'How long does it take from the moment you get a sales order until you're ready to process the invoice?' Regardless of what the answer is, do a little study and find out for yourself what it really is."

The first place to look for delays is in the transmission of invoice information from the sales staff in the field to the billing department. Many firms establish regional sales offices and warehouses to decrease the time it takes to deliver both invoices and goods; close proximity to the customer also gives salesmen and collection managers the benefits of increased personal contact. Unfortunately, this impedes centralization of customer information, which is important for ensuring that the billing process starts as soon after the sale as possible. Is the subsidiary's system meeting the needs

Better Receivables Management Through Automation

Computers can dramatically improve each step of the credit and collection function. For example, an Italian paper manufacturer set up an automated receivables function several years ago to handle its 50,000 domestic accounts. At that time, the firm was suffering an annual loss on bad debts of 1.2 percent of the net value of its sales, and it had DSOs of over 100. The computerized system maintains credit histories on its customers, permitting instant checking on credit limits, and automatically generates invoices when sales data is entered. The computer also sends out dunning letters to customers that do not pay on time. As a result, within a few years the firm reduced its DSOs to seventy-two and its bad debts to just 0.45 percent of its sales.

A French manufacturer recently purchased a receivables software package that it uses on an IBM mainframe. The firm's treasurer explained that the computer generates daily reports on past-due accounts, DSOs, and agings by customer. In addition, sales information is fed into the computer, which automatically produces invoices. The new system has already shaved several days off the collection cycle, primarily by speeding up billing procedures.

The French subsidiary of a U.S. steel company is establishing "a real-time receivables system," in the words of the firm's treasurer. "We've had our collections on computer for several years, but we get reports only every fifteen days. With the new system, we will be able to interrogate the computer through a terminal whenever we want. We will have our receivables situation every day to inform our salesmen of their customers' positions so they can try to get payment."

---

of both the sales representatives for access to customers and the billing department for fast access to information?

For example, the treasurer of a U.S. oil firm found that his Australian subsidiary's widely scattered sales offices sent billing information to headquarters in Melbourne "by courier or even mail, believe it or not. But now we're going to a completely new EDP system, putting in new hardware, a mainframe, just changing everything." Under the new system, all sales offices will have on-line hookups with the central computer in Melbourne, and sales agents will be able to key in orders daily, automatically invoicing their customers.

While the costs of such a system are high, the spokesman believes that "the payoff is going to be huge. Not just in working capital savings, but also in manpower." He estimates that the new system will cut four days from outstanding receivables. With annual sales of A$2 billion and borrowing costs of 19.5 percent, the automated system will save nearly A$4.3 million a year. In addition, the company expects to cut its headquarters credit and collection staff nearly in half.

Once the sales data is in the hands of the billing department, an almost infinite number of inefficiencies can crop up between each separate step in the invoicing process. Many companies turn to computers to eliminate these delays, which, although small, can snowball into day after day of additional—and easily avoidable—DSOs. One company that followed the review procedures outlined above and made significant savings through automation is a small German food producer. Its internal review revealed the following billing cycle:

Order-to-Invoice Procedures	Elapsed Time (Days)
Salesman receives order from customer	0
Warehouse processes and ships order	1–2
Warehouse mails order/delivery information to HQ	1–2
New order entered into on-line data system and processed	1
Order listing processed and proofed, errors corrected	1–2
Customer invoice prepared and reported to marketing	1
Customer invoice mailed and received by customer	1–2
Total elapsed time	**6–10**

The unusually long billing cycle of six to ten days was caused by the lack of automation between the distribution warehouses and the treasury department at corporate headquarters. The company reduced the time required to process orders and mail invoices from the minimum six days to just one or two days by installing on-line computer terminals at its warehouses, thus minimizing the time needed to transmit invoices to headquarters. In addition to labor and other savings, the firm calculated that by accelerating the collections cycle its new system generated the following savings:

Average daily sales	Dm30,000
× 5 days' savings	Dm1,500,000
× overnight rate	7.85%
= annual savings	Dm117,750

After the invoice has been generated, the next step is delivering the invoice to the customer. Invoices can be mailed, shipped with the goods, delivered by the driver or a company representative, or even transmitted on-line. Is the subsidiary using the fastest possible method? A review of the options will determine which one is fastest and least prone to foul-ups. The mailing of invoices can be decentralized at the plant level if this improves mail and processing time, or centralized at the head office, whose urban location may offer its own advantages.

Finally, although the formatting and content of the invoice do not create delays during the billing process, they are worth discussing here because they can result in problems later on in the receivables cycle. Some of the points to consider are the following:

- Does the invoice clearly state how payment is to be made—whether by check, draft or bank transfer—and to which account?

- Are there any ambiguities that might enable customers to interpret terms to their own best advantage?

- Are key points highlighted in red or boldface print?

- Does the billing staff know or maintain contact with payables staff at key customers to facilitate the resolution of problems and confusions as they occur?

To illustrate the sloppy invoicing that can delay later phases of the collection cycle, consider the words of a seasoned cash management consultant: "In at least a quarter of the cases invoices will say 'net thirty days'—net from what? From the date of the invoice? From the end of the month? From the last full moon? They never say. And to compound it they'll send the invoice out and at the end of the month they'll send a statement and it will say 'here's your outstandings' and it will have a term section which in half the cases will say 'net thirty days.' Well you've invoiced them on the fifth of the month and said 'net thirty days' and on the thirtieth you send out a statement which says 'net thirty days.' You've given him an additional twenty-five days. If you send a statement, make sure the due dates coincide with those on the invoice. It may be better not to send a statement. If you have two pieces of information the receiver will act upon the one that is most beneficial to him."

Phase Two: Accelerating Payments from Customers

The next phase in the collections cycle starts when the customer receives the invoice. The customer must now decide not only when to pay his bill but how to pay it. This section will focus on the methods customers use to settle debts to suppliers by reviewing the five main categories of payment instruments. An effective collection study must examine the receivables cycle by each instrument used, since each has its own costs, float, problems, and associated techniques for accelerating collections. Only then can companies encourage their customers to use the best possible instrument.

To illustrate the value of conducting a separate review for each instrument, consider the case of the Italian subsidiary of a U.K. tire manufacturer. An internal review revealed that collections via bank transfers averaged 9.2 days of clearing float, compared with just 4 days on checks. By asking customers to use only bank checks, the firm reduced its overall float to just 4.7 days—for a cash savings equivalent to 1.4 percent of its annual sales.

The first step in this phase of the review, then, is to identify the various collection instruments the subsidiary is receiving and break them down by percentage of transfers and cash volume. The processing costs, bank, postage and other fees, administrative and customer float, and bank clearing time should be measured for each one. Actual tests should be conducted with a sample of each instrument. Collections staff should be queried to answer the following questions:

- Do certain types of customers tend to use certain types of instruments (e.g., do large customers use checks, small ones drafts, etc.)? Why?

- Does the collections staff understand the clearing process for each type of instrument? Can they describe the pros and cons of each?

- Is the staff encouraging customers to pay with the fastest-clearing collection instrument available in that country? How?

The following case example demonstrates how this sort of review should be conducted and offers insights into the types of findings and recommendations companies should look for. The Italian subsidiary of a major U.S. computer manufacturer was the subject of a full cash management audit by staff from the group's European regional headquarters. To review the unit's receivables, the internal consultants examined its management of each payment instrument. They found that the breakdown by sales volume (totaling $57 million) was as follows:

ricevute bancaria	25%
checks	25%
bonifici bancari	25%
postal transfers	10%
quietanze	15%

The review was based on interviews with both collection managers and clerks and an examination of all relevant documents. After surveying the collection cycle for each type of instrument and drawing on external sources of cash management information and their own experience with cash management in other European countries, the consultants were able to recommend techniques for accelerating receipts through each available instrument.

(1) **Ricevute bancaria** are a very popular payment instrument in Italy. A *ricevuta* is a list of receivables prepared by the seller and presented to a bank for collection at least twenty days before the first maturity date. *Ricevute* are generally considered the most effective and inexpensive way to make collections for all but the smallest amounts, and many firms use them for 75–85 percent of their receivables. They are popular with suppliers because they remind customers to pay on time, reduce the amount of administrative work within the credit and accounting departments, and can be discounted with local banks at around two points below the normal overdraft rate.

But *ricevute* also have their drawbacks. They are subject to lengthy float delays, and banks credit the amount of the *ricevuta* not on the due date but an average ten to fifteen days later, although these terms are negotiable. Moreover, they do not constitute a legal obligation to pay, and banks often keep suppliers in the dark about nonpayment—which in the case of this firm constitutes an unusually high 20 percent of receipts, attributed to internal organizational problems—for as long as a month. Even worse, when a customer does not honor a *ricevuta,* a bank commonly charges the supplier interest on the credited funds from the day of maturity, rather than the day value is given.

The consultants advised the subsidiary to start by renegotiating their value-dating conditions, which, though considered good, could be better. In addition, they offered two tactics for speeding receipt: lodging the *ricevute* in separate sets according to the regions on which they were drawn, and depositing *ricevute* in the branch network where they originated. The subsidiary planned to incorporate these ideas into the receivables computer by creating a data base of customers' bank account locations.

It was estimated that two value days could be saved and that information on dishonored *ricevute* would be transmitted faster when only one bank was involved on both the paying and receiving ends.

Another method recommended by the consultants for reducing the delay in notification of dishonored *ricevute* required the subsidiary to do some of the banks' work for them by attaching a prepaid postcard to the *ricevuta* requesting the bank to return the postcard in the event of nonpayment. Alternatively, the subsidiary could ask for telex notifications in the event that particularly large amounts are dishonored. It was calculated from telex charges and interest costs that for amounts up to about L1 million this was a cost-effective approach.

Finally, the subsidiary was advised that customers who consistently sent bad *ricevute* should be required to pay by draft or charged interest for all resulting delays. The consultants cautioned, however, that "the commercial implications of doing so would have to be examined closely." Despite these problems, the review team concluded that *ricevute* were the preferred form of collection and that more customers should be encouraged to use them.

(2) **Checks.** The company receives most of its checks through two post office boxes. A review of the check collection cycle showed that the major source of float was mail delays, not bank delays. Most checks were being received through two post office boxes located in different towns. The internal processing of these checks worked as follows:

- 8:30 A.M.—Messenger picks up mail from first post office box.
- 9:30 A.M.—Same messenger picks up mail from second box.
- 9:45 A.M.—Messenger delivers mail to company headquarters.
- Noon—Checks arrive at accounting department.
- Afternoon checks arrived in the second mail at the accounting department, and deposit slips were prepared. The next morning, the checks were banked by the messenger after he delivered the mail. To eliminate internal processing delays, the consultants recommended that checks be photocopied as soon as the messenger delivered them. Deposit slips could then be prepared and submitted to the bank with the checks between 11:30 A.M. and noon for same-day value. The accounting department could use the photocopies for control and follow-up.

The consulting group also discovered that about 5 percent of the subsidiary's check receipts were sent to regional offices, which then mailed them to the headquarters. This resulted in an eight-day mail and administrative delay in depositing the checks. The solution: Checks received at regional offices should be deposited in accounts at branches of the subsidiary's main collection bank and photocopies forwarded to the accounting department for control purposes.

By comparing postage and receipt dates over a two-month period, the consultants learned that mail float averaged four to eight days. Furthermore, although sending undated checks is illegal in Italy, the review showed that many of the firm's customers indulge in this practice to obtain more float, leaving the supplier to date the check.

Transfer Instruction

Customer's Name _____   Date of Transfer _____

Bank Account No. _____   Reference _____

Please make transfer in favor of Company X, Roma
at: Bank A, Account No. 12345
or: Bank B, Account No. 67890
or: Bank C, Account No. 87654

with the prefixed value date for Company Y:
Four real days out of town after initiation
Two real days in town after initiation

Customer Signature: _____

To avoid these delays, the consultants told the subsidiary to ask customers to remit funds either by *bonificio bancario* with a prefixed value day for the beneficiary or by *ricevuta.*

(3) ***Bonificio bancario.*** When a customer gives instructions to his bank to pay by *bonificio* (bank transfer), his account is debited immediately, but the supplier's account is not credited for two to twenty days. The delay depends on the instructions given to the bank and the relationship between the paying and receiving banks. Credit can be transferred rapidly if the customer requests a prefixed value date, furnishes complete supplier and account information, or routes the entire transfer through the same branch system.

The consultants found that though the collections manager did ask customers to observe the above procedures, he did so on an informal basis with no regular reminder process. Thus, they suggested that a special transfer instruction form be included with the invoice (see above). Other recommendations included more intensive negotiations with banks for improved value dating and use of the same branch system.

(4) **Postal transfers.** The majority of the firm's receipts via postal *giro* (see p. 126) are made by public entities, which are required by law to pay by either post or *quietanza.* The postal system is unpopular with cash managers because it otters poor reporting facilities; although funds are value-dated early, with slow reporting it is difficult to transfer them out of the low-interest postal account into a more reasonable bank account. For example, a random sample of twenty-one transfers received by the company indicated that the average delay between the initiation of the transfer and the receipt of notification was sixteen calendar days, although the funds were usually value-dated on the day following the transfer initiation.

To speed the process, the firm was advised to negotiate a special service with its banks to permit customers to remit their transfers to the banks' postal accounts rather than the supplier's accounts. Not only would this reduce float time, but funds could be transferred into a regular bank account much more quickly, even before notification.

(5) *Quietanze.* The biggest problem with the *quietanze* (a combination payment instruction and receipt) is administrative float. Public entities mail *quietanze* to the subsidiary to be signed or request the firm to prepare one itself. The *quietanza* is then routed on to the accounts receivable department, where it is signed and dispatched to the paying bank. However, an examination of eighteen randomly picked *quietanze* showed an average delay between receipt and dispatch of over five calendar days. *Quietanze* that were rerouted to headquarters (where the authorized signatory resides) from the central sales office incurred a further delay of five to thirteen days. The consultants calculated that if *quietanze* could be turned over on the same day, the firm would realize a savings of $23,750 p.a.

The consultants' solution was simply to photocopy the *quietanza* to allow control procedures to be carried out at a later date; the original could then be delivered to the bank the same day. The consultants also suggested establishing a signatory capability at the central sales office to avoid the postal delays.

As this case study makes clear, each instrument generates its own kind of float and leads to different cash management techniques. Beyond some basic similarities, collection instruments and the clearing systems through which they pass vary widely from one country to another (see table on pp. 181–2 for a comparison of countries' clearing systems). Nevertheless, they can be usefully broken down into five categories. The following discussion reviews the collection instruments that are common to most countries and presents typical problems and their solutions.

(1) **Checks** are written obligations to pay issued by the customer. They are drawn either on the customer's account or on the bank's and are the predominant form of payment in countries such as the United States, the United Kingdom, Canada, Mexico, and Australia. Checks have inspired many cash management techniques because of the special forms of float that they generate. The most obvious of these is mail float, which can range from one day in countries such as the United Kingdom or Germany to over a week in Italy and Venezuela. On top of this, while other instruments are

Comparative Clearing Systems

Country	System	Operators	Comments
Australia	National clearing system for paper checks	Trading banks, Reserve Bank of Australia	Very effective, but nonbank institutions may be blocked from participating.
	CEMTEX clearing system for automated transfers	Trading banks	See above.
Brazil	National clearing system for paper checks	Integrated Clearing House	Checks drawn on nonparticipating banks may take 5–10 days to clear. Otherwise, system is very efficient.
Canada	National clearing system for paper checks	Canadian Payments Association	Highly efficient.
	IIPS international funds transfer system	Bank of Canada	Used for interbank foreign exchange transactions.

sent from the customer directly to the bank, the collection cycle for checks is lengthened by the inclusion of the supplier. This results in additional internal processing and transport delays at the supplier's location. Of course, checks, like other instruments, are also subject to bank float.

The check collection cycle can be outlined by measuring the following forms of float:

- **Mail float:** From the date of postage on the envelope carrying the check to its receipt by the supplier.
- **Internal float:** From the date the check was received by the supplier to completion of internal control procedures to its deposit at the bank.
- **Clearing float:** The time between deposit of the check and the receipt of the customer's funds by the supplier's bank.
- **Value dating** (where appropriate): The time it takes for the bank to apply good value to cleared funds in the supplier's account.
- **Advice delay:** The time it takes for the supplier to receive acknowledgment of good funds from its bank.

Global Cash Management

Country	System	Operators	Comments
France	National clearing system for paper checks	Paris Clearing House, Bank of France, Credit Agricole	Open to all financial institutions.
	SAGITTAIRE international interbank transfers	Bank of France	The system works like CHIPS.
	SIT interbank transfers	Major banks	Allows direct teleclearing. Excludes nonbanks.
Germany	*Giro* credit transfers	Bundesbank	Very efficient; composed of four separate decentralized systems.
	Genonet automated transfers	Credit cooperatives, savings banks	For automated processing of *giro* transfers.
Italy	*Stanza di compensazione* (local clearinghouses)	Bank of Italy	No national clearing system exists. Local checks are cleared through Bank of Italy's branches and through the local clearinghouses.

▶

The last three forms of float should be fought through more aggressive negotiations with the banks and improved reporting services. To minimize the pernicious effects of postal delays, subsidiaries might consider employing **courier services** or **in-house messengers** to pick up checks from customers or to rush them to their banks before value-dating cutoff times. A French food manufacturer, for instance, has a team of messengers who "run around to all our banks each morning to deposit checks before 10 A.M., so we can get credit right away." Courier services also reduce the risk of theft and loss. If customers mail checks and documentation, it may take weeks before a company can determine that items are missing.

Instead of employing couriers, companies can use **salesmen** in the field to pick up payments. This technique can backfire, however, unless companies educate their collector-salesmen on the time value of money and establish clear guidelines for collection procedures.

One firm, for example, set up a system under which salesmen collect checks in rural areas. To the chagrin of the treasurer, many salesmen simply kept the payments in their briefcases until they returned to headquarters from one- or two-week sales trips. By the time checks were actually deposited, more time had been lost than if the customers had mailed the checks. To solve this problem, the treasury instructed

Comparative Clearing Systems (Continued)

Country	System	Operators	Comments
Japan	*Zengin* credit transfers	Tokyo Bankers Association	Very efficient on-line system used mainly to process electronic credit transfers.
	Automated transfer clearing system (magnetic tape)	Tokyo Clearing House	Processes direct deposits but not direct debits, which are processed directly by individual banks.
	CAPTAIN Videotex transfers	NTT (Japanese Telecommunications Corp.)	Used for corporate banking.
	INS high-value transfers	NTT	Works like CHAPS.
United Kingdom	Town Clearing paper check system	Bankers' Clearing House	Restricted to transfers over $10,000.
	General paper check clearing system	Bankers' Clearing House	For high-volume, low-value check clearing.
	BACS automated transfers	Bankers' Automated Clearing Services Ltd.	Two days' notice required to enact transfer.
	CHAPS automated transfers	Supervised by the Bankers' Clearing House	Begun in 1984 for nationwide interbank transfers.

salesmen to deposit sizable checks (those large enough to justify the cost of transfer) at the nearest branch of the firm's main trading bank and inform headquarters immediately of the transaction.

Some companies even find it worthwhile to fly messengers to pick up large payments from remote locations. A cash manager at a U.S. pharmaceuticals company said, "There are some very big wholesalers in the pharmaceuticals industry, and it's a tough business. They play the float much more aggressively than we do. Because the sums are large, they like to pay us from a remote point. It's part of a game. They do it from different banks. We won't know which bank it's issued to until it gets to our lockbox, so we have an arrangement when they get in to get out a courier. If it's issued in some remote place in Texas we may send someone to pick it up. The $500 in airfare is more than covered by the cut in float. This happens twenty to thirty times a year."

Lockboxes help control not only mail float but internal processing float as well. First developed in the United States in the 1940s, lockboxes are simply post office boxes set up at strategic mailing points to ensure prompt receipt of checks. Under the

Global Cash Management

Country	System	Operators	Comments
United States	National paper check system	Federal Reserve System, private operators	Fed operates 12 regional banks; private operators operate more national systems.
	Automated Clearing House (ACH) transfer system	Federal Reserve System, NACHA, private operators	Originally cleared direct deposits and debits via tape; now handles electronic deposit transfers (EDTs) and corporate trade payments (CTPs).
	FedWire interbank wire transfers	Federal Reserve System	Guaranteed settlement.
	BankWire/CashWire interbank transfer systems	Private operators	BankWire transmits information only; CashWire settles funds.
	CHIPS interbank transfers	NYCHA (private ACH association based in New York City)	The major clearing center for international dollar transfers.
	CHESS interbank transfers	Private operators	Clearing center based in Chicago.

standard lockbox setup, customers mail remittances to post office boxes designated by the seller. The bank empties the boxes one or more times a day and transports the contents to the bank for processing. The checks are reconciled against invoices, and any discrepancies are identified in a bank report. The checks are then entered into the clearing account that day.

Lockboxes cut down on administrative delays, too. When checks are mailed directly to the collection department without the aid of a lockbox, they are mixed in with newspapers and general correspondence. In such cases, the mail room may take an hour or more to segregate and distribute checks; accounts receivable must then process these checks and make up a slip for deposit at the bank. Since delivery of mail often occurs late in the day, this may cause firms to miss bank deadlines for that day's value. In addition, lockboxes reduce internal handling expenses, since a bank-owned lockbox service collects the mail, processes the remittances, and deposits the checks directly into the company's account.

Lockboxes receive much more attention in the United States, a vast nation where over 90 percent of cashless payments are made by check, than in most other countries.

How to Make the Most of Lockbox Services

When picking a lockbox bank, companies should do the following:

- Require the bank to provide a photocopy of each check.
- Make sure the bank provides standardized balancing of checks to invoices and of total checks to bank credit tickets.
- Request a daily statement via an electronic terminal or magnetic tape of checks processed; the statement should include the amount of checks processed, the deposit date, and the funds availability date.
- Seek prompt crediting of the account, reflecting multiple collections and processing of checks received during the day. This ensures that the maximum number of checks received can be processed in time to meet the bank's and the interbank check-clearing deadlines.
- Arrange to have deposit tickets sequentially numbered to help identify any batches of checks that may have been lost or destroyed during processing.
- Inspect the bank's check-processing equipment to determine if it is sophisticated enough to handle high-volume processing with reliability, speed, and accuracy.
- Request that one person handle your company's work each day so that the individual is familiar with the unique character of your business and needs.
- Insist on prompt handling of inquiries.
- Require that all documentation forwarded to your company's office (e.g., photocopied checks/drafts and invoices) be sent in sturdy, secured boxes. Additionally, an index of each box's contents should be included.
- Review the bank's lockbox contract carefully to determine exactly what services the bank guarantees.
- Check the fees to be sure they are competitive.

In Canada, for example, the coast-to-coast branch networks of the major banks and efficient cash-concentration services make lockboxes somewhat less popular. Lockboxes are even less common in Asian and European countries because the banks do not offer them. The spokesman for a French manufacturer explained: "We want to use lockboxes, but they just don't exist in France. The banks do not offer them. They are ten years behind the times." Firms that cannot find a bank-operated lockbox system should consider setting up one of their own.

Companies typically locate lockboxes near their customers and in cities with good mail times. For example, in the United States, Chicago is preferred to New York as a lockbox site because of its excellent postal and airport facilities; New York suffers notoriously poor mail service. And because Manhattan is a congested island, it is not suitable for quick airplane deliveries.

Besides carefully choosing the best sites for speedy service, companies must take cash-reporting and pricing considerations into account. This generally leads firms to keep the number of lockbox systems they rely on to a minimum, although restrictions on interstate banking in the United States make this difficult.

A typical lockbox system is maintained by a major U.S. manufacturer of sophisticated machinery. The firm's treasurer considers lockboxes to be the next best thing to electronic funds transfers (EFTs), remarking, "I'd love an EFT system, but unfortunately, no one wants to pay electronically." Because the company is decentralized, with twenty divisions, it uses about eighteen different lockboxes from twelve different banks. But to increase efficiency and reduce fees, the company plans to cut this network back to about five lockboxes and three or four banks (it has hired one of its major banks to conduct a study on how this can be best accomplished). The funds from each lockbox bank are concentrated via electronic deposit transfers (EDTs) in an investment fund in New York. One of the firm's divisions handles about 7,000 receivables items a month, while the rest receive up to 3,000 each, for a total of $1 billion in annual sales. Assuming that its money is worth 9 percent, the firm saves $250,000 annually (less the cost of the service) for each day the lockboxes eliminate from the collection cycle.

Companies seeking to accelerate check receipts can also turn to an **intercept point** (a strategically located office that receives mail quickly and then deposits it locally) and a **concentration account** (a bank service that automatically consolidates corporate balances in various bank accounts into one central account). A good example of how they work in tandem is offered by a German automobile manufacturer. The firm has designated forty of its sales agents as collection, or intercept, points. Receipts from local sales are collected with one day of mail float and deposited locally in the branch of one of the three major banks with which the headquarters maintains a concentration account. If, for example, the Hamburg collection point receives a check, it deposits the check with a branch of Bank X in Hamburg, which credits the amount the same day. By 11 A.M. the next day, the money is transferred to Bank X's concentration account in Stuttgart, where the headquarters is located, for immediate value. Thanks to this arrangement, the firm has not only drastically cut float but has centralized excess funds for more efficient investment. (See chapter 6 for more details on the corporate use of concentration accounts.)

(2) **Bank transfers** are funds transfers initiated by an instruction issued by the customer to its bank to pay a specified amount to a specified supplier's account. They can be initiated via telephone, paper instruction, or a terminal in the customer's office. Bank transfers are attractive to suppliers because they eliminate mail delay. They also often entail shorter clearing or value days because they are electronically initiated between banks on a wire system.

The drawback of bank transfers is that the supplier does not know about them until it is notified (hopefully) by its bank of the receipt of good funds. Therefore, it cannot control or monitor transfers during the early stages of the cycle. According to the treasurer of a U.S. glass manufacturer's French subsidiary, "The customer may tell you he has already paid something on a certain date, but that doesn't mean anything. He may have signed the order, but it didn't reach the bank for four or five days. And

How to Compare and Contrast Collection Instruments

The use of checks, *giros,* and other collection instruments varies widely among countries. To help companies review the payment options in each country, the following checklist presents the key features to look for in measuring the benefits and drawbacks of each instrument:

- **Fees.** Banks often charge processing and clearing fees for collected funds that can range from zero to sky-high. As a general rule, banks tend to charge less for electronic or tape-based transfers than for paper-based ones. High fees can discourage payers from using an instrument that might otherwise be attractive to the supplier. For example, the main disadvantage of commercial bills in Italy is that the customer must pay a stamp tax. As a result, customers in a strong position often refuse to use commercial bills.
- **Internal processing.** Some collection instruments take longer to process internally, adding to administrative costs and float. For example, processing drafts can be a time-consuming and costly process for companies. "We're trying to get away from that," explained a spokesman for the French subsidiary of a U.S. computer firm. "You have to fill out the bill and mail the acceptance to the customer, and when you get it back you have to record it and get it over to the bank. It's a lot of work handling these things. If you don't need the credit, it's not worth it."
- **Clearing float and value dating.** Because different collection instruments often pass through different clearing systems or are handled differently by banks, their clearing times or value days can vary widely. For example, in Italy, *ricevute* take ten to fifteen days, checks one to eight, bank transfers two to twenty, and commercial bills twelve. Clearing days can be much more costly than bank fees, especially in high-interest-rate environments.

---

then banks naturally tend to keep the float, claiming administrative delays and all that." The Italian treasurer of a paper manufacturer agreed: "The customer is under no compulsion to pay on time. We use transfers only with the very best customers."

To analyze the collection of bills via bank transfers, companies must measure four different kinds of float.

- **Customer float:** the time it takes the customer to initiate a transfer.
- **Clearing float:** the time between the customer's initiation of the transfer at its bank and the receipt of funds by the supplier's bank.
- **Value dating** (where appropriate): the time it takes for good funds to be credited to the supplier's account.
- **Advice delay:** the time it takes for the supplier to receive acknowledgment of the transfer from its bank.

A special form of clearing float is mail float, which not only adds extra days to the clearing of checks but can complicate cash forecasting as well. The importance of mail float varies widely. For example, in the United Kingdom, mail float is only one to two days, but in Italy it can range from four to ten days or longer.

- **Ability to discount.** Commercial bills are negotiable and therefore can be discounted with banks, providing an easy source of financing in many countries. Italian *ricevute* and Japanese promissory notes can also be discounted at good rates.
- **Level of risk.** Some instruments constitute a legal obligation to pay and thus provide sellers with protection against customer default. In France, for example, if a customer cannot honor an accepted draft, he is put on the Banque de France's blacklist and can be taken to court. In Japan, a company that dishonors its obligation on a promissory note twice within six months is blacklisted by the local clearinghouse; thereafter, banks will sever relations and suppliers will switch to cash on delivery.
- **Reporting.** Instruments subject to mail float or inconsistent bank clearing make it difficult to forecast availability of funds. One of the reasons postal *giros* are unpopular with cash managers in many countries is that it is impossible to get telephone information on postal accounts (statements arrive in the mail). On the other hand, commercial bills and Italian *ricevute* can help suppliers because their fixed maturity dates facilitate cash flow projections.
- **Control.** Italian *ricevute* are popular because they are formally presented by the bank, and remind customers to pay on time while highlighting the fact if payment is missed. Checks do not offer such fringe benefits to help with collection. As the treasurer of a French pharmaceuticals concern warned, "You have no control over checks. If you call the customer, they can tell you that their payment is lost in the mail. And if they are far from us, it can take over a week to get here, even if they are telling the truth." Finally, as one subsidiary credit manager put it, "The big problem with checks is that you have to deposit them, and people lose them. For large amounts, we insist on drafts or bank transfers."

Much of the float on bank transfers can only be fought through negotiations on terms and use of the best possible banks. One way to quantify clearing float is to obtain the customer's assistance. When possible, ask a trusted customer for a sample of transfer initiation dates and times, and then match them with the bank's balance reports. Another approach is to conduct tests; instruct an operating unit or other entity to make transfers through certain banks at certain times and compare the results.

(3) **Commercial bills** are time drafts with a predetermined maturity. They are popular with suppliers because they can usually be discounted with a bank, providing an easy source of financing in many credit-tight markets. Sometimes they provide legal protection. On the other hand, processing drafts can be a time-consuming and costly procedure for companies, involving extensive handling and paperwork. Moreover, bank collection charges for commercial bills can be high.

Four key forms of float should be measured to determine the collection cycle for bills:

- **Acceptance delay:** the time from the supplier's issuance of the invoice to the date the draft is returned by the customer to the supplier.
- **Internal processing delay:** the time from receipt to deposit of the draft.
- **Clearing float:** the time it takes for the supplier's bank to process the draft and obtain the customer's funds.
- **Value dating** (where appropriate): the time it takes for good funds to be credited to the supplier's account.

To get the best value from commercial bills, subsidiaries must try to negotiate better value dating, fees, and financing rates with their banks. Furthermore, they must weigh the importance of financing and legal protection against the costs of internal processing of bills and bank fees.

Many countries have specialized instruments that offer a number of the same features as commercial bills. For example, in Japan and Korea, companies commonly rely on promissory notes. Under this system, a customer issues its supplier an IOU specifying the amount of the debt and the date payment is due. The supplier takes the note to a bank, which holds it until maturity. On the due date, the supplier is immediately credited. Promissory notes differ from checks in that they may be discounted with the supplier's banks and offer maximum security: A company that dishonors its obligation twice within six months is blacklisted by the local clearinghouse.

Companies in Brazil rely to a great extent on the *duplicata* system. Under this system, which involves a great deal of paperwork, a *nota fiscal* is prepared by the supplier. One copy is delivered to the buyer with the merchandise. Another copy, the *duplicata,* is forwarded to the bank, which then advises the customer of the branches at which it can be paid. The customer signs an acceptance acknowledging the terms of sale and the placement of the *duplicata. Duplicatas* can be and often are discounted, especially when the buyer is a chronically late payer.

(4) **Postal *giros*** are transfers made via postal accounts operated by the postal authorities, most commonly in Europe. They differ from standard transfers in that in order to use them, the creditor's account number must be known and there is no per-transfer charge, which makes *giros* an extremely inexpensive form of payment. In response to invoice terms, customers send preprinted punch cards with the supplier's name, account number, and amount due to the *giro* computer center to initiate a direct deposit. Alternatively, the supplier can mail a *giro* acceptance to the customer a few weeks before the due date; the customer fills in its own account number, signs it, and mails it back. In practice, customers are more willing to consent to *giro* acceptances than to direct-debiting systems (such as Bankers' Automated Clearing Services, BACS) because timing control is retained; a customer signs and mails the *giro* acceptance at his own discretion. Finally, the *giro* serves as a reconciliation device

when returned to the originator after being credited. The net effect is an extremely efficient and inexpensive instrument for reminding customers of and collecting payments.

The forms of float in a *giro* transfer are similar to those in a bank transfer. In the case of *giros,* however, the advice delay—the time it takes for the supplier to receive acknowledgment of the transfer from its bank—is often the most costly part of the cycle. Combined with low rates on balances, inadequate reporting is the major complaint many cash managers have about *giros.*

The Italian subsidiary of a U.S. computer manufacturer, for example, found that it took sixteen calendar days on average to receive notification of deposits in its postal account, although value was received much earlier. Such delays are expensive, because the accounts often pay trivial interest—in this case 0.5 percent. And to make matters even worse, overdrafts in some systems are not allowed, so a customer trying to maintain minimal balances can inadvertently bounce payments.

Fortunately, in response to increased competition from the commercial banks, some *giro* systems have begun to offer reasonable interest on idle balances, daily balance information, and in some cases even overdraft facilities. This improvement of services, together with the *giro*'s extremely low cost, makes it worthwhile for local collection managers to review the capabilities and potential benefits of local *giro* systems.

(5) **Direct debits,** also known as "preauthorized transfers," are transfer orders prepared by the supplier and presented to the customer's bank, which then credits the supplier's account based on standing instructions from the customer. Because this can be done on a same-day basis, the seller reduces or eliminates clearing, value dating, internal processing, and mail float. Only customer and advice delays need to be monitored and controlled. Suppliers usually initiate direct debits by providing their banks with payment vouchers or listings. In the more automated markets, collection may be made via specialized clearinghouses, such as BACS (see p. 129) in the United Kingdom or ACH (see p. 136–139) in the United States.

Direct debiting is particularly attractive to companies that have a high volume of recurring billings and want to automate collection. Some of the common users are finance, insurance, gas, electric, and telephone companies, which send out regular bills with only the amount charged. Many customers, of course, resist direct debiting because of the loss of control over disbursements that it entails; companies in dominant market positions are best able to encourage customers to pay via direct debiting. The key advantages of direct debiting are the following:

· **Elimination of payment delays.** All customer accounts are debited the day payment is due, because the initiative is taken from the payer and given to the payee. Also, since the supplier collects directly from the buyer's bank, administrative and postal delays are eliminated.
· **Administrative simplification.** Direct debiting offers tremendous savings by reducing paperwork and cutting clerical costs.
· **Improved cash flow forecasting.** Companies can more accurately monitor and

The Impact of National Payment Systems on Receivables Float

Besides understanding the pros and cons of various collection instruments, cash managers need to know the ins and outs of the clearing mechanisms in their country. Clearing systems facilitate the transfer of funds and transfer notifications between the supplier's bank and the customer's bank. Unless the two companies happen to use the same bank, the national clearing mechanism determines how fast the supplier's bank receives good value on funds transfers from the customer. In addition, in most countries banks formally or informally tack on "value days" to these clearing days for their own profit. As a result, companies must try to speed payments through the clearing system as well as reduce the banks' additional value days.

A useful illustration of the impact national clearing systems can have no corporate trade payments is the case of **Germany.** All domestic payments in Germany are settled through one or more of the four major clearing systems. The savings banks, the cooperative banks, and the post office each run a clearing system through their respective central institutions. The fourth system is run by the Bundesbank and clears payments between commercial banks as well as payments crossing from one system to another. In addition to these four systems, the banks with large branch networks have internal clearings for their branches.

These various clearings affect corporate clients because different types of banks use different clearing systems; therefore, value-dating conventions vary according to whether a payment is drawn and presented on a commercial, savings, cooperative, or postal account. Although clearings within each of the four circuits are relatively efficient, payments crossing from one system to another often suffer delays. Consequently, companies in Germany need to know what types of banks are involved in a transaction to determine how long—and how costly—the clearing delays will be.

The efficiency of national clearing systems varies widely. For example, because the Canadian clearing system is completely centralized, banks in **Canada** are able to grant each other next-day value on all corporate payments. Dominating the Canadian scene are five major banks; all have advanced computer and communications equipment that interacts with the automated check-clearing centers. As a result, companies receive same-day value for all deposits (technically, only intrabank transfers are truly

---

forecast their cash flows by pinpointing the exact amount and timing of incoming payments.
· **Lower bank costs.** Direct debiting cuts bank processing costs, since banks debit accounts by computer tape rather than by processing hundreds or thousands of transfer orders or checks each month. The bank may pass these savings on to the corporate user.

Because direct debiting reduces most of the float in the second phase of the collection cycle, subsidiaries should be encouraged to push customers to accept it whenever feasible. One firm taking advantage of direct debiting is the French subsidiary of a

same-day, but banks grant same-day value on interbank transfers and compensate their float loss in other ways).

In sharp contrast, **Italy** does not yet have a unified national clearing system. Thus, out-of-town items must be settled between banks on a cash-letter basis through correspondent accounts. Some in-town items are cleared through local clearinghouses *(stanza di compensazione)*. In addition, the Bank of Italy runs clearinghouses at ten of its branches and provides clearing services through branches in towns lacking a local clearinghouse of their own. Essentially, the domestic clearing system in Italy is a microcosm of the international payment system, with no direct method through which correspondent institutions can settle. As a result, it is difficult to predict when payments will clear, and value dating ranges from one to twenty days.

To speed up the clearing process, cut costs, and accommodate growing volumes, several countries are automating their clearing systems. For example, in 1968 the **United Kingdom** clearing banks established the Inter-Bank Computer Bureau for the exchange of magnetic tapes for just these reasons. Bankers' Automated Clearing Services (BACS), owned by the largest London clearing banks, was set up as a separate company in 1971 to further the work of the Inter-Bank Computer Bureau; it is now the world's largest automated clearinghouse. BACS operates on a three-business-day settlement cycle and handles mostly direct debits and payrolls.

In 1984 another automated interbank clearing system was established in London to improve the handling of high-value transfers. Known as CHAPS (Clearing House Automated Payments System), the system provides computerized clearing of payments between banks. CHAPS offers two advantages: It allows same-day settlement of interbank payments (with a minimum value of £10,000) and provides immediate confirmation of funds transfers to the paying and receiving parties.

CHAPS is a decentralized clearing system organized around a public utility (British Telecom) switching system. Each of the thirteen settlement banks has its own electronic gateway to the central network. Corporate customers can access CHAPS directly through one of the gateway banks. But since fees charged for using the system run from £5 to £10 per transfer, only companies that need same-day settlement of large transfers (e.g., commodities trading firms and companies that are major players in the money market) use CHAPS extensively.

U.K. office equipment rental company. At the end of each month, the firm's clients send the head office a form stating the number of times a machine has been used. The firm's computer then generates invoices and a tape, recording all the clients' usage bills. This is sent to the clearing system, and customers' bank accounts are automatically debited.

However, a company spokesman finds that the number of participants in the system fluctuates. "When the economy is booming and there's plenty of cash, we find that the percentage of clients letting us direct debit shoots up," he explained. "When times are bad and there's a squeeze on cash, the clients drop out." Indeed, many firms find that the main obstacle to direct debiting is their customers' natural reluctance to being forced to pay on time. As an incentive, one electronics firm is offering easier credit terms to customers agreeing to use the system.

Another company that switched to direct debiting for its premium billings is a U.K. insurance firm. Before the switch, the insurer offered a 3 percent discount if it could draw a check in the client's name on the premium due date. Now the company gets the payment on the due date through direct debiting, with no discount to the client. Ten days prior to a premium payment date, the client is notified by the company. On the due date, a tape is supplied to the appropriate clearinghouse. The program is working well, with only a 2 percent insufficient-funds rate, which is what the company experienced with check payments.

Phase Three: Clearing Payments Through the Banking System

The final events in the collections cycle take place at the bank. Once the customer's payment has been presented, there is almost always a delay before good funds are available in the supplier's account. Behind the delay is clearing float: the time it takes to physically transfer and record payment information from bank to bank. To compensate itself for the clearing service, the receiving bank may also delay releasing the money to the company. In many countries the term "value dating" refers to a predetermined clearing time period.

The clearing times at each bank can be determined by comparing the dates checks and other instruments are deposited (for certain instruments, this information may have to be requested from the customer) and the dates when good funds show up on bank ledgers and balance reports. It is important to pay special heed to apparent irregularities. For example, one company found that its major bank was delaying acknowledgment of a high percentage of its Friday deposits until Monday to pick up the extra two days' float for itself.

To determine if subsidiaries are minimizing delays in the collection cycle caused by clearing times at the banks, ask local managers the following questions:

(1) Are you reducing float by encouraging customers to deposit funds in a bank that you presently use yourself?
(2) Do you understand the clearing system in your country well enough to try to route collections through the most efficient clearing path? (See the table on pp. 128–129.)
(3) Have you tried to negotiate improved clearing or value-dating terms with your banks?
(4) Have you compared the performance of each of your banks?
(5) Do you carefully monitor your banks to make sure they are keeping to the agreed-upon terms?

A good way to start improving clearing times is by making certain that local staff are directing collections to banks they share with their customers. This avoids interbank clearing and requires only that the bank make ledger entries on the two compa-

Value Dating and Float for Intracountry Receivables

Country	Instrument	Supplier Credited	Customer Debited
Australia	Check[1]	Same day	Same day
	Check[2]	3–4 days	Same day
	Wire transfer	Same day	Same day
	Promissory note	Same day	Varies
Brazil	Check[1]	0–2 days	0–2 days
	Check[2]	9–10 days	0–2 days
	Wire transfer	Same day	Same day
Canada	Check	Same day	Same day
	Automated transfer	Same day	Same day
	Preauthorized payment	Same day	Same day
	Wire transfer	Same day	Same day
France	Commercial bill	4 days	1 day
	Automated commercial bill	4 days	1 day
	Check	2–5 days	2 days
	Wire transfer	1 day	1 day
Germany	Check[1]	0–2 days	1–2 days
	Check[2]	2–5 days	1–2 days
	Transfer order	2–6 days	Immediate
	Wire transfer	Next day	Immediate
	Direct debit	2 days	1 day
Italy	*Ricevuta*	7–15 days	1 day
	Check[1]	2 days	Same day
	Check[2]	3–8 days	Same day
	Wire transfer	Same day—20 days	Same day
Japan	Check	1–4 days	Same day
	Wire transfer	Same day	Same day
	Intrabank transfer	Same day	Same day
	Promissory note	Same day	Same day
United Kingdom	Check[1]	Same day	Same day
	Check[2]	2–4 days	Same day
	Wire transfer	3–7 days	Same day
	Automated transfer (BACS)	Same day	Same day
United States	Check	1–2 days	Same day
	Automated transfer (ACH)	Next day	Immediate
	Wire transfer	Same day	Same day

[1]Denotes intracity.

[2]Denotes intercity.

Note: Customer accounts are back-valued; suppliers receive forward value.

nies' accounts. As the spokesman for an Italian paper manufacturer explained, "The main way we cut collection time in Italy is to encourage our customers to use our banks. If it's all done internally by one bank, it should be quicker." The treasurer brought his value dating down from eight to ten days to just three or four this way.

The next step is to determine if local staff are consistently and effectively negotiating for better clearing times with every bank. Begin by comparing their terms with those other companies in the country are receiving and finding out if much time has passed since the last improvement occurred. The rewards of tough negotiations for better value dating and float time are demonstrated by these examples:

· The regional treasurer of a Hong Kong-based consumer products MNC was able to get his main bank to reduce funds availability on transfers from five to seven days to just one or two days "simply by telling them that there were other banks willing to do it for us. You've got to bargain out here. Keep the bankers on their toes."
· "Four days on drafts is what people who don't negotiate get," claimed the spokesman for a French food producer. "We have negotiated the value dates to just two or three days." A French mining company has achieved even better results. "You can bargain with your banker to get better conditions on drafts than the usual four days," the firm's treasurer stated. "And we do get better conditions. We get one day after the maturity date."
· Even though he represented a small firm, a German finance director succeeded in negotiating excellent clearing terms with his banks. "Value dating is usually standard, but you can squeeze something out of the banks if you try," he advised. "We get next-day value on both in-town and out-of-town checks, which is pretty good."

To achieve reduced value-dating times, firms must demonstrate their importance to their banks and be willing to offer something in return. As one experienced French treasurer advised, "Success depends on the amount of money you give a bank in business. With banks where we have major relations, it may be enough just to show how much business we already give them. For others, you can bargain: 'Well, if you give us only one or two days, we will give you more business than in the past. If you improve the conditions, we will improve the volume of the operations." To facilitate his negotiations, the treasurer installed a computerized system to monitor his business volumes with each bank. "That way," he said, "we can prove exactly how much we give the bank and why they should give us concessions."

An Italian firm negotiated better conditions with its banks by analyzing the value dating its five banks imposed on postal checks. The results were as follows:

	Average Value Days
Bank 1	5.9
Bank 2	3.0
Bank 3	2.0
Bank 4	2.0
Bank 5	5.0

Calculating the Impact of Value Dating

When negotiating value-dating arrangements with banks, companies should try to base the terms on calendar days rather than business days. The reason is simple: Under the business-day method, firms lose value itself over the weekends—a total of 102 days each year—plus bank holidays. Thus, value dating based on business days is at least 40 percent more expensive than that based on calendar days (for each working day during a 5-day week, there are 1.4 calendar days). A medium-sized electronics firm in France convinced just one of its banks to use calendar days and saved itself more than $17,000 p.a.

To determine the savings from switching to calendar days, companies can use the following formula:

1.4 × average daily collections × % of receivables collected by value-dated instruments × cost of funds = annual savings.

When companies are forced to accept the business-day method, they should calculate the true cost of the agreed float, which is based on the number of interest days. To adjust terms based on business days to those based on calendar days, companies can use the following formula:

$$\text{Adjustment factor} = \frac{I}{(C - H)},$$

where I is the total number of interest days per year (360), C is the total number of calendar days per year (365 or 366), and H is the number of weekend days and bank holidays per year.

With this information to support him, the firm's cash manager successfully negotiated with the slower banks to match the faster ones—or lose the business.

For companies with low business volume and limited banking business—an apt description of many small subsidiaries of MNCs—it may be difficult to negotiate faster funds availability with banks. As the spokesman for the Mexican subsidiary of a major U.S. MNC said, "I walk into a Mexican bank here, and they look at our account and they're dealing with Celanese and Alfa Group and all that. They don't even want to talk to me about negotiating float time; I'm just not that important to them. I can't say that I blame them." Because many small subsidiaries do not always have sufficient clout with their bankers, parent companies may have to get involved in the negotiations and perhaps dangle the carrot of increased business from the parent, either with the local bank or with a branch of the bank in another country.

Even if local companies are actively pursuing negotiations, parents should review how they monitor bank compliance. This is particularly important in high-interest-rate environments. According to the treasurer of a Brazilian company, "You must have control over the banks because they're simply unreliable here. If they know you don't have any control over them, they'll sit on the cash. So even though they're supposed to clear the accounts, they don't." Banks have many little tricks to increase float. In Germany, for example, where there are four major clearing systems, companies must beware of banks increasing their share of float by routing payments from one system to another for the least efficient transfer.

Dealing with Delinquent Debtors

Customers that simply refuse (or are unable) to pay on time can undermine even the most sophisticated receivables system. To cope with delinquent accounts, it is vital that companies maintain a reporting system that tracks slow-paying customers and indicates what actions have been taken to accelerate collections. To evaluate how well subsidiaries are dealing with delinquent debtors, parents should first analyze internal credit reports. The effectiveness of a firm's dunning procedures is most apparent from its record on collecting on accounts that are delinquent beyond thirty days, sixty days, and so on. Second, parents should make sure that subsidiaries are aware of the standard dunning methods, including issuing standardized letters and telexes, making telephone calls and personal visits, relying on outside collection agencies, and taking legal action.

The dunning process typically begins with a series of letters sent out immediately after the due date when no payment is received. The in-house review team should read these letters and compare them with others they have seen that they know are effective. The first letter can be a simple reminder, but successive letters must use stronger language and refer to the possible consequences of continued tardiness. Final notices should contain specific threats, such as the supplier's intention to take legal action.

Besides being well written, the dunning letter must be part of a regular, consistent procedure. Are letters issued on a timely basis to all delinquents, or is this done haphazardly? Is dunning coordinated with collections? Who is responsible for dunning, and to whom do they report?

A good example of a rigorous system is that of a capital goods manufacturer in the United Kingdom. Collection clerks write dunning letters by the eighth or tenth day of the month following the due date so that customers receive them by the fifteenth (in the United Kingdom, customers pay all of a month's invoices at month end). A second letter—written in fairly threatening language—is delivered on the twenty-fifth. By the end of the month, customers are informed that supplies have been cut off. Many companies automate this procedure to reduce administrative costs and ensure smooth, consistent notification. The danger here is that the response to form letters is predictably lax. Personalized letters created on a word processor can be much more convincing.

While letters are a good, inexpensive way of prodding many customers, large accounts are usually worth a phone call. But parents must make sure local dunning officers are not falling into the trap described by the treasurer of an Australian MNC: "The biggest area where companies fail is they don't get on the phone. Or they're apologetic and say, 'Look, I'm sorry for ringing you, but you seem to owe us money.' I know that when I get calls like that I just say, 'So bloody what?' and they'll say, 'Oh, sorry, I just thought I'd ring you anyway,' and hang up. But if someone says, 'I'll be around in half an hour to pick up the check,' quite often I'll get on it. Someone with good telephone technique can wring a lot of money out of people."

To pressure debtors even further, a personal visit may be necessary. Some companies use salesmen for this because they are already in the field and have established strong relationships with customers. They also have the advantage of appearing less threatening than a collection agent and can often pressure a customer without jeopardizing business relationship. Such an approach is preferred by the treasurer of a U.S. chemicals corporation in Japan: "Collection is part of our salesmen's job in Japan. They have to go out to late-paying customers and say, 'Look here, you have been late with your payments and we would appreciate it if you pay on time.'"

For the more uncooperative clients, however, it will be necessary to send an officer with more clout than a salesman. In Korea, for instance, a U.S. exporter cautions that "you've got to be careful who you send out. You have to send a manager or some top-ranking person; the companies just throw out salesmen."

Subsidiaries should be persuaded to try each of the above dunning techniques and find a combination that works for their environment. Goals should be set for reducing long-overdue accounts to encourage the staff to take initiative. If letters, phone calls, and personal visits still prove ineffective for some customers, the only solution may be to use a collection agency. Collection agencies can actually cost less than internal personnel because severe and unusual tactics may not be necessary on a regular and predictable basis, and an agency can be hired only when needed. An agency can also act as a buffer between the supplier and the customer and assume the blame for any friction generated.

On the other hand, outside collection agencies may not always be sufficiently flexible or knowledgeable about a customer's specific problems. In-house staff can better tailor collection approaches to take into account special client relationships by suggesting alternative plans, such as debt rescheduling, that an outside agency might overlook. One way of using in-house personnel while reaping the benefits of a third-party collector may be to move the collection function to a different unit. For example, a U.S.-owned services firm in the United Kingdom went so far as to create a collection subsidiary with a separate board of directors, address, and telephone number so that to customers it appeared to be a totally independent outside collection agency. About 90 percent of their overdue customers are goaded into paying when they receive notice from this "independent" agency.

When accounts have become unacceptably late, companies should also consider cutting all further deliveries to the customer—bearing in mind that such an action may undermine the client's ability to pay. For example, the Brazilian subsidiary of a U.S. power-equipment manufacturer compiles a daily "blacklist" of late clients and cuts all shipments to accounts that are more than ten days overdue. Said the treasurer: "With the cost of financing what it is, we'd rather lose sales than carry a customer on our books." This tactic is not always feasible, however, because of the need to maintain contact with customers to retrieve payment or to keep sales going.

The last resort is to turn collections over to the courts. It is important to examine

Future Vision: Using ACH for On-Line Collections

The ACH (Automated Clearing House) experiment in the United States reflects a recognition of the collection cycle as a complex process with many inefficiencies that create float. The ideal is to make the entire process of collection—from generation of invoice to customer payment to receipt of good funds at the bank—a unified, standardized, and highly controlled procedure. ACH promises not only reduced bank charges and next-day (and eventually same-day) value on receipts, but also dramatically quicker and cheaper procedures for internal billing and processing of payments.

ACH was conceived in 1968 as a unified mechanism for electronically clearing transactions between financial institutions while controlling float and reducing processing costs. Throughout the 1970s, groups of financial institutions created regional clearinghouses. Then, because ACH was an invaluable tool for disbursing Social Security payments, the Federal Reserve offered its banking system and communication lines to unite all regional ACHs into a nationwide network; it also gave the clearing system the volume it needed to become cost-efficient. It even subsidized transaction costs to encourage ACH use.

The main alternatives to ACH are checks and wire transfers. Checks are expensive to process internally—especially for low-value, high-volume transactions—and can be lost or mutilated. Checks also complicate cash forecasting for both customer and supplier, since float times on check collections vary widely, depending on where and at what time of day the check is deposited. Banks charge high collection and processing fees (sometimes 50 cents per item) and assign stiff penalties if checks are returned.

The ACH system, on the other hand, can electronically transfer funds directly into or out of an account, greatly reducing bank and internal costs. It also enables the supplier to predict clearing time, is much more secure, and ensures delivery of the funds by the next day.

---

closely the subsidiary's experience with legal solutions. The effectiveness of using the courts varies tremendously from country to country, and companies must have a clear understanding of the probable costs and the prospects for success before proceeding. For example, the credit manager of a U.S. manufacturer's French subsidiary almost never initiates legal action because "if you go to court, it can take six months to six years to settle, or it will go on endlessly."

The Brazilian system works like this: When suppliers start protest proceedings against customers whose payments have fallen far in arrears, a past-due debt is first placed with a lawyer outside the highly bureaucratic legal network. If this fails, the next step is to register a formal complaint with a notary *(cartorio)*, who in turn publishes the complaint and requests payment within forty-eight hours. If payment is still not made, a formal protest is initiated and the debt is settled in court.

Unfortunately, there are major drawbacks to this technique. Once the protest mechanism is activated, banks will normally cut off the debtor's credit lines. The

The other major payment option in the United States is a wire transfer via FedWire or BankWire. Like ACHs, wires are electronic messages carrying payment information between banks; companies typically initiate them with a phone call or via an in-house terminal. They guarantee same-day value on funds and cost anywhere from $10 to $20. But transaction costs for ACHs are much lower—about 10 cents per transfer—and the ACH format provides an almost unlimited amount of information (vs. 200 characters for wires). This information is invaluable for reconciling accounts, checking customer credit exposure, and so on. Furthermore, wire transfers cannot be so well integrated into the entire collections system.

One of the first companies to use ACHs to reduce transaction costs for delivery of regular, multiple accounts was a major insurance firm. According to the vice president for finance, when the firm switched from a paper-based collection system to an electronic one that debited premiums directly from customers' bank accounts, "the motivation was to cut internal processing costs." The switch resulted in big savings in paper-handling and check-processing costs. An added bonus was the elimination of late payments, so that float on mail time was reduced by as much as two weeks.

In addition to direct debiting, companies can use ACHs to replace depository transfer checks (DTCs) for transferring funds into concentration accounts. More significantly, companies can also pay and receive large, one-time invoices through the system. Companies participating in the pilot corporate trade payments (CTP) program started in early 1984 are initiating and settling transactions completely electronically between in-house terminals. This is an expanded invoice-information format as well as a settlement system that allows up to 4,990 "addenda records" (information units), each carrying ninety-four characters. Additional addenda records can be added to each transmission, providing a virtually unlimited amount of information.

Despite the allure of low-cost systems for collecting, however, the majority of U.S. companies continue to resist the move to ACHs. This is largely because payers are

▶

problem thus becomes circular: Without access to bank financing, the client cannot usually pay its bills, and further protests by other suppliers are likely to ensue. If the circle closes, the customer must eventually obtain a debt moratorium *(concordata)*, which typically lasts from one to two years. Moreover, protesting can be very expensive. In addition to legal fees of 20 percent, creditors lose a substantial amount in the time value of money because of backlogs in the legal system. Consequently, commencing legal proceedings in Brazil, as in most Latin American countries, is truly a supplier's last resort.

When the legal process is known to be long and inefficient, subsidiaries should avoid seeking redress through the courts. Fortunately, in some countries the mere threat of legal sanctions is effective. The subsidiary of a U.S. food manufacturer in Australia concludes its dunning process with a letter threatening a lawsuit. "That usually works," said a spokesman, "because if we sue, a notice appears in a legal gazette, and a lot of companies don't like that because people read it and say, 'Oh,

concerned over loss of float. As one cash manager remarked, "Everyone wants to get paid electronically, but no one wants to pay electronically. It's a good idea, but I really don't know if anyone wants to start it up."

But many companies are beginning to realize that the float game is costly for both the customer and the supplier. This is a key selling point for convincing customers to switch to ACH payments. "The tough part," remarked the vice president of an insurance company that now makes extensive use of both direct debiting and depositing, "is how to explain the disbursement float that you lose." But his analysis of his own firm's payments concluded that, while the firm lost over $140,000 of float annually by disbursing electronically, it ended up with net savings of $50,000 because of lower banking and clerical costs.

Another way to solve the float dilemma is to renegotiate settlement dates to account for the gains or losses that float used to offer. Rather than delaying payment by remitting a check via remote disbursement, the customer uses ACH and negotiates a later settlement date. He maintains full use of the funds, and knows where they are and when they will settle. The customer benefits from better reporting and eliminates paper-handling costs. The supplier suffers no loss of float because the new settlement date reflects the date checks actually used to clear;

Company X is going down the tubes.' Suppliers cut them off and banks take away their overdraft lines."

In Germany, the courts act fairly quickly on lawsuits. If the customer is found guilty, the government will force him to pay. One German cash manager stated that his customers are supposed to pay within 30 days and that he starts legal proceedings after 150 days. "This [the legal process] is very speedy here in Germany," he said. "And once the case is in court, the credit agencies take notice, and the customer is in trouble."

Case Examples: Two Successful Credit and Collection Systems

Company A, a subsidiary of a prominent U.S. electronics firm, is one of the largest foreign-owned operations in France. Its annual sales are split among three divisions: consumer goods customers, large corporate machinery customers, and small and medium-sized corporate customers. The firm has a network of thirty-five sales agencies throughout the country; about 60 percent of its receivables come from customers in Paris, and 40 percent come from clients in the provinces.

suppliers have found that they can even negotiate to get funds sooner than with checks.

Given its high transaction costs, frequent clearing delays, and the myriad opportunities it offers for creating float, it is difficult to imagine the paper-based and highly decentralized U.S. clearing system continuing into the twenty-first century. Once the objections of customers have been overcome, the ACH system of the future will probably look like this: Transaction and invoice data would be transmitted electronically from a terminal at the supplier's warehouse to its accounts receivable ledger to its ACH bank and the regional clearing center, into the customer's loading-dock computer and accounts payable ledger, and back again to the supplier with confirmation data—all with no human intervention. In addition, bar-coded goods would be tabulated and recorded by the system as they arrive and depart on loading docks. Funds and billing data would be transferred electronically, requiring no paperwork and suffering no mail or administrative delays. Ongoing developments promise standard formatting between CTPs and the ANSI X-12 format, which would allow the ACH connection to be further integrated into the entire invoicing and internal payments system.

ACH could revolutionize corporate collection systems. But the timing of the revolution depends on when large numbers of corporate cash managers and their bosses decide to take the ACH plunge. Even if corporate users do adopt ACH, Federal Reserve politics and battles over system formats could delay the ultimate triumph of electronic over paper systems.

All of the company's customers undergo a thorough credit check before salesmen are allowed to book orders. For new accounts, the firm's credit department taps the expertise of one of the French credit rating agencies. If the rating is positive, the salesman gets the green light. But if it is questionable or negative, the treasurer may demand a bank guarantee or recommend not selling to the prospective customer.

For established clients, the company closely investigates past payment histories. If an account has had delays of more than three months, the credit department recommends that the sale be blocked. Although agency sales managers can, in theory, ignore the department's advice, "they do so at their own risk—and very few are willing to do that," says the treasurer.

Credit and collection information is stored on a real-time, mainframe-based system that connects the company's agencies with the Paris headquarters via terminal hookups. When a sale is made, data is fed into a computerized file that shows the date of order, estimated delivery date, and whether the item is in stock. Two days before the order is delivered, the computer produces an invoice that is immediately sent to the customer, so that it is on his desk when the equipment arrives. Another file keeps track of payments by customer, invoice, and amount, enabling the firm to monitor payment patterns from day to day.

To handle its massive collections, the company has enlisted the support of its sales

Twenty-Nine Questions to Ask in a Credit and Collection Study

To help companies conduct an efficient credit and collection study, the questions below should be asked of each subsidiary by either a review team from parent headquarters or an outside consultant conducting the study.

Background, Organization, and Reporting

(1) Do you have any procedure manuals or guidelines you could share with us?

(2) How many customers do you have? Who are your major accounts and what percentage of receivables do they represent? Where are they located? What is the value of receipts by location?

(3) Who is responsible for collections? For billing? For credit? For terms? For sales? Who reports to whom?

(4) Where are bills sent out from? Where are they collected?

(5) Are collections part of the performance review of salesmen? Are bonuses and raises tied to collected accounts, not sales?

(6) How do you monitor your receivables? Are your systems automated? Does your monitoring system update receipts and pinpoint outstanding accounts without delay?

(7) What is the format of receivables reports? Are you assessing collection performance, including days' delinquent outstanding, aging of receivables, and current receivables levels? Do you think these reports are adequate for efficient credit and collection management? How would you improve them?

---

staff. It has established firm guidelines for each agency manager and individual salesmen that spell out targets for sales, installation of equipment, and prompt payment. As an incentive, all salesmen who hit their collection targets are given a bonus of one month's salary. Sales managers' performance ratings also include a collection factor, and awards are made at annual sales meetings to those agencies that have met or surpassed their targets.

Because of this heavy emphasis on collection, the company's salespeople try hard to collect, "particularly," said the treasurer, "toward the end of the month, to remind their customers of outstanding payments or to check up on why overdue amounts haven't come in." The result: The firm has an average DSO of thirty-two days on equipment sales, which are normally made on thirty-day credit terms. Unfortunately, DSOs for maintenance and other service contracts are a high forty-five days. "We can count on the salesman's personal thrust to get payments for equipment," the treasurer commented, "but this doesn't hold true for the service contracts. After all, the client doesn't see the guy after the first month and is likely to drag his later payments."

Because it has minimal borrowing needs, the company tries to avoid using commer-

Customer Credit Risk and Credit Terms

(8) Do you conduct regular checks on all customers through local credit agencies and bureaus, bank and supplier references, personal visits to customers' facilities, and other sources of credit information?

(9) Do you have many delinquent accounts? How much bad debt do you encounter? If there are problems in this area, why?

(10) What are the established credit limits by customer? How are these limits monitored?

(11) What are the standard terms of sale? Are there many exceptions to these standard terms? Does the finance department have input into the decision?

(12) Do you impose penalty fees for late payment? Do you offer discounts for early payment? How do you judge the effectiveness of these terms?

(13) What steps have you taken to make sure credit terms are not too tight or too lenient? Have you compared your credit terms with those of other companies in your industry?

(14) Do you negotiate tighter credit terms or, alternatively, raise prices to compensate for long terms?

(15) Please show us the invoice. Does it clearly state the due date, payment instrument to be used, and what account to send payment to? What is the payment due date based on—when goods are delivered or from date of invoice?

▶

---

cial bills. This allows it to avoid the administrative complexities of the French draft system. According to the firm's spokesman, 80 percent of the company's receipts are in the form of checks, 10 percent are drafts, and 10 percent are bank transfers. To reduce mail float and avoid the five days lost to value dating on out-of-town checks, the firm has its customers outside Paris send payment to the nearest agency. Checks are then deposited in collection accounts at branches of the company's main domestic bank, where they are subject to just two days' value dating. The funds are then automatically transferred to a central account in Paris.

Customers located in Paris send checks directly to the company's headquarters. As soon as the mail is opened, checks in excess of Ffr1 million are rushed to the bank and given same-day value. However, checks for smaller amounts are generally not deposited until the afternoon—after the cutoff time—and cannot be cleared until the next day. The treasurer explained this lapse in his cash management system: "We get about 1,500 checks each day, and we have to enter them all into our accounting system. We just can't speed up the processing any further."

Thanks to its tight credit and collection policies, the company has few seriously delinquent accounts. When a customer is in arrears, the firm allows a three-month

Twenty-Nine Questions to Ask
in a Credit and Collection Study
(Continued)

The Collections Cycle

(16) Describe the order-to-invoice process; what happens from the time an order is received to the time the invoice is sent out? How long does each step of the process take? What are the main delays? How efficient do you think the system is, and what steps would you take to improve it?

(17) Have you automated the entire collections process—from creating the invoice to dunning late payers to recording receipts—to minimize internal float?

(18) What payment instruments are received (checks, drafts, transfers), broken down by percentage of total amounts received?

(19) How long does it take from the time an invoice is sent out until funds are credited to your account for each instrument?

(20) Do you encourage customers to use the fastest clearing instrument available in your country? Have you asked customers to permit you to debit their accounts directly or to use ACH or other electronic funds transfer systems?

(21) Do you use courier services, in-house messengers, or sales representatives to collect payment from customers and speed documents to the banks before value-dating cutoff times?

---

grace period, during which it seeks "a friendly solution to the problem." After that, the treasury department sets up a repayment plan that includes interest charges. As a last resort, the treasurer turns the account over to in-house lawyers and finally to an outside legal firm for prosecution.

Company B, the Korean subsidiary of a U.S. manufacturer of diversified consumer and industrial products, has established a separate credit and collection department that reports to the executive manager of finance. This department has had outstanding success in trimming bloated DSO levels and eliminating bad debts.

To mechanize its cash management, the firm has purchased an IBM 34 computer. Using software provided by the parent, the company targeted accounts receivable as the first function to be computerized. According to the manager of finance, the company generates reports on aging of receivables, DSO levels, and "current accounts receivables" (i.e., receivables of accounts that are current). The firm has automated its credit analysis, storing all customers' credit limits, terms, and payment histories in the computer. In this way, Company B can check a customer's credit with the push of a button when an order comes in, and credit managers can stop shipment if the client is over its limit or paying slowly.

(22) Have you considered using lockboxes or intercept points to accelerate collections? Are you pooling cash or using concentration accounts to speed cash to an investment pool?

(23) Which banks are used as collecting agents? Where are they located? What are your average daily receipts at each bank?

(24) What are the bank costs—by bank—for processing drafts, transfers, and checks?

(25) Do you use the same banks as your customers to speed clearing or, in countries with multiple clearing systems, use banks within the same network?

(26) Do you regularly try to negotiate better value dating and clearing times with your collection banks?

(27) When do you receive notification that funds have been deposited and credited—by bank and payment instrument? How is the information received—telephone, mail, telex? How could this process be accelerated?

Delinquent Debtors

(28) Have you established formal dunning procedures? How do you dun customers (letters, telephone, telex)? When do you start dunning a customer? Who does the dunning?

(29) Is your sales force prepared to eliminate credit terms or even stop shipment for delinquent customers? Do the marketing and finance departments work closely together to ensure that sales are collectible?

The firm also automated its sales-order and invoice-processing procedures. In the past, sales orders were sent to the company's Seoul factory from two sales offices, one in Seoul and one in Pusan. Although the orders from Seoul could be sent over by messengers in automobiles, they were transmitted via registered mail from Pusan, which tacked on two or three days to the credit and collection cycle. Moreover, invoices were prepared manually, adding another day or two. Now, the company has on-line hookups from its sales office to the factory so that orders can be transmitted instantaneously. The computer prints out invoices and provides data on sales and inventory levels.

Even under its manual system, the company achieved a remarkable collection record. The subsidiary won a regionwide credit contest, outperforming its sister subsidiaries by exceeding targets in three areas: DSOs, ratio of current accounts receivable, and bad-debt write-off. There are four reasons for the company's success:

(1) The firm's credit department thoroughly checks the credit standing of its 300 customers. Salesmen fill out a customer information sheet that includes the client's business registration number, names of the top officers, business and banking refer-

ences, and a financial statement. For large customers, the credit staff uses the local company directory to obtain complete financial information. For smaller customers, not listed in the directory, the staff must contact other suppliers and banks.

(2) The company applies tight internal controls to credit terms. Terms are normally sixty days, although they are sometimes extended to ninety days for marketing reasons. The credit staff has the final say on all sales. Customers are informed from the start that "if they are going to buy from us, they will have to stick to the terms. That's it." If salesmen accept promissory notes made out for longer than sixty days, or if customers try to delay issuing promissory notes, "we yell at the salesmen and there is a lot of fighting with the customer." If problems persist, the customer will be placed on a cash-on-delivery (COD) basis (about 30 percent of the company's customers pay COD) or shipment will be stopped.

(3) The company imposes formal penalty fees for late payments—one of the few companies in Korea to do so. The firm applies penalty fees to twenty distributors, which must sign a contract clearly stating that payments exceeding the agreed-upon terms will be charged an interest rate of 2 percent per month. For its other customers, the company simply builds interest charges into its prices for slow payers.

(4) To accelerate the flow of funds to headquarters on cash and check collections, the firm's collectors deposit the money in the branches of two major local banks that have on-line hookups. Upon deposit, the funds are transferred to the firm's current account in Seoul "within ten minutes." Noted the spokesman: "If the collector notifies us, we can use them immediately."

4

Improving Export Collections

Once the domestic collection system has been reviewed and improved, the consulting team should turn its attention to export collections. Although many of the concerns facing intracountry collections are applicable to export receivables, cross-border customer receipts do pose additional obstacles for cash managers. The international cash or credit manager must not only establish procedures to protect the company from country risk but must also deal with such pitfalls as foreign exchange controls and poor credit-rating information on foreign customers.

The exporter needs to be familiar with a variety of export financing techniques, such as factoring, government export credit programs, forfaiting, confirmed letters of credit, and private export insurance; all of these vehicles can be used to transfer risk to the banks or other organizations. The exporter must also stay alert to more esoteric techniques such as countertrade.

Finally, and of particular relevance to the cash manager, export payment instruments are more complex than those employed for domestic sales. The collection cycle is usually longer, leaving more time for delays. It often involves two or three banks in two countries, which tends to increase clearing delays and bank errors. Mail float on check payments is longer, the need to bill in foreign currencies causes additional headaches, and discrepancies in documents can lead to stalled payments. These obstacles can add weeks of float to export collections, but they can all be avoided if good cash management practices are observed.

Despite the manifold challenges of export collection, it remains the neglected child of global cash management. The international credit manager in a leading U.S. chemicals manufacturer explained it in these terms: "International delays are regarded as inherent. A lot of companies throw up their hands and say there is nothing you can do about it. All you can do is eliminate as much risk as possible. That's a misconception; there are a number of days you can cut out."

Companies may find that their greatest opportunity for cutting float is in their export, not their domestic, accounts receivable. The credit manager offered an example: "A good comparison is to look at a domestic lockbox study; it typically saves one to one and a half days tops. It's such a mature product. That's not the case with export collections, where five to fifteen days or more is common, so it takes much less export volume to yield the same savings."

Understanding the letter of credit (LC) collection process offers many opportunities for cutting costs and float. For example, a major U.S. manufacturer with annual export sales of $200 million found in a review of LC processing that improvements in the way sight LCs were presented, negotiated, and collected could cut DSOs from twenty-eight days to just six or seven days, saving over $1 million per year. Any company that can cut down on discrepancies in LC documentation can also free up managerial and administrative time and strengthen the credit protection—which can be voided by discrepancies—offered by LCs. Improved LC processing also leads to better information on the status of collections, which in turn improves forecasting and hence investment and credit management.

Companies should be as aggressive in seeking ways to improve their export collections as they are in revamping their domestic receivables management. As one cash management consultant insisted: "It's common for the domestic cash manager to do lockbox studies every couple of years. The same approach should be taken for export collections." This chapter will show companies how to emulate such an approach. It will discuss ways of improving organization, policies, and reporting systems for export collections. Checklists and case examples will also be presented on evaluating systems for assessing customer and country risk, selecting payment terms, and reviewing and accelerating the collection cycle for export sales made on open account, documentary collection, and letters of credit.

Organizing Effectively for Export Collections

The export collection review should start with an analysis of organizational and policy-setting issues. Perhaps no other area of cash management suffers as badly from poor organization as export collections. According to one international credit manager, "Export collection tends to fall through the cracks in most companies." Many domestic cash managers do not track export collections until the payment arrives at a local bank. And as the cash manager of a leading U.S. communications company remarked, "I don't know how our export sales are collected. I am only concerned with those funds when they hit a U.S. bank in dollars."

The international credit manager, on the other hand, limits his attention to reducing risk. As one cash management consultant remarked: "The credit manager is interested in the security of the sale. His job is to keep bad collections down; that's how he's measured. There is a gap in how the export credit manager sees his role in cash management. Generally, he doesn't care about the process of getting the cash. There's a real vacuum there."

As a result, many companies do not have a manager with direct responsibility for the overall process of improving export collections. This often leads to costly mistakes, with officers working toward conflicting ends. A rather extreme example was provided by a cash management consultant: "The credit manager of a tobacco company said, 'I don't like to get those wire transfers.' He went back to the customers and demanded dollar checks, because it was something he can hold in his hand and mark against the customer's account." To uncover the pitfalls caused by poor organization, ask local managers the following questions:

(1) Do you have a clear idea of how well you are collecting export receivables and whether you are facing any payment delays?

(2) Have you clearly defined responsibility for such functions as customer credit analysis, country analysis, credit approval, setting credit limits, preparing documents, determining payment instruments and terms, and tracking payment status?

(3) Who is responsible for the cash management aspects of export collections? How is that person reducing payment delays?

(4) Have you laid down explicit export collection guidelines and procedures?

(5) Does the treasury department review credit and sales terms with marketing and accounting?

(6) Are export collection activities coordinated with other functions, such as marketing, currency management, freight forwarding, traffic, and trade finance?

Overcoming Organizational Problems

Honest answers to the above questions often reveal organizational and policy gaps that impede sound export collection practices. Many of these gaps can be filled by centralizing control of the entire export collection process in the hands of one manager—especially one with cash management expertise.

Many companies hand over the responsibility for export collection to the credit manager because credit decisions on foreign customers are so difficult—and critical. In these cases, make sure that the subsidiary's credit manager is well versed in cash management techniques. As one international credit manager said, "I fill a vacuum; there is no one in charge of export collections. I determine the payment instruments and the terms, and this very much influences how the cash will come back. I keep informed of cash management techniques that can speed up export collections, and I report to an assistant treasurer in charge of international finance and banking."

A good way to ensure that export collection activities are well coordinated is to have the credit manager report to—or at least consult with—the treasurer or cash manager. "They both have the same objectives in mind," said a cash management consultant. "Treasury is interested in cash and credit in information. Merge the two, and you have cash coming in on time and safely." For example, a U.S. food company has a pyramidal reporting structure that works as follows: Domestic and international credit managers from the units report to eight regional credit managers in charge of both domestic and international credit and collections, who in turn report to a corporate credit manager, who reports to the treasurer.

Of course, the flow of knowledge must run both ways. But because exporting is perceived as a mysterious specialty, many treasurers fail to monitor export activities or to educate themselves on the subject. "What I find," remarked one experienced consultant, "is that typically no one in the treasury department has any idea of what the export system looks like. The treasurer should be charged with making sure that there is an operating credit and cash management system in place that makes sense."

It is therefore critical to ensure that the export credit and collection function is coordinated with other related activities. Perhaps the most critical area to target for improved coordination is marketing. As in domestic collections, the marketing department is more concerned with making a sale than with cash management. A credit manager with a firm whose marketing department calls the shots expressed his concerns: "We've been forced to liberalize our terms for competitive reasons. It's not a credit decision, it's a marketing decision. If I had it my way, the terms would be tighter."

Some companies go so far as to have the export collection manager report to the marketing manager. One cash management expert warned that "the worst situation is having credit and collection report to marketing. You might as well sell to everyone on open account and give the merchandise away." Tempering this view, another consultant countered: "If you leave it totally up to treasury, the terms might be so tight that you would see a big decline in sales. The answer is that payment terms should evolve from a joint discussion."

In recognition of this need for cooperation, many companies have given the credit manager an advisory role. Some companies go even further and separate authority over the selection of terms and payment instruments. As one export credit manager remarked, "We play a coordinating role with marketing. They may come in and say the customer needs sixty-day terms to meet competition. We might say typical terms for that country are only thirty days. Frequently they go along, but we only have an advisory role on the terms; they have the final say. We have the final say on the form of the payment—whether it should be a letter of credit or open account."

Other critical organizational issues to examine include the level of communication between the export credit and collection staff and the order entry department, which must provide information to ensure that the orders are processed smoothly and quickly. The traffic department must also work well with the export staff to guarantee that goods are issued from the plant or inventory on a timely basis, all required documents are provided, and shipments are made under appropriate terms. Finally, the freight forwarder must coordinate its activities with the exporter's traffic and credit and collection departments to ensure that the bill of lading is sent promptly by the carrier.

Good communication will also reduce confusion over terms, payment instructions, and problems with collection letters (e.g., notification in case of discrepancies, which bank to use for documentary collections, etc.). Warned a consultant, "We've seen cases where companies were exporting and they didn't know who the freight forwarder was using for documentary collections in the United States. If you use a bank for documentary collections that is not your bank, you will get payment in checks. In one case, we found the forwarder putting the payment in its account and then paying the exporter. That's bad; you've killed your cash flow and you have a credit risk to the forwarder."

Developing Clear Policies

A well-defined organizational structure must be supported by well-formulated and explicit policies, as well as a well-trained staff. Clerical and other staff members should be grilled on their duties to make sure they are well equipped to handle their jobs; the smallest mistakes can give customers and banks an excuse to delay payments. Some firms have instituted in-house training programs to educate the staff. If a program does not already exist, make sure a policy manual is distributed that sets the ground rules for assessing credit risk, selecting payment instruments and terms, and enforcing sound collection procedures. The policies must deal with such issues as the following:

- Should the company sell to risky customers and countries? Define levels of risk.
- Is it worthwhile to pass the risk on to banks or other institutions despite the cost of doing so?
- If the company cannot pass the risk on, should it still make the sale?
- If it must assume risk, should it raise its selling price?
- How should payment terms be selected?
- Who sets policies for speeding up export collections?
- What instruments should customers and banks be encouraged to use so that payments get to the exporter's local bank promptly?

Policies must be explicit but, at the same time, remain flexible. "Ideally," advised one credit manager, "you may want to have very strict policies concerning such things as payment terms. But in today's world you can't have a strict policy. Because of competition, you have to be very flexible in the terms you use." A credit manager from a U.S. chemical manufacturer took that idea even further: "I think you have to be very adaptable in today's world. In exporting, everything is an exception."

Policies on applying discounts and penalties, choosing a currency for billing, and evaluating bank risk should be established, but authorization for making exceptions should be granted to one or more managers. For example, while most exporters prefer to bill in their own currency, many have found that they must modify this stance for marketing reasons. "We bill in U.S. dollars except in special cases," said a U.S. cash manager. "Exceptions are due to competitive conditions. Our marketing people will tell us that we will not get the sale because the dollar is too strong, and treasury will decide whether it will hedge."

Improving Reporting for Export Collection

It is important to review a company's reporting system for export collections to make certain that it is getting the information it needs. This information must be timely, detailed, and actively incorporated into the export management function. "Unnecessarily high DSOs occur because companies aren't keeping track of the instruments they are using and the float associated with them," said one cash management consultant. "They're just happy if the money eventually arrives."

To determine whether a reporting system is supporting or undermining the export collection function, ask local managers the following questions:

- Are there reports on DSOs and days past due on export sales?
- Are export sales broken down by country?
- Are export sales broken down by payment instrument?
- Are forecasts of export collections being made? Are they checked for accuracy and improved periodically?
- Are forecasts broken down by currency so that exposure can be anticipated?
- Is treasury hedging the company's exposure on export sales billed in foreign currencies?
- Is collection float tracked?
- Are you using reports and forecasts to actively manage export collections—taking a proactive rather than a reactive approach?
- Are reports and forecasts being transmitted from sales offices and local units via the most cost-effective and expeditious methods (i.e., telex, telephone, computer link, etc.)?
- Does the system show how payments are being received (i.e., wire transfers, checks)?
- Does the system tell you when to start dunning?

Identifying the Reports You Need

Missing or inadequate export collection reports can strangle a company's efforts to cut float and maximize investment earnings on export receipts. Essential information is provided by **daily balance reports** issued by collection banks for identifying the availability and the movement of funds. "The balance report shows the balances held in collection banks," explained a consultant. "Companies don't want the funds to just sit in a collection bank; they want the funds to go to a bank where they can use the balances to pay for services or to make investments. Treasury wants to make sure the funds are moved to their concentration bank."

Cash managers with substantial export receipts should consider using banks that offer intraday or real-time reports. "In most cases," a cash management consultant stated, "this is not important because the dynamics of the international clearing process are such that most of your payments clear late in the day, so you can live with previous-day reports. But companies with very large payments should ask for more frequent balance reporting. You could tell a bank that cannot do intraday to use those funds as a balance to pay for a lockbox or collections."

More so than the cash manager, the credit manager needs bank reports, which provide a detailed credit report—not just summary balances. The consultant cited above continued: "The export credit manager is not very concerned with balances; he is interested in knowing who has paid. He needs a report that will provide details on who paid, invoice numbers, amounts collected, and the country that payment came from." These detailed reports may be used for posting to accounts receivable. "Some banks can transmit information on remittances paid directly to a company to update the receivables. The report can be electronic so that the company gets it on the same day or the next day. It gives credit-by-credit information on the export collections that were paid into the exporter's account. One bank calls it an 'export paid collections report.' It gives detailed information on payment received, providing the invoice number, the reference number, the country, and drawee—enough information for the exporter to post and close the account."

Management reports (status or paid and outstanding reports) may help the exporter monitor and follow up on outstanding items. A cash management expert explained, "These can be paper reports rather than electronic balance reports. Your bank learns from the foreign bank that the item is ready to mature or that the buyer has made a local currency deposit with the local bank and informs the exporter of the change in status. These can be sent to the exporter on a weekly or monthly basis. Banks that have automated collection systems would load that information on their systems to generate a status report for the customer. The report consolidates all the exporter's outstanding collections. It is used to monitor receivables to see how the collections are coming along." Commented the credit manager of a U.S. MNC, "Our status reports are on the computer, but we can print them out and send them to our sales people to show them who's past due."

Export accounts receivable reports present DSOs and an aging of export receivables to help monitor management's performance on the export collection function. These numbers are often the best indicators that a serious overhaul of the system is needed. Advised one export collection consultant: "If your anticipated payments are in excess of ten days overdue, there is probably room for improvement. It may lie with the customer, with the banks, or with you. You have to look at the various stages to locate the delay."

DSOs should be compared with your firm's previous performance and with the experience of other companies exporting similar products to similar countries. In some countries, credit organizations (such as the Federal Credit Insurance Board [FCIB] in the United States), as well as industry groups, can give cash managers the opportunity to meet with their counterparts from other companies to compare collection performance. Exporters should attend these meetings or at least obtain the information published by these organizations. The aging figures point out the percentage of accounts that have become overdue; they are also useful for forecasting export collections, which, because of such factors as country risk and complex cross-border payment systems, is often less precise than forecasting domestic collections.

Possible improvements in the accounts receivable report include segregating collections by terms (LC, open account, documentary collection, etc.) and by customer and country in order to pinpoint areas that need special attention. Another way to fine-tune reports is to rely on measurements of days overdue (DSOs minus credit terms) rather than DSOs. As one cash manager pointed out, "DSOs are not a good measure of the performance of the credit or cash manager because they are determined heavily by marketing. The marketing department may extend terms."

Finally, be sure that the subsidiary is not making the costly mistake of neglecting adequate **backup documentation** on export sales—especially those associated with LCs. Because payment is often withheld until documentation questions are resolved, good files on the terms of the transactions and copies of invoices and other data can minimize collection delays. Such backup is particularly critical because customer inquiries are usually handled by the accounts receivable staff, which is not involved in the sales negotiation process.

The Benefits of Automated Reporting: A Case Example

To maximize the value of these reports, some companies have developed sophisticated automated reporting systems. For example, a leading U.S. chemicals MNC has a highly automated system that sifts through orders and spots those needing review. The credit manager described his company's system: "We have an automated credit approval system that is linked to our computerized accounts receivable system. It checks orders and kicks out those that fall outside certain parameters for follow-up by the credit department. I think it's the coming thing to cut down on the amount of paperwork. We've had it for one year."

The company's computer generates the report presented in Form A (p. 153). This customer status report contains a wealth of information, including the credit line assigned to the customer (CR LINE) and the date the credit line was assigned (C/L DATE). If the credit line was assigned more than twelve months ago, the order is automatically referred to the credit department. The form shows the payment terms (TERMS) used for the customer. In this case, they are 120-day sight draft documents against acceptance. If an order comes through with different terms, that order is kicked out for review by the credit manager. "We make exceptions in the current export environment, but those are the terms we generally give to that customer," said the company's credit manager.

Next is the Dun and Bradstreet (D&B) rating (D+B RATING). In this case, the company is not quoted in D&B. The form also identifies whether the importer is a subsidiary and the risk class assigned by the credit manager. (In this case, the blank space indicates that this is not a subsidiary.) "We have three classifications—A, B, and C," remarked the credit manager. "If this were an A risk, then orders under our credit approval system would clear automatically—regardless of the credit line assigned to that customer. We don't want to see those orders."

The report shows the dollar amount of invoices for that customer for the current year (INV YTD) and for the prior year (INV PYR). This reveals whether business with this customer is increasing or not. The report also gives the date of the first sale made to the customer (FST SALE) and the date of the most recent sale (LST SALE). It also shows the highest outstanding balance the customer has had this year (HYBAL) and last year (HI PYR) and identifies where the customer should send his check (PO BOX). The company has a lockbox at that location.

A very useful feature of this system is the automated dunning cycle. Considering customer and country practices, the credit manager assigns a dun date (DUN) to each customer, showing the number of days after the due date dunning will commence. "We have dun dates built into our reporting system," said the credit manager. "If we decide, for example, that a bill with a maturity date of September 4 will be paid in

Form A

```
FSCP                    CUSTOMER
REMIT 98219           STATUS REPORT              (C,D) 082789        AR07
PARENT 00000        CR LINE:     900000    C/L DATE:    070989     MGR          J-AS
                    TERMS:   120 SD/DA     D+B RATING:    NQ        RISK           C
                    INV YTD:     903108    FST SALE:     09/82      DUN:         10X
                    INV PYR:    1154000    LST SALE:    072789      STAGE:         0
                    HYBAL:       752358    LST CASH:    081389      LTR1:      999999
                    HI PYR:      685597    PO BOX:       PHILA      LTR2:      000000
                    ACTION DATE: 082889    STATEMENT:       S       OK:         75600
28258/28269         PAYS-DISC:     000%    PROMPT:        096%      LATE:        004%
PD 26AG LB99        AVG ELAP DAYS: 165     DAYS LATE:       1       CUR MO:         3
                    LST  -3   2   -2    1    1    2   -4     1       1    0    2    11
FUTURE CURRENT      1-30      31-60 PD     61-90 PD   90 + PD          BALANCE
331296  187306      192910         0             0         0          711512.00
```

INV DATE	INV NO	REFERENCE	AMOUNT	TERMS	DUE DATE	SBU	LTR
03/13/89	000-28258	PN/2060	40000.00	120 SD/DA	082589	095	
03/13/89	000-28289	VP/792	36200.00	120 SD/DA	082389	095	
03/14/89	000-28247	VP/797	39200.00	120 SD/DA	082389	095	
03/19/89	000-28276	VP/799	38400.00	120 SD/DA	082389	095	
04/01/89	000-28269	VP/780	39110.00	120 SD/DA	082489	095	
04/18/89	000-28349	VP/797	35200.00	120 SD/DA	091689	095	
04/18/89	000-28350	VP/795	36700.00	120 SD/DA	091689	095	
UPDTE?	RETURN?	PAST?	CLSED?	STMT?	GO TO:_____		

PAGE 1 OF 2 — OPEN ITEMS

seven days, it will automatically come out of our system if it is still unpaid on September 11. The dun dates depend on the payment practices we have experienced in a country. For example, we review accounts more quickly in the United Kingdom than in Ecuador because we know that there will be a long delay in Ecuador. This way, we won't waste our time dunning customers before they are likely to pay. We do factor the expected delay into the price of the export."

The form also shows what stage the customer is in if dunning has commenced (STAGE): whether the first or second letter or telex has been sent and the date it was sent (LTR). The credit manager explained: "We only have two letters going out. Then it's in the hands of the credit manager." However, the dunning process includes letters only for domestic sales, not exports. "For our domestic sales," he elaborated, "the computer would automatically generate a dunning letter. But we don't use letters for international sales. We use telexes. But I only telex the customer directly on rare occasions. In most cases, we will go to the sub and let them go to the customer."

In addition to a dunning date, the credit manager can input an action date. "I may want to go into an account on a particular date to check something out. If I want to see that account next Monday, I will put in that date and that date will appear on my action list for Monday. I can also enter a note showing why I want to see the account." In this example, the credit manager set 8/28 as an action date for following up on invoices that were due prior to that date. In the space for notes the printout shows that invoice numbers 28258/28269 marked for follow-up were paid on August

26 to lockbox 99. Thus, the credit manager will not have to follow up those invoices on August 28.

The form also shows that a statement is mailed every month to the customer and identifies the amount of orders that have been approved but not yet shipped and billed (OK). The balance outstanding plus the OK balance should be less than the credit limit (discussed above), or else the order is automatically kicked out for review.

The next line records the percentage of payments the customer made by taking a discount, paying promptly, and paying late. The credit manager explained his approach: "If he's not paying a substantial percentage promptly, we will go to him to find out why. We can also check against prior records to see if the percentage of late payments is increasing. This shows that you may have a credit problem with that customer."

Also automatically tracked are the average number of days that elapse prior to payment (AVG ELAP DAYS), the average number of days the customer has been late (DAYS LATE), the number of days he was late on his payments this month (CUR MO), and the average for each of the prior twelve months starting with this month (LST). Negative numbers show that the customer has paid ahead of schedule on that month.

"At the top of the form," the credit manager elaborated, "it shows that we gave this customer 120 days sight draft; sight draft means when he gets the documents in his country. In this case, the country is Australia. There are approximately forty days sailing time to Australia. When the shipment arrives, the customer accepts the draft, then 120 days later, he pays his bank and the bank wires the funds to us. On the average, it is taking 165 days for his account to turn over with us, which is 1 day late. The form also shows how promptly he has been paying for each of the twelve prior months. We look at this to see if there is a trend showing that the delays are getting worse."

Next, the form shows the balance outstanding. It shows the total due over thirty days from now (FUTURE) and the amount due within the next thirty days (CURRENT). Then the form displays the amount past due one to thirty days, thirty-one to sixty days, sixty-one to ninety days, over ninety days, and the total past current and future due amounts (BALANCE). In this case, $192,910 is entered in the "1–30" days past due column.

The form then identifies all open items: It shows the invoice date, invoice number, customer order or reference number, amount of the invoice, terms of sale, and due date. The due date can be changed. "The bank tells us when the sight draft has been accepted so that we can go into our system and adjust the due date to agree with the bank's records," explained the credit manager. The items with due dates prior to the date the record is called equal the amount past due. The credit manager can request a report that shows only the past due information by requesting a "D" report as opposed to this complete report ("C,D").

The report also keeps track of the receivables by strategic business unit (SBU). The report is updated every night for new invoices and new payments. "The bank's computer talks to our computer at night and tells it that such and such items were paid to our account," explained the credit manager. Finally, the form shows whether a dunning letter or telex has been sent on that specific invoice (LTR). In this case the dunning cycle has not yet been initiated because there are no items over ten days past due.

How Effective Is Your Credit-Analysis System?

Many companies incur very high bad-debt expenses on their exports because of inadequate procedures for credit analysis. If a subsidiary's bad-debt ratio on export sales is significantly higher than that on domestic sales, this part of the review should receive special attention. Start by asking the following questions:

(1) Is there a systematic approach to credit analysis? What is your credit policy?

(2) Is country risk analyzed apart from customer risk?

(3) What credit rating sources are you using? How reliable are they, and are there other internal or external sources that you could use?

(4) Do you have a high level of bad debt from export collections?

(5) Do you have blocked funds on export sales?

(6) Can you quickly change terms in response to changes in risk?

Unlike firms selling locally, exporters must consider two types of risk: country risk and customer risk. Country risk assessment demands a complex, broad-based analysis to determine a nation's prospects for economic growth and political and economic stability. A key concern is the potential for restrictive exchange controls leading to blocked funds. In many cases, the importer may be able to pay the required amount in local currency at the official exchange rate, but its government will not provide the necessary foreign exchange.

Analyze the sources being used to measure country risk, assess their reliability, and explore alternate sources. Depending on their resources, firms can conduct this analysis in-house or rely on the services of banks, accounting firms, and private consultants. Encourage exporters selling to a country where a sister company is operating to rely heavily on its staff for credit analyses. An organization of special interest to U.S. exporters is the FCIB, which publishes a semiannual survey of its members on commercial credit conditions in all regions of the world. While the survey takes into account economic, social, and political considerations, it focuses primarily on exporters' credit experiences in these countries.

The difficulties imposed by distance, international borders, foreign languages, and cultural differences greatly complicate customer analysis of importers. Most exporters rely upon a combination of commercial banks, credit rating agencies, and internal expertise for customer credit information. The treasurer of a U.S. electronics firm relies on every scrap of information he can uncover: "We have our credit department and we have the International D&B's, which are so-so as far as being effective. We deal with the foreign banks and some of our banking contacts. And if we have an affiliate in that particular country, they can make a check on their own through their own credit resources."

Using a Subsidiary to Analyze Export Credit Risk

Customer credit analysis in Asia is hampered by the scarcity and unreliability of published credit data in many countries. As a result, most companies are forced to analyze credit risk themselves, trying as best they can to obtain data from banks, local business references, and the importer itself. Too often the credit analysis is impressionistic and superficial.

Such weak credit analysis can lead to disaster, especially in risky environments, where debt/equity ratios can be as high as 50:1 and bankruptcies can occur suddenly. For this reason, some companies have established in-house credit rating systems that use available data to their best advantage. For example, the Korean subsidiary of a U.S. chemicals concern arranges indent sales on exports from the parent to that country. The firm has its sales staff fill out a sheet of information detailing the customer's banking references, capital structure, management, number of employees, sales, and so on. This information is supplemented with data from banks, other suppliers, newspapers, and a company directory (published only in Korean) that shows the financial statements of most Korean firms.

With this information in hand, the company's credit department compiles a list of financial ratios that includes gross income/sales, current ratio, quick ratio, net worth/total assets, debt/equity, fixed assets/net worth and long-term liabilities, sales per employee, and sales growth. The ratios are compared with industry averages that the firm has developed over time. Depending on its deviance from these averages, the customer receives a ranking, ranging from 0 to 100 points. A similar procedure is followed for a general rating, based on such considerations as the reputation of management and the prospects for growth. The point total for each category is then combined and divided by 2. A ranking is assigned based on the following table:

Point Value	Rank
80–100	A
60–79	B
40–59	C
20–39	D
0–19	E

The appropriate ranking is then fed into the company's computerized credit file and is used to set credit terms and limits. The information is updated once a year to ensure that the customer's credit ranking has not deteriorated.

Checking credit is more difficult in some countries than in others. The treasurer of a natural resources company had this comment on the difficulty of checking the credit standing of Asian clients: "There is scant credit information available in the region. So we draw very heavily on our local expertise. We ask them to make an assessment based on whatever information they can find—which is not always necessarily from the banks or a credit agency. It's often just hearsay or informal contacts they have with competitors and dealers." Unfortunately for exporters, the difficulty of gathering credit data on foreign customers goes hand in hand with the higher risks of export sales.

Setting Payment Terms

Once a foreign customer has been cleared for credit, the next step is to set the terms of credit and sale. When dealing with export sales, local management must decide on much more than the term and the price; it must also choose what payment instrument each customer should be willing to pay with and the currency of billing. These decisions are a natural extension of customer credit risk evaluation. Because of the increased hazards of dealing with faraway customers not subject to the laws of the exporter's government, riskier customers require specialized payment contracts to reduce the chance of default. Unfortunately, these instruments can be costly and time-consuming to both the exporter and the importer. While exporters need quick, secure payment, importers expect the lowest purchase price possible and the most favorable sales terms. To determine if the exporter is carefully weighing the amount of protection he needs against both the credit risk of the importer and the market risk of being uncompetitive, the review team should ask the following questions:

- How do you decide how much protection you require for each sale? Do you consider the size of the contract and the customer's payment history and credit rating?

- Do you factor your market position into credit terms? Do you know what terms are offered by the competition? How strong is each of your trading partners' negotiating positions?

- Do you compare your financing capacity to the importer's credit capacity?

- How do you measure country and customer risk, and precisely how do you factor them into terms?

- What is your bad-debt expense on export sales?

A Review of Collection Instruments

While customer credit risk has a particularly strong impact on the choice of collection terms, the overall customer relationship and level of business must be considered as well. For example, according to a financial executive at a U.S. electronics firm, "We very often start out a new customer on a letter of credit or cash in advance. Then, if his sales pick up or we think that he's fairly good, we might put him on a time-draft or sight-draft basis, depending upon their terms. And then, if he does really well, we might even sell to him on open account. So, in effect, we use generous terms as a selling incentive."

There are four basic methods of exporting goods for payment, and each has its own credit and collection implications. Review local management's use of each one to make sure that customers are being assigned options on an effective and consistent basis.

(1) **Cash in advance.** This method affords the exporter the greatest protection and the fastest collection, because the importer pays either before shipment or upon arrival of goods. Under cash terms, the exporter avoids tying up his own funds. On the other hand, this technique is very unattractive to importers and should be used only with the riskiest customers.

(2) **Open account.** The open account is the least secure payment method for exporters. It is not appropriate when the exporter wants to control the goods until the importer has formally paid or promised to pay because it does not offer real evidence of indebtedness, making legal action very difficult even if it is based on a dishonored, unpaid acceptance. On the other hand, open accounts are attractive because they offer speedier processing and payment and fewer administrative and bank costs than do the less risky payment terms such as LCs.

Before selling on open account, exporters must carefully evaluate the credit standing of the importer, prior collection experience, overall relationship with the customer, and the terms offered by competitors. The payment record and exchange control regulations of the importing country are also relevant. Open-account sales should be used with very safe customers in relatively risk-free countries. Intracompany sales are typically on open account.

(3) **Documentary collection.** By basing payment on documentary collection, the exporter is able to extend credit to its customer while retaining title of the goods until the importer has actually paid or has promised to do so at a future date by signing (accepting) a draft. A draft is an enforceable debt instrument that puts the exporter in a strong position in a court of law. Furthermore, payment may be quicker for the exporter when a bank presents a collection on its behalf, and the trade acceptance may be discounted for financing.

Companies often experience a number of problems with documentary collections, however. Banks are involved but only act as intermediaries: They do not guarantee payment but only attempt to collect the funds. There are thus certain risks inherent in documentary collections that companies must heed:

· **The importer may not accept the shipment.** After inspecting the documents presented by the collecting bank, the importer may reject them and refuse to pay or to accept the draft. Documentary inadequacies and product disputes are often cited; that is, the documents submitted by the exporter fail to comply with certain terms of the sale contract.
· **Documents may be released to the importer before payment or acceptance of the draft.** Ideally, under a documentary collection the importer obtains shipping documents only after he meets his payment obligation by either paying or accepting the

draft. In reality, the documents are sometimes released to the importer before he meets his payment obligation. For example, the presenting/collecting bank may be required to release the bill of lading to the importer so that he can obtain government permits for foreign exchange or arrange for customs clearance of the goods.

· **The importer may default on the trade acceptance at maturity.** The heart of the matter is this: Will the importer be willing and able to pay the trade acceptance at maturity? If he has not assessed the situation properly, the exporter could be left out in the cold. The only thing the trade acceptance gives him is an enforceable debt obligation. This is fine if the exporter does not mind going to court for what will probably be a protracted suit, but it does not guarantee payment—even at the end of a long legal wrangle.

· **Sovereign action of the importing country may delay or block payment.** Even if the importer is eagerly waiting to pay, government regulations may impede the transfer of funds abroad. The importer's government might decide to block payments for economic or political reasons or, in the worst cases, because of civil disturbance or war.

· **Payment may be delayed because foreign exchange is unavailable in the importing country.** If the draft is denominated in a currency other than that of the importer's country, the importer must exchange his local currency for the required foreign currency. But sometimes the required foreign currency is not on hand. The importer may have to wait his turn for funds before he can pay the exporter. Depending on conditions in the importing country, the waiting period can be long.

· **Exchange rate fluctuations may reduce the value of the collected funds.** When the sale is denominated in a currency other than that of the exporter, there is always the risk that exchange rate fluctuations will undermine the value of the receipt when the importer's currency is weak.

· **The importing country may have documentary requirements that delay the transaction.** The importing country may require import licenses, preimport approval for foreign exchange, and a host of other procedures that can be time-consuming and expensive for the exporter. If the exporter fails to comply with such documentary requirements, his goods could be delayed in clearing customs or even confiscated.

(4) **LC.** When doing business with those regions and customers that pose a greater risk, exporters should rely on LCs. As one financial executive remarked, "We sell to Asia and Europe often on open account, and we sell through LCs to Latin America. We used to sell through documents against acceptance to Latin America, but with all the defaults—Mexico, Venezuela, Argentina, Brazil—we switched to confirmed LCs."

An LC is an agreement in international trade under which a bank assumes a conditional obligation on behalf of its customer, the importer, to pay the exporter. Payment is conditional on the exporter's compliance with the terms specified in the LC. The exporter is required to present a number of documents, including bills of lading, commercial invoices, insurance certificates, and consular invoices. Then, in effect, the bank substitutes its credit standing for that of the importer, thereby

Procedures for Documentary Collection

When basing payment on documentary collection, the exporter uses the remitting bank as its agent to collect payment from an overseas buyer. The following steps must be taken to document the transaction:

(1) The exporter ships its goods to the buyer.

(2) After the goods have been shipped, the exporter submits three sets of documents to its bank:

- Any **shipping documents,** including the bill of lading, which convey title to the goods.
- A **draft** (bill of exchange) demanding payment from the buyer. There are two types of drafts: **sight** and **time.** The sight draft demands payment on presentation, while the time draft demands payment at a future date calculated as either days from the bill of lading date or from some other date (arrival, sighting of documents, invoice, etc.).
- **Instructions** to the bank to handle the transaction as either a documents against payment (D/P) collection or a documents against acceptance (D/A) collection.

(3) The exporter's bank—the **remitting** bank—sends the documents, draft, and instructions to one of its branches or to a correspondent bank in the importer's country, known as the **collecting** or **presenting** bank.

(4) The collecting or presenting bank tells the importer that the documents have arrived and that he can obtain them if he complies with the payment terms, which are either D/P or D/A collections.

---

assuming the full credit risk. The importer also benefits, because he is assured that he will not have to pay unless the exporter meets the conditions stipulated in the LC.

The LC can be either a **sight LC** or a **time LC.** A sight LC orders payment to be made upon presentation of a sight draft and the required documents. Under a sight draft, the bank pays or negotiates payment to give the exporter immediate funds. A time LC orders payment to be made at some specified time after the presentation of a time draft and the confirming documents. Under a time draft, the bank holds the draft until maturity before making payment. Or, if the exporter is not willing or able to wait until maturity for payment, he will ask the accepting bank to discount the draft and accept it immediately. The benefit of the time LC is that the exporter can extend better payment terms to the importer while realizing immediate cash from the sale through discounting.

An LC may be issued in either **revocable** or **irrevocable** form. The opening bank may cancel or alter a revocable credit at any time. Thus, the exporter assumes the risk that credit may be revoked for any reason until the advising bank receives the

D/P Collection

When an importer operates under a D/P collection, he must pay the sight draft before the bank will release the documents. Once the collecting/presenting bank has received payment, it will transmit the funds to the remitting bank to pay the exporter. D/P collection allows the exporter, through its banks, to retain control over the goods until the importer has paid.

D/A Collection

When the exporter has extended credit terms to the importer, the collection is made on a D/A basis. The transaction then takes place as follows:

(1) The exporter draws a time draft on the importer; the importer must accept it to get the documents.

(2) The importer/drawee writes "accepted" across its face and dates and signs it. By accepting the draft, the importer recognizes its legal obligation to pay the face amount at maturity—e.g., thirty, sixty, or ninety days after the date of acceptance. The accepted draft is known as a **trade acceptance.**

(3) Once the draft has been accepted, the bank releases the documents to the importer.

(4) Depending on the exporter's instructions, the bank will either hold the trade acceptance for safekeeping or return it to the exporter.

(5) At maturity, the bank presents the trade acceptance to the importer for payment.

(6) The collecting/presenting bank is paid by the importer and transfers the funds to the remitting bank for payment to the exporter.

---

appropriate documents. Because of this risk, revocable credits are rarely used except between parents and subsidiaries or as a method of obtaining currency under foreign exchange regulations. An irrevocable LC can be amended or canceled only with the express permission of **all** parties—the exporter, the importer, and the bank(s). Under irrevocable credit, the exporter has a bank pay on behalf of the importer once the exporter has fulfilled the documentary requirements of the LC.

An LC can also be advised or confirmed. An irrevocable LC issued by the importer's bank, known as the "issuing bank," may be **advised** to the exporter by a bank in his country, known as the "advising" or "paying bank." Most U.S. dollar-denominated LCs issued by overseas banks in favor of U.S. exporters are payable at a U.S. bank— the paying bank. It is important that the exporter realize that when the credit is advised but not confirmed, the U.S. paying bank has not given its own commitment to pay the credit. It pays only with funds provided by the issuing bank. If that bank does not provide the funds, the paying bank will not be able to pay the credit. There may be situations in which an issuing bank cannot pay. For example, political conditions in the importing country, such as a government action to block funds, might

Procedures for LCs

An LC has two distinct stages: (1) issuance and advising and (2) presentation and payment.

Issuance and Advising

The issuance of an LC and the advising of the exporter of its issuance has four steps:

(1) The importer and exporter conclude a sales contract that provides for payment by an LC.

(2) The importer instructs its bank—the issuing bank—to issue an LC in favor of the exporter.

(3) The issuing bank sends the credit to a bank in the exporter's country—the advising bank—which may also be asked to confirm the credit.

(4) The advising bank notifies the exporter that the credit has been issued.

Presentation and Payment

Once the exporter has been advised that an LC has been issued in his favor and he is certain that he can satisfy the terms and conditions of the credit, he initiates the following process leading to payment:

(1) The exporter prepares the goods for shipment and assembles the shipping documents and other documents required under the terms of the LC.

(2) The exporter presents the documents to the negotiating bank where the credit is available or to a bank that is willing to negotiate the credit.

(3) The negotiating bank reviews the documents to make sure they comply with the terms and conditions of the LC.

(4) If they do comply, the exporter is either paid (sight LC) or will be paid on a future date (time LC).

(5) The bank sends the documents to the issuing bank.

(6) The issuing bank examines the documents and, if they comply with the terms and conditions of the credit, reimburses the bank that paid the credit. In the case of a time credit, reimbursement is made when the bankers acceptance matures.

(7) The issuing bank gives the verified documents to the importer upon presentation of the amount due or upon consummation of some other financing arrangement.

(8) The importer presents the shipping documents to the carrier and takes possession of the goods.

---

prevent an issuing bank from paying the credit. In such a case, the exporter would still be subject to financial risk.

If the exporter does not want the burden of these risks, he may require that the irrevocable LC be **confirmed** by a bank in his country or a third country. The confirming bank thus adds its commitment to the original credit. When the paying bank has confirmed the LC, it is obligated to pay whether or not it obtains reimbursement from the issuing bank. From the exporter's point of view, this is the most favorable type of credit, as long as the confirming bank is trustworthy.

The central advantage of LCs is that they can reduce or eliminate customer risk. The chief disadvantage is that they are expensive, since they involve bank commissions and fees, as well as non-interest-bearing accounts in some countries. They are also time-consuming, because exporters and importers must ensure the accuracy of voluminous documentation. Finally, they do not guarantee prompt payment, as some importers seize on minor technical mistakes in the document, such as a misplaced apostrophe, to delay payment.

Choosing a Currency of Sale

When establishing payment terms, exporters must not only choose a collection instrument but also determine what currency to bill in. This decision has a strong impact on the riskiness of the transaction as well as the sale's attractiveness to the importer. International sales can be billed in the currency of the exporter, the importer, or a third country (e.g., a German exporter can bill a Japanese importer in dollars). Many exporters prefer to eliminate currency translation risk by billing in their own currency (although this risk can also be combatted by taking on a forward contract to cover foreign-currency billings). Importers, on the other hand, often prefer to be billed in their own currency. The billing choices break down as follows:

Exporter's Currency. From the exporter's point of view, this is the best option because it pushes the exchange risk and cost on to the importer. When the home currency is very strong, it may be politic to help reduce the exchange risk for the customer by billing in the home currency while negotiating a fixed rate of exchange. Alternatively, exporters can use a more systematic approach based on inflation differentials in the exporting and importing countries to fix the rate of exchange and offset the price impact of a strong currency.

Importer's Currency. Billing in a foreign currency not only exposes the exporter to currency risk but can add substantial delay to the collection process. The credit manager of a U.S. MNC offered a graphic description of the problems that can arise: "Once we received a check for 190,000 pesetas. We did not catch the check, and it went to our domestic lockbox. It went through as 190,000 *dollars.* It made it all the way to our New York bank, and then it was spotted. We had to correct all of our records and send the check out as a collection item. It took sixty days to collect on that check."

Despite such problems, there are occasions when it may make sense to bill in the importer's currency:

· **If it is a buyer's market.** The exporter might fear jeopardizing its relationship with the importer and would therefore bill in the importer's currency.

- **If the importer refuses to take on the exchange risk.** Billing in the importer's currency can be used when the customer cannot or will not hedge his transaction exposure. The exporter should factor the cost of hedging into the sale price.
- **If the exporter needs the foreign currency.** The exporter may have operations in the importer's country that need local currency for payables, or he may have payables of his own denominated in the importer's currency. For example, a U.S. information services firm with branches in several debt-ridden countries in Latin America, Asia, and Africa bills in soft local currencies and then uses them to pay off its local expenses.
- **If the exporter's currency is too strong to be competitive.** In the early 1980s, the overvalued dollar undercut the competitiveness of U.S. exporters. As a result, many exporters started billing in the importer's currency just to maintain sales.

Third-Currency Billing. Billing the importer in the currency of a third country offers two benefits: It can reduce foreign exchange costs when the exporter has payables denominated in the third currency, and it can reduce exposure risks if the third currency is related to his home currency.

For example, a U.S. manufacturer with yen payables for components sourced in Japan decided to bill its exports to Australia in yen. The arrangement has advantages for both the exporter and the importer. First, the U.S. exporter receives yen to pay its Japanese supplier and can thus hedge its yen payables and eliminate the transaction costs associated with forward contracts. Second, billing in yen puts the U.S. exporter on an equal footing with Japanese competitors exporting to Australia. A third advantage is that billing in yen reduces the currency risk for the Australian importer because of the government's policies on exchange rate management. The Reserve Bank of Australia manages the Australian dollar against a trade-weighted basket of currencies, with the greatest weight—as much as 40 percent—associated with the yen. The result is that the Australian dollar varies less against the yen than against the U.S. dollar.

The disadvantages of third-currency billing include the need of one or both partners to hedge the transaction. Furthermore, exporters who are paid in a third currency can incur very lengthy collection delays because the funds must clear through several banking systems and two foreign currency conversions.

An interesting approach to third-currency billing is to invoice in a basket of currencies. For example, some companies bill in European Currency Units (ECUs) for intra-group transactions among European subsidiaries; this is especially attractive for weak-currency countries such as France and Italy. ECU billing stabilizes transaction exposure for companies that do not hedge small transactions between European Monetary System (EMS) currencies and suffer periodic P&L hits when the EMS realigns. For companies that do hedge EMS exposures, ECUs cut the administrative costs of hedging. According to the treasury director of a French manufacturer, "We save a lot of money using the ECU by not having to hedge. We also save 15 to 20 percent in administrative costs by not having four or five exchange risks to monitor every day; we prefer having one."

Accelerating Export Collections

After a company has reviewed its procedures and policies for assessing customer credit risk and setting appropriate payment terms and currencies for billing, it should turn its attention to the actual export collection cycle. This cycle is very complex and contains numerous potential sources of delay. For ease of analysis, some consultants break the cycle into a preshipment and a postshipment phase. The preshipment phase starts with receipt of the sales order, continues through order entry and credit control, and concludes with shipment of the goods. The postshipment phase begins with the receipt of export documentation and ends with the receipt of payment.

To pinpoint possible inefficiencies in the system for collecting receipts on exports sales, companies should ask the following questions:

(1) How are payment instructions communicated to the importer? Are they clear?

(2) What are the speediest and safest money transfer methods? For example, what is the impact on the delay of receiving payment by wire compared with check? Are wire transfers used for large transactions that may justify the higher charge made on wires?

(3) How are payments monitored? How quickly is information obtained?

(4) Have importers been encouraged to use a bank with a good correspondent relationship with the exporter's local bank?

(5) Are billings made in the exporter's currency, the importer's currency, or a third currency? What impact does this have on collection time?

(6) What percentage of LC sales have discrepancies? What are the most frequent discrepancies that contribute to major delays? What steps are being taken to reduce errors?

(7) Which step in the collection cycle is causing the most delays? Are these delays measured and analyzed on an ongoing basis?

(8) How much delay is associated with each payment instrument?

(9) Have performance standards been set in such critical areas as the timing of document presentation and the number of discrepancies?

The Preshipment Review

Much of the preshipment stage of the collection cycle consists of in-house processing. Consequently, most of the possible improvements involve operational changes that speed up the work flow. The review team should interview the staff and observe the system, looking for oversights, bottlenecks, and problems. A cash management consultant provided an example: "We did a study recently that showed that no one was looking closely at LCs—whether they were confirmed or whether there were potential problems that might result in discrepancies and delays later on. One department thought that the other was doing it." The review should examine the following key factors:

- **Order entry and processing staff.** The review must identify each step in the process: Who is putting the order into the system? What information do they require for order entry? Are they getting the information? From where? How long does the whole process take? Delays at this stage of the sale will contribute to a longer collection cycle. Commented one cash manager, "You'll find sometimes there is a delay in entering orders because they don't have all the information coming from a sales office. You might want to develop standard formats to save on telex costs and getting clarification and repeat information."

In addition to looking for inefficiencies that result in lengthy processing times, the review team should pay special attention to LC procedures that may cause errors and hence delays at a later stage. Remarked a cash management consultant, "Sometimes they will get an LC and literally put it in a drawer and pass on the information to a traffic department. They'll say we need x amount of this at this location—get ready to ship it. But under an LC you need some things in triplicate and others in duplicate; you need inspection certificates and so on. You don't want to end up presenting your shipping documents and finding you were supposed to ship on the twenty-ninth of September and you shipped on the third of October. That's a major discrepancy, and discrepancies are the most serious cause of cash flow loss on LCs."

Advised another cash management expert, "The company should look at LCs as they are received and understand what the special requirements are so that they can meet them or immediately go after amendments if they are required. Don't wait until you're ready to ship before you ask for an amendment."

- **Credit control.** Because orders cannot be fully processed until the customer has been cleared by the credit department, there must be speedy approval procedures and good communication between the credit control and the order processing staff.
- **Traffic department.** Traffic personnel are responsible for numerous tasks that must be performed efficiently to reduce costly errors and delays. Typically, they deliver the export order from the order processing department to the bank, transport the goods from the plant or inventory stockpile, book freight or instruct the freight forwarder to do so, and make sure that documentation actually accompanies the freight (although in some companies this is the province of the credit and collection department).

Reviewers should check to see how long each step takes and how many and what types of errors are being made. For example, the traffic department may not be processing documents correctly or getting orders out before the deadline specified in the LC. It is particularly important that there be good coordination between traffic and freight forwarders.

- **Freight forwarders.** Companies should monitor and evaluate their freight forwarders on a regular and consistent basis. Careless forwarders can generate extensive delays in the processing of documents. A U.S. capital goods company effectively controls its five forwarders by demanding a record each month, showing, by invoice, the days elapsed between the bill of lading date (i.e., the shipping date) and the date the documents went out of their shop. They must also report how quickly they got LCs to the negotiating bank. For draft collections they state how quickly the draft was mailed to the foreign collecting bank.

Exporters should also take advantage of direct-collection systems, whereby the exporter sends documents to the importer's bank directly rather than via its bank, thus accelerating the flow of documentation through the banking system. This procedure can save one or two days. Many banks provide a supply of special bank stationery (collection forms) to the exporting company, which facilitates the technique. One U.S. company interviewed makes extensive use of direct collections; in the past, though, the firm had documents sent directly "to our bank in New York, and then they would send them out to Asia. We don't do that anymore. We just send it direct from the ports to the overseas bank to speed up the collection," reported the firm's cash manager.

The Postshipment Review

The review of the postshipment stage of the export collection cycle should distinguish between open-account sales and documentary collections on the one hand and LC sales on the other. This is a worthwhile exercise because the payment flows for open-account and documentary-collection sales are very similar, while those for LCs differ substantially. As one cash management consultant explained: "Draft collections and open-account collections are customer-generated payments. LCs are document-driven; that is, a negotiating bank will be allowed to negotiate your document and usually pay upon presentation. So if you can present clean documents with no discrepancies, you can be sure of getting paid."

A review of the cycle for open-account sales (see the flowchart on p. 170) should examine the following stages in the process:

· **Customer delay.** This is the number of days between the due date of the invoice or draft and the date the payment is initiated by the customer. Unfortunately, the latter date is not always easily obtained. As an experienced cash management consultant remarked: "That's one of the limitations of the study—ours and, to my knowledge, anybody else's study. If you have subsidiaries who are making payments, you can get that data easily. But if you are talking about third-party customers, you must either use your leverage and ask the customer to give you the dates or you can demand to see the payment receipts. But you'll only get those in countries with exchange controls requiring that an import license be matched against a foreign exchange requirement. The customer will get a payment receipt showing the date payment was made."

However, many exporters don't have the power to demand payment information from their customers. Moreover, it is likely that the customers who are least likely to cooperate are the worst offenders. As one cash manager remarked, "The problem

Extracting Review Data from Documents

Consultants rely heavily on computer analysis to identify problem areas in export collections—particularly for the postshipment review. The data should be gathered from a representative sample of transactions. Philadelphia National Bank, for example, uses a coded form to collect the needed information and puts it through a computer model. Twelve items are key in the information it gathers:

(1) The specific division responsible for the sale;

(2) The transaction type;

(3) The payment method;

(4) The credit terms expressed in days;

(5) The customer's or buyer's name;

(6) The foreign bank initiating the payment for open account payments, the foreign collecting bank for draft transactions, and the opening bank for LCs;

(7) The country of ultimate destination or where the payment originated;

(8) The date the payment was due (calculated based on terms);

(9) The date the customer initiated the payment, when available;

(10) The date the foreign bank initiated its payment (except when payment was made by corporate check);

(11) The date the exporter's bank or, in the case of checks, the company received the payment; and

(12) The date the company's account was credited.

---

is typically that the kind of company that has the leverage to get that information doesn't have a big DSO problem."

With less cooperative companies, the reviewer should try a more subtle approach to avoid irritating the customers. One technique reviewers can use is to send a letter to customers explaining that they are examining bank charges and delays in their country and need to know when they initiated payments. This letter can stress that the goal is to cut down on bank float, which benefits neither the importer nor the exporter. Thus, the customer does not feel threatened. According to the cash manager cited above, "This approach has worked well for us. However, at times the response rate can be fairly low because it requires that the customer take the time and effort to get you the information."

Because it is not always feasible to track every payment, companies should focus on following up on the most important ones. To encourage importers to telex the details of payments made (local banks used, amount, invoice numbers, etc.) on large transfers, exporters should consider offering a reimbursement for the telex fee. "It helps if they tell you which invoices they are paying, especially if they have multiple invoices," advised a cash management consultant. If the customer will not cooperate,

Global Cash Management

In lieu of the information noted in the last five items, the following information is captured for LCs:

(8) The on-board bill-of-lading date (sight) or payment due date based on the terms of the LC (time);

(9) The date the LC documents were presented to the negotiating bank for payment (sight) or payment due date based on the terms of the LC (time);

(10) The date the negotiating bank initiated its payment to the company;

(11) The date the negotiating bank's payment was received by the company; and

(12) The date the company received credit in its account for the payment.

In order to identify the sources of problems in export collections, the analysis of this data is sorted by the computer to distinguish among five sources of delay.

Customer: to distinguish between customer and bank delay.

Transaction type: to identify where specific payments were being delayed.

Payment-transmission means: to identify how often the company's payment instructions are being followed and to quantify the cash flow impact of compliance or noncompliance.

Foreign collecting bank: to determine, first, which banks are handling a substantial volume of the company's business and, second, how those banks are performing in the initiation of "on-time" payments.

Country of payment origin: to isolate for analysis the countries that received a substantial volume of the company's export business and the general experience resulting from that volume of export.

the exporter can try to get the information from the bank. Some banks will provide this information, but many will not. "Most foreign banks would never do it," stated a cash management consultant. Branches of larger multinational banks are more likely to cooperate, particularly if the exporter is a client of that bank.

Exporters can also conduct tests. They can ask a good, cooperative customer or a subsidiary (if one exists in that country) to make several payments through the bank in question and to inform the exporter of the date they initiated the payment. The exporter can then subtract this date from the date the bank remitted the funds to determine the length of the delay, which typically can be attributed to the bank. Working backward, the exporter can subtract this period from the date the bank issued payment to determine when the customer initiated the transfer.

If these techniques fail to uncover the date the customer remitted funds to the foreign bank, then the date the bank initiated its payment will have to do. If the customer sent a check directly to the exporter, the date on the check could be used. However, as any domestic cash manager can tell you, the date the envelope was postmarked is generally a more accurate measure.

Customer delay should be measured against the terms of the open account or

Open Account/Documentary Collection Delays

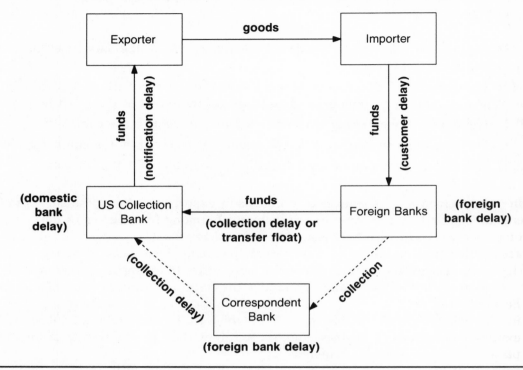

documentary collection sale. Open-account sales may call for immediate payment (e.g., cash against documents) or give the importer time to pay (e.g., thirty days from the bill of lading date or from the date of vessel arrival). To determine what customer due date should be used for cash-against-document sales, companies should estimate how long it takes for the documents to be processed in-house upon receipt of the bill of lading, as well as the document transit time.

For example, if terms are thirty days from the day of arrival and it takes ten days for the documents to be processed and shipped to the importer, the exporter should not expect payment until forty days have elapsed. The review should pay particular attention to the promptness of payment of time drafts, which are often delayed. "Instead of 90 days, they pay in 105," said a frustrated international credit manager.

Once the exporter has identified slow-paying customers and their average delays, he must encourage them to speed up their payments. Unfortunately, it is usually more difficult to get foreign customers to speed up payment. For example, unlike the domestic collections manager, the export manager rarely uses discounts to entice importers to pay promptly because, according to an export collections manager, "There are just too many complications when exporting to make a system of offering discounts work. For one, it would be very difficult for the importer to prove when he made the payment to the bank."

The "stick" approach of imposing penalty fees on late payments is also difficult to implement with international sales. "You can ask a foreign bank to charge interest on late payment," a cash management consultant observed, "but frequently the importer won't pay. There may also be tax implications on the interest earned. In some countries, the exchange authorities won't authorize foreign exchange to pay interest charges. So it's not commonly used by exporters." An alternative tactic used by many exporters is to raise the price to customers that take too long to pay.

Perhaps the best way to encourage speedy payment is to make sure that the importer understands the instructions. Exporters should consider establishing terms based on a set number of days from the invoice or bill-of-lading date rather than the date the vessel arrives. The reason: The date of arrival is difficult for the exporter to pinpoint.

Finally, exporters should track payment closely and start dunning if payment is delayed. The personal touch may be the best approach: "You get more mileage out of making a telephone call on a late payment than a letter or telex," advised a collections manager. It is important that dunning recognize different country-payment practices. For example, firms should start dunning customers in countries where prompt payment is the norm sooner than those in nations where delay is the common practice. The company described on p. 000 of this chapter provides a good example of how this approach can be automated.

- **Foreign bank delay** occurs between the date the customer pays the foreign bank in local currency and the date the foreign bank initiates a funds transfer to the exporter's paying bank. Because it can be difficult to identify the date the customer paid the foreign bank (see above), this float is often difficult to measure. One consultant claims that foreign bank delays are often responsible for 25 percent of the float up to this point. The date the foreign bank initiated payment is easier to obtain—either from the domestic bank or from cable dates, airmail payment order dates, and the like.

One way companies can determine if the fault lies with the customer or with the banks is to compare the payment histories of both participants. For example, if several customers use the same bank in a country and the payments of one customer consistently take longer to be remitted, then it is likely that the customer is delaying payment. If the exporter is experiencing delay with all its customers, then it is likely to be a bank problem.

Exporters can also examine country conditions to determine the cause of delays. Foremost considerations are the quality of banking services and the existence of currency restrictions, which can be an important factor beyond the control of both customer and bank. The day of the week the payment was initiated may be important because payments made on Friday in some countries will not be remitted until Monday due to banking conventions. According to one consultant, "First you decide if the fault lies with the exchange authorities. If the country is not experiencing foreign exchange problems, you are down to two other choices—the bank or the customer. Take Germany, for example. Is the bank causing delay? Probably not in Germany. It's probably a customer problem. Then you look at his payment history. If it has been clean all the way through, and then you get a bad payment, you go back to the customer and say, 'Payment was due on such and such. We think the bank held up the money. Can you ask them for a clarification of the date they ordered payment?' "

The ability of the exporter to improve the performance of the foreign bank depends on the leverage he has with the importer and the importer's leverage with the local bank. Importers should be encouraged to use a bank that will process the payment quickly. However, the exporter must be aware of different standards for bank delay in each country. "The local bank will get funds, and they may hang on to them for several days before they initiate some kind of payment instruction," said a U.S.-based consultant. "That varies by country. There can be good reasons, such as currency shortage. Also, some banks hang on to the funds longer than others. You should try to steer the business to the most efficient banks."

Furthermore, exporters should check to see how many banks were involved in the transaction. As a cash management consultant pointed out, "When a second or third foreign bank is involved in remitting payments because the foreign collection bank has no relationship with the drawee, the bank delay is much higher." Therefore, exporters should work with a bank in the United States that has a large correspondent network that will increase the likelihood that the importer's bank will have an account relationship with the exporter's bank.

· **Transfer delay.** The time between the foreign bank's initiation of payment and the receipt of funds by the exporter's local bank is known as the "transfer delay." The nature and length of this delay depend to a great extent on the type of transfer mechanism used. The following discussion will consider telex transfers, company checks (in open-account sales), bank checks, and bank mail transfers.

Each instrument offers clues to help the reviewer measure the amount of float it causes. Company and bank checks are dated by the drawer and the remitting bank, respectively (although not always accurately), and those sent directly to the exporter through the mail should have a postmarked date on the envelope. The date for a telex transfer may be easily obtainable if payment was made directly to the exporter's collecting bank. It will be less easy to obtain if payment was made through a common correspondent. Most electronic bank payment systems provide details on where the payment came from, the value, date, etc. Bank mail transfers also indicate the transfer date. Credit advices can be used to determine the date payments are received by the U.S. paying bank.

After the delays have been measured, companies must devise ways to reduce them as much as possible. For example, if the study shows that check payments are the greatest impediment to cash flow on collections, the company should encourage importers and foreign banks to remit payments via a speedier method, such as telex. To make certain that the best payment mechanism is used, exporters should print instructions conspicuously. Some firms use two-part colored stickers to get the attention of the importer's accounts payable staff; if checks are used, the bottom half of the sticker can be separated and stuck on the importer's own letterhead as a payment instruction to the bank.

A major U.S. chemicals company uses a big red stamp on the face of its invoices to communicate payment instructions. If possible, instructions should be given in the importer's language (which is rarely done except for sales to France) and should specify the currency and bank to be used. A sound knowledge of how overseas banks and accounts payable departments operate can be invaluable for communicating effective instructions. "One of the biggest problems companies have is the naivete of an export collections manager who does not know the worldwide banking system," remarked a seasoned cash manager.

The following payment instruments should be reviewed:

Telex Transfers and Bank Wires.   Telexes and wires are extremely effective for international funds transfers, and, as a general rule, importers should be encouraged to use them. Because the higher costs of these transfers can deter customers from relying on them, many exporters are willing to pick up the transfer costs. Despite their speed, however, wires and telexes are not always cost-effective for smaller sums. The credit manager of a U.S. MNC explained: "We will pay the charges because they tend to be less than the interest on the money. Our standard instruction for all items over $5,000 is to transfer either by SWIFT or telex to our bank. We give them the SWIFT number or telex number of the bank. Our customers know we will pay the charge." To determine whether a wire or telex transfer is cost-effective for a particular transfer, see the formula on p. 226.

Although wire and telex transfers can be sent, processed, and cleared on the same day, delays can occur at times. Problems are particularly prevalent in Latin America. For example, the treasurer of a U.S. producer of business machines told of a $5 million wire transfer from the firm's Argentine subsidiary to parent headquarters—a procedure that generally takes one night. "In this particular case, it went from an Argentine bank to a local office of a U.S. bank and then to that bank's office in the United States, where it was transferred to still another U.S. bank. It wasn't as clean a transfer as we normally would have, and, in this case, one bank just lost it."

The banks searched for the funds but were unable to discover quickly which bank had made the error. They eventually made payment to the firm and paid the interest lost during the time the funds were missing. In another case, half the funds under telex transfer from a subsidiary in Latin America to parent headquarters in the United States inexplicably ended up in Italy. The guilty bank also paid the firm for interest lost.

To ensure that such delays are minimized, some companies make funds transfers through the global branch network of the same bank. But this practice is not always possible or desirable: International banks do not have branches in every country, and customers may prefer to work through their own banks. When a single branch network is inappropriate, companies should use banks with strong correspondent links with the importer's banks. This will minimize the difficulties in tracking down stray transfers.

If the exporter's and the importer's banks are not direct correspondents, there should at least be a designated contact at the exporter's bank—preferably a bank officer. The bank should provide the importer with the name, title, address, and

International Funds Clearing and the Currency of Billing

To cut back on clearing delays on payments received from international customers, exporters should pay careful attention to the currency of billing. Whatever the currency, the exporter must give clear instructions to the importer and its bank on how payment should be issued. In most cases, instructions should specify that payments be made by an electronic transfer or telex—not by a draft, which can seriously delay clearing. For example, when Latin American banks mail instructions to their correspondents to request a cable transfer of funds denominated in the exporter's currency to the exporter's bank, the exporter may not get the funds for ten to thirty days. (A graphic illustration of this type of cable transfer appears in the chart below.) If possible, exporters should also encourage their customers to route payments through correspondents of their U.S. collecting bank.

Transfer from Argentina to the United States in Dollars

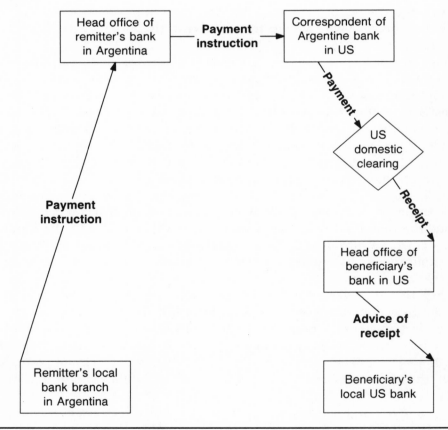

When a sale is billed in the exporter's currency, a check can be drawn against a bank in either its own or the importer's country—or even a third country. If it is drawn against a bank in the exporter's country, it is cleared domestically through the same process as other local currency checks. Checks drawn abroad, however, must be cleared abroad, and this can take a good deal longer.

For example, a U.S. exporter receiving a dollar check drawn against a German bank must collect the check in Germany, receiving either a dollar draft drawn against a bank in the United States or a request by the German bank to its U.S. correspondent (mailed or cabled) to transfer funds to the exporter's bank. All local currency checks drawn abroad must eventually be settled through the local clearing system. Therefore, exporters should demand that any checks used in payment be drawn on a bank in the exporter's country.

Cable Transfer from Venezuela to the United States in Bolivares

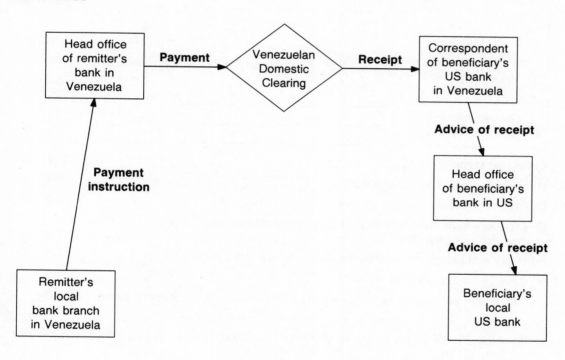

Exporters who are paid in the importer's currency will usually experience longer delays than those paid in their own currency. The illustrations of a cable transfer (see the chart above) and a check transfer (p. 176) made in the importer's currency

▶

show the payment routes involved. Checks in the importer's currency are usually drawn against banks in the importer's country, so they must be returned through a correspondent of the exporter's bank for collection. Companies that cannot persuade their customers to pay in the exporter's currency should consider five alternatives to speed up collections of foreign currency receivables:

Collection of Checks/Drafts in Importer's Currency

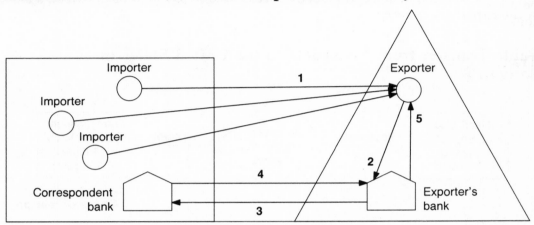

Collection steps	Days
(1) Importer mails check to exporter.	5–8
(2) Exporter presents check to its bank.	0–3
(3) Exporter's bank sends check to its correspondent bank in importer's country.	5–8
(4) Check proceeds from correspondent bank to exporter's bank.	2–3
(5) Bank advises payment to seller.	1–2
Total time from check issuance until exporter receives advice of final payment	13–24

- Use local staff or an agent in the importer's country to intercept the check and clear it locally.
- Contract with a courier (third party or bank) to intercept the check and deposit the funds locally.

telephone number of the contact officer so he can be advised when funds transfers are expected and can follow up if funds do not arrive on time.

For example, the Singapore subsidiary of a U.S. company always insists on same-day value on its international transfers and gives its bank at least five days' notice

- Instruct the importer to deliver the check directly to a correspondent of the exporter's bank.
- Use a hold account.
- Discount the check with your bank (if it is in a hard currency), building the cost of the discount into the invoice price.

Third-currency checks can be delayed for more than thirty days, and even telex transfers can take about four days to clear. (See the chart below for an illustration of a third-currency transfer.) If a check must be used, the exporter should insist that it be drawn on a bank in the country of the currency involved. These checks should be directed to a lockbox or to a correspondent of the exporter's bank in the third country rather than to the exporter's offices.

Transfer from Mexico to Germany (in Dollars)

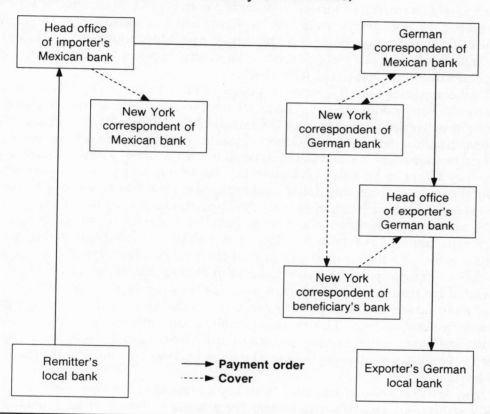

when transfers are expected. It also asks customers to put pressure on their own banks to advise when funds are sent. According to a company spokesman, "If our bank still manages to mess up two or three of these transfers, we just switch to another bank."

As this example stresses, companies experiencing bank problems should seek out a more efficient bank. When mishandled wire transfers are the fault of a bank, firms should insist on swift action and a refund on the interest lost due to delay. As the spokesman for a major U.S. manufacturer put it, "When transfers get lost, I call up the bank and scream, and say, 'If it's your problem, you sure as hell better clear it up and compensate me for your mistakes.'"

Company Checks.   Another common payment mechanism, particularly for open-account sales, is the company check. Unlike telex transfers (and bank drafts and mail transfers, discussed below), company checks are not debited from the importer's account immediately, but must wait until they are actually presented for payment at the drawee's bank by the exporter's bank. The importer gains the full advantage of the float. On top of clearing float, checks are subject to postal delays. For example, mail time from Latin America to the United States ranges from one to three weeks. "Companies should try to avoid being paid by check," advised a cash management consultant. "Fortunately," he added, "checks from overseas have become the exception and not the norm today." To encourage customers currently paying by check to switch to telex transfers, exporters can offer to pay the telex costs. Even this approach, however, does not always yield results. Remarked the consultant, "Government agencies frequently have policies on how they pay. Most will issue checks but not wire transfers." As a last resort, exporters can increase prices to compensate for the long collection time associated with checks.

Many companies use air courier or pouch services to minimize delays on check collections. For example, a U.S. chemicals producer employs a courier service for overnight deliveries of checks from Colombia, Chile, Guatemala, and Ecuador to its regional headquarters in Coral Gables, Florida. Another chemical company with regional headquarters in Coral Gables is considering the use of a similar pouch service offered by a Venezuelan bank. Numerous U.S. banks run daily pouch services, usually for local companies receiving dollar-denominated checks. But before using a courier, firms should compare its charges with the opportunity cost of mail float.

The international lockbox is another popular bank service for speeding up export check collections. This service provides local post office boxes, operated by the exporter's bank, to which importers can mail their checks. For example, a U.S. pharmaceuticals company established a lockbox in Hong Kong to cut down on the float generated by having Asian customers mail checks directly to New York. A U.K.-based financial service company built a chain of lockboxes throughout Europe, generating enormous savings. The system combines elements of lockboxes, intercept points, and bank courier services into an unusual cross-border setup. Sales agents in over 140 countries remit more than $500 million in checks annually to the company's lockboxes.

A corporate spokesman described three key advantages of the system: "We use the lockbox/intercept point/courier system for a combination of reasons. First of all, when you're in as many countries as we are, lack of access to sophisticated transfer methods dictates their use in certain geographical and business situations. Second, we've been able to reduce float by up to two or three weeks in regions where the postal systems are disasters. Third, by having the checks and drafts attached to the invoices, you have improved accounting control and reduced clerical needs."

Concentration accounts are also valuable for speeding up export check collections. A large Italian auto maker is currently working on an international banking arrangement structured around a series of concentration accounts to speed up collections from Saudi Arabia to Europe, which up to now have been torturously slow. Its goal is to simplify its circuitous correspondent-bank network, under which proceeds from Saudi Arabian sales are first sent to accounts in New York, only to be sent back to the company's main account in Italy.

Because of long transfer delays and poor reporting services, the frustrated firm sometimes must wait up to two months before it even finds out that the Saudi funds have been credited to its Turin account. According to the spokesman, "We're presently looking into setting up an international concentration system throughout the Middle East. All remitters would deposit funds into local branches of a U.S. bank with offices throughout the Middle East. The bank branches will have standing instructions to credit the regional bank office in Turin, on a daily basis, with compensated value."

Bank Drafts.   These are checks issued by a bank and delivered directly to the importer or its bank. These checks are drawn either on the issuing bank itself, a foreign branch, or a correspondent bank. Bank checks encounter many of the same float delays as company checks. The main difference is that it is not the importer, but its bank, that benefits from the float. This may make it easier to enlist the support of an importer to find a way to cut down on bank-check float—such as paying by telex.

Bank Mail Transfers   (airmail payment orders). These are routed and processed in the same way as telex transfers, except that instructions between banks are sent by mail rather than by wire. In addition to the delays of cross-border mail service, mail transfers are subject to more extensive processing delays than telex transfers because they are usually assigned a low priority. In fact, in some countries mail-transfer deliveries can take up to fifty days. As a result, exporters should discourage importers from using this payment mechanism.

Domestic bank delay is the time between receipt of the importer's payment by the exporter's bank and the date good funds are credited to the exporter's account. As a U.S. credit manager pointed out, "You have to find out when the foreign bank sent the payment, when your bank received it, and when it debited the exporter's account." The major way to reduce this type of delay is to review the bank's processing and, in the case of checks, to negotiate aggressively with domestic banks for better clearing time.

Improving the Use of LCs

Most companies find that they reap their greatest savings on export collection reviews from improvements made in the processing of LCs. As one export collections expert put it, "There is almost an inverse relationship between the mechanism that is the safest and the one that takes the most time from a cash management viewpoint. We have typically found that the most days can be cut by improving the processing of

How One Company Cut Down on Bank Float

With U.S. exports approaching 15 percent of the country's annual $7 billion in revenues, a major domestic chemicals company views the principal objectives of its international cash management system as the reduction of float time and currency exposure. Because it is especially concerned with export collection in Latin America, the company commissioned two banks to identify collections bottlenecks in six countries: Argentina, Brazil, Chile, Colombia, Ecuador, and Peru. The study examined the flow of funds for products shipped directly from the United States and sold on dated-draft terms (i.e., the customer must pay within a set number of days after the date of the bill of lading).

The firm's general credit manager explained how the review was conducted: "We did a lot of the legwork ourselves. First, we went to our customers to find out which bank was used and the date payment was authorized. The study focused on information from the customer's bank after the payment was made. It was necessary to determine how long the bank took to convert local currency payments into dollars, the date the funds actually were transferred to the U.S. bank, the method of transfer, and which U.S. bank received the funds."

The company asked the two consulting banks to visit each of its collection banks in the United States and examine their files to determine when and how payments were received. According to the credit manager, "We looked at the payment vs. collection differentials and were able to evaluate the time that might be eliminated. We decided that there was an opportunity to save a significant amount of dollars."

LCs because it is a document-initiated payment and the exporter has more control over the presentation process. Conversely, under open account and documentary collection, payment is initiated by the customer and most of the float is attributable to customer delay or payment method [e.g., check], which is more difficult for the exporter to control." (See the flowchart on p. 182 for an illustration of sources of collection delays on LCs.)

Thus, companies using LCs should place a special emphasis on the presentation stage of the review process. Unfortunately, many companies make the mistake of rigorously studying their procedures for processing sight LCs while paying scant attention to time LCs. The reasoning behind this, as one consultant put it, is that "sight LCs are typically the ones where you need to do the most because you don't have the time to rectify things later, as you do with time LCs." More specifically, it is not as vital that documents be presented promptly to the negotiating bank or that discrepancies be resolved quickly because payment will not be made until the terms in the LC come due. "If you have ninety-day terms, you have a longer period of time to resolve the problem and present the documents," said the consultant.

Because of the leeway provided by time LCs, then, companies are not likely to realize as dramatic a savings from their review as they may from a review of sight

The study found that there could be gaps of up to twenty days between the time the importer authorized payment and the date the foreign bank initiated the transfer. It was not always possible to discover the reasons for the delays. However, it was determined that some local banks contributed to the lengthy collection cycle by mailing payments to the U.S. banks rather than wiring them, as was requested. The company also found that many of its customers' banks did not have a correspondent relationship with its collection banks, but sent funds through an intermediary, for up to four days' additional delay. Finally, delays of four to five days were found at one of the local collection banks. The following solutions were proposed to resolve collection delays:

(1) Use only U.S. banks offering very good collection services. Favor those with local branches or subsidiaries in the importer's country or strong correspondent dollar-account relationships with indigenous banks. This avoids channeling customer payments through two or three banks before they reach the U.S. collection bank.

(2) Instruct customers to use local banks with a reputation for excellent administrative control, quick remittance capabilities, and good correspondent relations with U.S. collection banks. "You can't dictate to the customer which bank he should use," said a spokesman for the company, "but you can point out the advantages. For example, the customer should understand that accelerated payments will save administrative costs from tracking down delayed payments. It will also allow us to offer it a higher level of sales under the same credit line."

The company estimated that these reforms could cut average accounts receivable turnover by up to ten days for the equivalent of around $100,000 per year—considerably more than the cost of the study.

LCs. Still, improved procedures for time LCs can reduce administrative and follow-up costs and make sure that error resolution never takes longer than the terms stated in the LC. Furthermore, float delays between the negotiating bank and the exporter's collection bank are the same as those for sight LCs. For ease of presentation, the remainder of the section outlines the review for sight LCs, but these steps should also be used as guidelines for a review of time LC procedures.

Presentation delay occurs between the date of the on-board bill of lading or the airway bill and the date documents are presented to the negotiating bank for payment. The bill of lading is generated at the time of shipping by the shipping company and is then presented to the exporter's negotiating bank, which places a time stamp on it. Companies should track the difference between the date of shipment as shown on the bill of lading and the date of presentation stamped by the bank for a representative number of sales to determine the average delay. "Based on studies of many companies," said one consultant specializing in U.S. export sales, "we feel that there should be on average 3 business days [4.2 when adjusted for weekends] between the bill-of-lading date and the presentation of documents to the negotiating bank."

In addition to the exporter's processing, excessive delays are frequently caused by the carrier or the freight forwarder. The carrier may take several days to get the bill

LC Collection Delays

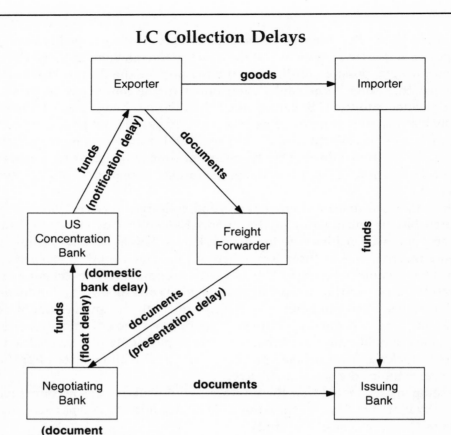

of lading to the freight forwarder. The freight forwarder may not present the documents as quickly as possible to the bank. Since the freight forwarder is responsible for coordinating activities with the carrier, it may often be held accountable for the entire presentation delay.

Some companies tighten their control over freight forwarders by physically checking the documentation before it goes to the bank. However, "this approach should generally be avoided because it can add to delays in processing," cautioned a consultant. A better solution is to have freight forwarders submit a regular report showing the dates of shipping, receipt of the bill of lading from the carrier, and the bill's presentation to the bank. An explanation should be required whenever the presentation delay is greater than, say, five days.

Other ways to speed up presentation include instructing freight forwarders to send a courier to pick up the documents from the carrier rather than waiting for the carrier to deliver the documents. It may also be worthwhile to use couriers to present documents to the bank. Finally, companies can consider bringing some of the freight-forwarding functions in-house. Said the consultant cited above, "This will give the company better control and should speed up the presentation process by one or more days."

Delays can also occur during the **document negotiation** process, which commences with the presentation of documents to the bank and ends when the bank negotiates and pays on the documents. The presentation date appears stamped on the LC transmittal letter, and the payment date can be determined simply by looking at the date on the check or wire transfer. Companies should try to find out what the standard for good performance is in their country; according to a cash management consultant, the U.S. standard is three working days.

If they have not done so already, exporters should implement routine follow-up procedures for past-due payments. A Canadian MNC, for example, contacts its negotiating bank for an explanation every time a payment or notification of discrepancy is not made within five days of presentation. Legally, the advising bank is supposed to pay the exporter within seventy-two hours after discrepancies have been resolved. Therefore, one export collections expert advises U.S. companies to "start tracing an LC three business days after presenting it. Except for New York, which uses the UCP [Uniform Commercial Practices], which call for a 'reasonable time period,' the UCC Code [Uniform Commercial Code] specifies that the payment must be made within seventy-two hours. After seventy-two hours, they have to pay you or say they can't because there are discrepancies. But many exporters are waiting longer."

Many U.S. banks do not abide by the seventy-two-hour rule. A cash management consultant advises exporters facing this problem to "go to your bank and negotiate, because there are banks that will guarantee to do it. I've talked to companies dealing in very large LCs that have gotten their bank to pay in twenty-four hours or less. Of course, your leverage is considerably enhanced with a larger payment, because the banks are afraid that a company will come back and ask for compensation for unwarranted delays. The policy should be the larger the credit, the faster you trace."

In many countries, when dealing with banks, the personal touch may be called for. One exporter suggested that "you take the clerk in the bank who handles LCs out to lunch occasionally. This will help your LC get to the top of the pile, particularly in small banks."

Many exporters use the special presentation services that some banks offer to keep track of the status of their LCs. The credit manager of a major U.S. MNC illustrated how it's done. "We use our bank's LC presentation programs so we no longer have to call them to find out the status of the LC. This saves us time because it can be pretty difficult to get to the right person in the bank. Our banks in New York and Philadelphia find out where our funds are, and, if there are any discrepancies, they report them to us and we take care of them. They also give us an analysis of what is past due. It's saved us an average of three and a half days on payment time."

In addition to unwarranted or administrative delays, the document-negotiation phase can also be lengthened by documentary discrepancies (i.e., omissions, errors, and contradictions). In fact, discrepancies are the leading cause of delays in LC processing. "LCs are much more risky than companies realize," a cash management consultant warned. "We find that 40 to 50 percent have discrepancies that will slow down payment." Furthermore, when documents submitted by the exporter are not in accordance with the terms and conditions of the LC, the exporter loses the credit protection of his bank and must rely on the willingness of the importer to accept the documents and pay.

Even minuscule discrepancies, such as a misspelled name on a bill of lading, may be grounds for the importer to refuse payment. A bank that agrees to pay when there are discrepancies runs the risk of not receiving repayment from the importer, whose obligation is contingent on the exact terms and conditions of the credit. In hard times or when prices are falling, importers may even use minor discrepancies to renege on a contract or to negotiate a lower price for the shipment.

An export review should pay special heed to the more common sources of discrepancies (these are enumerated in the box on p. 186). The review team should take the following steps:

(1) **Analyze where and how discrepancies are occurring over a representative period of time.** This is the first step that must be taken to identify the source of the delay.

(2) **Categorize each discrepancy as major or minor and determine the resulting cash flow loss and cost of the discrepancy.** A major discrepancy is one that cannot be readily corrected by the exporter for representation to the negotiating bank. The loss from extended payment time resulting from discrepancies can be measured by taking the actual negotiation time on erroneous documents and subtracting the average time for error-free documents.

(3) **Determine who is responsible for submitting the documents with major discrepancies.** "There must be accountability," advised one expert. "If an error is made by someone, that should get back to the person so he knows he made the error. Unfortunately, documents are very often done piecework, where one guy does one little thing, someone else does another, and when you get to the final set of documents it's tough to pinpoint who made the error."

(4) **Implement procedures for correcting these problems.** A cash management consultant suggests one possible approach: "Try to simplify the terms of the LC and concentrate on common discrepancies, especially those involving communications with foreign banks that cause a lot of delay."

(5) **Set standards of performance**—e.g., a 20 percent discrepancy rate—as well as procedures for the rapid correction of discrepancies.

(6) **Identify which negotiating banks identify the fewest discrepancies and are the quickest to make corrections.** Companies will find that some negotiating banks are more efficient in negotiation; customers should be urged to have their local banks designate them as advising/negotiating banks.

Fortunately, companies can adopt numerous techniques to improve their record on LC discrepancies. For example, the credit manager of a U.S. chemicals company that has successfully reduced discrepancies relies on "an LC checklist of steps and possible errors. We also devote a lot of time to working with our order department and freight forwarders to cut down on discrepancies. We have cut them to less than 25 percent."

Another approach an exporter can use to cut down on discrepancies is to assign an

LC coordinator in the traffic department to review the entire process. Furthermore, there should be training for all persons involved in the LC process to fine-tune their skills.

The time it takes to remedy a discrepancy can vary enormously, depending on the type of error and the country issuing the LC. In some cases, the exporter may be able to correct the discrepancy simply by resubmitting the documents and draft prior to the expiration date of the credit. As a general rule, if the advising bank or exporter can fix the discrepancy, the delay will be short. Other approaches include contacting the importer directly and asking it to amend the credit with the issuing bank or requesting the advising bank to telex the amendment to the issuing bank; the issuing bank will then contact the importer to obtain its consent.

In more difficult cases, exporters may have to follow these more elaborate procedures:

(1) **Request that the importer waive the discrepancy.** Serious delays can occur when the exporter has to go to the foreign bank and ask it to amend the LC or fix the discrepancy. The advising/paying bank can telex the issuing bank, notify it of the discrepancy, and request that the importer be contacted for approval to accept the documents as tendered. An importer is frequently willing to overlook a documentary discrepancy if it does not materially affect the shipment. In return, the importer may sometimes request a price reduction or other concession.

Even worse delays are encountered when documents must be sent back for review by the foreign bank. A cash management consultant elaborated: "The first thing to do is to go out and try to wire for approval of payment, because if you have to send the documents it can take a lot longer to get approval. Sometimes, however, banks want to see the documents. Sometimes it's the government that insists LCs issued by local banks must go back to the local bank for review; these are the worst. The documentation will have to go back to the foreign country and the delays can be enormous; they can go over 100 days."

Exporters should pay particular attention to those countries and banks that make the handling of discrepancies particularly difficult. "Some banks in Italy and Egypt are very difficult," one expert noted. Another pointed the finger at Nigeria: "If you deal with Nigeria and you don't have a confirmed LC, you have a problem. Even if you do have a confirmed LC but you made an error, a U.S. bank will not accept the document and the Nigerian bank probably won't allow the importer to waive the discrepancies."

(2) **Obtain a documentary-discrepancy guarantee.** When the exporter is confident that the importer will accept the documents with discrepancies and it does not want to wait for a waiver, it may ask its bank to issue a documentary-discrepancy guarantee. This is written in favor of the paying bank as a promise to reimburse that bank if the importer does not accept the documents. The exporter's bank issuing the guarantee retains recourse to the exporter, however, in the event that the guarantee is called.

(3) **Submit the documents on a collection basis.** The exporter may ask the advis-

Common Discrepancies in LCs

(1) Documents and drafts are presented after the expiration date of the credit.

(2) Drafts and documents are not presented within twenty-one days of issuance of bill of lading or other shipping documents.

(3) A document is presented against more than one credit.

(4) Common draft discrepancies include the following:

    (a) drawn on the wrong party;

    (b) not signed by the drawer (exporter);

    (c) drawn for an amount in excess of the amount of the credit;

    (d) drawn for an amount different from the invoice amount;

    (e) payable on an indeterminable date.

(5) Documents are not consistent with one another; for example, weight or descriptive marks and numbers differ from document to document.

(6) Documents called for by the credit are missing.

(7) Bill-of-lading discrepancies include the following:

    (a) does not show freight paid where the credit covers a (C&F) or the (c.i.f.) shipment;

    (b) a charter-party or forwarding-agent bill of lading is used when not specifically authorized;

    (c) does not show evidence of goods loaded or shipped on board a named vessel;

---

ing/paying bank to present the documents to the issuing bank and importer on a collection basis. The documents and drafts will be forwarded by the bank to the importer, who may or may not accept the documents and pay the draft.

Clearing Time. The clearing time is the period between the negotiating (payment) date and the date funds are received by the exporter's collection bank (which may or may not be the same as the negotiating bank). On an LC transaction, the exporter is paid by its local negotiating bank, so there is no float delay from the foreign issuing bank.

Delays depend on the means by which the negotiating bank makes the payment. As one expert advised, "You have to tell the negotiating bank how to pay you, because LCs will be coming from a lot of different banks, not just relationship banks. There is an interesting debate going on: If they don't pay the way you insisted, can you go back and claim back value? You can, but you're probably not going to collect it. The bank will say, 'We are working for the issuing bank, and not you.' By and large, however, U.S. banks will pay how you tell them."

If payment is made via check, the delay is generally longer. One company achieved significant savings by getting its negotiating banks to switch to electronic transfers.

Global Cash Management

(d) on-board endorsement is not signed and dated by the carrier or his agent;

(e) changes on the bill of lading are not signed by the carrier or his agent;

(f) shows goods shipped on deck where this is not specifically authorized in the credit;

(g) is not properly endorsed;

(h) is dated later than twenty-one days before presentation or the latest shipping date allowed in the credit.

(8) Insurance document discrepancies include the following:

(a) risks specified in the credit are not covered;

(b) currency denomination other than that of the credit;

(c) covers less than the c.i.f. value of the goods or, if such value cannot be determined, the amount of drawing or commercial invoice, whichever is greater;

(d) does not show the consignment exactly as required by the credit;

(e) shows the coverage effective only after the bill-of-lading or other shipping-document date;

(f) is not properly endorsed or issued by insurance companies, their agents, or their underwriters.

(9) Commercial invoices may have the following discrepancies:

(a) a different description of goods than that given in the credit;

(b) partial shipment when not authorized in the credit;

(c) an amount different from the draft amount;

(d) an amount that exceeds the amount permitted under the credit;

(e) made out in the name of someone other than the credit applicant.

"In the last three years," explained the credit manager, "we've pushed for electronic transfer of LC payments. The banks used to mail the checks to this office. Now they wire the funds to our concentration banks. By and large it's to the bank's advantage because they do not want to store and prefer not to process checks, due to the added expense and manpower requirements. We have picked up three working days on LC payments."

Finally, LC payments are subject to **payment processing** delays—the time between the collection bank's receipt of payment and the date the company's account is credited. Exporters must ensure that processing and notification are prompt.

The Export Collections Review: A Case Example

With the insights gained through two consulting studies and a great deal of post-review effort, a U.S. manufacturer with export revenues of over $1 billion was able to reduce float by 50 percent in many areas. The firm sells from twenty divisions to

Calculating Savings on Export Studies

Companies that invite outside consultants to review their export collections can expect to receive a highly quantified report highlighting the precise savings they will realize from adopting the recommendations. For example, an outside consultant reviewing the export-collection cycle of a major U.S. exporter based its analysis on 128 transactions over a five-month period, representing $17,725,909 in export sales. It recorded average DSOs of 10.662 days, for a dollar DSO of $189,009,351 (dollar export sales times days' delay—i.e., 17,725,909 × 10.662). The study identified seven areas where improvements could be made in the collection cycle:

(1) **Improve sight LC presentation time.** The consultant found that sight LCs were experiencing 7.1 days of float—2.9 days more than they considered acceptable (4.2 days). Excessive DSOs were calculated as the number of days that could be saved multiplied by the amount of the sight LCs during the test period:

$$2.9 \text{ days} \times \$4,491,203 = \$13,024,489.$$

Because the company did its own freight forwarding, the consultant estimated that an additional 1.2 days could be cut from the standard to save

$$1.2 \text{ days} \times \$4,491,203 = \$5,389,443 \text{ p.a.}$$

---

more than fifty countries around the world. Proceeds are received by lockbox and wire transfer, and terms include drafts, LCs, and open account. Controlling the flow of funds from each transaction is an extremely complex process.

To reduce collection time, the firm started by identifying and measuring its delays. Because export terms are largely determined by marketing considerations, shorter credit terms were not an option. Instead, the consulting studies had to focus on the role played by customers, foreign banks, U.S. banks, and internal processing procedures.

The first study was conducted to quantify each type of float and identify possible solutions. As a result, the company modified the way it prepared and mailed out documents, attempted to change customer payment methods, and concentrated its collection activity in far fewer banks. It estimated that the changes would slice as much as eight days of float out of its collection system.

The firm later decided to test and expand on the results of the first study. It was interested in better defining what happened in the foreign and U.S. banking systems and in more closely relating each float component to its export DSOs. It was also

(2) **Speed negotiation time.** The consultant concluded that the company could cut its discrepancy rate by 50 percent through better processing. Cash flow loss from lengthy negotiation on documents with discrepancies was calculated as

$$\$15{,}554{,}778 \times 0.5 = \$7{,}772{,}374,$$

where $15,554,778 was the net cash flow loss from discrepant documents.

(3) **Cut bank delays in paying.** The consultant found that the negotiating bank used by several customers routinely viewed time LC sales as 150-day sight-term items as opposed to 150-day bill-of-lading-term items. Since the items were sold on 150-days-of-lading terms, the bank's error resulted in delays of 2.8 days, or $2,432,287 in excessive dollar DSOs.

(4) **Reduce delays of a major customer.** The consultant found that one customer accounted for over 70 percent of the DSO delay on open-account cash-against-documents sales. Assuming that the documents took no more than fourteen days from the bill of lading to reach the customer, the customer did not pay until 24.777 days after the bill of lading was received. Therefore it averaged 10.777 days past due, for a dollar DSO of $17,672,791. The consultant recommended that the company use a courier to move the documents to the customer on the day after the bill of lading and call for payment ten days after document receipt, reducing the total cycle to approximately thirteen days. Savings (exclusive of courier costs) were calculated as follows:

$$\frac{24.777 \ (14 \ + \ 10.777)}{17{,}672{,}791} = \frac{13}{x}.$$

▶

interested in learning how consistent the float was and whether it could be accurately predicted in order to aid cash forecasting.

To make the results more representative, the company and the bank consultant decided to gather a very large data sample. Approximately 1,500 transactions were chosen. They included collections by draft and on open account, which covered the major portion of sales. The sample was also composed to reflect accurately the geographic distribution of receipts. Once the transactions were chosen, the information for each was pulled from various sources. Data was gathered internally from the traffic department and credit files; letters were sent to foreign customers asking them for payment information; and information was obtained from the exporter's U.S. collection banks. In all, about 35,000 separate pieces of data were collected.

To analyze the data, the consultant defined four basic components of a typical transaction:

· **Document processing.** This was the delay between the shipment date and the date of the draft or invoice. This float was thus directly under the firm's control.

Calculating Savings on Export Studies (Continued)

Solving for x yields $9,272,567. To complete the calculation, 17,672,791 (actual dollar DSO) − 9,272,567 (attainable dollar DSO) = $8,400,224 (excessive dollar DSO).

(5) **Use couriers or wire transfers to speed up check receipts.** The consultant found that collection delays on open-account sales totaled $18,884,993 in dollar DSOs, 94 percent of which represented payment by check. One large customer was responsible for more than half of this delay ($9,684,142). If it could be encouraged to pay by telex, the savings would be $9,684,142 in recaptured dollar DSOs.

(6) **Alter terms from date of arrival to day of bill of lading.** The consultant felt that the company should tighten its terms by switching from so many days after the vessel's arrival to a number of days after the bill of lading's date. This would reduce DSO days on such payments from 21.3 (with dollar DSOs of $10,919,052) to 4.5, for a savings of 16.8 days. The savings in dollar DSOs is quantified as optimal DSO days divided by optimal dollar DSOs equals current DSOs divided by current dollar DSOs:

$$4.5 \div x = 21.3 \div 10,919,052;$$
$$x = \$2,306,380.$$

Actual dollar DSO minus optimal dollar DSO equals excessive dollar DSO:

$$10,919,052 - 2,306,830 = \$8,612,222.$$
$$(\text{actual}) - (\text{optimal}) = (\text{excessive}).$$

- **Customer payment.** The study attempted to identify strictly customer delinquencies. These were defined as the time between the maturity of an invoice or draft and the time the customer actually made payment to its local bank.
- **International funds movement.** The study attempted to identify the delays in transmitting funds or payment instructions to the U.S. collecting bank. This was greatly influenced by how the instructions moved (i.e., by wire, check, payment order, etc.).
- **Bank delays.** The study quantified how long the collecting banks delayed in crediting the company's account. This component depended on the speed of each bank's internal communication system and documentary-collection department.

The consultant used a computer to sort and quantify various combinations of data. For example, weighted average days of delay with weighted standard deviations were calculated to measure the dispersion of each dollar of delay around the weighted mean and thus the predictability of the data. The weighted averages

(The consultant felt that if the exporter wanted to use a more conservative measure of savings, it could assume that at least 50 percent of the customers would agree to the switch in terms. The excessive DSOs would then be $8,616,222 \times 0.5 =$ $4,308,111.)

(7) **Improve collections from the Bank of China.** The Peoples Republic of China (PRC) requires that its LCs be presented at the Bank of China for negotiation. The consultant's expectation, based on prior studies, was that payments would be made ten days after the presentation date if reimbursed by a telex transfer and fifteen days later if reimbursed by mail transfer. The company experienced twenty-one and twenty-four day negotiation time on two LCs.

The consultant recommended that telex-transfer payments be part of the original contract; that the documents be subject to a prenegotiation review with the exporter's collecting bank (because correcting documents once they are sent is more time-consuming); that the company use a collecting bank that had special PRC collection procedures in place with respect to document delivery, tracing, and funds movement; and that it avoid using back-to-back LCs with its agent for sales to the PRC. These tactics were expected to reduce the delay to fifteen days, resulting in savings of $4,370,922 on dollar DSOs.

If the procedures recommended in these seven areas above are adopted, the total excessive DSOs would be $54,296,660 for the five-month test period. To compute the daily excess-DSO expense, the consultant divided $54,296,660 by 150 days, for daily excess dollar DSOs of $361,978. Assuming an 11 percent cost of capital, this yields $39,818 ($361,978 \times 0.11$) in yearly interest savings.

were compared with the firm's own calculations of DSOs as a further test of the data's reliability.

The results of the study vindicated the company's four-year effort to modify and streamline its export-collections system. The first study claimed that its findings would lead to a reduction of eight days of collection float. In fact, sixteen days of float had vanished. The second study explained the improvements as follows:

· There were virtually no delays in dating drafts. In the prior study, there were often several days between the time goods were shipped and the time drafts were dated. Since terms began from the date of the draft, the customer's terms were correspondingly extended by several days.
· Customers remitted funds primarily by wire transfer. Before the prior study, customers billed on open account often sent checks that added mail float of a week or more.
· The foreign documentary-collection banks were remitting funds by SWIFT or cable transfer rather than by check, as had been the case in the past. Less than 5 percent of the dollars came in by check.

· Cabled payment instructions traveled through fewer intermediary banks. In most cases, wires came directly to the firm's collection banks.

Despite these dramatic improvements, the study also found startling evidence of lengthy processing delays at its U.S. documentary-collection banks. For each bank, the analysis measured the time between the receipt of a payment instruction and the time the bank credited the company's account or transferred the funds. The delay ranged from 0.3 to 2.5 days, and funds from check deposits were sometimes credited 3.0 to 6.0 days after receipt, despite being drawn on U.S. banks. The company is using the results of this portion of the study to work with its collection banks to reduce the float.

The study also recommended other methods for fine-tuning the collection system. These include better clarification of payment instructions and the elimination of misdirected checks. In all, the study estimated that further efforts to cut the export collection cycle could eliminate an additional 1.5 days from the company's export DSO figures.

5

Paying Attention to Payables

All too often, disbursement management—the flip side of credit and collection—is a weak link in corporate cash management systems. In fact, parent companies typically pay little attention to their subsidiaries' disbursement practices; they delegate prime responsibility for such procedures to local cash managers and monitor payables activity infrequently, if at all. A BI survey of 302 firms with international operations shows that just 7.6 percent of parent companies play a major role in the day-to-day payables activities of their subsidiaries, while 39.6 percent set policies and review disbursement practices, and a majority—52.8 percent—have no involvement at all.

This lax attitude toward payables management is not hard to explain. Unlike accounts receivable, payables do not constitute working assets and thus have a less noticeable impact on profits and financing costs. Moreover, many companies believe that since payables are completely under their control, the function is easy to manage. As one U.S. cash manager summed it up, "We focus more on credit and collection because it's linked with sales and is therefore more visible. We also have less control over collections than payables."

But firms are paying a price for their failure to take a cogent, systematic approach to payables management. At one extreme is the example of a U.S. consumer products company with operations throughout the Asia/Pacific basin. The firm's Hong Kong-based regional treasurer conducted an audit of subsidiary cash management practices and discovered shocking errors in their disbursement strategies. "What I discovered was that some companies would get an invoice, approve it, and pay it the same week. So, I emphasized that the payables were not to be made until they had to be made according to the general terms of trade in the area." By implementing this standard textbook approach in Japan, the firm saved about $250,000. "It's a large operation there, there's a lot of money involved, and they were paying about thirty days in advance of terms. We saved all that money just by extending payment out to the full length of the terms."

At the other extreme are those firms adopting a consistent policy of delaying payment as long as possible. Although such a policy certainly maximizes a company's use of internal funds, it has serious drawbacks: Given the increasingly sophisticated and innovative receivables management techniques now being implemented around the world, it is unlikely that companies will be able to get away with such tactics for very long without injuring supplier relations.

The dangers of a simplistic approach to disbursement management are well illustrated by the experience of a U.S. cosmetics firm. According to a company spokesman, "To us a payables 'system' means throwing invoices into the file cabinet, where they're most likely to be lost. We have an unwritten policy of ignoring terms and waiting for suppliers to scream. I know—I just ordered some replacement parts, and the supplier told me he still hadn't been paid for the original machinery. When I told the controller, he said, 'I know.'" Already slipshod, the company's disbursement system is now on the verge of collapse. Suppliers "used to delay intentionally," he noted. "But now even that's backed up. I may never get my parts."

To avoid such costly errors, companies must begin to consider payables management an important discipline on a par with receivables management, cash concentration, investment and debt management, cash forecasting, and reporting and control. Good payables management is a delicate balancing act, allowing a firm to hang on to its cash without ruining supplier relations. It requires a detailed knowledge of individual country and supplier nuances, as well as the plethora of payment instruments and banking services available around the world. Finally, effective disbursement management necessitates a team approach involving not only the cash management department but also such related functions as purchasing and production.

Those companies willing to make the effort to improve their payables management will be rewarded handsomely. The annual interest savings to be derived from slowing disbursements—through negotiations with suppliers, efficient use of payment instruments, or selective delays—can be quantified by applying the following equation:

$$\frac{\text{Days gained}}{360} \times \text{annual payables} \times \text{investment rate} = \text{annual savings.}$$

Take the simple example of an Australian subsidiary with annual payments of A\$500 million. If the firm adds just one day to its disbursement cycle and secures a short-term investment rate of 16 percent p.a., its savings would be

$$\frac{1}{360} \times \text{A\$500 million} \times 16\% = \text{A\$222,222.}$$

Thus, even a marginal improvement in payables management can substantially alter a subsidiary's financing needs—and ultimately its overall profitability.

To help companies reap these benefits, this chapter will show firms how to audit and improve the following critical components of their payable function: (1) organization, (2) reporting, (3) payment terms and discounts, (4) internal processing, (5) timing of payments, (6) payment instruments, and (7) specialized banking services.

Conducting a Payables Review

An effective audit of a firm's disbursement management system invariably leads to smoother internal processing, increased control, and considerable cost savings. To make these improvements, the audit team will need to examine every aspect of the payables function, beginning with a review of such critical background information as the number and location of suppliers, total disbursements by category (e.g., payroll, suppliers, etc.) and currency, and the banks used to effect payments.

Next, companies should look into the payables organization (see p. 200), asking such questions as: How many disbursing locations are there? Who has input, and who actually makes purchasing decisions? Within each location, who is responsible for payment control? In addition, firms should collect and evaluate existing procedural manuals. The staff may want to conduct interviews with both managers and clerical staffs to determine how closely practice follows policy (see p. 201).

After reviewing policies, a payables audit should examine the firm's internal reporting system (see p. 204). All internal reports relating to disbursements, including CDOs and aging of payables, should be collected (see p. 205) and reviewed. Companies will want to ensure that all data is made available in a timely and accurate fashion.

The audit staff must also track sample invoices through the payment process. Glaring inefficiencies often arise in the way payments are routed. Companies should therefore investigate current procedures, eliminate unnecessary steps, and perhaps consider introducing automation to the payables flow (see p. 206).

Finally, a thorough audit must include a detailed breakdown of payment instruments and flows during a sample period—generally thirty days—including all payments made to tax and other government authorities, employees, local and foreign suppliers, and intracompany payments. Payments within each category should be classified by size because, in the words of a leading consultant, "It helps to focus attention where it's most needed—the largest payments of course commanding the most attention. You may be able to benefit from the 80/20 rule—80 percent of the benefits coming from 20 percent of the payments."

One advantage to this approach, according to another cash management consultant, is that "different people may be responsible for each type of disbursement. Breaking it up this way would show you who's in control of what." Moreover, by separating out the various categories of payments and instruments, companies can easily identify inefficient and costly practices.

Case Example: A Major Bank's Consulting Study

A good illustration of a payables audit is provided by Company A, a U.S. consumer and industrial products firm operating in Venezuela that contracted with a major international bank to conduct a review of its disbursement management system. The bank designed its approach to answer a fundamental question: Could Company A generate additional cash resources by lengthening the disbursement cycle?

Company A Disbursements, July 25–August 25

U.S. suppliers	$150,000	60% check drawn on U.S. parent 25% wire transfer 15% other
Local suppliers	$500,000	35% check drawn on remote account 55% local check 10% wire transfer
Taxes	$27,000	100% local check
Taurel	10,000	100% local check
Payroll	$15,000	60% local check 40% direct deposit
Other*	$10,000	80% local check 20% wire transfer

*Includes loans, investments, insurance, debit notes, and other miscellaneous expenses.

The first step was a breakdown of the firm's payments by expense category. The breakdown included payments to U.S. suppliers, domestic suppliers, Taurel (a government import-services bureau), taxes, payroll, and miscellaneous areas. The consultants chose a one-month period "free of any holidays, or anything out of the ordinary."

To detail the company's current system, the consultants conducted exhaustive on-site interviews with Company A's treasurer, controller, cash control clerk, accounts payable manager, accounts payable clerk, payroll manager, payroll clerk, and check dispatch clerk. Based on these interviews and analyses of banking statements and payment instruments, the bank consulting team developed the following recommendations.

· **Payments to U.S. suppliers.** Company A's largest U.S. suppliers are a nonrelated equipment firm and a sister international sales division (ISD), both requiring payment in U.S. dollars. Financing for purchases from the nonrelated source takes the form of bank-issued promissory notes, but ISD payments are all paid in full on the due date. The disbursements study begins with a look at these international payments. First, the consultants developed a graphic portrayal of the payment process, presented on p. 197.

As the diagram shows, sales from the third party are invoiced to Company A by telex, which initiates the search for financing. To obtain financing, Company A calls each of its banks and compares the offered rates on promissory notes. Once a bank is selected and a rate granted, Company A telexes the information to the equipment firm, which completes presigned promissory notes. The U.S. supplier then discounts the note at the proper bank on payment due date. The consulting bank examined this invoicing/financing arrangement in detail and found it to be efficient, with no significant effect on cash flow.

Payments to an Unrelated Equipment Firm

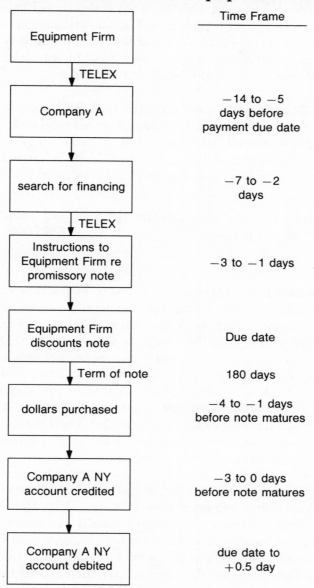

Time Frame

Equipment Firm

↓ TELEX

Company A

−14 to −5
days before
payment due date

search for financing

−7 to −2
days

↓ TELEX

**Instructions to
Equipment Firm re
promissory note**

−3 to −1 days

**Equipment Firm
discounts note**

Due date

↓ Term of note

180 days

dollars purchased

−4 to −1 days
before note matures

**Company A NY
account credited**

−3 to 0 days
before note matures

**Company A NY
account debited**

due date to
+0.5 day

But the consultants found potential for improvement in the next phase, as the notes mature (typically 180 days) and interest and principal fall due. The present system calls for purchase of dollars one to four days before the debt's maturity and a subsequent transfer to a Company A New York dollar account. The New York account is then debited on the due date for credit to the note-issuing bank or for intracompany transfer (to the ISD).

Paying Attention to Payables

The consultants analyzed transfer and bank floats associated with these payments.

- **Wire transfer float.** This was defined as the time elapsed between debiting Company A's local account for the purchase of dollars and subsequent credit of the New York account—an average 2.45 days. But this was found to be mostly attributable to the fact that the company's Venezuelan account was debited on Friday, while New York did not receive good funds until Monday.

To lessen the float time incurred, the bank initially recommended that Company A arrange for due dates other than Mondays to avoid weekend funds loss. But as the study progressed, the consultants surveyed the capabilities of Venezuelan banks and found that same-day wire transfers to the New York dollar account could be negotiated. The reduction in float was determined as follows:

Days' float saved $\times$ avg. daily payments (US$) $\times$ avg. reduction in daily float.
2.45 $\times$ \$282,000 $\times$ \$691,000.

- **New York balance float.** This was construed to be the time from New York credit to the due date on the note. While value generally arrives in the account "just in time," as a precaution Company A sometimes initiates wire transfers two business days before payment is due. The result is an average of 0.23 day for New York balance float. Applied to the surveyed period payments, this amounts to average— and, according to the consultants, unnecessary—daily float of B64,500 (about US$1,500). The bank recommended elimination of precautionary early transfers.
- **Payments to Venezuelan suppliers.** Company A's policy is to pay suppliers by check on specified days from specific locations. Instruments are drawn on banks near the disbursing plants. The company has three disbursement points: one in Caracas, one in Valencia, and one in the interior.

In the domestic category, about 70 percent of payments go to Caracas suppliers. These payments include common checks, LCs, and sight drafts, and can be claimed by suppliers' collection agents on Tuesdays from 2 P.M. to 4 P.M.

The Valencia plant buys from suppliers in both Valencia and Caracas. For Valencia disbursements, checks may be picked up on Tuesdays and Thursdays from 9 A.M. to 4 P.M. Valencia's Caracas-based suppliers receive their checks from the Caracas location; checks from Valencia are sent by courier to Caracas. For control purposes, a telex advising Caracas of the checks written is sent daily.

Interior suppliers are paid with checks drawn on interior banks. The checks are written in Caracas and sent by courier to the interior branch for distribution. These checks are intended to be available only on Fridays, but the consultants found that checks were being distributed throughout the week.

The bank's consultants advised Company A to shift its supplier pickup time to Friday afternoon to take advantage of weekend float.

Current Float Time

Caracas—Tuesday Payday

Day payment due	M		T	W	Th	F	Sa	S	
Day paid	T		T	T	T	T	T	T	
Days of float	+1		0	+6	+5	+4	+3	+2	=21 days
21 divided by 7	=3								
Average daily float	=3 days								

Valencia—Tuesday and Thursday Paydays

	M		T	W	Th	F	Sa	S	
Day payment due	M		T	W	Th	F	Sa	S	
Day paid	T		T	Th	Th	T	T	T	
Days of float	+1		0	+1	0	+4	+3	+2	=11 days
Average daily float	=1.57 days								

Interior—Payments Every Day

	M		T	W	Th	F	Sa	S	
Day payment due	M		T	W	Th	F	Sa	S	
Day paid	M		T	W	Th	F	Sa	S	
Days of float	0		0	0	0	0	+1	+1	=2 days
Average daily float	=0.29 day								

Float Generated by Friday Payment

All Regions—Friday Payday

Day payment due	M		T	W	Th	F	Sa	S	
Day paid	F		F	F	F	F	F	F	
Days of float	+4		+3	+2	+1	0	+6	+5	=21 days
Average daily float	=3 days								

- **Remote disbursement.** As explained above, the company's policy is to pay suppliers with checks drawn on local banks. The consultants were asked to review the possibility of paying local suppliers with checks drawn on banks in another clearing region—adding six days to the float cycle. The consultants reported that this would not be an acceptable course of action because of the negative impact on supplier relations. Most of Company A's suppliers are small and could not negotiate immediate credit on deposits (as Company A has done with its customers). The consultants were therefore certain that the cost would be passed on to Company A, rather than borne by the suppliers' banks (see p. 223 for a discussion of remote disbursement).

- **Payroll.** Company A's three branches pay their employees through a combination of cash and direct deposits. The bank examined Company A's payroll mechanism and found that no significant improvements could be made (see p. 223).

- **Taurel.** This is the customs agency to which Company A pays import duties, which are financed by promissory notes. As such, the payments to satisfy the notes are supposedly debited on the due date. In practice, the consultants found, bank error yielded an average of 5.7 days of disbursement float on these payments. The consultants found no way to increase this float further and therefore recommended no changes.

· **Taxes.** Venezuela imposes national and state taxes, which in either case must be paid by a check drawn on the Banco de Venezuela and on time. No improvement in float could be realized in this area.

How Effective Is Your Payables Organization?

The first step in any review of the payables function is to identify the major players in a company's disbursement management system. In this way, the audit team can quickly learn whom they need to interview and identify potential trouble spots in a firm's organizational structure.

The key to improving payables management is a well-trained local staff with clearly defined policies and procedures. Successful disbursement management is a team effort requiring fluid interplay among the treasury, accounting, production, and purchasing departments within a local operation. All companies conducting an audit of payables practices should therefore ask the following pivotal questions:

(1) Have you clearly defined responsibilities for such functions as requisitioning, purchasing, invoice processing, disbursing, and reporting and forecasting?

(2) Who within the treasury department is responsible for payables management?

(3) How does the payables staff coordinate decision making with other treasury functions—e.g., currency management and short-term borrowing and investments—and with the production, purchasing, and accounting departments?

(4) Does the treasury department review payment terms and discounts in conjunction with the purchasing staff?

(5) In case of conflict among the various departments involved in the payables process, who has final authority for the control of disbursements?

(6) Have you laid down disbursement management guidelines and procedures?

(7) Do you have a formal payables systems manual spelling out standard procedures?

By probing the foundations of the payables function in this way, companies can often uncover glaring organizational weaknesses that stymie efficient disbursement management. As one cash management consultant noted, "While credit and collections policies frequently collide with marketing considerations, disbursement management may be at odds with the purchasing function over such issues as negotiating volume discounts, the timing of the receipt of goods, and the discount for early payment."

For example, a private consulting group hired to audit the cash management system of a European manufacturing concern quickly learned that control over the company's payables process was fragmented among several departments with conflicting goals. The purchasing department, which reported to the production manager and was evaluated solely on its ability to obtain materials at the lowest possible price, placed its orders without input from—or reports to—the treasury department on terms, acceptable discounts, or currency of billing. The treasury department, which had control only over disbursements to foreign suppliers, tried to stretch its payments out as long as possible to maximize investment income and cut down on borrowing requirements. Finally, the controller department of the firm's plant, which also reported to the head of production, had authority for payments to domestic suppliers, loosely coordinated with the treasury staff.

As a result of this splintered organizational approach, the company was mired in a bitter dispute over payables that had reached the board level. The production manager was agitating for a standard policy of paying all suppliers on time across the board in order to end complaints and possible price hikes, while the director of finance fought to retain his department's control over disbursements. In the meantime, the company's currency exposures were spiraling out of control and unnecessary borrowings mounted because of the lack of coordination.

Case Example: One Company's Well-Run Payables Function

To avoid such conflicts, firms should establish organizational patterns to optimize—not inhibit—their payables function. A good example of a smoothly functioning payables structure is provided by a well-known U.S. consumer products firm. At the heart of its system is a quarterly management workshop that serves as a forum for improved interdepartmental communications, policymaking, control, and feedback.

The payables organization is adapted to each location's structure. According to the corporate treasurer, "We're in thirty countries with over 100 operations. So for each location, the organizational pattern can vary. The purchasing manager answers to either a production or marketing officer, depending on the operation." In the case of one sales subsidiary, no production manager is on hand, and purchases are made on an intracompany basis. "Basically, disbursements are handled by an accounts payable department," said the treasurer of the company. "And depending on the operation, this could be two people, or a larger group—five to ten people. The accounts payable manager answers to the director of finance. They have different labels in each operation, but in any case, the disbursements manager would report to some form of treasury manager."

To facilitate positive interaction among production, marketing, and finance, each subsidiary holds a quarterly strategy and policy workshop. As the treasurer explained, "Each of the local companies conducts quarterly meetings where workable budgets and policies are developed for the next quarter." With all managers assembled, the meetings address such critical concerns as what to do about changing terms or discount structures. The various department heads share their plans for the coming weeks, and working together as a team, the group constructs a workable strategy. To arrive at a strategy, "each manager constructs a three-month and one-year forecast for his area," the treasurer said. Production forecasts costs, marketing forecasts sales, and finance forecasts cash flows. Based on these projections, "from a cash management viewpoint, we can derive what our funding needs for the operation as a whole will be."

In the opinion of this treasurer, the key to effective payables is a spirit of cooperation among all the relevant functions. "There shouldn't be an adversary relationship. We work closely with purchasing, for example, on all financial matters. If there's a term question—we can pay this supplier in thirty days at this percent, or whatever—they'll just call us up, or stop by, and we'll talk. It's actually a very good relationship."

Practical Policymaking

To make certain their payables are being handled properly, firms should consider formalizing disbursement policies and presenting them to local management in systems manuals that contain step-by-step instructions. Such manuals are especially important in Latin American countries and other developing nations because of the high turnover of personnel; without the manual, corporations cannot ensure that their systems will continue to function smoothly when new employees arrive.

According to corporate cash managers and consultants interviewed by BI, the following broad areas should be addressed in any payables policy manual:

· **Payment terms.** "Purchasing needs to know what kind of terms are acceptable—which can translate into a policy," explained one U.S. cash manager. "For instance, the policy might be that minimum acceptable terms with packaging suppliers are thirty days." Since the treasury department is familiar with terms from both a collections and a payables point of view, it is in the best position to evaluate payment terms and set standards. "If we see something's in the wind—money is getting tighter or freeing up—we can recommend that policies be adjusted."
· **Discounts.** "In a stable country," according to a cash management consultant, "you could probably identify whether or not a certain supplier's discounts are worth the effort; you could say, 'Take the discount or not.' Where interest rates are moving you'd need more of a guideline." While it's up to purchasing to negotiate the best discounts, the payables department has to evaluate each case. Therefore companies may want to adjust discount policies on a monthly basis.

Another policy decision regarding discounts is when to take them. For instance, a 2 percent discount within ten days is often claimed by firms paying in fifteen. As the spokesman for a large building supplies manufacturer put it, "We generally take the approach that we'll take the discount even if we're late. Our policy is to put the burden on the vendor to say, 'Hey, you didn't earn that.'" (For further details on discounts, see p. 212).

· **Payment timing.** Delays in payment may help the short-term cash position, but compensating price rises may eventually appear—something the purchasing manager will not appreciate. "You have a choice of being a good corporate citizen or a pain," stated another cash manager. "Our policy is to pay on time wherever we are." But, he adds, "that also means trying to swing matters in our favor. If you're the only one who pays on time [in a certain country], you've got to get better terms. So our policy is to pay on time but to get the best terms."

The treasury manager for a U.S. heavy-equipment maker admits to a less noble approach: "The official policy is to make payments on time and not to create any problems with vendors. The unofficial policy is and always will be, 'We have to survive first.' And if for any reason we're in a cash crunch and we can't meet the payments on time, we'll stretch that payment out as long as we can—short of putting the vendor out of business or getting sued. When we get some money, we pay them off."

One well-known Australian firm has gone so far as to institute a formal policy on delaying payments to be carried out by its clerical staff. According to the firm's spokesman, "We decided that rather than rely on their [the clerical staff's] lack of intelligence, we'd just put down a little game plan that would prevent them from being silly or inconsistent." The game plan is a list of all the firm's suppliers, with notations such as, "Don't pay him until he starts harassing us" or "Pay thirty days late or sixty days or what have you." Payables clerks who violate these instructions "are just sacked, just summarily dismissed." (See p. 216 for an in-depth discussion of timing payments.)

· **Currency of billing.** Given the extreme volatility of currency markets, it is imperative that firms set guidelines on acceptable currencies of billing for purchases as part of an overall exposure management strategy. In the words of the treasury manager for a U.S. steel maker, "These tend to be long-term policies. With a net asset exposure in certain currencies, you'd want as many liabilities as possible. For instance, our policy may require more sourcing to be in deutsche marks." Without such a policy, purchasing managers would seek suppliers at the perceived lowest cost, without considering the impact on a firm's exposure.

BI research reveals that companies have more room to maneuver in this area than in the past. According to a survey of 302 multinational firms, while the majority of respondents (55 percent) are still invoicing some or all of their receivables in the currency of the exporter, nearly as many (47.5 percent) have been forced to absorb exchange risk by billing a portion of their receivables in the currency of the importer. A major French exporter of heavy equipment, for example, has given in to the demands of overseas customers for local currency billing. "They just don't want to bear the exchange risk anymore," stated the company's treasury director. "I can't blame them." Companies should take advantage of this recent trend by setting policies requiring purchasing managers to negotiate with foreign suppliers for billing currencies that best suit exposure management needs.

Naturally, payables policies must be flexible. As the treasurer for an international foods company put it, "What company in its right mind would say, 'No, you can't buy that'? Local operations are out there to make money for the parent. We're in business to maximize the shareholder's wealth, and that means conducting business—not adhering to strict policies. Companies with inflexible payables policies are the ones that can't react."

Centralizing the Global Payables Function

BI research reveals that for most companies, disbursement management is more decentralized than any other cash management function. "Payables decisions have to be made locally," explained the treasurer of a U.S. publishing firm. "We at headquarters sometimes make recommendations, but we don't get mixed up in the day-to-day workings, and we don't set policy. It makes a hell of a lot of difference whether you're operating in a stable, low-inflation country like Canada or someplace like Brazil—you can't run these things out of parent headquarters."

But a few companies are managing their worldwide payables more aggressively. For example, a $6 billion French multinational has devised a centralized disbursement system to fund subs in isolated parts of the world. The system is operated in conjunction with a major New York bank, and is part of a larger cash pooling arrangement concentrating $2.7 billion in liquidity. The French firm's treasurer believes that how cash moves out is more important than how cash flows in. "That's where you lose most of your money, most of your float," he contended. To control cash outflow more effectively, the firm set up a novel disbursement scheme.

"Because the company zeroes the balances of its operating units every day, nobody's got money in his pocket to spend the following day," the treasurer stated. "They need money to run their operations, and there are essentially two ways of sending money back to an account." The first way is through the use of overdraft accounts at the higher levels of the corporation, where there is good control over expenses.

Establishing Tight Payables Reporting Systems

An experienced consultant offers this advice: "You need to review payables if you can't, without a lot of trouble, get your hands on the following answers: What are my CDOs, broken down by operation and country? What percentage of my payments are made by which instruments? And, what float am I realizing from various payments? If your reporting system makes it difficult to retrieve information on payables, you've got a problem." If a person can't answer these questions, he needs an audit:

(1) Are local managers getting enough information to manage payables efficiently?

(2) Have adequate lines of communication been opened with all relevant departments, e.g., purchasing and production?

(3) Is order and invoice data reported regularly to the accounts payable staff?

(4) Are reports prepared frequently enough to provide a basis for aggressive disbursement management?

The second method of disbursement is called SLIPS (an acronym for the company's international payments system). This is based on revocable letters of credit, which are issued monthly to operating units for limited amounts.

The treasurer described this innovative disbursement approach: "An office in Jakarta knows that its average monthly expenses for payroll, supplies, and other costs come to about $50,000. We ask our bank to issue a revocable LC for about 100 percent of the amount, for a little leeway. The arrangement is noncumulative, so that if the office should only use $45,000 one month, it would not have the extra money to spend next month. We ask the local office to concentrate as many of its payments in as few days as possible in a month, perhaps three or four."

On these dates, the local office writes ten to fifteen checks for a total of $40,000. At the same time, the office draws a draft on the letter of credit. The checks are then sent to the suppliers and the LC draft to the bank. The money from the LC goes into the office's bank account and the checks are paid against it.

The treasurer pointed out two key benefits of the SLIPS system. "In our industry, we are nearly always out in the boondocks," he said. "A very local bank may never have heard of our company to start with and may not know what creditworthiness it has. So if they don't have the money right there in the bank, they won't clear the checks."

The system also gives the banks security without tying up too much liquidity. For one thing, SLIPS works by telex, so funds can move quickly. For another, the LCs are revocable, so if anything goes wrong, the firm can stop the payables system immediately. Hence, the company's risk is limited only to the monthly amount drawn by an individual sales office.

---

(5) Are you carefully tracking disbursement float?

(6) Are you using such measurements as CDOs and aging of payables to assess the effectiveness of payables practices?

(7) Are major cash outflows—e.g., dividends, tax and supplier payments—forecast to plan for funding?

(8) How are forecasts made?

(9) Do you forecast payments by supplier, amount, and currency?

(10) How frequently are forecasts prepared?

(11) Are forecasts measured against actual results and evaluated for accuracy?

(12) What actions do you take based on your reports and forecasts?

(13) Are payables reports and forecasts being transmitted via the most cost-effective and expeditious methods?

(14) Have you explored the cost advantages of automating local payables reporting and forecasting systems?

Case Example: Reporting for a Centralized Payables Function

A major player in the U.S. building materials industry has developed a well-honed reporting system to facilitate its payables management. According to the firm's cash manager, disbursements—including payroll and plant expenses—are completely centralized at parent headquarters. But "all of the documentation is done at the local level—matching invoices, preparing the paperwork, everything we need to get to the point where a check can be written."

To coordinate its centralized payables strategy, the firm has established a timely and detailed reporting system to keep parent headquarters in constant touch with twenty-five operating units. "Our accounts payable function at the local level processes payment information for use by our corporate accounts payable. They're a feeder mechanism—they channel payables information to parent headquarters."

The firm's reporting system includes the following functions:

· **Uncompared-item report.** Upon receipt of goods, the dock foreman compares the vendor's invoice with the contents. The invoice is stamped and forwarded to the operating unit's accounts payable staff. There, payable clerks compare invoices with purchase orders. Items that are "uncompared" because of price, quantity, or description are segregated and compiled in a special report. This report is given to the proper local manager for special attention.

· **The 501 report.** Items of a capital nature—i.e., anything to be capitalized and depreciated—are the object of a special authorization report. "Let's say you were going to spend a million bucks on something," a local manager explained. "Our treasury people would be tuned in through a report we have called a 501, which is sent to everyone in the approval process, including the cash manager." The report enables the cash manager to prepare for extraordinary items. Once completed, items on the report are handled under normal procedures.

· **Vendor-payment detail.** This report, produced daily by all twenty-five operating units, informs headquarters of all purchases. The listing includes vendor name, address, amount due, and due date. "Since terms are generally thirty days," the headquarters spokesman explained, "we have an excellent idea of our cash requirements." The checks are written against a central controlled-disbursement account (see p. 224), which, according to the cash manager at the firm's headquarters, averages 4,000 checks for a total of $20 million per week.

· **Payroll report.** Every two weeks, each operating unit sends its hourly payroll information to the parent. Checks for salaried employees are cut automatically.

The reporting system operates in both directions; headquarters also generates the following reports for the operating units:

· **Payment-status report.** As checks are issued, the parent informs local units of the amount and check number. The status is updated when checks actually clear. Because many of the operating units deal with the same suppliers, payments to vendors are often lumped together in a single check. In that case, the cash manager explained, "We include a listing for the vendor of all invoices being paid, and we also inform the units separately."

- **Budget-variance report.** Once a month, headquarters issues a statement informing managers of their current budget status. According to a division manager, "This helps us keep things under control. If we're going over, maybe I'd better look into it. But usually we know what's happening." The system has built-in tolerances, and if a unit goes beyond its budget, the cash manager resorts to the ultimate reporting device—"I give them a call."

According to the spokesman, the firm's tight payables reporting system and centralized approach to disbursement management yield several benefits. "First, we can see the cash position for the company as a whole, which enables us to maximize cash deployment. Second, it's made bank management much simpler and more cost-effective. Because we use fewer banks, our costs are much lower. And we don't have unused funds sitting around in a lot of banks. Finally, we have multiple locations that now don't have to worry about printing checks, issuing checks, reconciling bank accounts. They don't have to put forth manpower and effort because it's all done here."

How to Evaluate Payables Performance

A top-notch payables monitoring system should also include reports that help firms assess the effectiveness of their disbursement practices. One handy measurement is CDOs, the flip side of DSOs. CDOs may be calculated as follows:

$$CDOs = \text{accounts payable at end-month} \times \frac{\text{days in period}}{\text{payables in period}}.$$

Companies can use CDOs much as they use DSOs. By comparing CDO figures with local supplier-credit terms, a firm can determine whether it is stretching out payment as long as possible. Parent firms may also want to establish CDO targets for subsidiaries and give incentives to local cash managers who meet the targets. Aging of payables is another useful yardstick, similar to aging of receivables. It shows the percentage of payments that are made in fifteen- or thirty-day increments.

A good example of how companies can use these reports to improve their payables management is provided by the Korean subsidiary of a major U.S. chemicals firm. The subsidiary prepares a monthly CDO and aging-of-payables report for its two operating units. "In this way," the firm's finance manager commented, "we can see if we are making progress improving our working capital management. We set targets for ourselves and we try to meet them."

As shown by the form below, the subsidiary recently succeeded in stretching out its CDOs by five days over a four-month period. When asked how the firm managed to do this, the spokesman replied, "There is no trick. We must keep asking and asking, pushing and pushing with everyone." However, the report also showed that the firm was unable to upgrade its aging profile, maintaining a steady 32 percent of payments

FORM A CDOs Outstanding

	Operating Unit A	Operating Unit B	Total	
Date				
12/31	16	8	24	
4/30	26	3	29	
Increase (decrease)	10	(5)	5	
Payment profile 12/31				
0–15 days	2,221	23	2,244	(32%)
Over 15 days	4,868	—	4,868	(68%)
	7,089		7,112	
4/30				
0–15 days	390	24	414	(32%)
Over 15 days	887	—	887	(68%)
	1,277		1,301	
% Change				
0–15 days				—
Over 15 days				—

within fifteen days and 68 percent in sixteen days or more. "We must improve on these figures and raise the percentage of payments over sixteen days by a few points," remarked the spokesman. "It is difficult to actually delay payment, but we can do better with our supplier terms."

Another method of evaluating the performance of local management is to compare subsidiaries' DSOs with their supplier credit terms. The two sets of figures are often similar, especially where the supply component is related to the final product. The food industry supplies a good example, since wholesalers or retailers pay suppliers on very short terms, and the final customers pay equally fast. This is not true, however, of industries where raw materials have a low demand but the end product has a high demand. In any case, companies should make an attempt to receive supplier credit terms that are longer than their DSOs.

Automating Payables Reporting

In line with the worldwide trend toward automated reporting systems (see pp. 77–79), many companies are now tapping computers for payables data and forecasts. In this way, firms can receive daily or even real-time information on orders, invoices, and other critical payables items. For example, the Belgian regional headquarters of a U.S. chemicals firm has fully automated its European subsidiaries' disbursements so that they can identify exactly when payments are due. According to a company spokesman, "This is proving very beneficial in the United Kingdom, where we had a tendency to pay suppliers ahead of time. Now we can pay right on the due date. With weekly payments of five or six million dollars, it's a lot of money we're saving." Indeed, with regional disbursements of over $250 million per year, the company estimates that it is saving about $230,000 annually thanks to the system.

Another U.S. company found a payables computer program helpful for the opposite reason: avoiding late payment. Explained the firm's treasurer, "We were paying a lot of interest to suppliers for overdue payments—21 percent over the merchandise charges. That's where we were really losing. So we use the computer now to make sure we pay everything on time."

To reap these benefits, one consumer products firm is now installing automated payables systems in all its major subsidiaries. The reporting package will contain the following:

· **A purchasing control module** that converts requisitions into purchase orders and reports the data to accounts payable. The module helps the purchasing department evaluate vendors based on price, quantity, and on-time delivery. At the same time, it gives the accounts payable staff advance warning of upcoming disbursements.
· **Control and structure data**, including how vendors will be paid and at what organizational level. This module defines how accounting entries will be accumulated and contains information on material specifications, banking channels to be used, payment schedules, and account codes.
· **Vendor data**, including vendor numbers, names, and alternate payees.
· **Accounts payable data**, which contains information on these types of invoices: regular, prepaid, credit memos, debit memos, and contracts (e.g., rent).
· The system will also have such features as **reporting of current and future cash requirements by pay period and vendor, automatic check reconciliation**, and **user-oriented report writers** enabling the staff to create reports tailored to their own needs.

Successfully Negotiating Payment Terms and Discounts

Once the organizational structure and reporting system have been audited, companies should conduct a full-scale review of the disbursement cycle—beginning with payment terms. By analyzing supplier terms and discounts and comparing them with industry and country standards, firms can determine whether the purchasing department is pressing for the most advantageous conditions.

The rewards of skillful negotiations with suppliers can be substantial. For example, a German company used its clout to bargain with its suppliers for three-week terms rather than the standard two weeks. With this simple strategy, the company realized the following savings:

Weekly purchases $\times$ overnight rate = annual savings.
Dm1,730,000 $\times$ 7.85% = Dm135,805.

To identify such opportunities, firms should ask the following questions:

(1) What are your payment terms, by supplier?

(2) What discounts do your suppliers offer for early or prompt payment?

(3) Are discounts evaluated by comparing them with the cost of short-term debt or the opportunity cost of short-term investments?

(4) Have you compared your payment terms and discounts with those of other companies in your industry and country?

(5) Is your purchasing department pressing for longer credit terms or taking advantage of attractive discounts or lower prices for shorter terms?

(6) Do you use computer software programs to analyze terms, discounts, and prices?

(7) Does the finance department have input into strategies and decisions on payment terms?

Naturally, the main corporate goal in this area of payables management must be to negotiate the best possible credit terms with suppliers—especially in such regions as Latin America, where chronic credit shortages and restrictions on borrowings by foreign-owned firms make supplier credit a major source of financing. To this end, firms should review the indicative credit terms discussed in chapter 3 to determine whether their subsidiaries are negotiating with suppliers as aggressively as possible. Foreign firms and the larger indigenous companies are in a strong position to demand longer terms or lower prices than their smaller counterparts. First, such companies often have excellent payment histories relative to those of smaller firms. Second, their orders are often so large that suppliers would rather grant longer terms than risk losing sales.

As the cash manager of a Venezuelan subsidiary of a U.S. capital goods producer remarked, "I tell our supplier, 'You know that everyone is paying fifteen to thirty days late. So give us an extra ten or fifteen days. At least you know you'll get the money from us.' And they've gone along with this." A huge Korean trading company strives to make its "collection period shorter than our payment period." While the firm forces half its customers to pay cash on delivery, it pays cash only to 20 percent of its suppliers—and only if it can get cheaper prices by doing so. According to the corporate spokesman, "If we give them cash on delivery, we insist that the price be lower. When such negotiations are conducted, we decide how to pay, depending on the price."

Companies should also institute a policy for determining which quotation to take when two suppliers offer to sell the same product at different prices and terms. When faced with this situation, a Venezuelan consumer products firm calculates the present value of the two prices as follows:

$$\frac{P}{1 + i\,(N)/360} = \text{present value},$$

where P = sales price, i = effective annual interest rate, and N = credit period. Thus, if one supplier offered to sell a product for B500 on terms of sixty days, and another wanted to sell the same product for B495 with terms of thirty days, the company would make this comparison:

$$\frac{B500}{1 + 0.17 \times 60/360} = B486.22$$

$$\frac{B495}{1 + 0.17 \times 30/360} = B488.09$$

Taking Advantage of Discounts

Firms should also capitalize on the attractive discounts offered by many suppliers throughout the world. To determine whether the discount is worth taking, companies should compare the rate with prevailing financing and investment costs (see the box below). Because of sharply fluctuating interest rates, firms should conduct ongoing reviews of credit terms and the value of trade discounts. All too often, companies negotiate discount terms and then continue to pay early even when the rates have become disadvantageous.

As a rule of thumb, it generally makes sense to take a discount in countries with low or moderate interest rates and reject them in high-interest-rate countries. A major U.S. pharmaceuticals firm takes the discount in every case. According to the company's treasurer, "Unless you're talking about extremely high interest rates, [taking the discount] will always make sense. With a typical 2/10, net 30 you always want it. I mean twenty days for 2 percent is 36 percent per year, and with the U.S. borrowing rates, that's instant arbitrage." Or, as the Philippine cash manager of a U.S. firm reasoned: "Our opportunity cost, in terms of money market investments, ranges from 15 percent to 18 percent p.a. Now, your usual discount is 2 percent a month, or an effective annual yield of 24 percent. So it's always worth taking the discount."

But in hyperinflationary countries such as Argentina and Israel, only the highest cash discounts will be competitive with the rates available on local money market instruments. Sophisticated customers in these countries often forego cash discounts and park funds in more remunerative investments until payment is due.

Some advanced companies are using computers to evaluate and pay discount invoices. For example, the Brazilian subsidiary of a U.S. oil firm has an automated accounts payable system that lets it compare the economic advantages of paying early and receiving a discount with those of delaying payment until the due date. A German manufacturer of building materials also keeps tabs on payables by using a software package. All suppliers, invoices, and credit terms are listed in the computer to prevent oversights and late or early payments. "Our computer takes care of everything," said a spokesman. The package makes sure the company pays on time to take advantage of discounts, "because when we pay within a certain period, we can take a discount of 1, 2, or 3 percent. This saves us 20 to 30 percent per year."

When to Take a Supplier Discount

Deciding which supplier discounts to take means carefully comparing discount rates with the cost of money. One method for determining whether to take a discount is as follows:

Amount of invoice − amount of discount (i.e., percentage of discount × amount of invoice) = net payable.

$$\text{Net payable} \times \frac{\text{annual cost of borrowing}}{365} = \text{daily interest on net payable.}$$

Daily interest on net payable × days of financing (adjusted to reflect delays already being realized) = cost of discount.

Amount of discount − cost of discount = threshold for accepting discount.

A company should consider taking the discount if the threshold figure is positive and reject it if the figure is negative.

Streamlining Internal Processing

The success of any disbursement strategy hinges on the ability of the payables staff to execute internal procedures in a swift and orderly fashion. Without efficient processing of invoices and payments, companies run the risk of missing out on discounts, injuring supplier relations through chronically late payments, or, even worse, needlessly incurring additional financing costs through early payments. To determine the efficiency of internal procedures, companies should examine each stage of the invoice-to-payment cycle:

(1) Who receives the invoice, and how does he inform the payables staff?
(2) Are invoices matched against the prices and materials specified in purchase orders, and how long does this procedure take?
(3) Once an invoice has been approved, how much time elapses before it is booked?
(4) When does the payables staff receive payments advice from the accounting department?
(5) How long does it take to prepare and execute payment orders?

When making this calculation, it is imperative that firms factor in the true number of days they will forego by paying early—that is, the actual time they normally take to pay a supplier, rather than the stated credit terms. For example, if an invoice to an Australian subsidiary is for A$10,000 and the discount offered is 2/10, net 30, the amount of the discount would be A$200 and the net payable A$9,800. With a money market rate of 16 percent p.a., the daily interest on the net payable would be A$4.3. If local management is paying within an average fifty-nine days instead of the stated thirty, the number of days of financing foregone would be forty-nine (fifty-nine days minus the ten days specified in the discount terms). Thus, the cost of taking the discount is A$210.70. Subtracting this figure from the A$200 discount leaves a A$10.70 loss. The discount is not attractive and should be ignored.

Another item that must be considered when making the discount calculation is the grace period that suppliers often extend to customers taking discounts. Typically, companies will grant the discount even though the funds are a few days late. One Dutch firm, for instance, routinely pays suppliers five to ten days after the ten-day period allowed under its discount arrangements—and receives the discounts without complaints.

Therefore, if the Australian cash manager in the above example could take the discount while paying at fifteen days, the financing foregone would be only forty-four days. The cost would then be a positive A$10.80, and the discount should be taken.

(6) Has the possibility of automating payables procedures been investigated?

The dangers of inefficient payables processing are well illustrated by the experience of a European capital goods manufacturer. The firm recently analyzed its procedures and identified the following pattern:

Procedure	Average Number of Days
Receipt of mailed invoice from suppliers	5.0
Receipt of delivery information from warehouse (every Monday, the warehouse informs accounting of deliveries arriving the previous week)	3.5
Matching of invoices with purchase orders	3.5
Booking of approved orders	2.0
Screening of bookings	1.0
Listing of payments advices (run off the accounting department's computer every two weeks)	7.0
Approval of payments by controller	3.0
Preparation of payments	3.0
Miscellaneous delays	2.0
Total	**30.0 days**

Since the company's suppliers typically grant thirty-day credit terms, the firm should theoretically be able to make payment on or slightly after the due date. In practice, however, the firm often suffers much longer processing times.

As the company's controller explained, the analysis shows an "absolute minimum. If everything goes well, it takes about thirty days." But this does not always happen. "About 10 to 12 percent of the invoices are sent back to purchasing because the price doesn't match the order, and another 5 percent go back to receiving because the quantities don't match the order." The purchasing and receiving departments often take several weeks—and in some cases a few months—to straighten out the discrepancies. On top of these delays—affecting nearly 20 percent of the firm's invoices—"if a delivery comes in late in the week, it might not be reported until a week from the following Monday," adding a week to the cycle. Moreover, approved invoices are often not booked promptly and wind up being pushed into the next biweekly listing. "When we have problems, an invoice can take up to three months to pay."

The result: The company receives daily complaints from its suppliers, which the controller suspects are raising their prices to compensate for anticipated late payments. Even worse, several suppliers have actually stopped deliveries, albeit for only short periods of time.

This company is not alone in its problems. "It often takes two to three weeks before the documents get to me," lamented the cash manager of a large Philippine MNC that was being offered attractive discounts of 2 percent for payments made within ten days. "So I can no longer take the discount. You may want to pay early, but you end up paying late—not by design, but because it takes so long for our people to process." To get around these obstacles, the firm is installing an automated accounts package to identify upcoming disbursements eligible for discount, and it is establishing a computerized system to prepare checks. In the meantime, the spokesman has instructed his payables staff to expedite large payments to avoid losing discounts offered by suppliers.

Naturally, companies should avoid going to the opposite extreme by adopting procedures that result in early payment. For example, the Brussels-based regional treasurer of a U.S. chemicals firm discovered to his chagrin that his U.K. subsidiary had a policy of batching disbursements each Monday for all invoices falling due that week. This sloppy payables practice resulted in numerous payments being issued several days early, as shown in the following table:

Payment due	M	T	W	T	F
Payment made	M	M	M	M	M
Days paid early	0	1	2	3	4

Thus, on average, the company was paying its suppliers two days ahead of time. The firm has now installed an automated payables system that enables the U.K. subsidiary to pay precisely on the due date.

Automating Internal Processing

As these examples make clear, a growing number of companies are drawing upon computer technology to help improve their payables management. Perhaps the greatest attraction of automated systems is the sizable reductions they yield in administrative expenses. Such is the experience of the manager of banking and finance of the Belgian regional office of a multi-billion-dollar U.S. company that is implementing an on-line payables system throughout Europe. "It will reduce quite a bit of staffing," the manager noted. "We won't need people to prepare the payments and match them to invoices and then make sure an approval for payment has been obtained. Under the new system, it will be automatically done. It also reduces our reconciliation time and staffing."

The money that can be saved by automating just one aspect of the payables function was demonstrated by a bank consultant auditing the operations of an Australian manufacturing subsidiary. The consultant analyzed the firm's manual check-processing costs and discovered the following:

Item	Unit Cost
Stamp duty	A$0.10
Bank processing charge	0.18
Check stock	0.05
Secretarial cost at 4.7 minutes per check	0.90
Total cost per check	A$1.23

As this calculation clearly shows, about three-quarters of the total expense of check writing is attributed to manual preparation. As a result of this exercise, the consultant recommended purchasing a system that, at a low initial cost, would provide for the automated printing of checks several times a month. The system will also automatically update computerized accounting records and the cash forecast.

Another important benefit is increased control over disbursement procedures. The cash manager of a U.S. consumer products firm described the virtues of an automated payables package obtained from his bank: "We keep track of our payables on an electronic ledger. Every time we issue a check, we have the amount, the magnetic code, the invoice number, and this is transmitted to the bank via terminal. Then, as the checks arrive, the bank compares them to our ledger, and if there's a match, they pay out. It really streamlines our payables. The advantage of the arrangement is better control and the fact the disbursement account is fully reconciled at all times. If for some reason we want to stop payment, that can be done over the terminal as well."

A major U.S. retailer has gone so far as to automate virtually every aspect of its payables, including an electronic ordering system. According to a company executive, "Not all our suppliers have this arrangement, but we'll set it up if we have sufficient volume and they're willing." Not only is the payables ledger updated when the order is placed, but at some locations, a wand reads a bar code to record electronically the arrival of goods at the loading dock. "The receiving desk makes note of any damage or shortage, and this is included in a supplementary report titled 'adjustments.'" Informed of the receipt of goods, the system can then generate payment in the form of an electronic credit.

Despite the benefits of reduced costs, errors, and paperwork, many firms still resist automating their disbursement systems because they fear the loss of disbursement float. As the treasurer of a French chemicals firm wryly commented, "We find that the old, slow manual techniques are much better for us—if not for our suppliers." But firms wanting to delay payment can follow the lead of a well-known firm in the United Kingdom that has cleverly built payment delays into its computerized system. According to a company spokesman, "We computerized our payables, but we made sure that we stayed as inefficient as ever. We've programmed the computer to ignore the due date on invoices and produce checks as of the date we normally pay suppliers—which is well beyond the stated terms."

Firms that suspect they may be good candidates for automation might want to tap the consulting expertise of computer service companies, which is often given free of charge to help promote products. "Our cash management division out of our headquarters will actually go in for a couple of days and do a hard-core study," explained the spokesman for a U.S. software company. "For a large company, we'll take a look at the entire payables situation—invoicing, trade practices, discounts offered by their vendors—and draw them a picture right there."

Timing the Payables Process

With an effective processing system in place, companies can turn their attention to the actual timing of payments. For many firms, the options seem simple—either pay on time or delay. But developing an effective timing strategy requires a close examination of country and industry practices wherever overseas subsidiaries are located. Only by conducting a thorough review can companies avoid tarnishing their reputations or thoughtlessly providing suppliers with handouts.

To determine if your payables timing is effective, you should start by answering six questions:

(1) When does the payment clock begin ticking—from date of delivery of goods or date of invoice, or date of receipt of invoice?

(2) What are the accepted local payment practices?

(3) Are there special conditions that apply to your industry?

(4) Have you looked at your suppliers on a case-by-case basis to determine their attitudes toward delayed payment?

(5) Is it common for suppliers to charge penalty fees or raise prices when payments are delayed?

(6) How do your CDOs compare with your DSOs—i.e., are your own payment practices in line with those of your customers'?

How to Read Local Calendars. The first step in deciding when to pay is to identify the actual or implied due date—which can vary considerably from country to country and even from industry to industry. In the United States, for instance, most firms interpret the beginning of the credit period as the date stamped on the invoice. Thus, an invoice dated the tenth with thirty-day terms would be payable the following tenth, regardless of what day the invoice arrives.

But this is not the case in all countries. In the United Kingdom and Australia, firms typically pay from the end of the month of billing. "Our credit terms are officially net thirty days from date of invoice," complains the CFO of a diversified U.K. firm. "But nobody in this country takes any notice. They wait until they receive the invoice and then pay thirty days from the end of that month. That means they average forty-five days' credit." In these countries, a customer billed on January 15, given thirty-day terms, would not be expected to pay until the end of February. So thirty-day terms may, in effect, translate to as much as sixty-day terms, adding up to thirty days to the payment cycle.

Firms must also investigate industry-specific variations. For example, several years ago the Japanese subsidiary of a U.S. firm managed to capitalize on billing practices in its industry through sheer luck. Caught in a sudden cash bind, the company started paying its suppliers thirty days later than it had in the past. To its surprise, the subsidiary's suppliers voiced few complaints. The reason: It was common practice in the firm's industry for customers to start the credit cycle at the end of the month in which delivery was made, or even a week or two into the following month. Similarly, payments in the German steel industry are made on the fifteenth day of the month following billing, while the automobile industry pays on the twenty-fifth day of the month following delivery. (For more information on industry variations in major countries, see the chart on pp. 219–221).

But some companies may want to take matters into their own hands. The Asian regional treasurer for a Canadian natural resources firm told BI that he had an across-the-board policy of paying suppliers as of the end of the month that goods are delivered. "And then we smile if the supplier rings up and says, 'No, no, our terms are from the date of invoice.' We'll just say, 'Oh, sorry, we made a mistake.' If he says nothing, then it's sixty days from the end of the month. Let's be honest: You sure as hell get away with it 60 percent of the time."

In the Netherlands, the controller of a heavy-equipment manufacturer has unilaterally decided that the payment clock begins ticking when mailed invoices are received, not on the date of the invoice. Because of delays in the mail and suppliers' internal processing systems, this practice adds an average of five days to the credit terms. But for its largest supplier, a well-known electronics firm, the delays range up to ten days.

No matter what definition of the due date a company adopts, it should make sure payment is never made in advance without receiving an attractive discount. Surprisingly, this simple rule is often broken by even the largest companies. For years, a major U.S. pharmaceuticals firm has taken a relaxed attitude toward its payables. According to the company's cash manager, "Any time we see a check over $1,000, it gets special processing and will be timed to coincide with its due date. Anything

Paying Suppliers on Specified Days

One sure way of stretching out payments is to pay suppliers only on specific days. This tactic is common in regions where the mail systems are inefficient and suppliers make use of couriers for collections. In response, payables managers can agree to pay the couriers, but only on set days. Where acceptable to suppliers, the technique is an excellent delaying mechanism and can add days to a company's disbursement float.

The technique is especially popular in Latin America, where nightmarish mail systems force suppliers to use couriers. But rather than pay at any time after due date that a courier shows up, one Venezuelan firm pays its suppliers' collection staff only on Friday afternoons. According to a company spokesman, the firm has told its suppliers: "If you don't come on Friday you have to wait until next Friday. Our cashiers are open only on that day." As a result, on some days, "up to 50 percent of payments due are not picked up. And even if they are, since we pay in the afternoon, we get two extra days' float time over the weekend."

A Mexican firm using the technique chooses to pay suppliers only on Mondays. The firm has found that this is the day collectors are most likely to miss, thereby gaining the firm an additional week's float.

But the practice is not unique to Latin America. In the Philippines, for example, the subsidiary of a U.S. consumer products firm issues checks on Friday afternoons—after the banks have closed—to ensure the weekend float. In addition, the company always issues "cross checks," i.e., checks drawn on banks other than those used by the supplier—a technique adding as much as three days to disbursement float.

---

under that goes through our normal processing routine." The company sends lower-value checks through a system of invoice matching and authorization, resulting in payment within only fifteen days. The firm's system is far less than optimum because terms granted by its suppliers are generally thirty days.

Although the lost float is significant—the spokesman concedes that hundreds of checks per month are under the $1,000 benchmark—the firm continues to maintain its cavalier attitude. "To us, it's just not worth it to look at every single payment. We have a lot of other things to look at before we can look at a new system."

Do Unto Others. Most MNCs think twice before deciding to delay payment. For one thing, such firms are large and highly visible concerns that do not want to run the risk of damaging relations with local suppliers or government officials. Indeed, companies that seriously delay payment may endanger their supplier shipments and may even find themselves embroiled in damaging legal actions. This can have very serious consequences in such countries as Brazil, where banks normally cut off the credit lines of delinquent debtors involved in legal proceedings.

By stretching out payments, MNCs may also hurt smaller suppliers. As the head of a major bank's consulting group put it, "Certainly you don't bankrupt yourself to meet a payment—but neither would you want to use your market presence to bleed every drop." The treasurer of a huge French chemicals firm agrees: "We've been doing business with many of these suppliers for years, and it serves us no benefit to squeeze them for the little bit extra it gets us. Many of our suppliers rely on us as their major source of revenue. These are little mom-and-pop operations, and if we put the squeeze on them, it can make the difference between their survival and extinction. For us, the added profit might just buy a bigger Christmas party. It's not worth it."

Moreover, in certain countries paying on time is de rigeur. For example, in Germany and Japan there are unwritten rules requiring prompt payment according to agreed-upon terms. As the treasurer for a German construction firm noted, "Sometimes we stretch payment a little. But in Germany the most important thing is to preserve your reputation with suppliers." According to a spokesman for one of Japan's largest trading companies, his firm would never consider delaying payment to suppliers. "If we delay payment, we lose face, and we will lose our suppliers." Thus, in these countries, companies that adopt delaying tactics common in certain other countries may severely compromise their reputation.

In many other countries, however, the issue is not so clear-cut. In much of Latin America, in parts of Asia, and even in Europe, some companies have found that payment practices unacceptable in other nations are tolerated. When asked whether his company pays on time, the Latin American regional treasurer of a U.S. chemicals concern answered, "Yes, we're very good at paying, and we have a reputation as a prompt payer. But frankly, we are now looking at the idea of being less good, of delaying payment more often in accordance with normal country practices. I mean, we don't want to be accused of financing ourselves with the other guy's money, but if we find out that everybody in a particular country is taking terms plus thirty days, we don't want to be the only yo-yo paying on the due date."

Companies must therefore examine payment practices in each country in which they have operations. As one cash management consultant maintains, "Companies that haven't realized this and evaluated their payables management on a country-by-country basis are losing money. Delaying means just making sure you're fair to yourself and not treating your suppliers better than they treat you."

BI research shows that delaying payments is a common practice in the following countries:

- **Asia.** Despite the stringent adherence to terms that are prevalent in Japan, other Asian countries are noted for their delaying practices. In **Australia,** for example, delaying payment is practically a national pastime. An Australian treasurer for a foreign firm revealed his payables strategy in a BI interview: "Since most suppliers give thirty-day terms but don't start screaming until the sixtieth day, I've told the units to pay fifty-nine days for every possible account unless they're squeezing the man out of existence—you know, the small business that has to survive for its payroll. We weren't that way once, but I figured the cost is enormous to rigidly pay at thirty days. You can argue that paying on time keeps the wheels of trade rolling, but in reality every bugger does it to you, so I decided to take the advantage." The tactic yields significant benefits: "I figure we make A$1.5 million a year in interest recovery. So, suddenly the moral argument looks pretty weak, doesn't it?" A giant indigenous mining firm in the **Philippines** lets its payments "slide off when times

Getting Suppliers to Accept Checks

While checks are attractive for issuers, they are not widely used in many countries—especially in Europe. Despite this, some companies have managed to enjoy the benefits of checks in nations where they are not usually acceptable. For example, an Italian capital goods producer was able to wean its suppliers from bank transfers and *ricevute,* the country's preferred instruments, and began paying them all via check—creating a six-day disbursement float. The maneuver was aggressive, but according to the firm's treasurer, it met with virtually no resistance.

Suppliers haven't complained, the treasurer believes, "because psychologically they see the date on the check, and even if we continue to use the money for another five or six days, in their eyes we still paid on time. Actually, the float may be longer with some companies, depending on how quickly they deposit the check. In big companies, many people want to sign, look at, and enjoy the check." With annual payables of over $70 million and local interest rates at around 14 percent p.a., the spokesman estimates that his firm saves over $140,000 each year with the technique.

Another firm has taken Italian check writing even further. Since Italian banks back-value checks from the date of issue, the firm leaves the date on the check blank

---

are tight." Said the company's spokesman, "The regulations in the Philippines are very liberal on this." When suppliers complain or try to impose penalty fees, "we just say, 'You want to be paid? Give us a discount.'"

- **Europe.** Suppliers in the **United Kingdom** are accustomed to payment delays and rarely attempt to impose penalty interest charges. The assistant treasurer of a consumer products firm explained why: "Everyone in the United Kingdom wants the flexibility to say, 'I'm hard up this month; I'll forget to send his check off and wait for him to scream.'" Thus, firms can take advantage of the relaxed attitude toward prompt payment without seriously jeopardizing supplier relations. In **Italy**, cash managers live by the saying "To pay and to die there is always time." According to an Italian controller, "We have one American company that pays on time. Why? Because they have American habits. Here, it's just not normal to pay on time." Firms that would hesitate to delay payment in other European nations for fear of damaging supplier relations should immediately consider adopting a more relaxed policy in Italy.

- **Latin America.** This region, with its tight credit and high borrowing rates, is a haven for corporate delaying practices. In **Brazil,** one cash manager divulged, "most local companies feel the credit terms start on the due date." As a result, some foreign-owned firms are reassessing their attitudes in light of the country's high financing costs and lackadaisical local payment patterns. The treasurer of a U.S. oil company's Brazilian subsidiary spoke for many firms when he said, "Look, we're

and has the supplier stamp the date of receipt. "It's not really permitted," a spokesman confesses, "but it's common practice. When I send a check from Rome to Milan for payment, I save at least a week of value. We save millions of lire a year."

A German oil and construction firm successfully implemented check payments to suppliers in a country where suppliers generally demand wire transfers. According to the company's cash manager, the firm uses checks for payments over Dm500—where he considers the float gain worthwhile—and bank transfers for smaller amounts. "Checks usually take about five days to clear, including mail time of one or two days. Then, in a lot of cases, the mail is delivered to the supplier after lunchtime, and if he brings in the check the same day, value doesn't start till the next day anyway. Most suppliers don't even do that. They keep the check for one or two days before giving it to the bank, and then it takes another two days to clear."

All these delays add up to a five-day disbursement float on checks, whereas bank transfers take only three to four days to get debited. For this reason, says the cash manager, companies in Germany "that know anything about cash management and understand float use checks. The smaller companies may use bank transfers more because they are not well organized, and they don't realize they are losing money."

being let down on our side as suppliers. So once in a while we should be able to be less prompt on our payments. All the more, because we get nothing for it. Suppliers think it's nice to deal with us because we pay on time, but so what?" **Venezuelan** firms are widely regarded as the slowest-paying in all of Latin America. While inflation and interest rates are moderate in relation to those of Mexico and Brazil, the practice of late payment is deeply embedded in the Venezuelan consciousness. As the treasurer of a U.S. consumer goods subsidiary puts it: "It is a custom. They use all mechanisms known to man to delay payment."

Choosing the Right Payment Instrument

Knowing when to pay is only one part of the payables equation. The next critical decision is selecting a payment mechanism. From *ricevute,* drafts, *giros,* and checks to electronic funds transfers and direct depositing, companies face a bewildering array of worldwide payment options. To determine which instruments are best, a company must analyze each payment mechanism being used in terms of acceptability to suppliers, cost, float, and techniques that can be used to slow down disbursements.

As a way of making this determination, start by answering seven questions:

(1) What payment instruments are you using to pay suppliers, employees, and government entities (checks, wire transfers, drafts, etc.)?

(2) What are the total disbursements made through each of these instruments monthly and annually?

(3) What is the mail and clearing float—or value-dating times—for these instruments in each country?

(4) What techniques, such as remote disbursement, are being used to prolong the payment cycle?

(5) How long does it take suppliers to process the various instruments and present them for payment?

(6) What are the bank charges and internal processing costs for each instrument?

(7) Is the local staff taking advantage of such banking services as controlled disbursement and zero-balance accounts where available?

Taking Advantage of Checks. Checks—written obligations to pay issued by the customer—are a favored payment instrument throughout North and Latin America and in such countries as the United Kingdom, Australia, and the Philippines. Checks offer issuers such key benefits as total control over payment timing and relatively low costs. But the main attraction of checks is the mail and bank float they generate. Indeed, using checks in such countries as Venezuela can add days or even weeks to the payment cycle.

To get the most out of checks, firms must therefore carefully audit float times. According to one cash manager, "You should go straight to the primary sources of information—to the ledgers, or you look at the checks. With disbursements you are in control. You wrote the checks. You can look at all the documentation and put the pieces together." This can be an arduous task. "Nobody gives you the information you're after in any readily digestible form," a consultant noted. "You have to go in and crunch the numbers yourself. There's no secret to getting it done; you'll have to roll up your sleeves and get out the pencils."

But companies that follow this advice will find that the hard work pays off. For example, the Venezuelan subsidiary of a U.S. steel firm prepares daily computerized reports on payments, including one to monitor disbursement float. By keeping in constant contact with its banks, the firm holds funds until checks clear on accounts payable. The company's finance manager pointed out that "the float period in Venezuela can go anywhere from five to twenty-five days, depending partly on the bank and partly on when the collector deposits the money. Sometimes they don't deposit the check for as long as a week or two, but as long as they've got it they're happy." Thus, by closely monitoring and aggressively playing the disbursement float, a firm can keep funds invested in local money market instruments until the last minute without hurting its reputation with suppliers.

Another good example of an effective disbursement-float tracking system is that of the Australian subsidiary of a major U.S. MNC. The cash manager's staff regularly monitors clearings of their checks to suppliers and has identified the following pattern of disbursement float:

Business Days' Float	Average %
0	4.8
1	44.7
2	23.5
3	11.6
4	6.1
5	2.8
6	1.4
7	0.4
8	0.1
9–21	4.6
	100.0

With this information in hand, the cash manager matches probable clearing times to each day's payments and funds his disbursement account only with the amount needed to meet anticipated debits. In this way, the firm can keep funds invested in local money market instruments as long as possible without hurting its reputation with suppliers.

The firm also reviews its tax payments and has developed the following matrix:

Tax Office	No. of Checks per Month	Average Amount per Month (A$000s)	Average Days' Disbursement Float
Perth	2	30	14
Brisbane	2	40	9
Melbourne	2	70	20
Adelaide	2	15	12
Sydney	2	400	9
Central	3	200	6
Payroll	3	100	5
Total	16	855	

By taking advantage of the float on tax payments, the company estimates it saves an estimated A$4,000 per month in interest expense, or about A$50,000 a year.

Companies that monitor their check-clearing float closely, like the firms discussed above, will find they have far more funds available for self-financing or investment than indicated by their book balances. As an aid to this exercise, companies should refer to the tables on value dating on pp. 124–26.

Remote Disbursement.   To maximize check float, some aggressive firms use remote disbursement—the drawing of checks on banks located some distance from vendors—a technique especially popular in certain Latin American countries and in the United States. While technically paying suppliers on time, remote disbursement invariably adds days to the total disbursement float. For example, one manager who spoke with BI has manufacturing plants scattered throughout the interior of Venezu-

The Ultimate Tracking System: Controlled Disbursement

Companies with operations in the United States can greatly simplify the task of monitoring check-clearing float by using controlled disbursement, a service offered by many banks. With this technique, firms can keep funds invested until the last possible moment, because the bank allows them to fund each day's cleared checks precisely. Each morning the bank receives cleared checks from the Federal Reserve and local clearinghouses, totals them, and presents the net figure to the corporate client. The company then transfers funds to cover the cleared checks.

Said the cash manager for a North Carolina equipment firm: "All of our operations write checks on a central controlled-disbursement account, except for a few odd ones here and there where there's no significant activity." The cash manager explained that her bank's electronic reporting system informs her of funding requirements each morning by 11 A.M. "We have a terminal where we tie right into the bank's system. We find out what our clearings are and fund exactly that amount by wire transfer—also through the terminal. The disbursement account then returns to a zero balance."

The manager said the system is very easy to use and maximizes the firm's use of available funds. "We set this up because before we had no idea what was clearing on a day-by-day basis. We would guess, and when you guess sometimes you don't have enough in the account, which results in an overdraft. At other times you have too much—and with us a net borrower, we don't like to have excess cash. We wanted the balance in our disbursement accounts to be zero every day."

---

ela. When making payments, the subsidiary's headquarters in Caracas always issues checks drawn on banks near the plant receiving shipment. Since most of the firm's suppliers are also headquartered in Caracas, this adds up to seven days to the check-clearing process, freeing funds for investment with the local money desks.

According to a company spokesman, these tactics yield a safety margin for excess cash investments. When using local money-desk instruments, he stated, "We must have a float of at least five days; otherwise we can't invest." The reason? The money desks require a minimum term of five days for investment in repos.

Remote disbursement is not unique to the Americas. Although limited in application, some U.K. companies have developed remote-disbursement points to maximize mail and clearing float. A manufacturer of consumer products, for instance, issues and mails checks to London suppliers from a disbursement center located at its Northern Ireland plant. According to the firm's cash manager, "This procedure has several advantages. By issuing checks drawn on our bank in Northern Ireland, we gain an extra day of bank float. In addition, mail takes an extra day from there, so we gain a second day of float. We also use second-class post, which gains us another two days. So in total, we gain four days." With annual payables of several hundred million pounds, the spokesman estimates that the remote-disbursement strategy saves the firm over £250,000 each year.

Controlled-disbursement systems have survived an unintended assault from the Federal Reserve. In an attempt to stop remote disbursement, a policy of increased presentments became the rule at many disbursing locations. Originally, the Fed made the day's final presentment to paying banks 9 A.M., making it possible for banks to inform corporate customers of the precise amount needed to cover checks. But later presentments to locations with high volume made early notification impossible. Since the Fed monitors the level of disbursement activity in all cities, when a particular area reaches a break-even level (the float saved by an additional, later presentment meets or exceeds the cost of an additional courier), a later presentment is added.

Despite these circumstances, banks have found ways to offer controlled disbursement while working within the Fed's new policies. For example, a large U.S. pharmaceuticals firm worked out an arrangement with its southeastern disbursement bank. All forty of the company's U.S. operations maintain a checking account with the same disbursement bank. Rather than fund their average disbursement of $5 million per day on a same-day basis, checks presented are funded on the previous day—with the bank absorbing the float. What's more, the company keeps a constant compensating balance on deposit to cover the cost of clearing checks. As the firm's senior cash manager explained, the system runs almost by itself. "They don't even tell me if we're funding the account sufficiently; I don't even care. If I underfund, I underfund; on average it works out. If after a few months it turns out we're constantly underfunded, then they'll say, 'Hey, you're short.' And I'll say, 'Fine, here's an increase in deposits.'"

One Australian firm has set up a diabolical system designed to create check-processing delays. The firm's western Australia operation currently pays suppliers with checks drawn on a Perth bank account; float time averages three days. Under the new system, the check stock is changed. The new checks prominently display the Perth address at the top, but the encoding designates an imprest account in Sydney. Upon receipt, the supplier will deposit the check in his bank, which will send the check to the Perth branch of the disbursing bank, where it will be rejected because of the MICR encoding. The check will then have to be physically transported to the branch of record for the account to be debited—a process taking anywhere from two to six days. In this way, the firm more than doubles its disbursement float.

Unlike its effect in other countries, remote disbursement does not necessarily add to Australian suppliers' collection cycles. Because local banks normally grant same-day credit on deposits to major companies, the banks—not suppliers—absorb float.

A related technique, although rare, is for a foreign subsidiary to issue checks drawn on the parent company bank. This is generally used for cross-border payments, but the tactic can also be deployed locally. As the spokesman for a large U.S. consumer products company with extensive Latin American operations commented, "We'll try anything. There are companies in Latin America that will accept our parent's checks for domestic payments."

When to Use Wire Transfers

Although wire transfers are the quickest way to transfer funds, they are not always the most cost-effective. To determine whether a wire transfer is cost-effective for a particular transfer, it is necessary to compare the days saved in transit and local interest rates with the telex fee to pinpoint the value of the interest earned by keeping funds longer. To calculate the break-even point on wire transfers, companies can use the following formula:

$$\text{Break-even} = \text{telex cost} \times \frac{365}{\text{investment rate} \times \text{days saved}}.$$

For instance, if a company secures an investment rate of 10 percent, it can keep funds invested for another five days, and wire transfers cost $15:

$$\$15 \times \frac{365}{0.10 \times 5} = \$10,950.$$

A graphic portrayal of this calculation is shown in the chart on the following page.

Bank Transfers

Bank transfers are instructions to move funds between specific bank accounts. They can be initiated by several means—telephone, paper instruction, or even via terminal. Bank transfers can be within the same bank's network, or to other banks through clearing systems similar to those for regular checks.

Payables managers find several features of bank transfers unattractive. First, they give value to suppliers much sooner than checks, since mail float is eliminated. Second, while the paying account is debited immediately—and even back-valued a day or two—the supplier may not receive credit for days, with the bank keeping the float. Finally, bank transfers—and especially wire transfers—can be as much as $10–15 more expensive than other payment instruments.

On the other hand, some companies prefer bank transfers as an aid to forecasting. As the German treasury manager for a large indigenous firm explained, "Precisely what is it you're trying to accomplish? You're trying to keep your money as long as possible and earn all the interest you can. When you pay by check today you have no way of knowing what will clear. So we use wire transfers, and we know how much we have to invest exactly." A bank consultant agreed. "What you're looking for is to delay the payment for as long as possible," he commented. "So do that and then pay by wire transfer. The advantage is you know your cash position." The consultant feels European companies commonly use wire transfers because "the volumes are small. Three days' float on a small amount may not be of any interest whatsoever.

Float Saving vs. Cable Cost
(When Is It Cheaper to Transfer by Cable?)

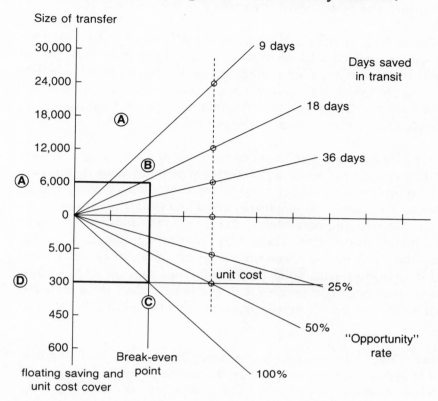

How to use the chart. Start with any given item size A, read across to days saved B, read down to "opportunity" rate of funds C, read back to float savings D. Do the savings justify the unit cable cost? For example, a $6,000 transfer accelerated six days, at 10 percent "opportunity" value for funds, would just cover a $300 cable charge. A smaller transfer, fewer days saved or a lower funds value rate, would not reach the break-even point. The chart can be read in any direction.

What they gain on float they lose on ability to manage cash position, so it's fairly easy to persuade a company in Europe to pay by wire transfer."

Another reason many firms choose to pay by bank transfer is simply that they are required to do so in some countries—e.g., the Netherlands and Germany. As one cash manager exclaimed, "Suppliers in Germany insist on wire or telex transfers. They simply won't accept checks." (But for another point of view, see the box on p. 222.)

Commercial Bills and Drafts. Essentially, a commercial bill is a paper statement of indebtedness. The bill's value, or quality, is determined by the degree to which it represents a legal obligation on the paying party or obligor. In some cases, an accepted commercial bill attains the status of commercial paper in that it can be discounted with a bank or transferred to another party. Commercial bills are generally seller-initiated instruments and thus provide much less control over disbursements to customers than checks or bank transfers.

The following are among the best-known examples of commercial bills:

· **Italian *ricevute*.** *Ricevute bancaria* (bankers' receipts) are a form of seller-initiated time draft. Issued with a prefixed settlement date, *ricevute* differ from most other commercial bills in that they are not a legal obligation on the buyer. To initiate the process, a supplier prepares a list of receivables and sends it to his bank. In turn, the bank prepares and delivers the *ricevuta* as a reminder to buyers of their maturing obligation. The *ricevuta* carries no recourse to the buyer.

Ricevute are extremely efficient for the seller when payment is made as agreed. But for the 5–10 percent (on average for all firms) of *ricevute* where payment is received late, or not at all, the system can be a supplier's nightmare. First, banks typically keep suppliers in the dark about customer nonpayment, inhibiting collection procedures. Second, banks commonly charge suppliers interest on the credited funds from the day of maturity, rather than the value date. These two features, combined with the lengthy ten- to fifteen-day bank float on even timely payment, can be turned to the buyer's favor. Payable managers with solid credit standings may be able to get suppliers to skip the *ricevuta,* negotiate longer credit terms (to reflect the supplier's fifteen-day bank float on the company's timely payment), and pay promptly by local bank transfer.

· **Brazilian *duplicatas*.** Under Brazilian legislation, every transaction involving the transfer of goods and services for money must be accompanied by a *nota fiscal* (see form on p. 229). This document is the only valid receipt for tax purposes, and, technically, tax incidence occurs at the time of sale. The *nota fiscal* is prepared with four copies, in some cases five. One copy is called a *duplicata*—literally, a duplicate of the *nota*—and consists of the upper portion of the *nota,* specifying credit terms, amount, purchaser, and seller (the nature of goods or services is not included). The *duplicata* is a negotiable instrument, basically a trade bill, which can be endorsed to third parties for collection.

Sellers send their *duplicatas* to a bank for collection. The bank then advises the buyer that a seller has placed a *duplicata* with the bank for collection and the branches at which it can be paid. The buyer signs an acceptance, essentially acknowledging the terms of sale and recognizing that the *duplicata* has been placed.

Under the *duplicata* system, a buyer faces severe problems should he default. The seller can instruct the bank to protest the *duplicata*— usually within forty-eight hours of the due date. In some cases, firms instruct the bank to cancel collection after a specified number of days and return the *duplicata* to them for collection.

· **French drafts and promissory notes.** Commercial bills are the most popular payment instruments in France, accounting for 80–90 percent of total corporate-to-corporate payments. There are two types of French commercial bills, both back-

DISTRITO:

N O T A   F I S C A L

Natureza da Operação:
Código Fiscal:
Data da Emissão:

FATURA		DUPLICATA		VENCIMENTO	FATURA
Valor CrS	Numero	Valor CrS	N.º de Ordem		

Condições Especiais:

EXTRAÍDO EM 9 VIAS

O(S) Sr.(s)
Endereço
Município   C E P.:   Estado
Praça de Pagamento
Insc. no CGC(MF) n.º   Inscrição Estadual n.º

VALOR POR EXTENSO	

Deve(m) a   o valor desta Fatura, pagável na
praça e vencimento acima indicados.

VENDEDOR:	AVISO DE VENDA N.º	Pontos	Comissão

NOTA FISCAL N.º/SERIE	DATA

DISCRIMINAÇÃO	TOTAL
serviços de locação de equipamentos correspondente ao período _____	
serviços de manutenção de equipamentos contrato n.º _____período _____	
serviços executados	
aplicação de peças e/ou acessórios	
equipamento Modelo N.º	

ISS   ICM   IPI

CONSERVAÇÃO	CUSTO	VALOR TOTAL DA FATURA CrS	

Em _____/_____/_____   _____
                                                          ASSINATURA

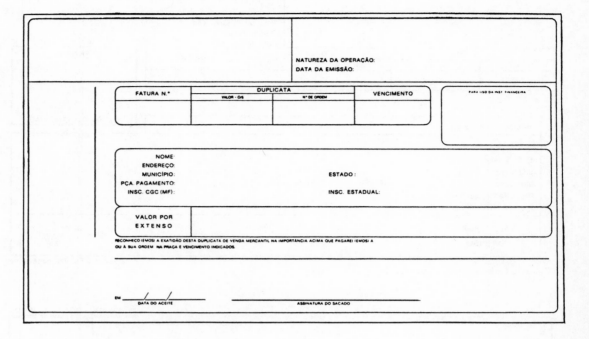

valued to payers' accounts one day from maturity: (1) *effets* or *lettres de change,* which are drafts issued by the supplier that become a valid payment instrument when accepted by the customer, and (2) *billets a ordre* (BAOs), which are promissory notes issued by the customer.

French suppliers prefer these commercial bills because not only can they be discounted, but they provide legal protection in case of default. According to a seasoned treasurer, "These are very secure. If a customer cannot honor an accepted draft, he is put on the Banque de France's blacklist and can be taken to court. The acceptance is proof that they owe us the money." Finally, the fixed-maturity dates of bills facilitate companies' cash flow projections.

In addition to paper drafts, firms can use automated commercial bills, which are cleared through an automated clearinghouse. These instruments replace the physical transfer of paper bills with the coded magnetic recording of drafts when they enter the banking system for collection. There are two kinds of automated drafts, corresponding to the manual instruments discussed above: (1) *lettres de change releve* (LCRs), which are presented on magnetic tapes by the supplier to the collecting bank, and (2) *billets a ordre releve* (BORs), which are issued by the customer.

· **Japanese promissory notes.** Promissory notes are the most popular payment instrument used in that country, accounting for nearly three-quarters of payment volume. Under the promissory note system, a customer issues its supplier an IOU specifying the amount of the debt and the date payment is due. The supplier takes the note to a bank, which holds the instrument until maturity. Promissory notes are magnetically encoded with payment information, and on the due date, an efficient Japanese clearing system automatically credits the supplier's account.

A company that does not honor its obligation twice within six months is blacklisted by the local clearinghouse. Thereafter, banks will sever relations, and suppliers will switch to cash on delivery. Often a single default has triggered bankruptcy. As the spokesman for a local steel maker put it, "If a company delays payment on promissory notes, companies and banks will no longer serve them."

What Cash Managers Should Know About Giros.

Giros, found throughout Europe, are instructions to directly debit a remitter's account and credit a beneficiary's. *Giro* payments have to be received in a specific *giro* account, frequently operated by a government or quasi-government agency such as the postal system. *Giro* transfers carry no per-transfer charge, making them an extremely inexpensive form of payment.

Although *giro* transfers are cheap, they have some serious drawbacks. Postal *giros* in Italy, for instance, offer almost no account information, which blocks efforts to monitor cash positions. The Italian subsidiary of a U.S. computer manufacturer, for example, found that it takes an average of sixteen calendar days to receive notification of deposits in its postal account, although value is received much earlier. Such delays are expensive, because the accounts often pay little or no interest—in this case, just 0.5 percent. To make matters worse, overdrafts in some systems are not allowed, so a customer trying to maintain minimal balances can inadvertently bounce payments. Inadequate reporting and unacceptably low interest on balances combine to put *giros* at the bottom of most cash managers' lists of payment instruments.

However, cash managers should be aware that many *giro* payment systems are now undergoing significant changes that may make them more useful for disbursement management. In response to increased competition from the commercial banks, some systems have begun to offer reasonable interest on idle balances and daily balance information—and in some cases, they even allow overdrafts. This improvement of services, when balanced against *giros'* extremely low cost, could sway cash managers to use *giros* more frequently.

What's more, payables managers may begin to see more and more suppliers requesting payment by *giro.* For instance, many collections operations are gearing up to use *giro* acceptances, an instruction to initiate a direct debit, as a collections technique (see p. 127–130). Payables managers may find the acceptances easier to work with than actual direct-debiting systems (such as BACs) because timing control is retained, although the supplier creates the instrument and a customer signs and mails the *giro* acceptance at his own discretion.

Giros can also be used for direct deposit of payroll, provided the information is in the form of disk or tape. While the employee must be persuaded to open a *giro* account, the advantage to the company is that *giro* transfers are free of charge. Once

Using EDI in Finance: Ciba-Geigy

Setting up an international presence is one thing for an MNC. Getting up-to-the-minute, accurate information about the company's performance is another. Gathering, analyzing, and distributing information is a herculean task for multinationals with operations in many countries. In the last decade, however, MNCs have improved information processing enormously by linking headquarters and field offices by computer.

Now, a few MNCs are taking another giant step in information processing by hooking up their financial systems electronically with suppliers and banks. Ciba-Geigy AG (CIGY), the big Swiss chemical company, is a pioneer in this area. It has developed, together with German banks, a cross-border electronic payment system between its Swiss headquarters in Basel and Germany. Next in line is automated cross-border invoicing; and two to three years down the road, the company plans to develop a trade document system that can be linked electronically to the banks.

Paying Electronically

For the past four years, CIGY has been routing payments electronically to German suppliers. As Werner Moser, deputy director of CIGY's finance department, explains, "We collect all payment data on the parent mainframe computer in Basel. Then the German payment information is downloaded to a personal computer in the finance department. The personal computer sends it by telephone modem to Deutsche Bank, Dresdner Bank AG, and Commerzbank at their Frankfurt headquarters."

At the same time, a telefax report with security information and the total amount of that specific run is sent to the Loerrach branches of these banks. CIGY uses Loerrach because it is the closest German city to several of its facilities just across the Rhine from Basel. The Loerrach branches then fax the approvals to the Frankfurt banks' headquarters, which make the payments out of CIGY's deutsche mark accounts to its German suppliers. For extra security, CIGY sends payment reports to both the Frankfurt banks' headquarters and the branches in Loerrach.

---

again, with *giros* paying typically low interest, the trick is to fund the account at the last possible moment.

Giros can also be cost-efficient for cross-border payments—especially smaller ones—provided the creditor has an account with the *giro* system in his own country. For smaller payments, there are two major reasons for preferring *giros* to commercial bank transfers. First, transfers can be made to a foreign *giro* account with no commission levied, as opposed to the normally fixed rate for commercial bank cross-border movements. Second, low-value international transfers usually attract large spreads. The currency conversion for a *giro* transfer can be made at rates even better than those for large transfers, generally splitting the current bid/offer.

Moser says the automated German payments take place twice a week. The German banks charge a quarterly fee based on the number of payments made during each three-month period.

CIGY has automated the transfer of most of its payments. About 85 percent are made through Telekurs, a Swiss data carrier in Zurich. Based on SWIFT conformity standards, fully automated payment details are currently collected on magnetic tapes and then shipped to and processed by Telekurs. However, Moser expects that the automated payments could soon be transferred by personal computer into the Telekurs system, possibly by the end of 1990.

The Next Steps in Automation

The next step, already under way, is the automation of invoicing. The chemical and automotive industries in Europe are rapidly developing electronic data interchange (EDI) standards, which should be ready early in 1990. In the chemical sector, ten major companies, including CIGY, Imperial Chemicals Industries PLC, and Rhone-Poulenc, Inc., are working together to set up standards for order processing, invoicing, and data exchange to allow electronic interfacing for invoicing.

Another high-priority EDI project is systemizing trade documents. CIGY is developing an internal system called Akkreditif Inkasso Documents Exchange (AIDA). AIDA will work this way: A customer opens a letter of credit with his bank and then sends the details by telex, facsimile, or letter to CIGY. This information is entered on the CIGY Vax terminal in the AIDA files.

Each CIGY department can then access the information on-line. The progress of documents such as invoices, insurance certificates, and bills of lading can be tracked through the various departments as the steps in the fulfillment process are carried out. When the goods are dispatched, all documents are ready to go with the shipment, and the file can be closed. The main obstacle to making AIDA workable as an electronic interface with the banks is the lack of standardization of trade documents. CIGY is working on the banks to use the CIGY in-house formats and hopes to get AIDA automated for external purposes in two to three years.

Electronic Funds Transfer Systems. Beyond traditional funds mobilization techniques, companies are enhancing the payables function by using the latest in electronic funds transfer techniques. Technological improvements and innovative bankers have joined to open avenues of electronic communication and funds movements that slash costs, streamline funds transfers, and increase security while producing reports and audit trails to aid reconciliation and bookkeeping. Throughout much of North America and Europe, and even in Latin America and Asia, companies are now able to benefit from two major innovations—terminal-based transaction initiation and automated clearinghouse debits and credits.

The Breakthroughs in U.K. Electronic Payments

National Westminster Bank PLC (NatWest) has rolled its guns into place for the battle over who will control, or at least hold the initiative, in the supply of EDI banking services in the United Kingdom. One of Britain's Big Four clearers, the bank has announced a trial in an EDI payments system between retailer ASDA Group PLC and candy manufacturer Rowntree PLC. The service will be run through a network operated by International Network Systems (INS), which holds 64 percent of the U.K. EDI network market. The bank plans to open the service commercially before mid-summer 1990.

Big Savings, Big Profits

What has held EDI back has been the inability to make payments that respond directly to electronic invoices. Currently, once an invoice has been delivered to a computer over a network such as INS, it has to be retrieved for payment to be made manually. This is because payments will typically involve more than one bank, because message formats have not yet been standardized, and because of difficulties in applying a security function.

The bank that can close that gap, and by so doing impose its own standards as generic, will get a head start in a service that, in a profitable industry, will be immensely profitable. Jerry Whitmarsh, EDI coordinator at NatWest, gives an example: "A bank in the United States was charging $0.06 a time for processing checks. It set up an EDI payment system with a particular company and started charging $2.50 per transaction. It could do this because the company itself was able to close down its accounts payable department and save $30 on each transaction. EDI solves business problems, and it is therefore possible to add much more value to banking services."

The NatWest/INS trial with ASDA and Rowntree will progress in two phases, says Brian Morgan, marketing manager for financial services at INS. The first will be the development of a range of new messages capable of conveying payment information, using TRADACOMS, a generic design methodology used on INS's TRADANET service for placing orders. It will be capable of carrying instructions in either the EDIFACT or UNGTDI "languages." The system, which INS plans to market as PAYNET, will be able to carry either language as long as the "envelope" (the part

---

There are two main benefits to using electronic initiation systems:

(1) **Time and cost savings.** Companies can eliminate vast amounts of internally generated paperwork, such as voucher requests, signatures, accounting verifications, and associated clerical costs, through automation of the transaction-initiation process. In the words of the treasurer of a Swiss chemicals firm, "Electronic initiation will speed everything up and reduce our clerical needs. We believe that our biggest cash

of the message that carries instructions for the network as opposed to the final recipient) conforms to the published standards for EDIFACT envelopes. "The network doesn't read the actual message," says Morgan.

The second phase will involve overlaying a security system to provide for payment authorization. "The bank has to be comfortable that the message has been generated by an appropriate person and has not been changed," says Morgan. The plan is for authorization to be made with a magnetic "smartcard" in conjunction with a numeric password, which is like getting money from an electronic teller with a card and a personal identification number. Information on payments due, which will be encrypted, will pass from a mainframe to a personal computer, which might sit, say, on the financial director's desk. Once the message has been authorized, it heads back to the mainframe and then on to the bank. Eventually, the bank hopes to run the authorization through the mainframe directly, although this is not yet technically possible.

Competing Systems

Richard Wainright-Lee, assistant head of electronic banking at Barclays Bank PLC and U.K. delegate to the European EDIFACT Banking Committee, while careful to express approval of progress in the EDI payments area, raises doubts about the NatWest initiative. At present, Barclays, another of the Big Four, is the other main contender in the fight to provide EDI services. Barclays opened its own gambit a year and a half ago with a trial payments system operating between Birmingham-headquartered Lucas Industries PLC, an automotive components and parts supplier and the biggest user of EDI in the United Kingdom, and West Midlands car maker Peugeot Talbot Motor Company, Ltd.

Wainright-Lee believes marketing an EDI payments system might be premature before the final development and publication of EDIFACT specifications, which are almost certain to be accepted as a standard in West European banking. In regard to legal liability, he is also skeptical about the use of an intermediary such as INS, as opposed to the direct company-bank-company route that Barclays has chosen. "There has been a lot of chat from INS in the press," he says. "But there are issues still to be resolved satisfactorily from the customer's point of view."

NatWest's Whitmarsh admits that INS has only about 1,400 users (out of a total

▶

management savings in the future will come from reduced manpower and man-hours by having an interactive terminal system."

(2) **Reduced errors.** To minimize confusion and costly mistakes, companies are looking to electronic initiation as a standardized method to initiate transactions—especially funds transfers—to intracompany and third-party accounts. "It will be a big help to us when we go to electronic initiation," the treasurer of a U.K. manufac-

U.K. network market of some 2,500, of whom 1,000 are with ISTEL Ltd. and 100 with IBM Corporation), of whom 800 would be NatWest clients. "But all a company needs to do is open a single NatWest account," he says. "Most companies big enough to be interested would already have accounts with all the clearers, even if they are primarily clients of only one or two."

Morgan of INS adds that the EDIFACT language to be used in the NatWest/INS system conforms to draft specifications already published and that the final version is "a long way off." On legal liability, INS will be responsible only for delivering messages unaltered, while the operation as a whole will be underwritten by NatWest. NatWest and INS hope to have their system taken on universally and lead the markets by fully publishing both the language and the security specifications finally adopted in the ASDA/Rowntree trial. NatWest and INS intend to throw the system open to other networks and to other banks.

Getting others to follow may not be so easy. "It is important to provide an open, even-handed, public service," says Wainright-Lee. "Some parties are readier than others, but many are not certain what they would do with a payments service. We will open a service when the public is ready."

Bloody Competition

NatWest obviously thinks the public is ready. When it starts its service in the summer of 1990, it will trigger a mean battle among banks to provide EDI services. According to Keith Blacker, EDI coordinator at Lucas and chairman-elect of the U.K. EDI association, EDI right now is a "small snowball" that is about to pick up speed. So far it has caught on primarily in the retail and automotive industries, sectors where companies handle large numbers of different goods sourced from many different suppliers. It is used to place orders and to send out invoices. In car making it allows assemblers to practice precise just-in-time inventory systems. In retailing it allows supermarkets and chain stores to respond rapidly, down to the day and even the hour, to what customers are buying, reordering items almost as soon as they are bought and quickly ditching stocks that aren't moving. Blacker is certain that this is not the end of it: "The retail and automotive industries have been natural starting places. But it will eventually affect a wide range of industries everywhere."

---

turer explained. "Then we can standardize the whole operation, rather than make transfers based on the telephone in some cases, telex in others, and so forth. It's hard to keep track of all our different payment routines." In addition, the service ensures that instructions are carried out exactly when firms want them to be, rather than when a bank officer gets around to it. This is especially critical when bank manual transfer and investment systems get backed up as clearing deadlines approach.

Funding Disbursement Accounts: ZBAs and TBAs

No matter which instruments are being used, companies should assess the benefits of integrating zero- and target-balance accounts into their cash disbursement systems. Relative newcomers to the cash management scene (at least outside the United States), zero- and target-balance accounts automatically keep corporate disbursement accounts at a zero or preset minimum (target) balance. With a zero-balance account (ZBA), funds are drawn from the interest-bearing master account and transferred to the disbursement account only as needed. In this way, idle funds earn maximum interest. Target-balance accounts (TBAs) are similar to ZBAs, except that a target balance (e.g., $10,000) must be left in the non-interest-bearing disbursement account. The arrangement is generally paid for by fee, or in the case of TBAs, the targeted balance is the bank's compensation.

These services are catching on globally, although some banks are still reluctant to offer the service. As one German banker admitted in a BI interview, "It is not time yet. The banking sector in Germany has a strong profit field in non-interest-bearing accounts. Why should we give it away? If there is pressure from the market, then possibly we will deliver the service."

But the evidence shows that persistent companies can obtain ZBAs even in Ger-

▶

But companies interviewed by BI also believe there are a number of potential drawbacks to electronic initiation:

(1) **Lack of accounting control**. Many firms are worried that electronic initiation will remove the audit trail they need to track their transactions. According to the finance director of a French consumer goods firm, "We are afraid to transfer funds directly over a terminal because we like very much to have a piece of paper. With our system, after the exchange takes place by phone, a ticket is filled out that goes to the accounting office. This back office feeds the data into the computers, which prepare all the reports, forecast, and issue telexes. There is a double system of back office—ours and accounting. We are manipulating billions of dollars. I prefer to have a system with a second control step."

(2) **Lack of free-form capabilities.** Corporate treasurers have found that electronic initiation is fine for standard, periodic transfers but less useful for one-time transactions. The Brussels-based regional treasurer of a U.S. electronics firm, for example, has experienced long delays on nonrepetitive payments made through an electronic banking system. "If it's a type of payment you always make, you build up a permanent kind of instruction that goes very quickly. If it's something you do very occasionally, what they call free-form, you have to go through a whole process, which takes longer than taking a piece of paper and filling in a transmission order. It's the security and all the different information the terminal asks you on the nonrepetitive payments."

many. For example, a German travel-service company worked out a combination concentration and ZBA with its major bank. The firm's finance director explained: "All the local units in Germany have two basic accounts: a collection account and a disbursement account. Each night, at midnight, all the balances in the units' collection accounts are automatically swept into a concentration account that the parent company maintains at the main branch of the bank that all the local units use. This account earns interest fairly close to market rates.

"In addition, each local unit is responsible for its own disbursements, issued through its individual ZBA. When a payment is presented against a local unit's ZBA, the funds to meet that payment are drawn from the head office's concentration account—just enough to fund the specific payment."

This system is successful because of a sophisticated on-line hookup among the bank's branches. The benefits to the company are threefold. First, the group as a whole receives high interest rates on the pooled funds by concentrating them into one account. Second, the local disbursement accounts can maintain zero balances until funds are actually needed. Third, making the local units responsible for their own disbursements—though the funds to meet them come from a parent account—permits the local managers a degree of autonomy while simultaneously providing the parent company with overall liquidity.

The treasurer of a U.S. parent company is also bothered by the difficulties caused by nonrepetitive payments. "The problem with the system in terms of doing transfers is that it is a standardized format. We're paying banks in different amounts and different currencies, and the transfer instructions may change. For the time being, we are not using this option via our terminal until it becomes more flexible so that we can input different receivers of funds and different transfer instructions."

(3) Lack of security safeguards. The treasurer of a French oil company expressed the feelings of many firms when he said, "We have a great fear of theft through these systems. Safety problems are a major concern." In fact, the spokesman has decided that he "will not sign an agreement with a bank for an electronic initiation system until the banks add a clause assuming responsibility for foul-ups and security breaks once the transmission has been properly entered by our company."

The Brussels regional office of a U.S. chemicals company was so dissatisfied with its bank system's security features that it developed its own security code. The firm's assistant treasurer described how it works: "It's an algorithm—a combination of codes arranged vertically and horizontally and of various random calculations, so that no one can accidentally unscramble it. Our bank has installed calculators next to the receiving units specifically designed to decode our algorithm."

However, there seems to be a growing feeling among other companies that the security safeguards built into a terminal transfer are comparable to traditional test-key features of a tested-telex transfer and callback on the telephone. As the treasurer

Slicing Disbursement Costs Through Direct Deposits

One of the ways companies are saving on operations costs is by directing high-volume, low-value payments through a direct-deposit system. Such systems—available in many countries—are especially attractive for payrolls, phone bills, tax payments, and other recurring payments.

For instance, companies in the United Kingdom make direct deposits to employees and government authorities by submitting computer tapes to their banks two days before the value date so that the necessary processing can be carried out. On the date specified, same-day settlement is effected. The direct-depositing system is efficient and far less expensive than issuing checks. According to the firms interviewed by BI, banks charge 20–30 pence for each check; direct deposits cost only a few pence.

A spokesman for a major French firm explained how his company employs the French version of direct deposit: "We make an annual forecast by category and due date for the major payments—income tax, monthly sales tax payments, monthly payroll, and regular payments to suppliers. Then we use direct depositing, where possible. The service is much quicker, it enables us to forecast our cash more accurately, and it cuts red tape." Payment instructions are registered on a computer tape, which is sent to the banks four or five days before the end of the month.

Direct depositing is also readily available in Mexico, where companies simply advise their banks each pay period of the amount to be deposited in employees' accounts. In Brazil, banks accept a list of intended payments from corporate clients (known as *bordereaux*) and then transfer funds to the payee. The payment listing is not limited to payroll transfers into that country and can be used for all types of disbursements. The transfers are usually made via magnetic tape, which is delivered by courier or mail rather than transmitted from computer to computer.

---

of a Dutch capital goods manufacturer put it, "Most of the terminal systems now include a password and a set of special codes at different steps in the transaction order, so it's the same as what you have on a tested-telex transfer. There is always the possibility that the terminal codes can fall into the hands of a nonauthorized employee, but that can happen with telexes, too."

(4) **Lack of international capabilities.** Some companies complain that bank initiation systems often cannot handle cross-border transfers outside the customer's home country. For example, the finance director of a Swedish natural resources firm stated, "Today, we can make transfers domestically, and in the near future we can initiate payments from Sweden to New York or whatever. But no one has offered us the possibility of transferring funds from Australia to South Africa, which would be initiated from our terminal in Sweden."

(5) **Lack of compatibility among bank systems.** As in the case of automated balance reporting, companies want their banks to develop a standardized electronic initiation system to make the various services compatible. As the treasurer of the U.K.

subsidiary of a U.S. auto manufacturer said, "If I were to start initiating transactions by terminal for my investments and borrowings, I would need to add compatible equipment between us and 175 U.K. banks. Although we only use four operating banks, I invest with more than 171 other banks."

Putting It All Together: One Company's Payables Management System

Although cash collection and concentration receives the lion's share of corporate attention, some savvy cash managers have also elevated disbursement management to a fine art, thereby minimizing the cost of the payables process and maximizing disbursement float. An instructive example of aggressive payables management is provided by Company B, the French subsidiary of a large U.S. agricultural equipment manufacturer. Because the firm operates in an industry that has been particularly hard hit by the economic downturn of the last few years, its treasurer must resort to every disbursement trick in the book to boost the company's sagging bottom line. Thus, Company B's highly developed payables strategy can serve as a model for other firms trying to upgrade their disbursement management.

The centerpiece of Company B's disbursement management is an **automated and centralized payables system.** The firm's computer generates checks, drafts, and bank transfer orders for domestic operating units and monitors all payment terms and instruments. As the treasurer explained, "All the suppliers are coded in the computer. Their outstanding invoices with the due date and the amount are recorded when orders are placed. The computer calculates how much is falling due every day and the payment methods to be used." When a payment is made, the computer automatically eliminates the invoice from the queue. In addition, Company B's computerized payables program produces a series of reports that permit the treasury staff to monitor both individual outstanding disbursements and total CDOs (the flip side of DSOs), which are currently about sixty days.

The automated system also enables Company B's treasurer to match the firm's cash outflows and inflows, thus optimizing borrowing and investment tactics. Without the computer, this would be a complicated procedure, since the company's production cycle causes extreme fluctuations in revenue during certain times of the month. The spokesman clarified the situation: "I have more supplier payments falling due on the tenth and the fifteenth. So I try to match up discounting receivables with the amount of disbursements that I know I have. I keep operations so that they have invoices on one side of the desk and checks on the other. You put the checks in when you know that you have the invoices covered. This is why we went from making disbursements at the plant level to making them by our centralized finance people: more finance control."

Another key element in Company B's payables strategy is the **negotiation of payment terms with suppliers.** According to the spokesman, these negotiations require a delicate touch in France. "You walk a tightrope with suppliers in terms of getting the maximum terms out of them, while they look at cash flows and try to grant as short a credit as possible. You are both working toward different objectives. When business is slow, the suppliers may have to bend a little bit more, because competitive conditions make it a buyer's market. Also, when there are plenty of substitutes for a product and you can easily shift from one supplier to another, the supplier is much more vulnerable."

The treasurer has an easier time, naturally, negotiating with suppliers of products for which he can tap a multitude of sources (e.g., screws). But for more specialized items, such as radiators that have to be made to a specific design, he is locked in to one supplier and has little room to maneuver.

But Company B often **delays payment** beyond the formal credit period to obtain a cheap source of short-term credit. "We stretch and delay payment to suppliers as much as we can within the latitude of a relationship while still meeting our obligations," the treasurer candidly admitted. He conducts periodic reviews through the automated payables system to determine how successful the firm is in this area. However, he acknowledges that the tactic can be risky and should be used cautiously. "As a treasurer, I don't think of stretching payment terms in isolation; it is part of a relationship. In advising our materials management group, I have to stress the maximization of stretching payments in the context of what is possible, product by product."

For example, the treasurer learned by accident that he could delay the payments of one plant longer than he had thought. A few years ago, when business conditions were at a nadir in the farm industry, the plant survived only by stretching payments for two to three weeks on 40 percent of its $10 million in monthly disbursements. After the crisis passed, Company B continued to lag the plant's payments, although to a lesser extent. Reasoned the spokesman, "From $4 million, they have continued to lag a couple of million. Obviously, a couple of million dollars a year at today's interest rates could come out to a quarter million on interest savings annually. And this is just from learning that we had a little more leeway to lag without disrupting their relationships with suppliers."

On the other hand, Company B occasionally takes advantage of some **suppliers' discounts** for paying early. "We have operations that are making a profit and can afford to take attractive discounts," the treasurer disclosed. "They are arbitraging, so to speak, by borrowing from their bank and getting the greater discounts from their supplier. But we also have operations that are still very strained and are sometimes forced to incur a penalty for late payment." The penalty fees are generally higher than bank borrowing costs. The finance staff calculates the various costs for each situation

In an effort to maximize its disbursement float, Company B carefully **chooses the right payables instruments.** The treasurer can choose the payment method because of his firm's strong market position: "We are in the driver's seat because our volumes are so big. A significant fraction of our suppliers are wedded to our operation; we may be 75 to 80 percent of their sales." He tries to avoid drafts because he has more flexibility to delay payments with a telex or check. "If a draft matures on a certain date and you don't pay it, the company has legal recourse to protest it, and if it has discounted that draft with its bank, the bank, similarly, has a legal right to protest," the treasurer explained. "But if I don't send the check on time, there is a whole array of familiar excuses: 'Our computer shut down last night,' 'The mail is late,' 'If you haven't received it in a week, I'll send you another one,' and so on." In sum, if a company pays with something other than a draft, "the supplier doesn't have the control."

The treasurer sometimes decides to forego these advantages even when he is in a strong bargaining position, because many small and medium-sized companies cannot finance themselves without drafts. As he put it, "The smaller suppliers need the drafts, because that is how they finance their business—and we have to work with them hand in hand. If we've provided 80 percent of their business in a good relationship for many, many years, they have no choice but to accept checks; otherwise, they couldn't survive. But we have to support them and vice versa."

6

Managing Bank Balances and Relations

Of all the functional areas of cash management, none offers greater potential savings than bank management. For one thing, banking costs constitute a heavy—and highly visible—financial burden for all companies. For another, local managers are all too often unfamiliar with the latest techniques and services that can be used to reduce these costs.

The experience of a leading U.S. computer manufacturer illustrates the dramatic benefits that can be attained through improved management of banking activities. According to the firm's Geneva-based regional treasurer, the company has for several years conducted in-house reviews of each of its European subsidiaries. Since these audits began, the firm has been able to save an average of $300,000 per year for each subsidiary in banking relations alone—more than 50 percent of the total savings from the studies. "It's the most critical area," the spokesman stated. "With the first audit you always get very big savings."

The company has found that the biggest savings come from three main areas:

· "Number one is the way the bank is treating your account—the value-dating conditions," the treasurer commented. "For instance, in the United Kingdom it's common to make different charges for in-town and out-of-town checks; it can be up to three days for out-of-town checks. We can negotiate that to one-day value—or even same-day, depending on the leverage we have with the bank."
· Next is the type of commission structure applied to the company's banking business. "If, for example, a bank is charging you commissions on an item-by-item basis, while the general condition is a monthly fee in that country, then you negotiate a monthly fee."
· Foreign exchange charges are the third major area of savings. "It depends on the country. For example, in Spain, the Spanish banks apply a commission to foreign exchange transactions. You can negotiate yourself out of that one if you're clever enough—or opportunistic. We're both."

To help companies achieve similar results, this chapter will analyze every aspect of banking relations, from internal organization and monitoring systems to effective balance management and bank-performance evaluation. Most importantly, it will show how companies can drastically reduce their banking costs by applying advanced techniques and systems, such as cash pooling and concentration accounts, and negotiating aggressively for lower charges and improved services.

Auditing Banking Relations

To reap the benefits of improved bank account and relationship management, companies must first conduct a review of their complete banking relations. Firms should gather information from parent, regional, and subsidiary managers to construct a chart listing the name and location of all foreign and local banks used by the corporation and the services each institution provides. The box on p. 244 shows the overview of bank relations put together by the in-house consulting team of a U.S. electronics manufacturer during an audit of its German subsidiary.

This exercise is important for two reasons. First, it familiarizes audit teams with the company's full range of bank relations and facilities and provides the foundation for further, more detailed research. Second, it helps companies take a holistic approach to banking services by identifying redundant or marginal accounts and by pinpointing opportunities to negotiate better terms and conditions with banks on a worldwide basis.

Once this background data has been collected, firms should investigate the following critical components of bank relationship management:

- **Organization, objectives, and policies.** Companies should interview local managers to learn how the function is organized and which staff members are responsible for monitoring and forecasting bank balances, tracking banking costs and evaluating services, and investing and borrowing short-term funds. Equally important, firms should probe attitudes toward banking relations in general. If, for example, local managers are primarily concerned with credit requirements, they may be overlooking the cost and quality of transaction services and not taking advantage of such specialized cash management schemes as ZBAs and concentration accounts. Companies should also review corporate banking policies to make sure that subsidiaries are adhering to them.
- **Bank balance management.** Companies should look at cash position sheets, bank statements, and detailed and summary balance information for each account and bank. The review team should find out how frequently and by what method the information is obtained. Most critically, it must determine if the cash manager has access to data not only on ledgers but also on value-dated and available balances as well as transfers and deposits. Bank balance reports and internal cash-position and forecasting reports must be carefully compared to analyze the cash manager's handling of the data and to "determine the integration of bank account statements with internal cash reporting and control procedures," as one consultant put it. Firms can use these reports on a daily basis to chart the credit and debit positions

Bank Relationship Overview

	Banking Services	Currency
U.S. Banks		
Chase Manhattan Frankfurt	US$ forward transactions	US$/Dm
	Disbursements to Japan, Singapore, and Hong Kong	
Chase London	Transfers Europe/United States	US$
	US$ hold account	
Citibank Frankfurt	US$ forward transactions	US$
Bank of America Stuttgart	US$ forward transactions	US$/Dm
	Dm call account	
	Dm collections over Dm500,000	
German Banks		
Commerzbank Stuttgart	Dm check collections	US$/Dm
	Dm wire collections	
	US$ collections by telex	
	US$ wire collections	
	US$ transfers to Vienna office	
	Dm money transfers to customers	
	Dm investments	
	Overdrafts	
Volksbank BBN	Payroll account	Dm
	Account for stock program	
	Account for standing orders	
	Account for manual wires	
	Account for cash withdrawals	
Kreissparkasse Friedberg	Account for collections	Dm
	Account for cash withdrawals	
	Account for standing orders	
	Account for Dm check disbursements	
Raiffeisenbank	Account for standing orders	Dm
Albtal Waldbronn	Hold accounts	Dm
Dresdner Bank Stuttgart	Account for DIB funds	Dm
Postcheckamt Frankfurt	Customer nonpayment account	Dm

in each bank account over, say, a four-week period. The results will show if the unit is holding idle balances or maintaining simultaneous debit and credit accounts.

· **Banking costs and services.** The audit team should examine account analyses provided by banks in some countries or internal reports that track the volume of business given each institution and the direct (e.g., fees) and indirect (e.g., value dating) costs of individual services. This information will enable firms to evaluate overall bank performance and variations in cost and service among the banks. Companies should also determine whether subsidiaries are assessing the quality and cost of banking services on a regular—at least annual—basis.

With this information, a firm can devise strategies to reduce expenses and optimize services by reducing—or in some cases adding—banking relations, negotiating more aggressively or switching to more cost-effective cash management facilities.

Consider Country Nuances

Naturally, the efficiency of local banking systems and the severity of particular banking problems vary by country. This is an important consideration for companies to bear in mind when pinpointing areas for improvement in individual subsidiaries. For example, the table below lists the most common banking obstacles in nine Latin American nations. Based on a survey of 101 companies with operations in the region, the statistics reveal that lengthy check-clearing times are especially common in Mexico and Peru, while Brazil is by far the worst country for excessive compensating balances. Venezuela has the dubious distinction of being the country that makes the most balance-reporting errors.

The same sharp variations exist in other regions. In the Far East, Japan, Hong Kong, and Singapore are all considered paragons of banking efficiency. On the other hand, Indonesia, Korea, and the Philippines offer consistently dismal service. Even in Europe, the quality of banking services can fluctuate widely, as can be seen in the following ratings made in a BI survey of 302 MNCs. Countries are broken down by the percentage of firms that placed them in each category:

	Excellent	Good	Fair	Poor
Belgium	12.0	46.4	33.1	8.4
France	5.3	32.5	44.5	17.7
Germany	18.4	50.0	26.2	5.3
Italy	5.8	20.5	49.4	24.4
Netherlands	10.6	51.2	33.7	4.4
Spain	0.8	15.0	39.2	45.0
Sweden	11.5	46.0	34.5	8.0
Switzerland	17.6	59.2	18.3	4.9
United Kingdom	17.8	59.2	21.6	1.4

Identifying Bank Problems

During the course of the review, companies should keep their eyes open for the following snags and snafus in their bank relations:

· **Too many relations.** In the days before cash management leaped to the fore of corporate consciousness, companies freely added new bank relationships to ensure credit availability and competitive investment and deposit rates. Many companies felt a loyalty to their banks that went beyond cash management concerns, and in many countries the banks still call the shots for their corporate customers. Said the director of a Brazilian subsidiary of a European pharmaceuticals manufacturer: "Our finance people said we should not work with more than five banks, because it involves too much time and money. But they found out you just can't do that here. I guess we have fifty banks. And we are serving the banks, rather than the other way around."

Bank Operations Problems in Latin America (Percent of Respondents)

	Most Troublesome	Somewhat Troublesome	Not Troublesome	Most Troublesome	Somewhat Troublesome	Not Troublesome
	Delays in Posting			**Difficulty in Getting Balance**		
Argentina	13.0	34.8	52.2	8.3	41.7	50.0
Brazil	21.6	41.2	37.3	6.3	29.2	64.6
Chile	15.4	23.1	61.5	0.0	16.7	83.3
Colombia	30.0	25.0	45.0	0.0	52.6	47.4
Ecuador	25.0	0.0	75.0	0.0	9.1	90.9
Mexico	11.8	32.4	55.9	3.1	31.3	65.6
Panama	12.5	12.5	75.0	0.0	0.0	100.0
Peru	22.2	44.4	33.3	6.3	37.5	56.3
Venezuela	32.0	20.0	48.0	18.2	27.3	54.5
Regionwide	**20.6**	**30.4**	**49.0**	**5.8**	**30.9**	**63.4**
	Mishandling of Wire Transfers			**Errors in Balances**		
Argentina	20.8	45.8	33.3	5.0	25.0	70.0
Brazil	10.6	23.4	66.0	0.0	18.8	81.3
Chile	7.7	23.1	69.2	0.0	18.2	81.8
Colombia	15.8	31.6	52.6	0.0	33.3	66.7
Ecuador	9.1	18.2	72.7	0.0	18.2	81.8
Mexico	27.3	27.3	45.5	0.0	29.4	70.6
Panama	0.0	14.3	85.7	0.0	0.0	100.0
Peru	6.3	25.0	68.8	6.3	37.5	56.3
Venezuela	12.5	45.8	50.0	10.0	40.0	50.0
Regionwide	**14.4**	**29.9**	**55.7**	**2.2**	**25.9**	**71.9**
	Excessive Compensating Balances			**Excessive Float Times**		
Argentina	0.0	15.8	84.2	20.8	29.2	50.0
Brazil	34.0	31.9	34.0	14.0	54.0	32.0
Chile	0.0	0.0	100.0	15.4	15.4	69.2
Colombia	22.2	16.7	61.1	31.6	10.5	57.9
Ecuador	9.1	9.1	81.8	9.1	18.2	72.7
Mexico	29.7	18.9	51.4	14.7	50.0	35.3
Panama	0.0	0.0	100.0	14.3	14.3	71.4
Peru	0.0	26.7	73.3	23.5	58.8	17.6
Venezuela	0.0	20.0	80.0	26.1	34.8	39.1
Regionwide	**17.3**	**20.0**	**62.7**	**18.7**	**38.4**	**42.9**

Cutting the number of banks is one of the best ways to improve cash flows and reduce costs. By using a manageable number of banks, firms avoid excess-cash build-ups and simplify administrative control and balance reporting. Determining the ideal number of banking relations is discussed on p. 287.

· **High banking costs.** Banking fees, compensating balances, and value-dating practices represent a major—and rising—cost for companies around the world. For example, in many Asian and Latin American nations local banks commonly demand compensating balances of 25–30 percent for loans and have not established firm fee schedules for corporate services. In Europe, high funds-transfer fees can cost firms dearly. Negotiating better terms from banks is reviewed on p. 281.

- **Poor reporting.** In many countries, cash managers face enormous barriers to obtaining timely and accurate data on which to base their account management. For example, the treasurer of one of Australia's largest firms complained, "It happens with some frequency that we can't find out what our balances are. The computer breaks down—at least that's the banks' regular excuse. So, for our money market investments we have to estimate what the balances might have been." The road to better reporting is explored on p. 259.
- **Numerous errors.** In developing countries, mishandled transfers and outright errors in account information are rampant. Remarked a Mexican cash manager who spends much of his time tracking down mishandled wire transfers, Mexican banks "just hold on to funds; they don't send us the slips that we need to check up on them. Sometimes they just deposit the money in the wrong account by mistake." And according to a spokesman for the local office of a major U.S. exporter, Korea "is probably the worst in Asia for just losing your money. You can't locate funds transfers; it happens all the time."
- **Limited cash management services.** Because many banks continue to resist cash management, special services such as electronic balance reporting, concentration accounts, and ZBAs are frequently unavailable to local cash managers. In such cases, companies must approach their banks with ideas rather than wait to be approached. As one treasurer put it, "You have to take your creativity to the banks and say, 'How about it? Can you do it?' With the banks here, it depends on who you are and what you say." Obtaining better cash management services is discussed on p. 262.
- **Idle balances.** A combination of poor reporting and forecasting and inadequate internal skills leads many companies to maintain idle balances that earn little or no interest. To make matters worse, firms frequently maintain simultaneous debit and credit balances, resulting in increased interest costs. Pointers on improving balance management appear on p. 256.
- **Excessive clearing delays.** Delays on obtaining value on customer checks and other transfers can be due either to bad bank communications and an inefficient national clearing system—as in the ploddingly slow environment of Italy—or to banks' efforts to hang on to an inordinate amount of float. Either way, the result is the same: Companies can't earn interest or use customer receipts to invest and may even have to borrow while waiting for funds to clear.

Organizing for Banking Relations

Without effective coordination and clear banking policies, firms cannot hope to achieve the quantitative and qualitative benefits of efficient bank account and relationship management. But all too often companies take a fragmented approach to banking relations, dividing the function between headquarters and local staff and even among different departments at the parent and subsidiary levels.

To avoid the administrative complexities and unnecessary costs of mismanaged bank relations, the following questions should be answered:

(1) What are your objectives in managing bank relations?

(2) Who is responsible for banking relations at the parent, regional, and subsidiary levels?

(3) What role does the parent or regional headquarters play in monitoring or managing local bank relations?

(4) How do you coordinate the banking needs of various departments within your company (e.g., treasury, export sales, etc.)?

(5) Who has the authority to establish new relations or sever old ones?

(6) Have firm guidelines or policies—on such matters as the number of banking relations, the use of foreign vs. local banks, and bank selection and evaluation criteria—been set? What are they?

(7) What steps have you taken to minimize bank risk?

Leaving It to the Locals

BI research indicates that most companies keep a tight rein on banking relations in their home countries but give primary responsibility for the function internationally to local subsidiary management. According to a BI survey, just 14.4 percent of parent and regional headquarters play an active role in the day-to-day management of their subsidiaries' banking relations, and a surprisingly high 16.3 percent have no involvement at all. The treasurer of a large U.S. food producer spoke for many companies when he said, "Here at headquarters, control of our banks is centralized. It's when you look overseas that we delegate a great deal. We set general policies, but the managers in each country actually pick and choose to fulfill their needs."

The explanation for this trend is simple. In the opinion of many corporate treasurers, local staffs are closest to their banking markets and therefore are best equipped to make decisions. As the spokesman for one U.S. multinational candidly admitted in a BI interview, "If we started telling people in Amsterdam or Geneva which banks they can and cannot use, we'd have a hell of a revolt on our hands. They believe, and I tend to agree, that they're the most qualified to evaluate who is the best in their region."

But those firms that take a close look at their subsidiaries' management of bank relations often find that decentralization has its drawbacks. This is especially true where a parent has multiple operations in the same country. For example, a private consulting firm reviewed the cash management activities of a highly decentralized European firm. In one country, the company had a manufacturing plant, a sales unit, and several branches—each with its own banking relations, investment and borrowing activities, and current accounts. Because of the lack of coordination among the various entities, the company was losing tens of thousands of dollars a year in needless borrowings, low rates on investments, excessive banking charges, and underutilized internal funds.

A bank consultant made a similar discovery when he audited the banking relations of a major U.S. electronics conglomerate. "I've seen the case in France where a firm was operating with eight large, independent, separate subsidiaries—not one really knowing of the others' existence. They were in completely different business lines.

Finally, during a treasury study for the group, they looked at banking relations and found that having eight separate accounts at the same bank was not an optimum strategy."

To avoid such pitfalls, a well-known international computer manufacturer has developed an effective organizational structure for banking relations that attains the benefits of centralization without stripping local managers of all responsibility. For its European operations, the firm has subsidiary cash managers report to a regional banking manager located in Geneva. The banking manager, in turn, reports to a regional treasurer who reviews all major decisions with the corporate treasury staff.

According to the firm's Geneva-based European treasurer, "We have a very decentralized organization. The local cash manager is responsible for all of the treasury activities pertaining to his country. But before anything is done concerning a banking relation, it has to go through us. Local managers have control of day-to-day operations, but we oversee the overall game plan."

The firm exercises central control through a model internal audit process. "We go through a review of each site twice a year—a sort of performance evaluation. We have a report where we enumerate our relationships and evaluate them. It shows all the different banks and all the lines and services available. It outlines the charges, performance, everything." In addition to the semiannual banking relations review, the firm has its trained treasury analysts personally visit local operations every five years. "We look at conditions we get from local banks and local transfer methods and whatever, and we then come out with a very clear idea as to what type of services we are getting and what we should be getting. We then modify our banking relationships." Through these audits, headquarters has a detailed map of banking activity and can identify and correct any inefficiencies or inadequacies.

Setting Bank Relations Policies

One sure way for companies to improve their control over banking relations is to set clear policy guidelines for all their operations. As the treasurer of a major U.S. consumer goods firm advised, "If you just let your treasurers go off on their own way, your banking business can grow out of control and become uncoordinated. It's helpful to sit down with your local people, and I think they appreciate policies as much as you do. The people we've dealt with appreciate knowing the game plan; they may not agree with it, but at least they know what it is. Our people feel confused when they're sitting overseas and don't know what the policy is."

Well-defined banking policies are especially critical for newly acquired operations. According to a U.S. treasury manager, "We bought a company about a year ago. It was out of the blue; all of a sudden their people walked in one day and found they were working for us. They were in a quandary, wanted some direction, and they asked us, 'What are your policies?' We'd have felt pretty stupid if all we could say was, 'They're in our head.' But since we had these policies well written and worked out, they knew right from the outset what they could and couldn't do."

Although specific policies will vary considerably from one company to the next, all firms should consider laying down guidelines in the following areas:

- **Which banks to use.** Local managers often feel they are the best qualified to select banks, but they usually lack the overall perspective of headquarters management. As the treasurer of a major Canadian resources firm explained, "My local people might get what looks like a good deal from one of their relationships, but we might be working on some cash management project where that bank just doesn't fit."

At the very least, the corporate treasury staff should have a strong say in picking the international banks subsidiaries use. In addition, firms should consider limiting the power of local managers. "They can't open a new bank account, open or increase a line of credit, negotiate a term loan, points or anything like that, without approval," a U.S. treasurer asserted. "Any major change must be okayed by headquarters."

- **How many banks to use.** Although the optimum number of banks in any given country varies with each subsidiary's cash management and financing needs, firms should strive to keep relations from getting out of hand. One U.S. treasurer insists that "our people limit their business to just a few banks, and we have input on what those are going to be. They can't use too many banks, and we make that clear."

The finance director of a U.K. consumer products company takes a similar tack during annual reviews of his subsidiaries' relations. "We look at the volume of activity, the charges, and we look for opportunities to consolidate. The locals understand that if they can't justify an additional relationship for a sound business reason—a service, or credit, or trade financing—then there's no reason for the relationship."

- **Issuing guarantees or comfort letters.** Parent companies must also have control over the issue of bank-directed comfort letters. As the treasurer of a U.S. paper products firm advises, "People just can't go out giving guarantees here and there. We need control to know who's obligating our company."

While the parent may agree to let the subsidiary issue letters, the treasurer explains, the decision must conform to certain loan covenants. "You have to list all U.S. and foreign loan guarantees. It somewhat limits your borrowing here if your balance sheet somewhere else is tainted by loan guarantees."

The Bank Risk Specter

Beyond a doubt, the policy area of greatest concern to MNCs today is bank risk. Fears about the stability of the international banking system have dramatically increased over the past few years. The troubles of Continental Illinois National Bank & Trust and the savings and loan industry in the United States and of Schroder, Munchmeyer, Hengst & Co. in Germany, along with the constant press coverage of the debt crisis, have forced many firms to rethink their guidelines for minimizing bank risk.

To protect themselves against possible bank failures, many companies are now setting up sophisticated credit-risk rating and control systems. For example, a U.S. auto maker's U.K.-based regional headquarters regularly assesses the credit risks of

How One Rating Agency Approaches Bank Risk

The managing director for an international bank-risk-analysis firm points out that U.S. and European clients have a different approach to the issue: The former are primarily concerned with a bank's solvency, while the latter are more interested in the probability of official support in the event of bank difficulty. As a result, the firm supplies both a bank credit rating (A-through-E designation) and a "legal rating" (on a scale of 1 to 5), which represents the firm's judgment of the extent of official government commitment to the bank.

There are very few banks rated 1, since this grade means there is a legal commitment from a government to stand behind the bank's depositors. Even though the major French banks are state owned, for example, they do not necessarily qualify for a 1. They are generally given a 2 rating, as are the U.K. clearing banks. This signifies that the banks are "virtually certain to be given full support."

To arrive at the legal rating, the director explained, "we look to see how the authorities have handled bank crises in the past. Virtually every country has had these. Second, we visit the central bank and ask about their policy. And finally, we evaluate relevant laws, traditions, and practices in the country."

Other reports offered by the agency include the following:

· **Country risk assessment of the bank's foreign branches.** The need for this report arose specifically from the case of blocked dollar deposits in the Philippines.

---

its banks by examining balance sheet ratios and using such outside agencies as IBCA and Standard & Poor's. Using this analysis, the firm sets limits on the amount of funds it deposits with its bank on a worldwide basis.

According to the firm's treasurer, "A bank sets limits on its exposure to a corporation like ours based on credit analysis. We similarly set limits on the banks we deal with for investments. We say there is a reasonable credit risk with anybody. We evaluate each bank we deal with according to certain standard ratios, and we will not invest beyond a certain limit, say x percent of net worth or whatever." The company is currently trying to integrate its system with the corporatewide data base "because the banks we deal with are multinationals as well. If our limit is $100 million worldwide with one bank and I invest $50 million, I need to know where in the world anyone else is investing with that bank so that we don't run the risk as a corporation of going beyond our limit. What I'd like is to have the limit constantly updated worldwide in real time."

When developing bank risk policies, firms should keep these points in mind:

· **Consider using outside credit ratings.** To ensure security and to exploit market inefficiencies in yields, companies should consult bank rating agencies for investment of their excess cash. While admitting a bias, one rating-agency official does

- **Comparative banking statistics.** This report compares various financial ratios among nearly 400 banks. Profitability figures are adjusted for Third World banks, since hyperinflation makes it easier for these institutions to show high rates of return.
- **Special reports.** These have included reports on the hidden reserves of Japanese banks and the banking implications of the U.K. budget and tax changes.

In the case of Latin American debt, the firm takes a very cautious approach. According to the spokesman, "We view every bank with loans to countries that have rescheduled debt, or need to do so, as having potential problem loans. We have lowered ratings for banks having high levels of loans in the region because of that risk. We take tremendous account of provisioning policy; good profitability that results from inadequate provisions against future losses is a bad sign."

In rating the twenty Third World banks it monitors, the agency makes a special qualification. "They are the same as any other banks in a statistical sense, but when one is involved in rescheduling problems with its government, we put a star beside it in the rating. This implies that the country might be unable to meet its foreign currency commitments even though the bank might be sound on a balance sheet basis."

Because of the differences in disclosure and accounting practices outside countries like the United States and Canada, the firm relies on unpublished information to compile its ratings. But there have been surprises. For instance, the recent collapse of one German bank sent shock waves through the agency. "On more than one visit," said the director, "management said things that we later found to be wrong."

---

not believe that companies should go to the trouble of inventing their own rating systems: "I honestly don't believe it's worth a company's time to develop its own system of evaluating bank risks. A bank's disclosure is generally quite bad. A corporate treasurer simply can't analyze bank risks by sitting in his office in Houston."

According to another experienced risk analyst, "You can't judge a bank by the numbers. There are about three countries in the world where there is enough published information: the United States, the United Kingdom, and Canada. But when you get to continental European banks and Japanese banks, published information tends to be very incomplete and could even be misleading if one is not a well-trained accountant familiar with the country's reporting requirements."

Moreover, rating banks is also time-consuming. An accurate rating involves gaining a detailed understanding of banks by visiting bank CFOs, accountants, internal auditors, and the heads of major departments, such as the international division.

The argument for using outside rating services is, therefore, based on economies of scale. The rating agency cited above, for example, employs seven full-time bank analysts and has a research budget of $500,000 a year. Another major rater of banks has a full-time staff of thirty analysts.

- **Develop internal expertise.** Despite the arguments in favor of using outside agencies, companies themselves must have the expertise to use the ratings and be able to analyze bank risks themselves. "If I were the treasurer of an MNC," a private bank rater commented, "I wouldn't want to be in the position where I say I relied on the analysis of somebody else and the bank ran into difficulties."
- **Establish a cutoff risk point.** Corporate depositors receive a higher return on deposits from a bank with a low credit standing than from one with a high standing. The managing director of an international bank rating agency believes that corporate treasurers should simply ask themselves whether they are prepared to take the risk or not. "Multinational companies should place a high premium on not losing money," argued the bank analyst. "They should not deal with a bank below a certain rating."

Whether a corporation uses bank ratings from outside services or develops them internally, it must superimpose its own risk preferences on the rating scale. The first step is to choose a cutoff point based on management's risk preference. For instance, one U.S. company deals only with banks rated A, B, or C on a major rating firm's A-through-E scale. Another U.S. firm will not invest with banks rated lower than B by a U.K.-based bank analysis firm.

- **Take bank ratings one step further.** A company may profit from a quantitative exposure-limiting guideline. For example, one firm weights banks according to net worth by taking 5 percent of A-rated banks, 4 percent of A/B-rated banks, and so on down to 1 percent of C-rated banks. The investment ceiling, then, is a factor of both the bank's rating and the relative size of its net worth. According to the company's cash manager, "With two different banks having the same net worth, if one was A-rated and one was C-rated, we'd have a higher limit with the A-rated bank."
- **Go beyond quantitative factors.** Sometimes a manager's subjective judgment should be considered when setting exposure guidelines. The European treasurer of a U.S. MNC explained the factors he takes into account: "To start with, it's statistical. But then we have to make some choices, because we cannot just take the top banks in the areas where we have business. We have some sentimental choices, you might say."
- **Don't be fooled by higher yields.** It is critical that firms determine whether higher yields reflect higher risk. As the treasurer for a U.S. consumer goods firm points out, "Our people from time to time sit on a great deal of cash, and they want the highest rate possible. A bank may offer the best terms, but who knows how long before they collapse? For that reason we set limits on where funds can be placed, and the amount that can be placed with any one bank."

To give subsidiaries flexibility, limits can be swapped. Managers seeing an opportunity at the local level often cannot react because of corporate guidelines. A financial manager for a major U.S. MNC recommends that companies allow units to exchange limits as a matter of policy. "There are times when we bump up against the limits because other people want to use a bank more than we do," he said. "Then it's a matter of negotiation. New York says, 'You've got $20 million that you're not using with Bankers Trust; can we use it?' It's done informally and formalized later on."

· **Be aware of repudiation risks.** It is important to know not just the credit risk of the bank but the political or sovereign risk of the country where the bank is domiciled. For instance, a Philippine division of a major U.S. bank froze its inter-bank deposits following the government takeover of foreign exchange. Many of the bank's depositors complained, and one sued. The episode made it clear that depositors must consider sovereign risk as well as credit risk.

Companies should also consider the deposit guarantees in effect. The financial officer of one German MNC reported that, although his firm does not carry large liquidity, it prefers German banks for cash investments because deposits are guaranteed for up to 30 percent of the bank's equity.

Offshore markets such as the Cayman Islands are really "nondomestic" areas, where the risk of invasion may be the biggest consideration. However, for an offshore money center like Manila or Panama, depositors must be aware of the economic performance of the country as well as the political risk.

Case Example: One Firm's Bank Risk Policies

One large Swiss MNC has been averaging Sfr4–5 billion in surplus funds available for investment during the past two years, generating a great deal of income. With so much cash to invest—and so much exposure—the company needed to develop a policy on evaluating acceptable bank risk. According to the firm's senior vice president of finance, "We started the system ten years ago, because we had a lot of cash to invest in various banks."

The firm's policy is to diversify deposits by country. Most of the company's liquidity is in Swiss francs, invested in Swiss banks, but the firm also invests in the United Kingdom, the United States, and Germany. "We do that to a certain extent to diversify our risk," according to the financial executive. "In these countries, country risk is minimal as far as our investments are concerned."

Because liquidity is centralized, all investment decisions are made at corporate headquarters in Switzerland. "Our subsidiaries usually borrow funds from banks to cover their working capital, so they have no liquidity to invest and no judgment to make on that issue. Because all liquidity, wherever it's possible—there are a few exceptions—is centralized."

The firm does not use rating agencies to evaluate individual banks. As the vice president said, "We make our own judgment. We have strong ties with the banks. We know the management of the banks, just as they know us quite well."

Bank ratings are done in-house once a year. Explained the finance vice president, "You look at the balance sheets of fifty banks. You don't need a big staff, just one person and a free morning. We also analyze the quarterly reports and look for large divergences from the annual reports."

The company's finance staff evaluates selected banks using three ratios: liquidity, capitalization, and return on assets. Each ratio is measured against an established norm. The three ratios' percentages are then converted into coefficients and multiplied to yield a general coefficient for each bank. If the general coefficient falls below an internally established level, the bank will be removed from the company list or the level of investment will be capped at a lower point.

With the ratios in hand, the company looks at how much it can invest in the various banks. "We know our own affinities," the finance officer commented. "We may exclude one bank or another for such reasons as the future trend, the trend of the past, or market capitalization, or we may also include a bank that does not meet the criteria entirely. And obviously at this point we are more careful, more cautious than we were five years ago. But we still invest large sums in bank deposits."

However, in times of uncertainty, the group treasurer may decide to alter its policy and reduce the total investment with banks: "We simply say that 50 percent of our cash should be invested in governments."

Another way of limiting bank risk is by trying to match investments with credits. For instance, if the firm has a Sfr100 million credit with a bank, and an identical investment, its risk is zero.

As a final measure, the firm limits its short-term investments to no more than 10 percent of a bank's equity. "Of course the banks limit themselves, too," the finance director commented. "They don't take any more from a single customer than a certain proportion of their assets."

But the finance executive feels the evaluation process for any bank has to be more subjective than just crunching numbers. "We know the management of the banks, and we evaluate whatever that's worth. Then, even if the figures look good, we may still adjust our decision based on our view of management. So it's not a purely mechanical evaluation. We can make an evaluation that is beyond the purely mechanical."

Maximizing Internal Funds Through Better Balance Management

For companies the world over, the number one cash management objective is to prevent buildups of idle funds to reduce borrowing needs and costs. And the best way to accomplish this is by paring bank balances to the bone. As a German treasurer put it, "Idle balances are extremely expensive. Take an example like Spain, where inter-bank rates have been as high as 25 percent. Since our goal is to raise financing at the lowest cost, the easiest method to do that is just to use our own funds better."

The need to keep balances to a minimum takes on a special meaning for companies operating in hyperinflationary nations. In Argentina, for example, where borrowing rates currently average 550 percent p.a. and current accounts pay no interest, the cost of maintaining A10 million in idle daily balances would be A55 million a year.

Regrettably, companies that closely review the bank balance management of subsidiaries are often shocked by the sloppiness of local managers. For instance, the corporate treasurer of a major U.S. consumer goods manufacturer had this to say

Bank Account Activity: Actual Daily Cleared Balance (G '000s)

Days in Month	Bank A		Bank B		Total A + B	
	Dr Bal	Cr Bal	Dr Bal	Cr Bal	Dr Bal	Cr Bal
1	(760)			188	(760)	188
2		598		172	0	770
3		144		261	0	405
4 FRI		275		315	0	590
5 SAT		658		319	0	977
6 SUN		658		319	0	977
7		11		318	0	329
8		22		304	0	326
9		36		489	0	525
10		20		575	0	595
11 FRI		47		408	0	455
12 SAT		1,328		409	0	1,737
13 SUN		1,328		409	0	1,737
14		78		395	0	473
15	(498)			396	(498)	396
16		437		429	0	866
17	(1)			453	(1)	453
18 FRI	(102)			374	(102)	374
19 SAT		704		383	0	1,087
20 SUN		704		383	0	1,087
21	(163)		(43)		(206)	0
22	(112)		(62)		(174)	0
23	(760)		(46)		(806)	0
24		201	(39)		(39)	201
25 FRI		158		128	0	286
26 SAT		836		152	0	988
27 SUN		836		152	0	988
28		836		152	0	988
29	(274)			123	(274)	123
30		190	(36)		(36)	190

about his local financial manager in the Philippines: "The local manager insists on keeping $300,000 in a non-interest-bearing current account to meet upcoming disbursements. He forgets that he will receive the proceeds of his cleared checks coming up. He always forgets that. We have had people drumming this into his head for four years; even I have come in and sat down with him. It's psychological."

To prevent such costly mistakes, audit teams should ask the following questions:

(1) How frequently and by what method do you get information on balances from your banks?

(2) Are bank reports accurate, timely, and sufficiently detailed? Do they indicate ledger, available, and value-dated balances? Are electronic banking services available?

(3) Do you calculate cash positions daily? How is the calculation made? Is the accuracy of these forecasts checked by comparing them with bank statements?

(4) What are the average daily balances for each account? Have target balances been set? What are they, and why are they set at that level? Are local managers over- or undershooting targets?

(5) Do you compare daily borrowings with credit balances? How often do simultaneous debit and credit positions exist?

(6) Do you pool funds among operating units? Are concentration or offset accounts available in the country?

(7) Do local managers take advantage of target accounts, ZBAs, or automatic investment facilities to minimize the buildup of idle cash?

(8) What are the local borrowing and investment instruments, and what do their costs or yields amount to?

Assessing Balance Management

To evaluate a subsidiary's balance management, audit teams must first identify all the accounts a subsidiary has established and then collect copies of bank balance, cash position, and forecast reports over a representative period—e.g., four weeks. Using this information, firms can construct a chart permitting easy comparison of all credit and debit balances in each account on a day-to-day basis.

For example, the in-house consulting team of a major U.S. electronics company several years ago carefully tracked the balances maintained by its Dutch subsidiary at two banks over a thirty-day period. This analysis, the results of which are shown on p. 257, helped the firm identify two costly errors:

(1) **Simultaneous credit balances at one bank and overdrafts at the other.** While the amounts held during the survey period were relatively small, the consultants believed that the potential expense of miscoordination between bank accounts was too high to risk.

(2) **Average daily credit balances of G604,000.** Although the subsidiary had negotiated a favorable 8 percent p.a. interest rate on its balances, the audit team discovered that the firm was simultaneously running an overdraft at a third bank—at a rate of 10 percent. The consultants calculated that the annual opportunity cost of maintaining the credit balances was:

$$G604{,}000 \times (10\% - 8\%) = G12{,}080 \text{ p.a.}$$

A similar study conducted by a major U.S. bank for a small German manufacturing company revealed much more glaring weaknesses. During the cash management review, the consultants uncovered numerous instances of simultaneous credit balances—paying just 0.5 percent p.a. interest—and debit balances, costing 8 percent. The following cases were highlighted as typical examples:

Global Cash Management

	Average Balance **Surplus (Overdraft)**
Bank A	Dm1,873,000
Bank B	Dm(610,700)

The consultants pointed out that in the case of Bank A, where high credit balances were maintained, the firm was forgoing investment opportunities of 11 percent p.a. Since credit balances paid 0.5 percent, the firm's opportunity cost was calculated as follows:

$$Dm1,873,000 \times 10.5\% \ [11.0 - 0.5] = Dm196,665 \ p.a.$$

The company was also overlooking the possibility of shifting funds from Bank A to Bank B and thus avoiding overdraft charges of Dm48,856 (Dm610,700 × 8%).

The consultants' conclusion? "No consistent policy or strategy exists for planning and timing the receipt of funds with disbursements and investments. We believe the overdraft balances and, consequently, interest expenses can be significantly reduced by coordinating investment maturities and customer remittances with disbursements and funding requirements. This requires daily monitoring and reporting of cash flows and balances. Forecasting receipts, disbursements, investment maturities, and funding requirements, along with actual bank balances, is essential to maximize the return on the firm's cash resources."

The Importance of Reporting and Forecasting

As this last example makes clear, the key to effective balance management is timely, accurate, and detailed bank information. This is especially true in countries where surplus balances earn little or no interest. According to the treasurer of a French engineering and construction firm, "Since you can get market rates only on six-month deposits, and since current accounts do not earn interest, we need to know very quickly what our real account position is in order to invest."

To ensure that cash managers have all the information at their fingertips when they need it, firms should instruct their banks to provide previous-day—or, where possible, same-day—balance information early each morning. Ideally, this should include both detailed transaction information (credit or debit amount, description, and account number) and summary balance information (total ledger, collected, and available balances for each account). Samples of these reports appear on pp. 260, 262, and 263.

Most importantly, companies should make certain their banks clearly distinguish between ledger and collected balances (i.e., posted totals vs. immediately available funds). A surprisingly high number of firms still mismanage their cash by, for example, basing their actions on book balances rather than factoring in float or value dating to determine available balances.

Consider the case of the Latin American subsidiary of a U.S. office machines manufacturer that until recently managed cash this way. According to the corporate

U.S. International Industries Summary Balance Report

Grouped By: Account Number
Within: Bank

Closing		Opening		Float		
Ledger Balance	Collected Balance	Available Balance	Float One Day	Over One Day	Total Credits	Total Debits

Chase Manhattan Bank, NA
BANK CODE: CHASE ACCOUNT NUMBER: 9991234567 ACCOUNT NAME: AAA ACME MFG CONC ACCT

12,432,542.76	10,198,642.76	12,398,642.76	2,200,000.00	33,900.00	9,220,151.04	5,462,014.66

BANK CODE: CHASE ACCOUNT NUMBER: 9991987654 ACCOUNT NAME: AAA ACME DISBURSEMENT

6,874,961.80	6,100,061.80	6,725,061.80	625,000.00	149,900.00	8,951,180.98	6,372,053.11

BANK CODE: CHASE ACCOUNT NUMBER: 9992543210 ACCOUNT NAME: ASIAN EXPORT ACCOUNT

3,849,098.23	3,642,598.23	3,840,598.23	198,000.00	8,500.00	4,582,391.46	3,249,500.11

Chase Manhattan Bank TOTALS:

23,156,602.79	19,941,302.79	22,964,302.79	3,023,000.00	192,300.00	22,753,723.48	15,083,627.88

Manufacturers Hanover Trust Company
BANK CODE: MHT ACCOUNT NUMBER: 83641027 ACCOUNT NAME: AAA MFG DISBURSEMENT ACCT

0.00	0.00	0.00	0.00	0.00	987,504.41	987,504.41

BANK CODE: MHT ACCOUNT NUMBER: 83641028 ACCOUNT NAME: ZZZ MFG CONCENTRATION

4,438,209.66	3,556,209.66	4,432,209.66	876,000.00	6,000.00	3,450,873.23	2,472,309.73

BANK CODE: MHT ACCOUNT NUMBER: 83652079 ACCOUNT NAME: ZZZ MFG DISBURSEMENT

2,673,309.66	2,638,309.66	2,670,809.66	32,500.00	2,500.00	3,447,065.98	2,500,600.00

Manufacturers Hanover TOTALS:

7,111,519.32	6,194,519.32	7,103,019.32	908,500.00	8,500.00	7,885,443.62	5,960,114.14

Security Pacific National Bank
BANK CODE: SEC PAC ACCOUNT NUMBER: 28400525 ACCOUNT NAME: AAA ACME MFG CONC ACCT

1,710,509.35	1,665,209.35	1,710,409.35	45,200.00	100.00	988,700.29	2,860,371.75

BANK CODE: SEC PAC ACCOUNT NUMBER: 28400529 ACCOUNT NAME: ZZZ MFG LOCK BOX ACCOUNT

1,200,980.00	750,300.00	1,200,480.00	450,180.00	500.00	868,580.68	688,754.30

Security Pacific TOTALS:

2,911,489.35	2,415,509.35	2,910,889.35	495,380.00	600.00	187,280.97	3,549,126.05

GRAND TOTALS:

33,179,611.46	28,551,331.46	32,978,211.46	4,426,880.00	201,400.00	32,496,448.07	24,593,168.07

Source: Chase Manhattan Bank.

treasurer, "A couple of local bankers convinced our guys that regardless of what amount you actually have in the bank, you have to manage your bank account based on the books. And they were sitting there with maybe $1 million in the bank and only $100,000 on the books." Fortunately, headquarters caught the error during a periodic internal audit of all its subsidiaries, and the problem was quickly corrected.

In many countries, firms are confronted with bank reporting of consistently poor quality; reports arrive late in the day with obsolete information, often riddled with errors and not clearly distinguishing between available and ledger balances. Even in Sweden, a local finance director was moved to complain, "You can't rely on bank systems now. They don't report quickly enough. If we relied on them alone we would be maybe Skr20–30 million off on our net balances each day. You never find out about an incoming payment until it's too late to do anything about it."

Companies in other countries face much more trying circumstances. According to

Global Cash Management

a spokesman for a Korean manufacturer, "The banks will not provide us with balances daily. The practice is that they send us a statement only at the end of the month. For the daily report, we must keep track of things ourselves." And in Venezuela, although banks will provide daily balance information to select customers over the phone, many companies using this system have fallen prey to criminals who have fraudulently tapped into the service to obtain information for falsifying checks.

Despite these obstacles, sophisticated companies have managed to build effective bank-balance monitoring systems in even the most difficult countries.

In Mexico, for example, major advances in electronic banking have also clearly helped to improve the information flow. But strong and consistent reporting is still required to back up the system, given the reality that Mexico's banking system is still prone to errors. Finance managers, in fact, recommend nothing less than daily monitoring of bank balances. This, they say, will reduce the chances of serious errors and guarantee that any bank foul-ups are caught within eighteen hours. And if a discrepancy is detected, one finance director recommends the following: "Call the bank immediately and demand compensation. Every day you wait, you lose." (The interview with this finance director was interrupted by the treasurer, who had just caught a large error. The finance director called the bank right away, and his firm's account was credited on the spot.)

Even better, companies should take advantage of the electronic banking services now spreading throughout North America, Europe, the Asia/Pacific region, and even parts of Latin America. In a fast-growing number of countries, firms have a broad array of advanced features to choose from, including microcomputer-based systems, multibank reporting services, and automatic reconciliation (see p. 49 for further information on electronic banking). And in those nations where local banks are resisting this trend, companies should make the upgrading of bank reporting services a top priority and lean hard on their banks to provide reports that enhance, rather than undermine, their ability to manage balances. The treasurer of a major Italian firm demonstrated the right attitude: "We're going to keep putting the pressure on our banks until they come through for us."

However balance data is collected, companies must incorporate the information into daily cash position and forecast reports (see sample forms on pp. 47 and 58). By transcribing the day's beginning bank balance onto the form, adding anticipated cash receipts for the day, and subtracting anticipated disbursements, cash managers can estimate their closing balance for the day. Without this estimate or forecast, they will not be able to keep accounts within targeted levels or avoid simultaneous credit and debit balances. (Cash forecasting is discussed in greater detail on p. 56.) It is especially important that firms compare cash forecasts with actual results.

For example, the in-house consulting team of a U.S. company recently reviewed the balance management procedures of its Italian subsidiary. The consultants found that the firm telephoned its banks every day to find out what its ledger balances were and adjusted these amounts by known debits and anticipated credits. But the process was sadly lacking in accuracy: The company suffered idle daily balances of nearly $800,000, some of it earning a mere 0.5 percent.

To remedy the situation, the consulting team advised local management to track

U.S. International Industries
Detail Transaction Report

Grouped By: Account Number
Within: Bank

Bank Code	Account Number	Account Name	Description	CR/ DR	Credit Amount	Debit Amount
Chase Manhattan Bank, NA 9991234567						
CHASE	9991234567	AAA AMCE MFG CONC ACCT	Incoming Transfer	C	5,008,763.00	
CHASE	9991234567	AAA AMCE MFG CONC ACCT	Incoming Transfer	C	2,137,110.00	
CHASE	9991234567	AAA AMCE MFG CONC ACCT	Security Credit	C	1,000,000.00	
CHASE	9991234567	AAA AMCE MFG CONC ACCT	Incoming Transfer	C	683,745.53	
CHASE	9991234567	AAA AMCE MFG CONC ACCT	Check Deposited	C	297,868.41	
CHASE	9991234567	AAA AMCE MFG CONC ACCT	Security Credit	C	91,879.41	
CHASE	9991234567	AAA AMCE MFG CONC ACCT	International Credit	C	785.00	
CHASE	9991234567	AAA AMCE MFG CONC ACCT	Outgoing Transfer	D		3,872,008.00
CHASE	9991234567	AAA AMCE MFG CONC ACCT	Security Debit	D		1,000,000.00
CHASE	9991234567	AAA AMCE MFG CONC ACCT	Outgoing Transfer	D		312,098.80
CHASE	9991234567	AAA AMCE MFG CONC ACCT	Check Paid	D		253,688.71
CHASE	9991234567	AAA AMCE MFG CONC ACCT	Misc. Debit	D		23,560.40
CHASE	9991234567	AAA AMCE MFG CONC ACCT	Misc. Debit	D		658.75
		TOTAL: 9991234567			9,220,151.04	5,462,014.66

and adjust balances carefully for bank float: "Compare forecasts with the actual balances shown on quarterly statements and try to account for variations to allow more accurate calculation of float." In this way, the firm could set optimal balance targets despite inadequate servicing by its banks.

Improving Balance Management Through Cash Pooling

Companies can dramatically increase their control over bank balances, while at the same time refining their borrowing and investment strategies, by implementing cash pooling techniques. Under a pooling system, operating units transfer surplus funds to a central corporate account, where they can be invested or shifted to other subsidi-

Bank Code	Account Number	Account Name	Description	CR/DR	Credit Amount	Debit Amount
9991987654						
CHASE	9991987654	AAA AMCE DISBURSEMENT	Check Deposited	C	4,763,711.80	
CHASE	9991987654	AAA AMCE DISBURSEMENT	Incoming Transfer	C	2,135,163.00	
CHASE	9991987654	AAA AMCE DISBURSEMENT	Lockbox Deposit	C	719,000.00	
CHASE	9991987654	AAA AMCE DISBURSEMENT	Foreign LOC	C	605,880.00	
CHASE	9991987654	AAA AMCE DISBURSEMENT	Foreign Rmtnc. Cred.	C	448,976.25	
CHASE	9991987654	AAA AMCE DISBURSEMENT	Security Credit	C	122,314.00	
CHASE	9991987654	AAA AMCE DISBURSEMENT	Security Credit	C	56,135.93	
CHASE	9991987654	AAA AMCE DISBURSEMENT	Security Credit	C	100,000.00	
CHASE	9991987654	AAA AMCE DISBURSEMENT	Check Paid	D		4,556,873.20
CHASE	9991987654	AAA AMCE DISBURSEMENT	Outgoing Transfer	D		1,000,000.00
CHASE	9991987654	AAA AMCE DISBURSEMENT	Payable Thru Draft	D		565,883.04
CHASE	9991987654	AAA AMCE DISBURSEMENT	Security Debit	D		150,000.00
CHASE	9991987654	AAA AMCE DISBURSEMENT	Outgoing Transfer	D		99,346.87
		TOTAL: 9991987654			8,951,180.98	6,372,053.11
		TOTAL: Chase Manhattan Bank			18,171,332.02	11,834,067.77
			GRAND TOTAL		18,171,332.02	11,834,067.77

Source: Chase Manhattan Bank.

aries. By centralizing balance management in this way, a corporate group can more easily monitor and manage cash flows and also obtain higher yields on its cash investments than any individual unit could achieve on its own. Cash pooling also cuts overall borrowing costs by funding cash-poor operations internally.

Cash-pooling systems, tailored to a company's organizational and cash flow patterns, range from unsophisticated to state of the art. Some are highly structured, with daily or weekly cycles and fixed bank channels; others are informal, with operating units remitting surplus funds to the center as they arise. Pooling systems can be organized centrally, regionally, or along divisional lines, and they may or may not be related to intracompany trade accounts. Moreover, pooling can be initiated by the central treasury department, by subsidiary staff, or by a bank as part of a concentration account service.

Through cash pooling, firms can also concentrate expertise at headquarters and

Establishing Internal Procedures for Better Balance Control

To upgrade balance management, companies should consider instituting the following proven techniques:

· Segregate banks by function (e.g., use one bank for disbursements, another for deposits over a certain amount). A detailed breakdown of a Venezuelan company's bank accounts, segregated by function, is shown in the table below.
· Set a target level for collected balances in each bank account. The target should take into consideration balance charges for credit facilities and operating services.
· Instruct local banks to provide daily information on their *opening* ledger balance. Midday balances are not useful to the cash manager, since they may not include all debits and credits for the current day and do not specify which—if any—are missing. Furthermore, it is uncommon for banks in Latin America to report on a collected-balance basis. Instead, collected balances should be estimated by assuming that a certain percentage of deposits clears in one business day, a certain percentage in two business days, etc., based on experience and discussion with local bankers.
· Have the accounts payable department maintain auxiliary records showing the value of checks released each day. Amounts should be broken down by method of payment (e.g., checks picked up by the supplier's messenger and checks mailed), so that disbursement float can be estimated.

---

relieve subsidiary or unit managers of the responsibility for making complex borrowing and investment decisions. As the treasurer of a major French chemicals firm said, "All the cash is managed at the mother company, and the affiliates have no problems managing their cash. We at headquarters know what is going on in the markets, and the affiliates can concentrate on what they know best—production and sales."

The enormous potential for savings that cash pooling offers is amply demonstrated by the experience of one of Germany's largest manufacturers. The company's cash-pooling recipe has three ingredients: (1) daily pooling of excess funds from seventy-five collection points in Germany to a few central accounts; (2) centralized borrowings and investments by headquarters; and (3) netting of all domestic intracompany cash flows.

The impressive rise in the company's interest earnings on group investments shows the effectiveness of cash pooling. In one year alone, net interest income rose from Dm343 million to Dm458 million—an outstanding performance when compared with the firm's total aftertax profit of Dm738 million and an adjusted net profit of Dm328 million in the same year. Pooling has also helped the company reduce bank float on receivables. "At today's interest rates, losing one day's float on average can easily mean a loss of Dm11 million," according to the company's finance director, who is responsible for the group's liquidity management. The firm

How One Company Assigns Bank Accounts According to Function

Location	Bank A	Bank B	Bank C	Bank D	Bank E	Bank F
Caracas	D/S (v)	P+ (50)	P—	Pb (5)	Pe (V)	Ni (1)
Caracas				Nc (1)		
Maracaibo		P+ (20)	P— (5)			
Puerto La Cruz	P+ (20)	P— (5)				
Valencia		P+ (20)	P— (5)			
Puerto La Cruz	P+ (20)	P— (5)				
Caracas	D (v)	P+ (20)				
Los Teques			P— (5)			

SYMBOLS:

P+ For payments above B3,000

S Overdraft

Nc Payroll—Caracas

D/S Deposit (with overdraft)

P— For payments under B3,000 on the basis of revolving funds

Pb For payments below B1,000

Ni Payroll—Interior

Pe Special payments

D Deposits

( ) Opening balance in thousands of bolivares (v = variable)

---

can achieve such dramatic cost savings because of the size of its cash cycle, which averages Dm130 million a day.

Another good example of a cash-pooling scheme that shows the strong linkages between balance management and improved investing and borrowing is provided by a large French producer and processor of raw materials with over fifty domestic subsidiaries. The firm has set up a pooling arrangement for its seven largest subsidiaries, which account for over 90 percent of its annual sales. It is managed by a central finance department at the firm's Paris holding company. Under the pooling system, subsidiary treasurers report to the group treasurer each day via telephone, informing him of their cash needs or surpluses, as well as of anticipated receipts and disbursements for the next few days. Treasury staff uses these reports to make a cash forecast for the current and following two days. In addition, subsidiaries submit a detailed monthly cash forecast for the next four months and an annual forecast for the next year, broken down by quarter.

With these forecasts, the firm's corporate finance department determines each local subsidiary's net surplus or deficit and either moves surplus funds on a daily basis to the accounts of needy subsidiaries or transfers them to Paris for investment. "It is much easier—and cheaper—for us to lend to a subsidiary for ten or twenty days than to have them go to a bank," the firm's treasurer explained. Moreover, through an

The Do-It-Yourself Approach: Hewlett Packard's Cash Management System

Since 1985, Hewlett Packard has been using a proprietary software system, HPCash, to keep track of movements in its bank accounts. A sizable number of other companies with HP computer systems have subsequently adopted HPCash for their own use.

The HPCash system allows a company to take advantage of lucrative overnight investment opportunities and utilize idle fund balances. It improves bank account analysis by providing accurate charges and interest earnings. And it tests bank efficiency and helps negotiate better bank conditions by providing accurate account information.

HPCash permits a corporate user to interface directly with its banks' reporting systems and gain access to bank information including value dates about its own accounts. European headquarters and the major subsidiaries just hook up and dial into the banks' computers.

Utilizing this data from the banks and from selected internal systems (accounts payable, accounts receivable, and forex), HPCash issues confirmation letters and telexes, accounting reports, decision-aid data, and a series of cash-position reports, which provide information by account, bank, currency, entity, and type of funds. With these reports, the subsidiary treasurers are able to detect cash management opportunities at a glance. HPCash is also able to issue reports with sophisticated graphics that aid trend analysis and provide formatting for "what-if" scenarios.

---

agreement with its main domestic bank, all transfers are made on a same-day basis. "It can take as long as three to seven days to get funds in from the provinces," he added. "The cash-pooling system saves us money just on these same-day transfers of the net excess."

But the spokesman emphasized that the system is totally voluntary: "We do not force the subsidiaries to participate. We try to create an atmosphere of trust and confidence between us and them. We say that we are working together toward the same goal: greater profitability for the group as a whole." Subsidiaries are also encouraged to participate in pooling through preferential rates on borrowing and investments. "However, we are not about to make a gift to anyone; the rates are better than money market rates, but close to them," he noted. Smaller subsidiaries outside the arrangement can also borrow from the central pool, subject to the approval of the treasurer, but at rates that are less attractive than those available to their larger counterparts.

Banking Aids to Balance Management

Companies seeking to upgrade their balance management can also turn to their

Among the reports the HPCash system generates are the following:

- An **audit report** presents daily details of all transactions from all accounts. The information includes amounts, reference numbers, source of transfer, etc.
- **Value-dated balances,** in both detailed and summary form, clarify exactly how much cash is available at any given moment and thus prevent errors. Treasurers are then better able to monitor float and bank clearing times. Value dating is extremely critical for managing cash—especially in Europe, where dating is negotiable—because of its influence on real banking costs.
- **Deposit, borrowing, and forex positions** are presented according to maturity dates, daily position, and amounts outstanding by bank and by borrower. This format alerts staff to pending due dates on time deposits and loans and tracks currency requirements for forward forex contracts. Treasurers need this information to make an accurate determination of their borrowing and investment needs.
- A **weekly cash position report** presents the cash position by entity and country and compares actual positions to previous forecasts, leading to better forecasts in the future.
- **Accruals, interest, and commissions** are detailed to reconcile internal records with bank fees and interest payments on deposits and loans. Some banks in Europe do not generally provide detailed account analyses of charges and interest payments, making it difficult for firms to detect errors.
- A **bank activity statistics report** indicates daily receipts and payments by account, bank, and total. It presents average balance and activity volume, lists interest and

▶

bankers for assistance. In many countries, banks offer concentration accounts that automatically consolidate corporate balances held in various bank accounts into one central account. Although the purpose of concentration accounts is always to pool corporate funds, their form varies by country and by bank. Some banks leave the actual funds in local accounts and merely post a net balance to the main account; these are often referred to as "offset accounts." Other banks, usually in countries where there are no overdrafts, zero out all the local balances and shift all funds to the central account.

By using concentration accounts, companies can achieve the standard financial benefits of cash pooling: greater investment yields, increased flexibility in shifting liquidity, and reduced borrowing costs. But concentration accounts also have another advantage: They eliminate the managerial time and costs of monitoring each corporate account and of instructing bank branches to transfer funds to a main account. Remarked the money manager at a French firm: "The benefit is that the banks will do it automatically, because we don't want the clerical costs."

There are two basic types of concentration accounts:

(1) **Intrabank concentration accounts** consolidate balances at the local branches

commissions, and reports on the status of credit lines. This helps treasurers detect idle balances and unnecessary credit lines. It also assists in evaluating the utility of each account.

HPCash also has on-line analysis screens for several accounts. These split the data in several ways and give users fully digested information that is very close to a recommendation for action.

Foreign exchange management is fully integrated into the HPCash system. While the program doesn't carry out actual trading or make decisions, it contains sensitivity analysis tools that can help indicate purchases or sales of foreign exchange.

When the forex trader has made a deal, he enters it on the screen. Automatically, a confirming telex goes out, the deal is recorded in the HPCash forex file, and the accounting department is notified. There are automatic accruals at month's end, noting interim gains and losses. As the firm's regional treasurer points out, "There is a significant security improvement since the forex deal is entered, etc., all at one time. Once it's in the system, you can't extract it. So there's much less risk of unauthorized transactions.

"With the HPCash system, we could have access to figures on a daily basis if we wanted. Currently, we look at these sums on a weekly basis across Europe. This leaves the subsidiaries with the micro approach to manage customer accounts and overdraft lines. At the European and corporate headquarters level, we watch the liquidity of the whole company."

HPCash is capable of linking a large number of reporting banks and accounts. In fact, one HPCash system client, a U.K. conglomerate, feeds in information electronically from 400 accounts every day. Some of these accounts lie within the same bank, some with a number of other banks. So it's difficult to say exactly how many banks HPCash can interface with; currently there are linkups with virtually all the main banks and the main countries.

---

within one banking network, with the net balance made available at a central corporate account.

(2) **Interbank concentration accounts** help consolidate funds held in numerous accounts with multiple banks by automatically concentrating balances from unrelated banking institutions in one bank account. These accounts must be set up through prior agreement with the participating banks.

No matter what kind of concentration account a company decides to use, there are often hurdles that must be cleared before the systems can be effective. The most common problems firms encounter when they attempt to establish a concentration account are the following:

Cash Flows Among Pooling Participants

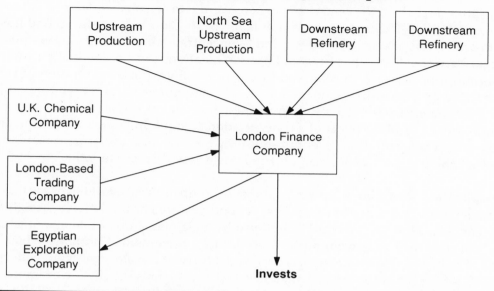

- **Internal resistance.** If funds are being concentrated from more than one subsidiary or operating unit in a country, firms may meet resistance from their affiliated companies. Subsidiary or unit personnel may dislike losing control over their funds and fear that their performance cannot be adequately evaluated when they are part of a concentration system. They may also resent losing contact with bankers as their financing and investing duties are removed from them.
- **Bank resistance.** Bankers sometimes resist offering concentration services because they reduce idle balances and, therefore, bank earnings. When companies do convince a bank to offer the service, they may then face the further problem of hurting their relationships with other banks—relationships that may be necessary for financing and other reasons. For example, to use a concentration service a medium-sized European company had to reduce the number of its local banks from nineteen to just one. As a result, the company was sharply criticized. The financial manager described the conflict: "There are a lot of banks dissatisfied with us because we chose only one bank. It is difficult to explain to the banks why we are compelled to use only one bank. But the bottom line was that the concentration bank system we use can give me this automatic service and same-day value. Using nineteen banks could not."
- **Poor bank capabilities.** In some countries, the poor state of advanced reporting systems has made it difficult or impossible for banks to consolidate funds automatically. As the treasurer of an Italian auto manufacturer explained, "When we pool funds, it's by our subsidiaries' initiation. You see, the Italian banking system is quite old. We, not the banks, are the pooler of funds."
- **Bank risk.** Some handle cash concentration cautiously because it contradicts their

basic philosophy: to minimize bank investment risks. Rather than one central account, these firms prefer an assortment of bank accounts. As a corporate spokesman for a French MNC remarked, "There were two lessons we learned from the Herstatt failure. The first lesson is that bankers are fallible. And the second lesson is to watch out and make sure we don't concentrate all our funds in one place."

· **Legal barriers.** A variety of tax and other regulations can undermine the value of concentration services. In some countries, for example, the concentration of funds generated by local units is considered a dividend remittance and is therefore subject to government taxation. Lack of overnight investment opportunities for pooled funds can also dull the luster of a concentration account. In France many companies do not find concentration accounts appealing because local investment regulations restrict the payment of interest on funds held less than six months.

Despite these obstacles, a growing number of companies the world over are making effective use of concentration accounts. A good example of a relatively straightforward concentration system is that employed by a German automobile manufacturer. The firm receives funds from an intricate lattice of agents in Germany, which are billed as branches. The company has designated forty of its sales agents as "collection points," which use a set list of banks to effect funds transfers. If, for example, the Hamburg collection point receives a check, it deposits the check with Bank X in Hamburg, which credits the amount the same day. By 11:00 the next morning, the money is transferred to one of three concentration accounts in Stuttgart, where funds are immediately available for use by headquarters in Stuttgart. Consequently, the firm has drastically cut float and centralized excess funds at its parent headquarters, where they can be much more efficiently invested.

A Swedish automotive company uses the offset-account schemes of four different banks for all its domestic subsidiaries. The system includes the company's krona and foreign currency accounts held in Sweden. All bank transactions of the Swedish company's local units are booked on local bank accounts. Each day, the banks offset the debit and credit positions of the various subsidiaries' accounts and post the net balances to the next level, which are divisional accounts. The divisional accounts, in turn, are also offset, yielding a net groupwide balance at the parent level, the highest point of consolidation. The money desk at parent headquarters monitors the daily activities through its banks' computer-based reporting systems, which provide available balances (including value dating) and full details of all transactions. The beauty of the setup, according to the money desk manager, is that "we know at all times what our position is, and we never have idle balances at the subsidiary level."

Once the funds are consolidated, the company uses the system to shift liquidity within the group, reducing external borrowing needs and costs. Cash-poor subsidiaries can tap internal credit lines at below-market financing rates. An interesting feature of the system is that the parent sets an internal interest rate for each division, which is free to charge whatever rate it wants to its subs. "We can use different interest rates throughout the pyramid," said the money desk manager. The internally set rates are supplied to the banks, which include them on the account statements of individual subsidiaries. The national interest rates are earned and charged for each subsidiary as though they were the actual bank rates.

A U.K. financial services subsidiary also utilizes cash concentration to cut transaction and related banking costs and to enhance earnings through improved liquidity management. The system pools cash from four major wholly owned subsidiaries (see the diagram above). Of the four, two are "upstream" field operations, which produce, transport, and market raw crude, and two are "downstream" operations, which refine and then market finished petroleum distillates. The pooling system is completed by the participation of other smaller entities, including a London-based trading company and a U.K. chemical company (an exploration company based in Egypt also participates, but as a borrower only).

The U.K. pooling system was developed in conjunction with a major U.S. money center bank. The daily cycle begins with concentration and collection of funds from the accounts of all subsidiary units. The funds are not actually intermingled, but the effect is the same. The pooled funds are construed neither as dividends nor as loans by the authorities because, as the treasurer explained, "the bank has separate accounts for everyone. It is just that there is an overall net balance that is looked at by [the bank] at the end of the day. But each of the constituents has its own separate account. So there is no intermingling of funds other than the banker's taking the net of all the credits and debits and giving us our balance." Essentially, the bank manages all of the subsidiary balances together, thus simulating a central "concentrating" account without the accompanying legal complications.

The operating units' debits and credits are compared every day and netted to obtain balances that are posted to a central account in London. The bank provides the company's central treasury with the individual balances, but the treasurer can invest the funds in any combination he wants. The pooled funds are not considered a loan to the central treasury, as they clearly remain the property of the subsidiaries. The central treasury merely performs the service of managing the subsidiaries' investments.

An intracompany interest rate, whether for a formal loan or just as interest from the cash pool, is determined in what the treasurer calls a "retrospective manner." This is based on the return London receives from its combined portfolios. Assume, for instance, that the U.K. trading firm had excess liquidity of $10 million, and an operating unit in the North Sea needed $10 million for capital expenditures. As the treasurer explained, "We find out what we've actually earned [on the investment portfolio for the loan period] and then we knock an eighth of a percent off that and pay them the difference." If the return on investment for the London portfolio were 10 percent, the trading firm would get 9.875 percent interest for lending the $10 million, the North Sea unit would pay the full 10 percent for use of the funds, and the finance company would earn the spread as compensation for administrative work.

Could the subsidiaries match the rates available from the center on their own? The treasurer thinks not, insisting that the center significantly improves group cash management by providing markedly improved investing and borrowing rates. Referring to the money market rates the center pays, the treasurer said, "They may well have been able to match us, but then they might not. We in treasury believe that we have concentrated within this unit the mechanics to receive the best rates available. We can go around and test rates with half a dozen banks until we find what we think is a good rate. The other units haven't got the facility or expertise to do this themselves. [And neither] do they wield the market leverage we have here [at the center]." This is a result of the large volume of cash London invests daily—as much as $10–20 million. On the borrowing side, the treasurer said, "they can't borrow at as low a rate as we offer. I mean you're talking about market rates there."

The second advantage this centralized treasury system has over the subsidiaries' own efforts is the reduction of administrative costs through efficient loan processing. "We cut down on the paperwork. From an administrative point of view, it is indeed easier to use us," the treasurer explained.

Forecasting the amount needed to fund operations and the remaining amount available to invest requires that the London finance company be informed of expected cash positions. Forecasts of cash positions therefore include sales projections for the ensuing quarter, as well as constant updates regarding when large invoices are to be disbursed or collected.

Even though local units have their own disbursement accounts with their own checkbooks, the funding decision rests with the financial services company. The services company can pinpoint the amount to be disbursed on any given day by a combination of notification mechanisms, including phone calls from the local units and receipt of invoices.

"Because of the volume of transactions at the local level, we can't be expected to survey every account," said the treasurer. "They have the checkbook, we control the balance. But these accounts are merely notional. It's up to us to make sure they're funded satisfactorily, though we can be overdrawn—as long as there are sufficient funds in the aggregate. It's the net at the end that the bank looks at."

The system makes a provision for overdrafts for subsidiaries that don't always generate a positive cash flow. To illustrate the mechanics, assume a subsidiary's account to be in debit balance at day's end. "If a unit is overdrawn," the treasurer explained, "it remains overdrawn. But we ourselves will recognize that it's going to be overdrawn and will leave a larger balance on one of the other subsidiary accounts to cover that. As far as the bank is concerned, although individual accounts may be in debit, we aim for our other accounts to be in credit, so that the net for the bank at the end of the day is also in credit." There is no penalty charged by the bank for this feature; however, the subsidiary account is debited interest by the parent, thereby injecting discipline into the subsidiary's cash management. If central treasury finds the subsidiary to be in continual overdraft, it will reexamine the situation to determine if additional funding is necessary, in which case a "proper loan agreement between that company and one of the companies in a credit position" would be orchestrated by the treasurer in London.

Excess funds accumulated in the cash pool are invested immediately by the center's staff. "As funds come in, we have the people next door putting it right on the money market," said the treasurer. The London center is kept well abreast of subsidiary cash requirements and can therefore make decisions about whether to invest funds overnight or in slightly longer-term instruments, with maturities of up to three months. "We're dealing with the margin, that is, the funds that aren't needed for current obligations," the treasurer explained.

ZBAs and Automatic-Investment Facilities

In addition to concentration accounts, companies can use a number of other special account services from their banks. **Zero-balance accounts (ZBAs)** and **target-balance accounts (TBAs)** draw funds from interest-bearing accounts into disbursement accounts as needed. This allows idle funds to earn maximum interest while still remaining available for funding payments to suppliers and other creditors on a daily basis. While ZBAs are usually paid for by fees, permitting the disbursement account to remain unfunded, TBAs leave a specified amount in the low- or non-interest-bearing payables account to compensate the bank for the service.

Some companies have negotiated ZBAs that work in tandem with a concentration account. As explained by the finance director of a German travel service company, "All the local units in Germany have two basic accounts: a collection account and a disbursement account. Each night, at midnight, all the balances in the units' collection accounts are automatically swept into a concentration account that the parent company maintains at the main branch of the bank that all the local units use. This account earns interest fairly close to market rates.

"In addition, each unit is responsible for its own disbursements, issued through its individual ZBA. When a payment is presented against a local unit's ZBA, the funds to meet that payment are drawn from the head office's concentration account—just enough to fund the specific payment." This system is successful because of a sophisticated on-line hookup among the bank's branches.

The benefits to the company are threefold. First, the group as a whole receives high interest rates on the pooled funds by concentrating them into one account. Second, the local disbursement accounts can maintain zero balances until funds are actually needed. Third, making the local units responsible for their own disbursements—though the funds to meet them come from a parent account—permits the local managers a degree of autonomy while providing the parent with overall liquidity control. ZBAs and TBAs are discussed in greater detail on pp. 237–38.

The automatic-investment services offered by banks can also help firms avoid idle funds and minimize managerial time and expense. Like ZBAs and TBAs, automatic-investment services spare the cash manager the responsibility of monitoring accounts and shifting funds around. As the treasurer of an Italian service company said, "Until our reporting systems are so efficient that we can make accurate investment decisions, we need to rely on local investment services. But the investments have to fit our overall investment strategies."

A major industrial goods manufacturer demonstrates how this service can work. The firm negotiated with its bank to set up an automatic-investment plan and set the minimum interest it would like to receive. If the bank is unable to meet the rate, it contacts the company. The rate of return takes taxation into account, because most of the investments are in government paper. According to the firm's treasurer, the arrangement's main advantage is flexibility. "You can exploit all the opportunities to get tax-free interest without any commitment on the duration of the investment. If I want the money back tomorrow morning, it's no problem; they will divest immediately." The bank charges a fixed monthly fee of around $200–300 a month. "They wanted a percentage, but we negotiated hard to get the fee."

Many cash managers, however, avoid automatic bank or money market investment services because they prefer to actively manage their cash themselves. As a U.S. cash manager put it, "We enter the markets ourselves. If a corporation is paying people to manage its money, then they're the ones who should be doing it." To evaluate the potential savings automatic-investment services can offer a subsidiary, consider the quality of local reporting, interest rate differentials, and the work load and skills of local managers.

Managing Complexity: A Case Example

With the help of a futuristic software package that ties together electronic balance reporting, cash forecasting, balance targeting, and a series of concentration services and investment accounts, a multi-billion-dollar U.S. services company has perfected its management of a coast-to-coast network of over 750 domestic accounts. In a nutshell, the software package matches all cash receipts against balance targets, calculates the daily cash flow, and funnels money through three concentration accounts into two special investment accounts. And, according to the firm's vice president, "It's all done without anyone touching it."

The system works like this: Each of the 750 local banks calls the firm's computer, which is operated by a computer service and time-sharing company, by a certain hour every morning to convey the closing balances of the previous day. The service company communicates this information to one of three concentration banks, indicating the amount of excess funds in the account and the amount to draw out. The regional concentration bank collects the funds and transfers amounts over its target balance to an investment bank.

Of the three concentration accounts, two are money center banks used for excess funds investment; the other bank concentrates funds regionally and moves them by wire transfer into the investment banks. Transfers are made via depository transfer checks or electronic funds transfers. Pricing bids on investments are evaluated regularly, so that nonconcentration banks can also be used for investment. Once the funds are in an investment bank, the firm's investment managers decide how to invest based on the daily cash position report.

The vice president offered an example of how this might work: "Let's take a bank in Nebraska. They call in this morning with their balance and transaction information. Say they have $100 and we had deposits yesterday of $50. It goes into the computer, where it is matched against a formula we have for gauging cash flows. After all information is accumulated by the service, excess funds are transmitted to a concentration bank, which draws down funds from each bank that called in. At 4 P.M., the time-sharing service transmits daily printouts of what happened to the home office."

The computer tracks every target, transfer, and balance and handles all day-to-day operation of the system. As the vice president explained, "The computer is making the adjustments; we merely put the parameters in. During a monthly period, if we take too much out one day, it adjusts the next day; it's always adjusting to the target you have. If we want to keep $75,000 on an average daily basis and we put too much in today, it takes it out tomorrow. If we find we have more cash flow coming into an account than we forecast, we will dial up and tell the computer to change the target. You can go in there and intervene manually whenever you want to change the target, and then the system just self-adjusts."

This massive flow of money is controlled and monitored by small groups of three to seven people in each domestic division who function as "cash control centers." The centers key up the electronic reporting services of the concentration banks, which control the 750 "local country deposit accounts" across the country, to obtain their cash positions. They also receive reports from the investment banks on the previous day's invested funds and the day's opening balance, and from the computer service company on what happened with each account and the specific problems that require attention. At the end of the month, all of this data is used to generate a consolidated report on the period's cash flows and collected balances, along with the standing of each account in relation to its year- and month-to-date balance targets. "This report is shipped to me at corporate headquarters," the vice president commented. "This is one check and balance we have in relation to balance levels." The cash controllers also get daily exception reports, which show banks that are over or under their targets by plus or minus 5 percent. "If that happens," the vice president explained, "they look at their list to see what the daily cash flow is through that bank. Is it what we estimated? If not, the cash control center will call the computer and change the target number at that bank."

The vice president is proud of the system's performance, boasting, "We built this ourselves. There is probably no other company in the country that has a system like this. The key to account management is to have control of money and reports." Although the package cost $2–2.5 million, the company calculated that in its first year of operation alone it generated $14.5 million in extra daily cash flows that could be invested for high yields. However, "the more important thing to us was that at 3:30 in the afternoon we knew what was going to be in our concentration accounts the next morning," the executive said. "What a feeling to know that you have that money to get into the market early in the morning! And if we knew we were having a problem with a bank, we knew before they did."

Tracking Banking Costs and Evaluating Services

Once a company has brought its balances under control, it can turn its attention to other banking costs and services. Specifically, firms should identify and rigorously monitor all banking charges, including both direct (e.g., fees, commissions, and interest rates) and indirect (e.g., value dating and compensating business) costs. They should also set up a system for evaluating the overall performance of their banks. The following questions can be used to evaluate performance problems:

(1) Do you regularly review and evaluate banking costs and services? What method do you use?

(2) Do your banks furnish regular account analyses that break down transactions and fees?

(3) Do local cash managers systematically calculate the value of your business to a bank, including forex transactions, LCs, float, etc.?

(4) Do you negotiate costs—such as reduced check-clearing times or lower compensating balances—with your banks or press them to switch to billing by fees?

(5) Do your banks consistently quote competitive rates on money market investments, short-term borrowings, and foreign exchange transactions?

(6) Are they willing to custom tailor their services, or do they offer systems only "off the rack"?

(7) Do they transfer funds efficiently and provide other services to accelerate domestic and export collection?

(8) Do they offer advanced services, such as electronic banking, concentration accounts, and ZBAs or TBAs?

How to Monitor Bank Costs

In some parts of the world, tracking bank costs is relatively simple. For example, U.S. banks routinely provide corporate customers with account analyses that detail the full cost of cash management services. These handy monitoring tools—an example of which is shown on pp. 278–79—enable firms to review the services supplied by their banks, the applicable charges, and such offsetting items as idle balances and float.

Naturally, companies should examine account analyses carefully for possible mistakes. In the opinion of a consultant for a major U.S. accounting firm, time spent in this way is well worth the effort: "We had a very large corporation hire a person to review account analysis, and in the course of two years he saved the company over a million dollars, mostly from fees the company would have paid if errors hadn't been uncovered—errors mostly in the balance levels." According to the spokesman, "In an account analysis, banks talk about float and collected balances. Float is often deliberately exaggerated because the greater the float, the less the collected balance. Since the earnings allowance credited toward fees is based on the collected balance, understanding the collected balance serves to minimize the offset to service charges. Unless this is caught, the bank makes more money with their service charges because they're giving you less credit."

But such problems are minor compared with conditions outside the United States. In many countries, banks do not keep accurate track of collateral business and rarely provide detailed descriptions of balance requirements and fee structures to their corporate customers. Complained the Hong Kong-based regional treasurer of a major U.S. consumer products group, "I've tried to get information out here. You know, what reserve requirement is being applied against your account, what sort of float the bank is giving you. What the earnings credit is. What the cost of services is. In the United States, all that's laid out right in front of you. Out here, they don't understand what the hell I'm talking about. Their eyes sort of glaze over."

Even in countries with sophisticated banking systems, companies may find it very difficult to obtain account analyses. In Japan, for example, a large bank interviewed by BI sets a profitability benchmark for each industry and determines whether a particular firm is meeting that figure. It does this by subtracting the interest paid on deposits from the value of all transactions, including loans, foreign exchange, and all other collateral business. But the account breakdown is for internal use only; companies are simply informed during a semiannual review whether or not their patronage is profitable for the bank. If not, the company is asked to make more deposits or to pay higher rates on loans.

In the absence of account analyses, companies must make every effort to keep tabs on their banking business themselves. In the words of the banking manager for a U.S. electronics firm, "Where it's not available, we take an eyeball approach. This doesn't imply a cursory examination. What we would do is completely dissect a month's banking business and figure out what the value dating is, what the fees for each type of movement are, and compare this with our understanding of the arrangement. When we're satisfied we know how we're being charged, and that the charges are accurate, we have a benchmark for comparison. From then on we can construct our own statement based on the volume of each kind of business and make a decision whether or not the charges in a given period are reasonable. Anything that changes dramatically without a corresponding change in volume attracts closer inspection."

An excellent example of an internal account-activity analysis—which could serve as a model for all companies—is employed by one of the Philippines' largest indigenous firms. According to the company's cash manager, "Even the most sophisticated bank here is doing a poor job of knowing just how much collateral business we have given them. So we track it and have been doing so for five years." The firm has ongoing discussions with its bankers to determine the precise value of each type of banking activity: "We ask them for formulas, which business they like better, and why." Armed with this information, the firm "makes up a report once a month that has everything—including the kitchen sink." Among the items listed in the report, broken down for each bank, are the following:

(1) **Interest payments on loans.** To calculate the profitability of its borrowings, the firm subtracts the bank's cost of funds from the total interest expense. This calculation is geared to each bank—"Some banks are better managed and have a lower cost of funds"—and to each loan transaction. For example, the company had learned that certain types of export financing credits, which can be rediscounted with the central bank, yield a spread to banks that can be seven percentage points higher than that on a normal short-term loan.

(2) **Volume of foreign exchange trading.** The rate for each transaction should be listed, along with the spread and any fees and commissions.

(3) **LCs, including commissions and fees.** Because of the high credit risks in many countries, the use of LCs can represent significant business to local banks.

(4) **Money market investments and bank deposits.** Firms must factor in the loss

Account number	Control number	1 Number of days	Month
34-227	Summary	in this cycle 29	April

Balance Analysis

2 Average ledger balance	254,517.
3 Less: uncollected funds (float)	325.
4 Average collected balance	254,192.
5 Average investable balance	221,783.
6 Earnings allowance @ 8.08 %	1,423.61
7 Less: total activity charges	1,425.71
8 Earnings allowance excess or (shortfall)	(2.10)
9 Collected balance required for activity charges	254,536.
10 Collected balance excess or (shortfall)	(344.)

Activity Charges

DESCRIPTION	VOLUME	RATE	CHARGE
Debits	21	.10	2.10
Credits	54	30	16.20
Checks deposited - Transit	33	09	2.97
- On-Us	30	05	1.50
- Local	37	05	1.85
Return items		1.00	
Cash deposited	3.5	1.25 /m	4.37
Account maintenance	2	12.00	24.00
Stop payments		6.00	
Zero balance charge - automatic		10.00	
Account reconciliation - Total		30.00 + 06/item	
- Partial		25.00 + 04/item	
Check sequencing - Standard		20.00 + 015/item	
- Priority		20.00 + 025/item	
Currency and coin issued			.83
Wire transfers — (see attachment)			142.00
Balance reporting			
Balance reporting telephone calls		2 50	
Foreign cash letter			
Foreign transit items			
Safekeeping			
Multiple cut off statements		1.75	
Lockbox processing			
Return Items Spec. Instr.			40.00
Controlled Disbursement Chg			1,189.89

Total activity charges	1,425.71

Balance Requirement for Loan Relationships

	Current month	Year to date
Collected balance available (line 10)		
11 Collected balance required for loan relationship		
12 Excess or (shortfall) for balance requirement		

Earnings allowance based on average T-Bill rate for previous three months.

An Account Analysis Statement is a periodic (usually monthly) review of services performed and balances maintained by our customers. The statement reflects

1. Activity charges and an
2. Earnings allowance which provides a credit for balances maintained.

The following definitions briefly describe the terms used in the Account Analysis formula.

1 **Number of days in this cycle.** The number of days in the period covered by this analysis.

2 **Average ledger balance.** The average balance maintained in a checking account. It is the sum of each day's ledger balance divided by the number of days in the statement period.

3 **Uncollected funds (float).** "Float" is deducted from the average ledger balance. It is the average daily amount of funds in the process of collection.

4 **Average collected balance.** The average ledger balance less uncollected funds.

5 **Investable balance.** The average collected balance less the reserve requirement of 12.75%.

6 **Earnings allowance.** An earnings allowance is calculated based on balances maintained in a checking account which provides credit for bank services. The following formula is used to calculate earnings allowance:

$$\frac{(average\ investable\ balance) \times (current\ cycle\ earnings\ allowance\ rate) \times days\ in\ cycle}{365} = earnings\ allowance$$

Earnings allowance is calculated on a daily basis and rounded to nearest hundredth percent.

7 **Total activity charges.** The total charges for bank services in this period.

8 **Earnings allowance excess or shortfall.** The net of service allowance less activity charges.

9 **Collected balance required for activity charges.** The following formula is used to calculate the amount of collected balance needed to cover total activity charges in the period:

$$\frac{Total\ activity\ charges - earnings\ rate \times \frac{365}{No.\ days\ in\ cycle}}{-\ (1 - reserve\ requirement)}$$

10 **Collected balance excess or shortfall.** Excess — a higher balance than necessary to pay for total activity charges was maintained for this period. Shortfall — a lower balance than required to pay for total activity charges was maintained for this period. (Line 4 less Line 9)

11 **Collected balance required for loan relationship.** The balance level required to comply with loan agreements.

12 **Excess or shortfall for balance requirement.** Excess — a higher balance than necessary to pay for both activity charges and loan relationships. Shortfall — a lower balance than required to pay for both activity charges and loan relationships was maintained for the periods indicated (current month and/or year to date).

of interest on balances left in current accounts, as well as the profit margins that banks have on time deposits and other interest-bearing investments.

(5) **Bank float.** Companies should monitor each bank carefully to determine exactly how long it holds on to deposited checks before crediting them to central accounts. The opportunity costs of check-clearing times should be factored into the bank profit calculation.

By compiling such a detailed report, firms can quantify the extent of business with each of their banks. "We know precisely how much business we are giving to each of the banks we use," said the cash manager. With this information, the firm can negotiate below-market interest rates on loans: It simply shows the banks that they are receiving an adequate rate of return from collateral business. At the time of the interview, the company was paying only the interbank rate but was giving the banks an additional 5 percent in collateral business, which the spokesman had learned was a fair profit margin. Whenever his banks complain about the extremely low interest rates the company pays, the cash manager just pulls out his monthly report. Said the spokesman: "Most of the time, they walk away with their heads down, because we tell them, 'We're already giving you so much business that you've either got to reduce the rate or give us more loans at the same rate.' And we can prove it to them."

Some companies are tapping the latest computer technology to monitor their banking costs. For example, a French automotive company set up an automated program several years ago that records all bank compensation—including fees, spreads, commissions, and value dating—and calculates the firm's level of business with each of its banks. Moreover, the computer estimates the profitability of the firm's business to the banks based on an estimate. The company's treasurer explained the system and its benefits:

"We mark every bank movement that comes through our accounting system. Anything that comes inside the system, including value dating, gets entered into the computer, so every month we know exactly what the banks make with us. The only thing we don't really know is their internal costs, so we make an approximation. For example, we consider that the size of a bank's network will affect its cost of funds," he elaborated. "We think that if a bank is losing money on us, that is a problem, because it will stop working with us. The point of this project is to help us treat a bank exactly like any other supplier. It's very useful in negotiations, because you know what you can ask for and what you can't."

The U.K. subsidiary of a well-known U.S. manufacturer also stores all its bank activity on computer, both to track costs and to compare performance. In the area of foreign exchange trading, for example, the computer generates reports on every currency transaction, showing the quotes of each bank contacted and the winning rate. Boasted the treasurer: "Every single quotation we get from every single bank is kept on file. We can see the size of the deals moving through banks, and we can see who is competitive and who is not. I mean, if they're off five or ten pips from the winning quote, they didn't win; but if they're forty-one pips off, that's just unacceptable. We're wasting their time and they're wasting ours." The computer also calculates each bank's success rate in offering acceptable quotations.

Minimizing Bank Costs

After companies have established sophisticated monitoring systems, they will be in an excellent position to negotiate with their banks for reduced compensation. Firms should adopt the following strategies to cut their banking costs:

· **Don't be afraid to ask.** Banks often charge premium prices for services simply because no one has challenged them. But as a U.K. treasury manager pointed out, "It's the squeaky wheel that gets oiled, isn't it?" The group treasurer of a prominent Italian firm concurred: "You negotiate with your banks every day; you have to fight for the best conditions. The banking system here is scandalous in what you can lose by not bargaining for good terms and conditions."

Large companies are the most likely to extract optimal terms from their banks. According to the treasurer of a mammoth U.S. subsidiary, "For the banks, it is important to have good relations with us, for the name and the image. A few years ago, I analyzed our relations with a certain bank and realized that they were making no profit from us. But they want to work with us because of our name." The director of finance of a major concern made the same point: "We ask our banks not for the best conditions, but better than the best. We are better than sovereign risk. Countries should pay more than we do."

· **Familiarize yourself with local market conditions.** A U.S. chemicals concern sharply reduced the banking costs of its Italian subsidiary by gathering information on interest rates and value-dating conventions for a number of its prime customers. Using this data as a benchmark, the company conducted tough negotiations with its banks to beat the prevailing market conditions.

In some countries, it is possible to tap the resources of local associations when investigating banking terms and conditions. As a French treasurer explained, "There is an organization of French treasurers, and when you are plugged into that association, you learn what rates or terms are for top-, medium-, and low-quality customers. You can improve your rates considerably."

· **Try the "total package" approach.** Companies can also slash banking costs by showing banks the full value of their business. Under this approach, firms identify all of the services being provided by a particular bank—forex, funds transfers, LCs, etc.—and negotiate costs for services based on the total volume of business.

For example, the CFO of an Italian auto maker negotiates "the cost of each type of transaction—all the fees, spreads, value dating, interest rates, and so on. And when we do that, we promise a certain level of business. We say to the banks, 'If you grant us these terms, we'll grant you this volume of business.' " Along the same lines, firms can even develop a global approach by including worldwide business from both the parent and subsidiaries in negotiations with international banks.

- **Minimize compensating balances.** In many countries, banks ask for compensation for loans and cash management services in the form of balances in non-interest-bearing accounts. In Mexico and Japan, for example, compensating balances range from 20 to 30 percent of the total amount of a loan. Savvy cash managers adopt a three-pronged strategy to pare balances to an acceptable level:

(1) **Set balance targets.** Balance targets can be set by determining the appropriate level of compensating balances needed to appease banks. This is generally based on a percentage of the total credit line extended from a bank, plus sums to compensate for special services. Cash managers then simply need to monitor balances regularly to make sure that deposits do not exceed target levels. Sometimes firms can successfully reduce balances by setting lower balance targets, usually without alienating their banks.

(2) **Negotiate.** Compensating balances are often subject to negotiation, particularly if a company is a valuable customer of the bank. For instance, when asked the amount of compensating balances required by banks in Japan, the spokesman for a large trading company responded: "It depends. It's a struggle between the bank and the customer. We minimize the compensating balance until our banks begin to complain." A Japanese banker shed further light: "In the past, we sent our employees around to customers to solicit deposits. We would ask for favors. We stressed our long-standing relations. But now it doesn't work."

(3) **Use the average to your advantage.** Since banks calculate balance requirements on a monthly basis, it may be possible to meet them without giving up the use of funds. As a U.S. manufacturer's regional treasurer for Latin America put it, "When the open market in a country is very small and the rates are low, I will not invest below a certain minimum. Instead, I keep that money on deposit and tell the banks, 'Hey, look how nice I am.' You know, the banks take the average for the month, they don't take a particular day and compare it with their requirements. So, I build my average balance on a monthly basis without locking it in. One day I'm zero, the other day I'm probably 70 percent when the open market is very low."

- **Press for reduced float and value dating.** Bank float can rob firms of funds availability in many countries. In such nations as Mexico, Venezuela, Spain, Italy, the Philippines, Thailand, and Indonesia, checks drawn on banks located in remote areas can take weeks to clear to headquarters accounts in the capital city. Fortunately, BI research shows that in many countries, aggressive cash managers have been able to obtain same-day or next-day check clearing from their banks. As the treasurer of the Brazilian subsidiary of a U.S. company put it, "If the banks don't credit my accounts within twenty-four hours, I change banks. That's just the way it works in Brazil."

The same approach can work in industrialized countries as well. In France, for example, where value dating is typically four days on drafts and two to five days on checks, most companies can improve on these times. "Value dating is definitely negotiable," said the treasurer for the French subsidiary of a U.S. electronics firm. "The banks tell you what is standard, and you take it from there."

Global Cash Management

"Four days on drafts is what people who don't negotiate get," claimed the spokesman for a French food producer. "We have negotiated the value dates to just two or three days." A French mining company has achieved even better results. "You can bargain with your banker to get better conditions on drafts than the usual four days," the firm's treasurer stated. "And we do get better conditions; we get one day after the maturity date."

· **Insist on fees where possible.** Rather than compensate their banks through balances or value dating, an increasing number of firms are asking their banks to charge fees. The European treasurer of a U.S. electronics firm explained why: "Compensating balances and all that are so hard to monitor. I want to know what each and every activity costs me, and I only want to pay for the services I get. When you deal with a bank, you should deal with them on such a basis that you know exactly what each and every transaction costs you. No overall hidden cost structure, but a structure where all transactions are known."

Although banks in many countries resist charging customers on the basis of a clear fee structure, the spokesman has had considerable success. "We've been able to negotiate this in every country in Europe. Obviously with varying degrees of success; you may get into certain compromise situations. But try."

Evaluating Banking Services

Companies that do not review the performance of their banks invariably suffer from lost interest revenues, overpriced services, lost work hours, and inappropriate or redundant services. To avoid such pitfalls, it is essential for companies to monitor and evaluate their banks rigorously at least annually. In the words of the banking manager of a U.S. consumer products concern, "We check each bank thoroughly once a year—even if it means working Saturdays."

Consultants and cash managers interviewed by BI recommend that companies ask the following questions when evaluating their banks' services:

Responsiveness

- Is there an account officer assigned to field your cash management inquiries?
- Is it necessary to initiate second and third follow-ups before an original inquiry is properly addressed?
- Is the bank's response timely?
- Is there backup when your account officer is out of the office?

General Services

- Do you hear from your bank at times other than when the bank wants to raise prices or if a problem exists?
- Are you approached by your bank about new ideas for improved servicing of your account?

How One Company Grades Its Banks

Asking the right questions about your bank's cash management services may not be enough. One large financial service company, for example, has developed a quantifiable system for reviewing the services provided by its banks. And because the system produces numerical ratings, it allows the company to stack one bank's service against another's. Here's how it works.

The annual review examines ten key bank servicing categories. Each category is assigned a weight of 1 to 3, representing the relative importance of the service to the company: 3 is "very important," while 1 is "minimal importance."

Each bank's performance during the year is graded on a scale of 1 to 4: 4 is "excellent," 3 is "good," 2 is "fair," and 1 is "poor."

In completing the review, the weight of each service category is multiplied by the quality rating of the bank in that category. A bank's "grade" represents the sum total of these products.

This test allows the company to grade each bank's services and permits easy and objective comparison between the different bank relationships. To highlight the intangibles that cannot be quantified, the numerical results may then be combined with subjective analysis.

The results of an annual performance test like this can be used to persuade a poorly performing bank to get its act together—or risk losing the company's business. The company may also wish to give more business to banks that are top-rated performers.

- Does your bank understand the complexities of your business and those of your competitors?
- Does the bank offer a full range of cash management services, such as cash collection, concentration accounts, ZBAs and TBAs, electronic information reporting, courier services/cash letters, lockboxes, foreign exchange, consulting services, and so forth?

Customized Services

- Is your bank amenable to provide customized cash management services to meet the specific needs of your company?
- Does the bank absorb, in whole or in part, the costs incurred in the development of these customized services?

Pricing

- Is the pricing of your bank's cash management services consistent with industry standards?
- Are you offered a variety of pricing formats, e.g., fee-based, compensating balances, certificate of deposit purchases, value dating, etc?

- Does your bank provide, via account analyses, information regarding how much it is charging you and for which specific cash management services?

Credit

- Are your needs for short-term/overnight lines of credit consistently honored by your bank?
- Does your bank provide long-term loans at preferential rates?

Funds Transfers/Check Clearing

- Are the outgoing funds transfers timed appropriately to give you the maximum use of funds?
- Are your incoming and outgoing funds transfers handled accurately?
- Are deposited checks and drafts cleared on a next-day basis or at an equally acceptable time?
- Does your bank's operational staff assist you in locating lost funds transfers?

Errors and Compensation

- Does your bank make frequent or repetitive errors in processing wire transfers or checks and drafts, handling documentation, or balance information reporting?
- Are your bank's errors, resulting in lost interest, compensated to your account with full back value?

Technology

- Does your bank have a high level of computerization, allowing you to draw upon its technological capabilities?

Rationalizing Bank Relations

At the end of a banking audit, companies must answer a final—and critical—question: How should bank relations be restructured to attain the best cash management services at the lowest possible cost? Based on an in-depth analysis of their banking needs and expenses, firms may want to increase or decrease the number of their relations, change the mix of foreign and domestic banks, or even take on some banking functions themselves. Any of these actions are sure to have a profound impact on a firm's traditional banking relations.

Changing Dynamics of Banking Relations

In the past, life for bankers was easy. They enjoyed close, long-standing relations with corporate customers, ballasted by personal ties and credit requirements. Breaking bank relations was practically taboo, since many firms regarded them as sacred. "Bank relations were like a marriage," ruminated a German finance director. "When you went with one bank, you automatically lost all the other girl friends you had in your past. That is why the decision as to whom I gave business was so difficult. Especially after the war, when it was not wise to disappoint those banks that were in early to help and assist us." Another German cash manager expanded: "Banking relations were more than a marriage. It was like in the Middle Ages, when you were given a wife—an arranged marriage, if you will. We inherited all kinds of banking relations that had existed for many years."

But the times are quickly changing. A BI survey of 302 international companies ranked the three most important criteria for bank selection and evaluation. According to the survey results, the top choices, rated on a weighted-average basis, were efficiency and quality of service, competitive pricing, and responsiveness. Length of relations ranked *last* among the eleven criteria listed in the questionnaire.

It is therefore not surprising that companies are beginning to alter their banking relations dramatically. The same survey showed that over the past few years, 37.4 percent of respondents increased the number of their banking relations, while 25.2 percent decreased them; only 37.4 percent made no change at all.

BI research clearly shows that cash management concerns are often the catalyst for corporate change. As the finance director of a French consumer goods company put it, "I think our banking relations are entering a new stage. Once, credit and personal relations were the most important things. But now we have come to a second stage, where we must consider the quality of a bank's services, and especially of their cash management." The treasurer of a U.K. natural resources firm also spoke of this new frontier: "History used to be the main factor—how much a bank helped us out when we were in hard times. But now we're doing quite a lot of soul searching, trying to figure out how important some of these relations are. What we are looking for now are banks that can help us in our cash management."

As a result of this new attitude, companies are beginning to take a much tougher— even confrontational—stance with their banks. An Australian cash manager expressed this perspective succinctly: "We can't go to a customer and say, 'You've been buying our products for twenty years; you have to keep buying them no matter what.' They'll just say, 'Well, I'll buy these over there, they're cheaper and better.' Why on earth shouldn't banks be treated the same way?" An Italian cash manager asserts, "If you can't find the services you want, then you have to make a little noise. If nobody listens, you go to the next bank. There's nobody hungrier than a banker who's just lost an account."

Even Japanese firms, which maintain closer relations with their banks than companies perhaps anywhere in the world, are becoming more demanding. Remarked the Swiss-based European regional finance director of a leading Japanese electronics firm: "If Japanese banks in Europe will develop convenient or really advantageous services, we will use them. But they are not considering what the customer is really requesting or really needs. There is not enough competition, as in the United States. Japanese banks are protected by the government. They should be very happy. But if their systems do not change, I will never use them."

Determining the Optimal Number of Banks

In this new, more experimental climate, companies are taking an especially hard look at the number of banks they use. The problems many firms face was summed up by the director of the Brazilian subsidiary of a European pharmaceuticals company. When asked how many banks his firm used in Brazil, he replied, "I have to laugh. When I was in China, I had two banks, and they really had to work for me. Then I came here, and I had to work for the banks. I had to give presents—Christmas presents—to the banks. It made no sense to me. Our finance people said we should not work with more than five banks, because it's too much time and money spent. But they found you just can't do that here. I guess we have fifty banks. And we are serving the banks, rather than the other way around. It's a most peculiar situation."

The spokesman's finance team understood well that using too many banks leads to sloppy cash management. As a consultant from a Big Eight accounting firm put it, "One of the big trends in bank relations is the consolidation and reduction of accounts. When you have fewer accounts, you can reduce overall costs, establish credit control, make management people more productive, and reduce the opportunity for idle funds to develop." In the opinion of many consultants and corporate cash managers, firms should strive to use no more than five banks in each country of operation.

Companies find that reducing bank relationships to this level boosts the bottom line in the following ways:

- **Improved control.** Many firms complain that trying to keep track of a bank's activity is a full-time job in itself, and with every increase in the number of bank relations, more effort is required to track banking activity. According to one seasoned cash manager, "Some banks make a lot of mistakes. So we must constantly check banking conditions, the value dates, the commissions, and the calculation of interest rates. Obviously, the task is easier when fewer banks are involved." The Italian treasurer of a U.S. chemicals firm agreed. "We cut down from twelve banks to five, because with a lot of banks you need a lot of people to monitor all the banking transactions involved. Using fewer banks makes my life easier all around. It's just too costly and time-consuming to maintain so many accounts."

- **Reduced banking costs.** The experience of a large, indigenous Philippine firm that has successfully trimmed its banking connections is instructive. When the firm's cash manager began implementing his program, the company was using twenty banks. He also found reporting practices to be extremely lax, with regional staff habitually leaving large balances with local bank branches. He quickly determined that the company actually needed just nine banks to handle its massive collections and severed ties with the other eleven. By working closely with the remaining institutions, the firm was able to reduce idle balances dramatically, from a daily average of P140 million to just P10 million in one year—saving itself nearly $2 million.

- **Easier use of cash management services.** Too many banks can also hamper the use of basic cash management services. For instance, a Japanese firm using over 120 banks found that this prevented the creation of concentration accounts, one of the

Choosing the Right Bank

When restructuring their banking relations, companies should develop selection criteria geared to the capabilities of local and foreign banks in each country. BI research shows that savvy firms judge banks based on the following factors:

Local Banks

(1) **Access to cheap local financing.** According to an Italian treasurer, "Our prime concern is to get low-cost financing. And inside Italy, the Italian banks are more competitive on loans and investments than foreign banks. They can provide loans at two points below the prime rate and usually offer higher interest on deposits."

(2) **Extensive local branch networks.** In the words of one U.S. treasurer, "We don't want to have a salesman or collector running around with checks in his pocket for a week. So we select or deal with banks that have as many branches as possible—and that means using major local banks."

(3) **Fundamental cash management services.** The credit manager of a U.S. chemical firm explained this criterion: "When you choose a local bank, whatever the country, you look for the basics. How good are they at moving money around? How long do they sit on checks? Do they offer concentration accounts? They usually don't have the capacity for electronic banking or good consulting yet."

(4) **Connections with local government and monetary authorities.** According to the spokesman for a major U.S. pharmaceuticals firm, "Local banks usually have better political connections than foreign ones and can be excellent sources of information

---

most basic cash management tools. Their long-range goal is to reduce the number of banks they use to two or three.

To obtain a concentration account, one European service company recently reduced the number of its banks from nineteen to just one. As a result, the firm was sharply criticized by its bankers. The financial manager described the conflict: "It is difficult to explain to the banks why we are compelled to use only one bank. But the bottom line was that the concentration bank system we use can give me this automatic service and same-day value. Using 19 banks could not."

· **Increased leverage.** An Italian company has concentrated its banking business with seven domestic and two foreign banks. According to the spokesman, "An Italian company of our size would usually use forty to forty-five banks, but we prefer to give a lot of business to each one. If you have a good negotiating position because of the business you offer a bank, you can get fantastic conditions in Italy."

Another firm that successfully trimmed its banking relations is the Brazilian subsidiary of a U.S. oil firm. According to the company's treasurer, the bank cut its

on upcoming credit restrictions, foreign exchange controls, banking regulations, and even currency devaluations."

International Banks

(1) **Efficient funds transfers.** According to the Asian regional treasurer of a U.S. consumer products group, "We pick foreign banks mainly on the efficiency of their facilities in wiring funds and making the necessary conversions, their strongest point."

(2) **Low-cost hard-currency loans.** According to the spokesman for a major U.S. firm with operations throughout Latin America, "We can get dollar loans through local banks, but usually they're more expensive. We may have a portfolio with an international bank of, say, $250 million. So if I call them up and say, 'Hey, I want a spread of such and such,' they say, 'Fine,' and that's it. If I talk to a local bank about it, they say, 'Forget it, we can't handle it.' "

(3) **Advanced cash management services.** Companies must often turn to international banks for the latest services, including electronic banking, multilateral netting, and consulting. As one Italian CFO complained, "In terms of cash management, the local banks here are in a prehistoric stage of development."

(4) **Financial innovation.** According to a French treasurer, "We look to foreign banks for their imagination and creativity." An Italian cash manager concurred. "The foreign banks are more innovative than Italian counterparts. They have introduced evergreen lines and a number of new investment instruments. They are the ones coming up with new ideas in this area."

---

relations from about twenty to nine. Finding that its balances were still getting out of control, it further pruned its relations to five banks. Said the spokesman: "That's just about right. We get along much better with our banks now that we've concentrated our business. Our balances are higher with each one, so we have more leverage with them."

When to Increase the Number of Banks

Although employing an excessive number of banks is a cardinal sin among cash managers, using too few banks also has its drawbacks. As one Australian treasurer pointed out: "A lot of companies out here tend to say to their bank, 'You're my mate and I'll deal only with you.' And the bank says 'Oh, fine, and you'll always get the best treatment.' But it gets to the stage where they just ignore you. The banks have a funny attitude out here. It's like, 'We're your principal banker, so who cares how high your rates are?' They're funny animals, these bankers."

Thus, in certain countries firms may want to increase their relations—or at least not cut them back too much—for the following reasons:

- **To satisfy credit needs.** Where credit is tight or scarce, maintaining relations with a large number of banks may be the only way for a firm to obtain adequate financing. According to the treasurer of a major French oil firm, "Credit is the main factor in our banking relations. Given the size of our borrowing needs, we are practically forced to work with a large number of banks."

Strict credit controls in developing countries may limit the amount banks can lend to a company, forcing cash-strapped MNCs to expand the number of banks they have accounts with. "We have between five and twenty banks in each country," said a spokesman for a U.S. chemicals firm with subsidiaries throughout Latin America. "In a lot of cases, a particular bank may not want to extend credit or may have limitations on how much they want to loan to an individual account. So we might maintain twenty different banks, thinking that we can play one against the other for terms and also be able to borrow as much as we need."

- **To spread risk.** As has already been discussed (see p. 251), many firms are concerned about bank risk and prefer to spread their business among many financial institutions. The regional treasurer of a U.S. chemicals firm in Latin America commented, "We are much more conservative in Latin America than in the United States. The reason is that when you deal with soft-currency banks, one is good today, six months later it's not good anymore." One automotive giant in Italy uses thirty-eight banks. Its CFO said, "It would be a big mistake to have only three or four banking relations in this country. No one should concentrate all their risk in a few banks. It doesn't make sense."
- **To increase bargaining power.** In certain countries, it may be easier to bargain for better terms with a large number of banks than with just a handful. A spokesman for a major Italian manufacturer summed up this attitude best: "You don't have the negotiating power or leverage when you use a few banks. Italian banks are secretive; they don't like to work together. They are quite tricky. So you can play one off against the other. If a bank doesn't feel that there is competition for your business, it will get lazy and not respect the terms. If you use a lot of banks, you can keep them all under control."

This is especially true in countries where companies traditionally use just one main bank. In Germany, for example, until recently firms have concentrated their business with a "house" bank. As one finance director explained, "You have to force the banks here to offer good cash management services. By turning to other banks, we can tell our main bank, 'They offer us better, cheaper service. Now we'll give you the chance to do the same.'"

- **To comply with cultural norms.** In Japan, for example, many credit-starved companies developed relations with as many banks as possible during high-growth periods; even though growth has slowed, those relations have been cemented over time, and it may be more beneficial to continue the tradition than to weed out those lesser-used banks. As one Japanese manager said: "I'd be afraid to cut any banks. We wouldn't buck tradition. I wouldn't even bother to experiment; maybe someone else will, but not me—it's taboo."

The Japanese approach to banking relations is not without its benefits. Good corporate customers can usually get credit when they need it and often receive assistance beyond the call of duty. For instance, one domestic bank interviewed even went so far as to arrange construction of a headquarters building for a major client.

Bypassing Banks Through Better Internal Systems

Some innovative companies have discovered that they can cut costs and simplify their banking relations by reducing their dependency on banks through sophisticated internal systems and treasury management vehicles. In the process, these firms are structuring their finance departments to serve as central banks for their corporate groups, usurping the traditional role of banks. For example, the treasurer of a German metal manufacturing firm that is installing cash-pooling schemes throughout Europe described his department as "the bank of our companies. That means the companies do not have loans with banks; they owe money only to the central finance department." The vice president and group treasurer of a Swedish capital goods firm called his department "the banking connection for all our companies. We accept deposits from subsidiaries and act as the group's short- and long-term lender."

A growing number of firms are competing directly with banks in this area by formally establishing captive finance and in-house factoring companies. For example, a U.S. electronics firm has set up an in-house factoring company in Geneva that purchases intracompany receivables at discount rates at least as good as those the exporting subsidiaries could receive from their banks. In addition, the factoring operation shifts liquidity within the corporate group by leading and lagging payments. According to the firm's financial statement, the factoring operation showed annual net profits of $600,000. In addition, the company saved the corporate group $750,000 in reduced forex losses, $150,000 in funds transfer costs, and $333,000 in lower borrowing expenses. Thus, the in-house factoring company achieved total profits and cost efficiencies of nearly $2 million.

A major U.S. consumer goods conglomerate has established a finance company in Geneva that pools the group's excess cash for investment, makes intracompany loans, and assists in currency management. According to the firm's general manager, last year the operation cost about $2 million to run and realized profits of the same amount—for a return on investment of 100 percent, not taking into account the advantages of concentrating profits in Switzerland's low-tax environment.

In the most extreme cases, some firms have actually opened their own banks. One German industrial group interviewed by BI, for example, recently formed a bank, and a major French corporation has increased the equity of its existing internal bank to give it more lending capabilities. And the idea is spreading. Said the treasurer of a French oil company: "We're looking very carefully at establishing a bank. It's a profitable business; why shouldn't we take advantage of it?"

Setting Up a French Finance Company

One way to beat the banking system in France is to become a bank yourself. By establishing a finance company, firms can participate in the interbank market and thus have access to restricted overnight investment opportunities. Finance companies can also be used to shift liquidity within corporate groups, easing the burden of the country's tight credit conditions.

But there is a catch: Finance companies, like everything else in France, are regulated by the central bank, and permission to operate is difficult to obtain. "In theory it can be done; in practice it can be very tough to do," one banker said. Large domestic—and especially nationalized—companies have been the most successful in negotiating with the Bank of France, although a handful of foreign companies have also received the green light.

To set up a finance company, firms must hire legal counsel and apply to the Bank of France, which makes its decisions on a case-by-case basis. Companies must be able to convince the authorities that their finance company will not damage the franc, or they may offer a quid pro quo, such as providing jobs through investment in a depressed area. One large French food manufacturer wants to set up a financing

---

Case Example: How One Company Reshaped Its Spanish Banking Relations

Several years ago, the treasury group of a major U.S. manufacturer decided the time was ripe to review the cash management systems and procedures of its Spanish subsidiary. However, the in-house audit team dispatched to Madrid quickly discovered that because the Spanish banking system had for years been "an isolated fortress in Europe" and a "rigid cartel," enormous savings could be realized by focusing the study on the firm's management of its accounts and relations with its banks. Moreover, the recent entry of foreign banks into the country and the liberalizing moves by the Bank of Spain had opened "the first cracks in the banking fortress," setting the stage for a complete overhaul of the subsidiary's banking relations.

The consulting team began its audit by gathering all internal data and bank reports. With this information, the consultants compared the cost of services and evaluated the performance of each subsidiary's banks. For one important bank service—foreign exchange trading—the team found that the average range between the highest and lowest bids amounted to thirty points and often exceeded thirty-five to forty points. By marking the low and high bids, the consultants could easily determine which banks consistently offered the best rates and how much the rates varied.

Next, the consultants reviewed the company's management of bank balances. The subsidiary had established as many as three different accounts (current, overdraft, and payroll) at twenty-two banks. The audit team took random sample periods of six weeks to six months and analyzed the bank statements for current accounts "with a view to identifying *actual* balances by value date as opposed to ledger balances

company but is proceeding very cautiously. As the firm's treasurer explained, "We lack the international scope of some of the major nationalized companies, which makes it harder to justify establishing such a company. Still, as long as the government foresees no danger of our company damaging the French franc, we have a good chance of gaining approval. We must move slowly, though, and have a solid case to put forward to them."

Finance companies are regulated like banks, but they are not permitted to transact business with entities outside the parent's group. In addition to easing access to the money markets, they are useful for coordinating intracompany flows through cash-pooling schemes. "We have set up a finance company that is controlled directly by the cash management department of the group, which keeps the finance company informed about the cash position of the group. So the finance company will either raise money from the banks on its own and then distribute it, or it might take money from one subsidiary and transfer it to another, even internationally," the finance director of a French oil firm explained. "The finance companies are separate entities: first, to have a location to centralize funds, and second, to be able to access the money market and the interbank market, which is possible only for certain legal entities in France."

---

shown in daily bank mailings and the accounting cash position." A running tally was kept of debit balances, credit balances, and net balances at each account on a daily and overall basis. The total number of days each account spent in debit and credit was also recorded.

As a result of this exhaustive investigation, three major sources of high banking costs were revealed:

(1) The company often ran up enormous credit balances—in excess of P200 million per day—at a number of its banks. These high idle balances resulted from underestimation of customer collections, discounting of drafts while current accounts were already in a credit position, and the proliferation of different bank accounts to accommodate foreign exchange activity. During the review period, credit balances earned a mere 0.1–0.25 percent, less a tax of 16 percent on interest income.

(2) The subsidiary also frequently overdrew its current accounts, resulting in stiff penalty fees. "This indicates a time lag between cash outflows and their coverage through customer collections or interbank transfers," the consultants concluded. "Also, it may reveal that the subsidiary does not factor value-dating conditions into its cash planning."

(3) Finally, the firm held simultaneous credit and debit balances at different banks and even within the same bank. As shown in the table above, the consultants calculated that average credit balances in current accounts represented 15 percent of overdrafts and 6 percent of the firm's total borrowings.

Using the results of its analysis, the audit team made the following recommenda-

Current Accounts as a Percentage of Credit Accounts

| Bank | Balances (P'000s) | | Current Account as a Percentage of Overdraft Account |
	Current Account	Overdraft Account	
1	66,740	(129,784)	51
2	9,831	(99,901)	10
3	6,507	(74,807)	9
4	2,397	(96,100)	2
5	5,890	(195,231)	3
6	8,614	(70,423)	12
7	1,631	(14,000)	12
8	28,101	(206,814)	14
TOTAL	129,711	(887,060)	15
Total current account as a percentage of total borrowings (P2,185,193)			6

tions and then helped the subsidiary implement them, saving it several hundred thousand dollars within a year.

- **Reduce the number of bank accounts.** According to the consultants' final report, "It is just impossible to control so many accounts and do a professional cash management job. The organization spends too much time reconciling a multitude of accounts (accounting records) instead of efficiently managing a few from a treasury viewpoint." They recommended selecting just one bank as the main concentration account for disbursements and collections.
- **Monitor and assess bank performance rigorously.** The consultants advised local managers to prepare comparative tables showing the cost of banking services. With this information in hand, the subsidiary would be equipped to negotiate more aggressively for the best terms on loans, value dating, etc. In the case of foreign exchange trading, although banks commonly demand forex business as partial compensation for loans, the team recommended "granting foreign exchange business solely on outright price performance."

Local managers were also instructed to establish procedures for filing copies of all bank statements for continuing review and to "cut relationships with banks that cannot provide statements on a regular basis."

- **Negotiate concentration accounts.** By having the banks automatically offset credit and debit balances, the subsidiary could greatly reduce its interest expenses. The consultants encouraged the firm to switch accounts to foreign banks, which were much more eager to offer the service than local ones.
- **Draw on the power of the parent when negotiating loan rates.** The team advised the subsidiary to offer parent guarantees when arranging loans with its banks. In this way, instead of being treated as a small local company, the firm would receive the credit rating—and the prime rates—of a large MNC.

7

How to Implement a Cross-Border Cash Management System

After you have investigated your company's worldwide practices concerning cash reporting and forecasting, credit and collection, payables management, bank relations, and short-term investment and borrowing—and have taken the necessary action to improve these critical procedures at the subsidiary, regional, and parent levels—you are ready for the final step toward successful cash management: the creation of a global treasury system. As one cash manager explained, "We've got our systems working well on a country-by-country basis. What we want now is to bring them all together into a cross-border system."

With financial liberalization quickly gaining in Europe and elsewhere, more and more firms are turning to global cash management vehicles to reduce financial costs and upgrade managerial control. Whether these vehicles are simple cross-border cash pooling systems or more complicated reinvoicing or in-house factoring operations, they can boost a company's bottom line by hundreds of thousands of dollars—even millions—by cutting borrowing needs, reducing currency risks and costs, minimizing float and funds transfers, increasing investment yield, minimizing taxes, and maximizing the use of internal funds.

Here are just a few examples of the dramatic quantitative and qualitative benefits companies realize by refining cross-border cash management techniques:

- **One French oil services firm set up an innovative global cash-pooling system to funnel cash automatically from local bank accounts into regional concentration points, thereby improving allocation of corporatewide cash resources, minimizing banking delays on funds availability, and significantly lifting investment returns.** Using the concentration services of two major money center banks, the system pools cash from hundreds of operating units and effectively directs global cash to a centralized investment facility in Amsterdam. The arrangement is so effective that remote service crews from Djakarta to Wyoming can generate receipts of over $2.5 billion per year, yet there is never more than $1 million floating in the system at any time.

· **A well-known U.S. consumer goods producer established a state-of-the-art finance company in Geneva that serves as a centralized cash mobilization and strategic treasury center.** The director of the finance company explained the reason the vehicle was created: "With today's environment, it's absolutely essential that we're able to move funds where they're needed. Here we do subsidiary financing, manage credit and collection, and at the same time minimize currency risks and our balance sheet exposure." The finance company, which also pools and nets corporate funds, ultimately saves the firm millions of dollars a year—thanks to lower financial costs and higher investment returns.

· **Another leading U.S. MNC implemented an in-house factoring operation to replace a reinvoicing center that was becoming increasingly difficult to run because of transfer-pricing headaches.** One year, this firm's Geneva in-house factoring company showed profits of $600,000. In addition, the factoring operation saved the corporate group $750,000 in reduced forex losses, $150,000 in funds transfer costs, and $330,000 in lower borrowing expenses. Thus, the factoring center added nearly $2 million to the company's P&L.

Six Approaches to Better Global Money Management

Although the actual techniques and systems must be tailored to a company's size, industry, and organization, your firm has six basic options for improving control of cross-border cash flows:

(1) **Cash pooling.** This technique allows companies to transfer the surplus funds of subsidiaries to one or more central corporate accounts where the money can be invested at higher yields or allocated to cash-poor subsidiaries, thereby reducing corporatewide borrowing costs.

(2) **Hold accounts.** One of the more popular global cash management devices, hold accounts are particularly useful to exporters and importers with large volumes of receipts and disbursements in the same currency. These accounts—which, if exchange controls permit, can be set up domestically or abroad in a foreign currency—are used to accumulate foreign currency receipts from exports. These funds can then be used to pay for imports or other expenses denominated in the same foreign currency, thereby reducing the number of necessary currency conversions and hence foreign exchange costs.

(3) **Leading and lagging of payments or receipts.** This is used to change the timing of intracompany trade flows, allowing firms to shift corporate liquidity, reduce borrowing costs, and protect against currency risks. Leading refers to prepaying import payments or receiving early payment for exports; lagging relates to delaying import payments or receiving late payment on exports. Most countries impose controls on the use of leading and lagging, setting limits on the time period intracompany accounts can be prepaid or delayed and establishing guidelines on the interest that should be charged.

(4) **Netting.** Perhaps nowhere in cash management is there an opportunity to cut costs as readily as through the implementation of a netting system. This allows

Growth in Specialized Cross-Border Vehicles

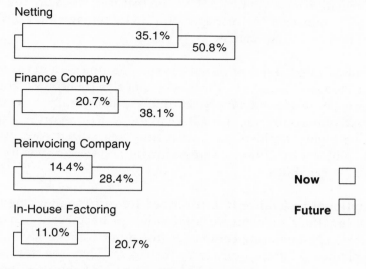

Source: *New Directions in European Cash Management,* Business International.

companies to "net" intracompany payments so that fewer transactions will occur. Firms have realized that they can sharply reduce the number of foreign exchange transactions and funds transfers by offsetting payments among subsidiaries within a corporate group.

(5) **Reinvoicing companies.** One of the most elaborate steps a company can take is to set up a reinvoicing system. These companies act as an intermediary to take title from the manufacturers and sell to other subsidiaries or to third parties. By controlling the currency of billing, a reinvoicing center can be used to centralize exposure management or enhance marketing.

(6) **Factoring/finance companies.** Some companies prefer to use in-house factoring, whereby receivables are purchased and discounted, in lieu of reinvoicing centers to centralize cash and exposure management. Others have developed sophisticated finance companies that can be used for reinvoicing, factoring, and other aspects of international cash management.

Hurdling Operational Barriers

When assessing the appropriateness of these cross-border cash management systems, companies must weigh the financial advantages against the hassles of setting one up. As a treasurer who learned his lesson the hard way warned, "If you're going to link into one of these central spider's webs, you have to do a great deal of groundwork—and it takes a group of disparate individuals and a lot of time and effort."

There are five major hurdles that companies must overcome when implementing a cross-border cash management system:

(1) **Steep start-up and operational costs.** Depending on a system's capabilities, start-up costs can range from tens of thousands of dollars to as much as $5 million. "The more information you want, and the more features, the more this thing is going to cost up front," counseled the manager of a Swiss reinvoicing center, which cost several million dollars to implement.

The more sophisticated and centralized a system becomes—and the more information that is collected and managed—the more expensive it becomes. Pooling systems, for instance, can be developed simply to follow a decentralized remit-when-you-have-excess-cash philosophy, requiring little in the way of reporting capabilities. But they can also be highly sophisticated, with fully centralized control—a "send-us-that-$100,000" philosophy. The costs are contingent on the complexity of the reporting system and its capabilities.

(2) **Organizational resistance to centralized treasury management.** Some companies find within their own organizations the greatest barrier to establishing a treasury vehicle. "The operating companies just don't want to give up any of their functions," explained a European treasury manager. "They see this as headquarters wanting to get a better look over their shoulder." The location and size of the subsidiaries may also affect their ability to participate in a cross-border cash management system. For example, a BI study of cash management practices in Asia shows that while companies tend to centralize control corporatewide, the majority of firms are decentralized for cash management in Asia. As the treasurer of a U.S. conglomerate in Asia said, "We're highly decentralized in Asia, and the main reason is sheer distance. Our affiliates are very far away, and besides, they are relatively small, so we just let them take care of their own needs."

(3) **Tax regulations and exchange controls.** Tax rates and regulations vary sharply; the United Kingdom, for instance, charges a 35 percent income tax and a 25 percent withholding tax, whereas Belgium grants ten-year tax holidays for treasury-coordination centers and levies no withholding tax. Beyond that, many countries impose tax restrictions that reduce the ability of a treasury vehicle to reinvoice intracompany sales, to factor export receivables, to shift corporate liquidity, and to carry out other cash management activities. The most notable example is the U.S. Tax Act of 1984 and the subsequent Tax Reform Act of 1986, which wreaked cash management havoc on many U.S. firms. As one frustrated U.S. treasury manager remarked, "Our timing was extremely bad. We set up our factoring operation based on the idea that it would handle both foreign- and U.S.-sourced receivables. So when they changed the tax laws, factoring no longer made sense."

Exchange controls are also a nuisance. Some countries in Europe (e.g., Greece and Turkey), in Asia (e.g., the Philippines and Korea), and in Latin America impose foreign exchange regulations that make it difficult or impossible to hold local funds offshore, net intracompany trade, lead and lag, or conduct other sophisticated cross-border cash management functions.

(4) **Poor banking systems and high financial costs.** The banking inefficiencies in

some countries and the high financial costs of operating in others impede global cash management. Excessive fees and spreads on foreign exchange and loans, high money-transfer costs, and compensating-balance requirements are just some of the complaints lodged by cash managers. In the words of one European financial executive, "Sophisticated banking services and systems are vital for international cash management. Countries like the United Kingdom and Switzerland are popular because of their banking systems. The banks in countries like Italy are a disaster."

The Asian banking system harbors a seemingly endless and often baffling diversity of banking traditions, regulations, practices, and services. Banks and services run the gamut, from the highly evolved international money centers of Hong King, Singapore, and Tokyo to the obstructive financial systems of Indonesia and the Philippines. The controller of a German subsidiary in Korea remarked, "The local banks are so time-consuming, so difficult, there's so much paperwork involved." But Asia is a pleasure compared with the woefully inept state of banking in many Latin American countries. Branches lack computer hookups, money transfers are mishandled, accurate balance reporting is hard to find and, to top it all off, errors are the rule. "It's just the worst," said a regional treasurer of a U.S. chemicals company of the Venezuelan banking system. "You name it, it's the worst. The banks in Venezuela are just thoroughly inefficient."

(5) **Currency volatility.** With an international cash management system, a firm must collect, disburse, invest and finance, and trade in a wide variety of currencies—which move up and down against one another, exposing the firm to exchange risks. From 1979 levels, the steamrolling U.S. dollar had appreciated about 70 percent against the deutsche mark and 60 percent vis-a-vis the U.K. pound by mid-1985. Because of the dollar's strength, many U.S. firms and their subsidiaries switched to billing in the importer's currency in order to maintain market share. But this exposes firms to increased currency risks and leaves the complicated task of forecasting and trading currencies up to local finance managers, who are generally oriented toward accounting or operations and not equipped to manage currencies.

In the United States, Statement No. 52 of the Financial Accounting Standard Board (FAS No. 52) focused attention on subsidiaries' transaction exposure—both from third parties and within a company. Subsidiaries are exposed whenever they have to pay or receive payment in a nonfunctional currency (the local currency is typically chosen as the functional currency). As a result of these concerns, companies are seeking treasury systems that will facilitate the monitoring, forecasting, and management of transaction exposure.

Building a Successful Cross-Border System

To help your company sidestep these financial pitfalls and build a successful cash management system, this chapter describes cross-border techniques and vehicles that can be used to improve cash management. The description is supplemented with case studies of some of the most sophisticated cross-border cash management systems in the world. In addition, the chapter shows companies how to determine whether these vehicles can benefit them.

The chapter also analyzes restrictions such as exchange controls, taxes, and banking practices that can hinder the development of a successful cross-border system, and it shows companies how to leap many of these hurdles. Critical behind-the-scenes issues such as the impact of these systems on organization, policies, and performance evaluation are also addressed to assist companies in putting together an effective system to boost their bottom line.

Taking Advantage of Cross-Border Cash Pooling

Despite its many benefits, cross-border cash pooling is often overlooked by MNCs. Cash pooling comes in many forms, each unique to the regions of operation, organizational structure, and cash-flow patterns of the firm. These range from unsophisticated to state-of-the-art systems. Some may be highly structured, with daily or weekly cycles and fixed bank channels; others are informal, with operating units remitting surplus funds to the pooling center as they arise. They can range from simple domestic cash pooling, as previous sections have discussed, to a fully integrated global cash pooling system. This section examines cross-border cash pooling.

Pooling funds on an intracountry or even regional basis is common. But the transition to a global system can be difficult. There are three difficulties involved in implementing cross-border cash pooling:

· **Exchange controls.** Many companies do not try pooling because they believe they will face insurmountable government restrictions: "Exchange controls make it impractical to pool cash cross-border," remarked a financial executive at a U.S. consumer-goods MNC.
· **Taxes.** Other executives are wary about transferring funds from one subsidiary to another unless the funds are tied directly to a payable invoice or are part of a multitiered ownership structure (i.e., an intentional payment of dividends by one affiliate to another). The reason for caution is simple: Tax authorities could presume that the amount transferred from one legal entity to another is a "constructive" dividend for the parent. If so, the transfer would be treated as income for the parent, with the resulting adverse tax consequences.

Pooled funds might also be treated as loans. In this case, however, the company could be faced with tax problems. The pooling center would have to pay interest to the subsidiary sending the cash. The income tax on the interest earned and withholding tax on the interest paid out might offset any benefits derived from pooling. Furthermore, pooled funds would have been converted to another currency and invested, which complicates the issue of the appropriate rate to be paid to the lending subsidiary. The tax authorities must be satisfied that the rate is an arm's-length rate, given the additional foreign exchange risk. Also, companies might face other government restrictions that differ according to the country involved.

· **Administrative controls.** Cross-border cash pooling also entails the administrative burden of keeping track of such things as where and when the interest income was generated and the amount of interest expense incurred. This can be expensive, because different countries have different regulations on intracompany loans.

While there are difficulties involved, cross-border cash pooling can be very beneficial, and companies are successfully using this cash management technique. Funds can be invested at a higher rate of interest, and borrowing needs and taxes can be reduced. "Establish the cash pool in a low-tax country and use the dollar as the functional currency," suggests the assistant treasurer of a leading U.S. MNC. "The tax can be as low as 3 percent if the proper elections are made and no funds are loaned to the United States." Withholding taxes on interest can frequently be reduced or minimized by operating the cash pool out of a finance company in a country that maintains extensive tax treaties, e.g., the Netherlands. Denominating all loans to and borrowings from the cash pool in the currency of the lender or borrower can protect the subsidiaries from exchange risk. Cross-border cash pooling may even be used as a foreign exchange management tool. For example, a loan by a foreign subsidiary to the cash pool may be declared a hedge of the net investment in that country.

Despite the restrictions, many companies find that they have enough flexibility to justify cross-border cash pooling. Subsidiaries in most countries can borrow from a cash pool if the company is willing to accept the withholding tax and tenor requirements. Many countries also allow subsidiaries to make cross-border deposits to a cash pool. These countries include Australia, Canada, Germany, the Netherlands, Singapore, Switzerland, and the United Kingdom.

Some alert companies have found ways to reap substantial rewards through cross-border cash pooling. For example, a U.S. manufacturer of electronic equipment found that its European subsidiaries were having difficulty getting the best investments and borrowing rates. The assistant treasurer elaborated: "The local money markets just weren't serving us well. Our subsidiaries are not all that big, and they often have relatively small sums of money to invest. I found that we were having a hard time placing funds of less than $100,000 at market rates for brief periods of time." Adding to these problems, cash-poor subsidiaries lacked the clout to get the best rates on short-term loans.

The solution was an ingenious cash-pooling scheme involving cross-border sweep accounts and automatic investment. As the treasurer explained, "What we have is standing instructions—where exchange controls permit, in the United Kingdom, Germany, Belgium, Switzerland, and the Netherlands—for our European banks to sweep our U.S. dollar accounts, on a daily basis, into an account in Luxembourg in the name of the subsidiaries." Luxembourg was chosen as the site "because the investment community there is smaller, and we can get more personal attention."

Once the funds arrive, they are managed by a major U.S. bank, which automatically invests them overnight. "All subsidiaries have Luxembourg accounts in their own name," the treasurer added. "The bank uses the accounts on an aggregate basis for investment purposes."

Interest is paid to the subsidiaries based on the pool's actual return. "One subsidiary might have only $50,000," the assistant treasurer explained, "while another has

$3 million, but the bank will give them both the same overnight U.S.-dollar Eurorate of interest." As a result, the center's rate is far better than any deal the subsidiaries could negotiate themselves.

Cross-border cash pooling is not necessarily global in application. Some firms find it worthwhile to develop regional systems tailored specifically to the locale. In the Asia/Pacific region, the most favored sites for regional pooling centers are Hong Kong and Singapore, because of the absence of exchange controls and easy access to the Asia-dollar market.

For example, a U.S. consumer products MNC has established a regional headquarters in Hong Kong to coordinate the activities of its subsidiaries in Hong Kong, Japan, Korea, the Philippines, Singapore, Taiwan, and Thailand. Every Monday, the units report to regional headquarters their receipts, disbursements, opening and closing balances for the previous week, and a forecast for the current week. On Tuesday, after consolidating the information, headquarters telexes the subsidiaries' banks to convert local-currency surplus funds into U.S. dollars and remit them to Hong Kong. According to the firm's regional treasurer, "We pool all excess cash here. If any unit needs money, we then push out whatever they need or invest it here."

However, exchange controls have forced the company to modify its pooling system for the Philippines and Taiwan. A spokesman for the firm commented on the Philippines: "Once our unit knows they have some excess cash, it takes them two or three days to get the documentation to the central bank, so there's a timing gap there. I've had to make the system work as well as it can there. They just tell us on Wednesday how much they can send to Hong Kong." In Taiwan, where the subsidiary is required "to present a mountain of documentation" to the central bank for permission to remit surplus funds, control is much more difficult. "There is a large gap between the time we request approval and the time they approve it, and we never know what the approval date will be. So we have said to Taiwan, 'When you have the authority, just send the money out that day,' and that's what they do."

Another example of an advanced pooling system is that of a Far Eastern airline company with offices in almost every Asian country, as well as the United States and Europe. At the end of each week, all units telex corporate treasury with details of the week's receipts from ticket sales and disbursements for catering, fuel, and payroll expenses. They also provide their anticipated inflows and outflows for the coming week, together with their surplus funds position. In large offices, where excess cash piles up more quickly, reports are submitted every two or three days. The treasury staff then instructs the subsidiaries to remit funds either in Singapore dollars to corporate headquarters, where they are invested in the offshore or domestic money markets, or in U.S. dollars to a New York hold account, where they are used to pay down U.S. dollar borrowings contracted for the corporate group.

Like the U.S. consumer goods firm, the airline has had to modify its system for several countries. According to the manager of finance, "In Taiwan and Korea, we can wait maybe three weeks or a month before getting approval to remit. They quibble on every item, and that jams up your money." As a result, the firm monitors these units and instructs them to invest surplus funds locally, earning interest until approval for remittance is received. Although these operations cannot participate in the pooling system, the weekly reporting cycle imposes a beneficial discipline and gives corporate treasury better control over excess-cash investment procedures.

The Australian regional headquarters of a U.S. pharmaceuticals firm has put the finishing touches on a cash-pooling system that includes operations in Hong Kong, Singapore, New Zealand, and Malaysia. According to the regional treasurer, subsidiaries will utilize overdraft facilities wherever possible and "just shoot funds back to headquarters. This will give us excellent control and maximize cash usage." By keeping subsidiaries in a net-deficit position, headquarters can use their funds to pay down Australian dollar borrowings, which are among the most expensive in the region. In this way, the pooling arrangement is expected to shave several percentage points off the company's regional borrowing costs.

Pooling Trade Flows Through a Reinvoicing Center

To avoid tax and exchange control problems, companies often opt to pool cash by managing their trade accounts. For example, Company A, a leading U.S. manufacturer, designed its cash management system to link its cash pooling system with its reinvoicing operation. The fast-growing firm decided to start a cash pooling system in the early 1970s to mobilize its international cash flows, which were swelling because of the firm's phenomenal 40 percent annual sales growth. "Idle cash was the last thing in the world that we wanted," said the manager of money and banking for the firm. The excess funds could have been used to finance operations springing up in North America, Latin America, Europe, and Asia. But because the company was still small at the time, it could not justify training treasury personnel in every subsidiary; consequently, the sales offices were collecting cash and sitting on it. As a remedy, the company wanted a simple system that did not require a sophisticated staff to administer—one that provided the firm with the greatest return for the least amount of management time. The solution was a weekly cycle of cash management.

Each Thursday the subsidiaries prepare a report of their projected cash positions in the coming week, including their bank balances (if any) and anticipated receipts, minus disbursements. The forecasts sent by the European subsidiaries to the reinvoicing center in Holland include receipts from all external and intracompany sources, as well as payments to third-party vendors and payroll and other operating expenses. Of course, accounts payable and receivable vary from week to week—some subsidiaries have a payroll only once a month, for example—and some payments may not arrive when anticipated. But the forecasts, according to a company spokesman, have been reliable.

Because it is usually in a cash-generating position, a sales subsidiary generally informs the appropriate treasury manager of anticipated net receipts. On Monday, the subsidiary borrows its projected net cash position through an overdraft facility (or through a demand loan in countries without overdraft facilities) and transfers the funds to the firm's reinvoicing center in Amsterdam, which sends them to the appropriate headquarters' bank account.

The following is an example of how the company's system works: On Thursday, a German sales subsidiary forecasts its receipts and disbursements for the week. For example, forecast receipts of the equivalent of $10 million in deutsche marks, projected disbursements of $6 million, and a zero bank balance would net a cash position for the week of $4 million. On Monday, the subsidiary goes into overdraft and transfers the $4 million to the reinvoicing center. As the anticipated receipts come in, the subsidiary pays off its overdraft so that by Friday it has no bank balance, loans, or investments outstanding over the weekend.

Meanwhile, the reinvoicing center examines its overall European cash position and tells the U.S. parent how much it can expect to receive in dollars on Monday. On that day the reinvoicing center's bank is charged with the amount, and the parent's bank is credited with it. Thus, the use of the company's European reinvoicing center facilitates cash pooling. As a spokesman explained, "The reinvoicing center does not hold the cash; it is sent to the United States and paid against its U.S. intracompany trade account. By having it centralized at the reinvoicing center it is much simpler, because we only receive one payment on our intracompany account."

Since all the cash that is remitted is against trade payables, there are no tax complications. "It is not like pooling and investing the funds of several legal entities, which can lead to tax and other problems; they are simply paying intracompany invoices," said the spokesman. "As long as we abide by the countries' guidelines, we don't have any problems getting the funds out. We make sure local regulations are followed."

Subsidiaries that are net users of cash—i.e., production plants—follow a similar procedure, but in reverse. When calculating the weekly receipts-less-disbursements forecast, cash-poor subsidiaries will show a net disbursement figure. The subsidiary submits its cash requirements on Thursday and, beginning on Monday, goes into overdraft to meet its necessary payments for payroll and other expenses during the week. On Friday, the subsidiary receives funds from the parent to pay off the overdraft and any unprojected disbursements that may have come due. At that point, as with the cash-generating subsidiary, the subsidiary should have zero cash, loans, and investments.

But the system is not always so precise. Frequently, a sales subsidiary takes in more money than expected and has to transfer net receipts more than once a week; occasionally, a sales subsidiary is hit with unprojected disbursements or late receipts and must use overdraft facilities. Similarly, manufacturing subsidiaries may have to make an unexpected or unusually large payment during the week; in that case, the parent sends the funds earlier than Friday.

The Dutch reinvoicing center includes the company's European subsidiaries in Austria, Belgium, Denmark, Finland, France, Germany, Ireland, Italy, the Netherlands, Portugal, Spain, Sweden, and the United Kingdom. But some countries are more difficult to operate in than others. According to a company spokesman, while this "makes it more cumbersome, the alternative for a cash-generating subsidiary is to build up the cash locally, which is not what we want."

Higher Interest Income. Company A's forecast, funds transfer, and investment system has a valuable result: While the parent has the full amount of the funds to invest for the entire week, the subsidiary's overdraft line is constantly declining as receipts are collected and used to pay down the facility. Thus, if the loan is repaid in equal installments, the average balance will be half the sum borrowed.

In practice, the net interest income will be smaller or larger, depending on the difference in borrowing and investing rates. On an overall basis, the company believes interest income is generated. The system of weekly cash cycles enables the firm to concentrate its cash at headquarters, where it can be invested at more favorable rates than if each subsidiary had invested individually (because the parent invests a much larger amount for a set period of time).

Company A believes this fundamentalist approach is most effective for its purposes because it is simple and systematic and does not result in transaction-exposure risk for the subsidiaries (which borrow only in local currencies). Moreover, concentrating the cash at headquarters allows the company to reap the benefits of large investments and to draw on the expertise and worldwide perspective of its money manager. "We believe that, even though the borrowing has a cost," a spokesman commented, "we can pool the funds and invest them at a higher rate."

The system also enables the parent to act as the corporation's "central bank." According to companywide policy, none of the subsidiaries make any borrowing—except for the overdraft facility, which is essentially a very short-term cash management tool. The parent fills all the subsidiaries' longer-term financing requirements, either by permitting delayed settlement of intracompany accounts or by raising funds itself in the international credit and capital markets and funneling the proceeds abroad. Moving the cash quickly also reduces the net amount of funds the parent must borrow.

A Cascading Cash Pool. Using what its treasurer calls "cascading cash pooling," Company B has established a daily cycle for pooling the cash flows of its worldwide operations. The system pools the cash from hundreds of local operating units and ultimately concentrates liquidity into the accounts of seven regional holding companies, where the monies can be most effectively managed. "After all," the treasurer said, "money is the only thing that's totally fungible—so why would you want to spread it out?"

A combination of two major money center banks provides the network of concentration accounts, which move cash from local units through various intermediate accounts all the way to the greatest possible concentration at the holding-company level. These seven regional balances, which are ultimately maintained in New York, are then invested by an Amsterdam subsidiary, which was established expressly for the purpose. The treasurer claims that his company operates with so little cash outside the pool that "the subsidiaries are expected to operate with absolute zero in their accounts, and in most cases they do."

Mapping the Cash Pool. Because Company B is a large firm, its operations are managed from three regional headquarters in Houston, Tokyo, and Paris. Paris is parent to the seven regional holding companies described in this case. The three regional headquarters, in turn, are governed by two main offices in New York and Paris.

The Paris treasurer is assigned the task of managing Europe, Asia, and South America—handling what he calls "a mixed bag of currencies." The mixture is actually a series of high-value/low-volume payments from over eighteen countries, with the majority of these in dollars. The second-largest group is composed of European currencies, and this is followed by a trickle of others from the rest of the world.

Company B's drive to concentrate cash uses just about every conceivable legal tactic. The firm pools cash domestically in countries with stringent exchange controls and uses cross-border pooling where permitted. Either way, Company B daily draws the liquidity from its hundreds of operating units throughout the world and concentrates cash into the accounts of the seven special holding companies. The accounts are maintained in New York but attributed to the various holding companies, which receive cash from the regional operations. Because of a desire to simplify the exchange function, the treasurer explained, "the final structure we'd like to see is one holding company per country in Europe."

The cascade begins when a local operating unit receives payment for one of its field servicings. "The crew would bill the owners of the oil rig, requesting that the bill be paid in dollars, which are deposited with the local Bank A or Bank B branch," the treasurer explained. (Bank A holds the majority of accounts and deposits.) These payments trickle in and are immediately zero-balanced in that unit's name to the next-largest unit's account, and so on. The automatic sweeping of local balances eventually creates a deluge at the central operating account within each country. From this point, three developments are possible.

First, the pooled cash can be invested domestically. "If we pooled cash within a country," the treasurer said, "in 90 percent of the cases it would be invested in that country's local markets." This is particularly the case in countries with exchange controls.

Second, in countries with exchange controls, the company takes domestically pooled funds and declares a dividend to that country's respective holding company. The decision to remit a dividend is based on corporatewide tax position, withholding tax by the country in question, and company liquidity requirements. Another variable is the availability of foreign exchange in illiquid environments, such as Brazil or the Philippines. Dividends paid to a holding company enter the corporatewide cash pool and are invested by the Amsterdam investment company.

Third, where permissible, Company B pools cash on a regional, cross-border basis. As the treasurer explained it, "If you take, for example, the Far East, there are virtually no forex controls, and business is generally conducted in U.S. dollars. Here we can pool regionally. There is no real cross-border pooling, except in the countries that are absolutely free of exchange controls." But in Europe, he notes, there are "very few countries where we can do this. I can only think of Germany and the United Kingdom." It is through a combination of these three mechanisms that Company B keeps cash pooled and maximizes the return on excess company liquidity.

To illustrate with a hypothetical situation, suppose a service crew's account in Germany receives a customer payment in dollars. That balance is automatically transferred, or "zero-balanced," to the next-highest domestic unit and then the next highest and so on, until it reaches the highest level of Company B in Germany. Similar operations for each nation where Company B maintains a presence would take place

Global Cash Management

throughout the world, resulting in single concentrated balances in every country of operation. At this point, the units in the "middle" siphon cash needed for current expenses. The remainder from each country's operations is either invested domestically or remitted to the holding-company parent as a dividend. Countries with no exchange controls remit excess liquidity to their holding company to be invested by Amsterdam. In this case, all interest earned is the property of the subsidiary. Next, the balances of the seven holding companies are transferred to one bank, Bank B, which places its receipts with Bank A, creating a single, consolidated cash pool for all operations. This pool, consisting of seven separate balances, can then be invested by the Amsterdam subsidiary, yielding optimum returns by taking advantage of economies of scale.

The Amsterdam facility performs what the treasurer calls a "purely fiduciary function" in that it can move a unit's funds in and out of accounts, but only in the name of the holding companies. In turn, each holding company is itself a profit center.

Pooling Cash Through Bank Concentration Accounts

As the example above illustrates, companies seeking to improve liquidity management through cash pooling often turn to their bankers for assistance. One of the main services these firms look for in their banks is concentration accounts, also known as "off-set accounts." These accounts, which may be set up domestically or internationally, automatically consolidate corporate balances held in various bank accounts into one central account. Prior chapters have explored the use of domestic concentration accounts. Because the difficulties in setting up cross-border concentration accounts run the gamut from international tax and regulatory barriers to operational and organizational snags, fewer banks offer cross-border concentration accounts than domestic accounts. However, to meet the rising need for these services, more banks are developing international concentration services to be offered to customers over the next few years.

The following examples illustrate how concentration accounts assisted companies with cross-border flows. MNCs should assess their own ability to adapt these tactics.

- A leading U.S. money center bank set up a cross-border cash pooling system for a U.S. MNC with subsidiaries in Europe and the Middle East. The units were paid in dollars and were always in a surplus position but lacked the expertise to invest the funds locally. Further, the returns available in the local markets weren't competitive. To compensate, the company set up New York dollar accounts for each subsidiary with a U.S. bank and directed customers to remit by wire transfer to these directly. The New York accounts are ZBAs, which daily funnel into a large concentration account. From this point, funds can be invested anywhere in the world—the responsibility of the parent's London operation. For bookkeeping purposes, the subsidiaries monitor the New York account electronically to see who paid into the account. The cash pool included funds from Europe and the Middle East.

Three Caveats

Although concentration accounts are becoming more common, they are not always easy to set up—particularly on a cross-border basis. There are three key problems that companies should watch out for:

(1) **Financial regulations.** Cross-border movement of funds may be difficult to achieve where there are caps on the amount of funds that may be taken out of a country. Furthermore, some countries, such as Italy, Denmark, and France, do not permit cash to move cross-border to a central pool unless there is an underlying commercial transaction.

(2) **Tax constraints.** Tax regulations vary by country. In some instances it is preferable to declare the transfers as dividend remittances, while in others they should be considered trade payments.

(3) **Organizational snags.** Companies, particularly decentralized ones, may encounter problems because subsidiaries may be opposed to the loss of control under an automatic transfer system.

· To speed up collections from Saudi Arabia to Europe, which had been tortuously slow, a large Italian company is currently working on an international banking arrangement structured around a series of concentration accounts. The firm is trying to solve the problem of a circuitous correspondent-bank network, under which proceeds from Saudi Arabian sales are first sent to accounts in New York, only to be sent back to the company's main account in Italy. Because of long transfer delays and poor reporting services, the frustrated firm sometimes has to wait up to two months before it even finds out that the Saudi funds had been credited to its parent Italian account.

Fed up with this inefficient system, the company is taking the bull by the horns. "We're presently looking into setting up an international concentration system throughout the Middle East," a company spokesman commented. "All remitters would deposit funds into local branches of a U.S. bank with offices throughout the Middle East. The bank branches will have standing instructions to credit the regional bank office in Turin, on a daily basis, with compensated value."

· A U.K. financial-services company used a similar approach to get around a serious bottleneck in moving funds from Libya to its New York subsidiary. To avoid costly transfer delays, the company opened a concentration account with the London branch of a Middle Eastern bank. Under this arrangement, funds deposited in local Libyan banks are automatically transferred to the London bank, which, in turn, automatically transfers the daily balance to a New York bank.

"By segregating the Libyan funds into their own separate concentration accounts, bad telex transfers are easily recognized," the cash management officer reported. "And because of the special regional ties of the Middle Eastern bank, problems can be resolved rapidly." As a result of this concentration account, the company was able to reduce clerical time spent on investigating missing funds transfers and to reduce float and lost interest revenues—by up to two weeks—on funds transfers that used to get caught in the bottleneck.

Setting Up Hold Accounts

MNCs can reduce the costs of foreign exchange transactions and global funds transfers by establishing foreign currency collection accounts, or "hold accounts." Simply defined, hold accounts are foreign currency-denominated bank accounts held locally or overseas by an exporter. They enable companies to accumulate export proceeds in a single currency, which can then be used to pay for imports billed in the same unit. Thus, hold accounts obviate the need for two exchange transactions: one to convert the foreign currency receipt into a company's home currency and another to convert the home currency into that of the foreign invoice.

Because of their many benefits, hold accounts are one of the most commonly used devices for managing cash and are particularly valuable for companies with heavy foreign exchange trading volume or sizable international sales.

How Companies Gain from Hold Accounts

Hold accounts provide a wellspring of advantages, enabling a company to

(1) Reduce foreign exchange costs, including central bank and commercial bank charges and commissions;

(2) Cut funds transfer costs by keeping funds offshore rather than remitting them to an exporting subsidiary;

(3) Minimize currency risks by automatically offsetting short currency positions and by reducing exposure to exchange rate fluctuations between the time of sale and repurchase of a currency;

(4) Shorten the float delays that occur when funds are remitted from the importer to the company's home country and from the home country to the exporter;

(5) Decrease float time for foreign currency clearing, e.g., by instructing worldwide importers to remit all U.S. dollar proceeds to New York, pounds sterling to London, etc.;

(6) Meet borrowing needs or finance investments by using hold accounts in conjunction with cash pooling or other investment strategies; and

(7) Generate income in countries where favorable tax rates on earned interest prevail, such as Switzerland and the Netherlands.

The advantages of hold accounts are further illustrated by a $1.5 billion European airline company with sales in more than thirty-five countries. Over recent years the

Calculating the Cost Effectiveness of Hold Accounts

To quantify the cost benefits of a foreign currency hold account, a company first calculates the interest earned on any foreign currency held plus the cost savings from reduced foreign exchange commissions. From this number are deducted bank charges and commissions on the account (e.g., compensating balances and any interest that would have accrued if the funds had been invested locally). Any losses or gains from the movement of the local currency vis-a-vis the foreign currency are also deducted or added. Tax differentials are factored into the calculations if different tax rates apply on foreign-sourced interest income vs. interest income generated domestically (e.g., withholding taxes on interest earned offshore).

---

company has arranged a creative package of hold accounts that ensures high investment returns. The company's field financial manager described the mechanics: "Let's consider the United States. We have all sorts of deposits into our local collection accounts from the sale of tickets. Additionally, we have to make a lot of U.S. dollar payments for purchasing spare parts and engines. So there is no reason to take dollars out of the United States to our home country and then go back again and pay off bills."

The airline has reduced its dollar accounts in the United States to two: a hold account and a controlled disbursement account. Controlled disbursement allows the firm to keep dollars invested until checks are actually presented for payment. The combination of cash management techniques allows the firm to avoid conversion costs, to earn money market interest rates on excess funds, and to minimize idle balances.

The Netherlands-based finance company of a U.S. industrial firm also relies on hold accounts as part of its overall strategy to hold down borrowing costs. Instead of repatriating export collections, the company prefers to use the funds to reduce its lines of credit in each currency. "What we do here is simple," the firm's funding manager stated. "We maintain collection accounts in seven different currencies. Those collection accounts are located in the country of that currency, so that we minimize any float that would result from the clearing of those funds. At the same time, we maintain an overdraft account with the same bank so that when the collections come in to us, presumably there's an overdraft balance outstanding somewhere that those collections will act to reduce."

Locating Hold Accounts: Regulations and Practices

As stated earlier, there are two basic types of hold accounts: foreign currency-denominated accounts held locally by exporters and those held abroad, usually in the currency of the country in which it is established. A Swiss company holding U.S. dollars in Geneva is an example of the first; the same Swiss firm holding U.S. dollars in New York illustrates the second.

Like all bank accounts, hold accounts are subject to government regulations. Because these may vary depending on the depositor's residency status, hold accounts may be broken down into four categories (for the sake of these examples, assume Switzerland is the country in question):

- Foreign currency accounts held domestically by a resident (e.g., U.S. dollars held in Switzerland by a Swiss company);
- Foreign currency accounts held abroad by a resident (e.g., U.S. dollars held in the United States by a Swiss company);
- Local currency accounts held domestically by a nonresident (e.g., Swiss francs held in Switzerland by a U.S. company); and
- Foreign currency accounts held domestically by a nonresident (e.g., U.S. dollars held in Switzerland by a U.S. company).

To decide where to establish hold accounts, companies must take government regulations into consideration, along with other country-specific factors (local tax rates on interest, compensating balance requirements, deposit rates, and banking practices and capabilities). When choosing hold account sites, firms must also consider any extra communication difficulties in monitoring and managing the accounts. In time, improved electronic bank hookups via SWIFT and automated balance reporting services of many European banks will make this less of an obstacle.

Leading and Lagging Your Way to Better Cash Management

MNCs should review their use of one hedging and financing technique that is unique to their multinational status: adjustment of intracompany accounts through leading and lagging. The technique can be used for several purposes:

- **To shift liquidity.** Subsidiaries with excess cash can lead payments to those that need cash. For example, a U.S. capital goods company can examine the cash position of its subsidiaries, and if one is in need of funds, the parent can have another subsidiary that is a customer of the cash-poor subsidiary pay its bills before they are due.
- **To facilitate exposure management.** The goal here is to direct funds away from depreciating currencies to appreciating currencies. "If we expect a currency to depreciate we try to rush the funds out before the devaluation," remarked the treasurer of a U.S. consumer goods giant. "But you can't always do it, because a country that is in trouble will tend to place restrictions on currency outflows." Furthermore, if funds have to be borrowed or taken out of invested funds, then the loss on the interest should be compared with the expected depreciation to determine whether it is profitable to lead. A firm would simply reverse this process, leading to a buildup of local-currency assets, if it expected a revaluation of that currency.

Borrowing and Investing Rates

	Effective Tax Rate	Investing Rate		Borrowing Rate	
		Pretax	Aftertax	Pretax	Aftertax
United States	34%	9.1%	6.01%	10.5%	6.93%
Germany	56%	7.2%	3.17%	7.8%	3.43%

· **To reduce financing costs.** Many MNCs find that it may be cheaper at times to fund the subsidiaries that need cash through leading and lagging than by having them go to a bank and borrow funds. They will have the cash-poor subsidiary lag intracompany payments and instruct affiliates that are customers of that subsidiary to lead payments to the subsidiary in need of cash. "We like to finance our subsidiaries through leading and lagging intracompany payments. We find that it's generally cheaper than borrowing from a bank," said the treasurer of a U.S. food and beverage company.

To conduct leading and lagging effectively, a cash manager must be informed of short-term money and currency market trends; be aware of the tax rates in effect in the area; be familiar with the finances of each affiliate, including the sources and availability of funds; be sensitive to the way the company allocates profits (because leading and lagging can have an effect on the recipient or sender of funds in this regard); and be well versed in current local banking practices and exchange controls.

Calculating the Effective Cost of Leading and Lagging

Many companies that are willing to lead or lag take a "seat of the pants" approach. When they find that a subsidiary is cash poor, they have it defer payments on trade accounts or have subsidiaries with weak currencies lead payments. But effective leading and lagging is more complicated, and companies should examine all the variables involved, such as interest costs, tax rates, and currency volatility, prior to deciding whether they should lead or lag.

To make the correct leading and lagging decisions, a cash manager must determine the differential in the effective aftertax interest rates adjusted to currency movements. This is derived by subtracting (1) the local aftertax interest rate of the company bearing the exchange risk, plus or minus the expected aftertax change in the exchange rate to the company bearing the exchange risk, from (2) the local aftertax interest rate of the company not bearing the exchange risk. If the interest rate differential is positive, the corporation as a whole will either pay less on borrowing or earn more in interest through investing if transfers are made. If the differential is negative, the corporation will pay higher rates for money borrowed or earn less on the money it lends. In other words, a positive sign means that payment should be led to a receiving country; a negative sign, that payments should be lagged to a paying country.

The table above highlights some of the key data needed to make a decision on intracompany payables between a U.S. parent and its German subsidiary. The borrowing rate is the rate at which the subsidiary can procure short-term financing, and the investing rate is the rate at which the subsidiary can invest excess cash. The effective aftertax rate is obtained by the following formula:

$$\text{Interest rate} \times (1 - \text{local tax rate}).$$

This interest rate is then adjusted by the expected annualized aftertax currency change to arrive at the effective aftertax interest rate adjusted for currency movements, as shown in the table on the following page.

When a subsidiary is in a surplus position and receives payment, it can invest the additional funds at the prevailing local investment rate. If it is in a deficit position, the payment received can be used to reduce borrowings at the effective borrowing rate. If the paying subsidiary is in a surplus position, it loses cash that it could have otherwise invested at the effective investing rate. If it is in a deficit position, it has to borrow at the effective borrowing rate.

The following example illustrates how this works. Assume that the German firm is to pay the U.S. firm (the U.S. and German tax rates are 34 and 56 percent, respectively), and the companies are in a tax-deductible position. Also assume that the German company expects the deutsche mark to appreciate by 3 percent (or by 1.32 percent after the German effective tax rate) against the dollar. The company should use the expected exchange rate, which may or may not be the forward rate. The effective aftertax dollar-equivalent interest rates are as follows:

U.S. borrowing rate = 6.93%   German borrowing rate = 4.75%
U.S. investing rate = 6.01%   German investing rate = 4.49%

If both the U.S. and the German firm are in a surplus position:

$$6.01\% - 4.49\% = 1.52\%.$$

If the U.S. firm is in a surplus position and the German firm is in a deficit position:

$$6.01\% - 4.75\% = 1.26\%.$$

If the U.S. firm is in a deficit position and the German firm is in a surplus position:

$$6.93\% - 4.49\% = 2.44\%.$$

If both the U.S. and the German firm are in a deficit position:

$$6.93\% - 4.75\% = 2.18\%.$$

Thus, if both companies are in surplus or deficit positions, or if the U.S. company is in a deficit position and the German company is in a surplus position, it would pay to shift funds from Germany to the United States (i.e., lead payments from Germany).

Effective Aftertax Dollar Interest Rates

	Effective Aftertax Dollar Investing Rate Adjusted for Expected Currency Movements	Effective Aftertax Dollar Borrowing Rate Adjusted for Expected Currency Movements
U.S.	6.01%	6.93%
Germany	4.49%	4.75%

The reverse (lag payments from Germany) would be beneficial if the U.S. operation were running a surplus, while the German company had to borrow funds.

This matrix does not take account of the costs of adjusting intracompany cash flows by changing transfer prices or fee and royalty payments. These are more complex to determine, and such techniques may lead to potential legal problems.

Corporate Practices in Leading and Lagging

Attitudes toward leading and lagging vary sharply among companies. Some firms avoid leading or lagging under any circumstances. A food and beverage concern, for example, sets fixed terms of thirty days and does not allow leading and lagging for any reason, including cash-shortage and exchange rate considerations. "We want to impose a strict discipline on our subsidiaries," remarked the company's assistant treasurer. Firms must decide whether such a trade-off is always justified. One company with a strict policy against leading and lagging will modify its rules when a subsidiary is faced with an imminent devaluation of its currency.

Companies should consider developing leading and lagging strategies in light of political considerations. The fact that calculations show that a company should lead or lag at a specific time does not mean that it is prudent for the company to do so. According to one financial executive, "Leading and lagging frequently to minimize funding costs is not a wise policy. Why expose yourself to the scrutiny of government authorities to save an eighth of a percentage point?"

The following are some examples of various leading and lagging strategies uncovered by BI researchers.

· Company C, a multinational chemicals firm, has its corporate treasury and regional headquarters make leading and lagging decisions jointly. The company generally goes along with regional recommendations because the regional staff is closer to the local situation. It arrives at leading and lagging decisions after balancing the local entities' need for funds, the related interest cost, and the expected exchange rate in a break-even analysis. The future exchange rate is the unknown. The break-even analysis shows that if the exchange rate—between the lira and the deutsche mark, for example—reaches a certain cross-rate, accelerating payment becomes attractive. But if the exchange rate penetrates that level, the company is better off delaying payment and earning interest in Italy, because the net effect would be greater companywide earnings. If the economic analysis indicates that leading is advantageous but a subsidiary needs the funds or cannot borrow to accelerate the payment, then leading is constrained.

- Company D, a high-technology company, uses leading and lagging to fine-tune cash movements when appropriate. For example, when the subsidiary has more cash than necessary to pay the intracompany trade bills that are due (mostly to the U.S. parent), it leads intracompany payments. "We use leading and lagging as part of the system," a spokesman for the company explained. "The goal is to get the cash from the subsidiary to the U.S. parent." On the other hand, if a subsidiary forecasts a debit position on intracompany accounts, it can lag payments.

When a situation arises in which the subsidiary has so much excess cash that it cannot lead without violating government limits, the parent company considers other alternatives. If it appears that the excess cash is only a short-term problem, the parent instructs the subsidiary to invest the funds locally. If it is clear that the cash will never be repatriated through the intracompany trade accounts, the parent company may have the subsidiary send the cash as a dividend or an intracompany loan. "It would depend on country and tax regulations," remarked a company spokesman. "They might lend funds to another subsidiary. There is no one solution."

- Company E, a multinational pharmaceuticals firm, frequently reviews and changes intracompany payment terms but currently allows leading or lagging in special circumstances. Corporate treasury makes decisions about leading and lagging, but not on a monthly basis. Rarely will the company make a spot decision to accelerate payments for a particular month. Subsidiaries generally pay according to the original terms because they have access to enough credit; the parent company always makes sure they have access to cash so that they can meet their obligations. Subsidiaries that have difficulties getting cash because of high interest rates in their domestic markets are exempted from this general company policy; these subsidiaries may be allowed to lag for a month.
- Company F, a U.S. chemicals giant, has a netting system that shows the cash position of each affiliate. If an affiliate has too much or too little cash, it may move the money by changing payment terms within the limits set by government exchange controls. The company also uses leading and lagging to manage its currency exposure. "For example," a company spokesman explained, "if we expect the Swedish krona to devalue, we will push the transfers out of Sweden and reduce their payment terms. We call that a 'miniclearing.' It is outside the normal schedule that we do every month. It's an emergency clearing to avoid being hit by a devaluation."

Do You Need a Full-Scale Euro-Treasury Operation?

Large European MNCs such as ICI, British Petroleum, BAT, Peugeot, and Renault long ago established their own treasury centers, which feature money market and foreign exchange dealing rooms. However, while there are significant benefits, the costs can also be rather high. Would such a strategy pay for other MNCs? The following represents the experience and analysis of Robert K. Ankrom of Treasury Associates, Ltd., UK.

At What Cost?

The cost of a dealing operation can be significant. The initial start-up cost will reach about $750,000 for a Reuters or Telerate screen, direct-dealing boards, computer hardware and software, etc. Afterward, annual running costs are about $1.5 million a year (taking into account salaries, office space, utilities, etc.).

Staffing requirements are critical: First, there has to be someone knowledgeable in the foreign exchange and money markets. There must then be someone familiar with local banks and markets where the company has its operating subsidiaries. In addition, there should be at least one clerk who knows bank operations. Finally, there must be backup personnel to cover for sickness, travel, and holidays.

None of this manpower comes cheap. Good treasury people are much in demand. A team of three treasury people, a secretary, and a clerk will cost about $300,000 in

Limits on Leads and Lags in Selected Countries

Because corporate leading and lagging decisions have a direct impact on balance of payments and exchange rates, government controls over this type of cross-border transaction may be strict and given to abrupt change. Usually, countries experiencing balance-of-payments difficulties try to restrict prepayment on imports while extending the lead period permitted on the early receipt of export proceeds. But even if the balance-of-payments outlook improves for the country, such restrictions may remain in force.

Cutting Costs and Improving Control Through Netting

Simply defined, netting is a technique for settling intracompany—and sometimes third-party—obligations. Under a netting arrangement, creditor and debtor positions are offset within a corporate group, with the net amount transferred from the net debtors to the net creditors. This simple technique can yield substantial benefits, as the cases below illustrate.

salaries and benefits. On top of that will be initial capital costs (furniture, computers, Reuters screens, etc.) of $250,000 and annual running expenses (space, utilities, telephones, supplies, etc.) of $200,000.

When it comes to recruiting, there will have to be sufficient growth prospects: The scope and size of treasury operations will have to be promising. Competition for staff will come from local MNCs and international banks, which are well placed to provide the prospects and professional interest demanded by top-caliber people.

In the face of this competition, foreign companies often have to settle for less experienced or even inexperienced personnel. In such a case, a firm's new hires may well look on the firm as a training ground. Retention becomes a problem, and companies run the risk of funding the early mistakes but not reaping the later rewards.

Obviously, the activities of European treasuries have to be tailored to the realities of local recruitment. In many cases, ambitious goals should be prudently scaled back to more modest levels.

Critical to success, however, is the level of activity. Before starting up, one has to ask if there is sufficient activity to command the best rates and services from European bank dealing rooms and to attract and retain top-quality dealers. The savings from an efficient dealing operation will reach, at minimum, twenty-five basis points on the entire volume transacted. Generally speaking, to recover the start-up costs and to justify the ongoing costs, a volume of at least $100 million in foreign exchange per month is necessary. With a lower volume of trade, a company could neither attract skilled dealers nor be taken seriously in the interbank dealing market, and the undertaking would be a wasted investment.

- "We have an offset ratio of 71 percent as far as the number of transactions are concerned and a 60 percent reduction in volume," boasted the financial manager of an Italian manufacturing giant. Even though it was installed just over a year ago, the company's netting system has already had a dramatic impact on the bottom line: Annualized savings are in the range of $500,000, according to a company spokesman. The Italian firm opted for a bank-designed netting package but now prefers to run the system itself because the costs of using the bank proved prohibitive.
- A multi-billion-dollar Dutch firm has slashed its intracompany trade flows by an incredible 85 percent by implementing its netting system. The company, in fact, is ideally suited for operating a multilateral netting system; it sells only 10 percent of its output locally and prefers to sell its exports to foreign subsidiaries rather than to third parties.
- A well-known Swiss MNC was able to reduce the number of its worldwide funds transfers and forex conversions by two-thirds, amounting to Sfr120 million per month. The company's system, which has been operating for three years, was designed by a major U.S. money center bank.

These are just a handful of the numerous success stories that explain the rising popularity of netting among companies. Given the sizable benefits of netting—which can save firms up to $1 million a year in reduced financial costs, depending on the size of the corporation—it is no surprise that it is one of the most commonly used vehicles for cross-border cash management. MNCs that do not have a netting system should move quickly to explore the usefulness of netting.

Because of the ingenuity of companies and banks, netting has evolved over the years into a complex cash management tool that can be adapted to meet a company's needs and organizational structure. But the variety of approaches can be classified into two basic categories—bilateral and multilateral netting.

Bilateral Netting

The simplest form of cross-border netting is the bilateral offsetting of payables and receivables between operations in two countries, usually between a parent and a subsidiary, but sometimes between affiliates. The concept of bilateral netting is simple. Consider the following simple intracompany transaction as an example:

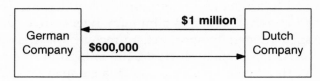

The German subsidiary of a U.S. company sells goods worth $1 million to its Dutch affiliate and bills the Dutch company for the deutsche mark equivalent of $1 million. The Dutch subsidiary sells the German affiliate $600,000 worth of goods billed in guilders. To settle these obligations in the absence of netting, the Dutch company would sell guilders worth $1 million in exchange for deutsche marks, which it would then remit to the German company. In turn, the German firm would buy $600,000 worth of guilders to remit to the Dutch company. Total foreign exchange transacted and funds transferred would be equivalent to $1.6 million.

To offset their payables bilaterally, the subsidiaries would first determine which was the net payer and which the net receiver. Clearly, the Dutch company is a net payer of the equivalent of $400,000.

Therefore, the Dutch company would exchange $400,000 worth of guilders for deutsche marks and remit the marks to its German affiliate, relieving the German company of any currency exchanges or transfers. The percentage of payables offset is calculated as follows:

Gross payables and foreign exchange	$1,600,000
Net payables and foreign exchange	400,000
Foreign exchange and funds transfers avoided	$1,200,000
Percentage of payables offset	75%

Direct cost reductions associated with this offset stem from two sources: the cost of executing a foreign exchange transaction and the cost of transferring funds across borders, including float times. Foreign exchange transaction costs vary according to the size of the transaction, the depth of the market for a particular currency, any special concessions the company may have negotiated with its banks, and other similar factors.

The charges associated with funds transfers vary widely, owing to government-imposed transfer charges or cartel-like agreements among banks concerning money-transfer commissions. A U.S. corporate treasurer may be surprised to learn that while he can transfer millions of dollars to his overseas affiliate for the cost of a telex—about $15—his affiliate might pay hundreds of dollars to remit a like sum abroad.

One company using a bilateral netting system is a U.S.-owned automotive company with sizable European operations. With this system, intracompany balances are built up and settled on a bilateral basis through three treasury offices in Frankfurt, London, and Detroit. The company's financial manager described the system: "Say the United States exports to one of our German companies. When it comes time to pay at the end of ninety days, the German company will instruct Frankfurt to pay the appropriate operating unit in the United States. However, they're not going to go out and make a physical payment. They'll go to the Frankfurt office, which will instruct the U.S. corporate treasury to credit the operating unit through the intracompany accounts. So far, no cash is moving at all. We do have balances between this office and the Frankfurt office, which we will then build up or settle as we determine. But the local German unit has met its requirements to the U.S. unit to which it owed money."

Some companies have carried bilateral netting one step further by developing multiple bilateral offset systems. Specifically, firms in which there are large numbers of two-way trade flows between the parent and subsidiaries in various countries, but not among the subsidiaries themselves, may opt for a multiple bilateral system over a multilateral netting arrangement.

For example, a German chemicals concern, with $15 billion in annual turnover, has constructed a multiple bilateral netting scheme that integrates third-party suppliers into the intragroup settlement system. The firm's finance manager described how the system works: "We at headquarters in Germany may owe a supplier money in the Netherlands; our subsidiary in the Netherlands may owe us money. So, we net the difference, and the subsidiary pays the balance to the supplier. This reduces bank charges and conversion costs. We can do this sort of bilateral netting with each country that we have operations in." When asked why the company doesn't simply use a multilateral system, the spokesman said, "Up until now there have been few two-way flows between the subsidiaries."

Multilateral Netting

More complicated than the bilateral method, multilateral netting involves the offsetting of intragroup debit and credit positions across a variety of currencies and countries. With this technique, each corporate participant pays or receives a net amount, usually on a regular cycle. Because multilateral netting may include many participants with complex trade flows among them, it usually requires a group coordinator to consolidate information on group receivables and payables, as well as to make final settlement of trade accounts.

While bilateral netting may be easier, circumstances often require multilateral netting arrangements. The chart below gives an illustration.

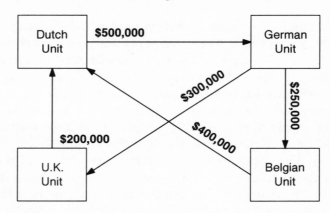

There are no opportunities for bilateral netting in this situation; no company both buys from and sells to any one affiliate. The German subsidiary owes $250,000 for goods bought from the Belgian subsidiary and $300,000 to the U.K. subsidiary; it will receive $500,000 for goods sold to the Dutch subsidiary. The Belgian subsidiary owes the Dutch subsidiary $400,000 and will receive $250,000 from the German subsidiary. The U.K. subsidiary owes the Dutch subsidiary $200,000 and will receive $300,000 from the German subsidiary. The Dutch subsidiary owes the German subsidiary $500,000 and will receive $200,000 from the U.K. subsidiary and $400,000 from the Belgian subsidiary. The benefits of multilateral netting are determined in the same manner as those of bilateral netting—by deciding whether a given subsidiary is a net payer or a net receiver vis-a-vis the other participants. A look at the treasury accounts will make this clear.

Dutch Unit*		German Unit*		U.K. Unit*		Belgian Unit*	
Rec.	Pay	Rec.	Pay	Rec.	Pay	Rec.	Pay
600	500	500	550	300	200	250	400
Net 100			50	100			150

*In $ thousands.

The example shows that the Dutch and U.K. subsidiaries are net receivers of $100,000 each. The German subsidiary has to pay $50,000 and the Belgian subsidiary owes $150,000.

The offset available from this scenario is as follows:

Gross payables and foreign exchange	$1,650,000
Net payables and foreign exchange	200,000
Foreign exchange and funds transfers avoided	$1,450,000
Percentage of payables offset	87.88%

320

Without netting, the gross payables would be $1,650,000. However, with multilateral netting, the payments would only be $200,000, saving the company in foreign exchange and funds transfer costs associated with $1,450,000 worth of payables. In addition, only three funds transfers need to take place (one from the German unit for $50,000 and two from the Belgian unit), as opposed to five transfers that would be necessary without a netting system.

Direct Settlement vs. Clearing Centers

There are two ways to settle intracompany accounts and tap the benefits identified in the example above: (1) by direct settlement or (2) via a clearing center.

Direct Settlement. With the direct settlement method, the netting center calculates the net amount owed by the debtor subsidiaries, which then send the funds directly to the creditor units (see illustration below). The paying companies are responsible for purchasing foreign exchange and transferring funds through their own correspondent network.

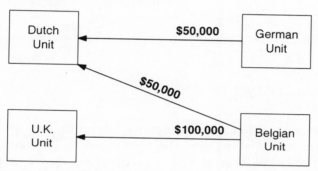

One benefit of direct settlement, often cited by firms with limited netting operations, is that it is easier and cheaper to run. As the financial director of one small MNC commented, "We could save money by combining everything into one center. But when we figured out all the costs of having a clearing center, the savings didn't amount to very much for us."

Another reason companies use direct settlement is that it gives subsidiaries a higher degree of autonomy than a clearing center allows. With direct settlement, subsidiaries continue to maintain control over currency trading, selecting the banks for funds transfers and other cash management chores—which are obviated by the clearing center arrangement. Thus, direct settlement has less of an impact on the organizational structure of the finance function.

Although direct settlement may be right for some companies, especially those with fewer trade flows and greater concern for decentralization, it has four main drawbacks:

(1) Remittance channels are not consistent. A paying unit may be asked to remit to different receivers each month, increasing the chances for errors.

(2) Subsidiaries may need to make multiple transfers, which boosts transaction fees and increases the company's exposure to bank float and transfer errors.

(3) Because currency conversions are handled individually by each subsidiary, foreign exchange spreads and commissions may be unfavorable.

(4) Importing subsidiaries will be exposed to currency risks if billed in the exporter's currency, and exporting subsidiaries will be exposed to currency risks of receiving payment in the importer's currency.

Clearing Centers. To eliminate these inefficiencies, many companies—particularly those with large, intricate trade flows—prefer to use clearing centers through which intracompany accounts may be settled (see illustration below).

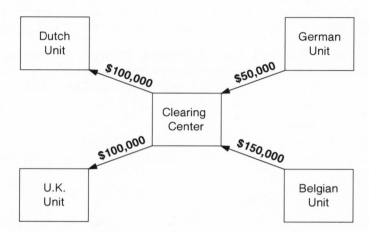

With this settlement technique, the net payers remit their obligations in local currency to the clearing center; in turn, the clearing center buys the foreign exchange necessary to pay net creditors in their local currencies. Hence, net debtors need to make only one payment (rather than several, as with direct settlement), thus reducing funds-transfer costs. Similarly, net debtors need not engage in currency trading; foreign exchange is managed at a central location, where treasury expertise and economies of scale may be applied to gain the best rates. Since debtors pay in their own currencies and creditors receive payment in their own currencies, subsidiaries are free from exchange risks. As an added benefit, clearing centers delineate single channels for payments both from and to netting participants. This facilitates reconciliation of intracompany accounts and expedites investigations into misrouted payments and other banking errors.

Under the clearing center arrangement, multilateral netting operates on an agreed-upon cycle, usually monthly (but sometimes every two weeks), and is composed of four stages:

· **Notification date.** Normally seven to ten working days before the agreed-upon settlement date, each subsidiary notifies the clearing center of all intracompany payables (expressed in the currency of invoice) it intends to settle during the cycle.

· **Approximate-position date.** Two working days later, the center notifies each subsidiary of its receivables, confirms the amount of its payables, and advises the subsidiary of its approximate net position.

Global Cash Management

- **Transaction date.** The clearing center enters into foreign exchange contracts to sell the currencies of the net payers in exchange for the currencies of the net receivers. On the basis of these contracts, the clearing center notifies the participating companies of the exact amount to be paid to or received from the clearing center on the settlement date and the rates used to compute these amounts.

Upon receipt of this information from the clearing center, each paying company contacts its local bank to effect the remittance for value on settlement date. Simultaneously, the clearing center instructs its banks to initiate payments to all receiving companies.

- **Settlement date.** The clearing center receives payment from the paying companies and makes payment to the receiving companies. The maturing foreign exchange contracts return the clearing accounts to a zero balance, and the settlement is completed for the month.

One company that prefers to net via a clearing center is a large automobile manufacturer in Italy. "We have a clearing center in Switzerland," said the firm's CFO. "We move the funds on a predetermined cycle twice a month. We use this for intragroup payments as well as third-party suppliers. The center coordinates all the transfers and foreign exchange. We can use any bank to carry out the movement and conversion of funds. All the payments and all their receipts are made in local currency. At the end of the cycle, the bank accounts of the clearing system go to zero and we move all the funds, with same-day value."

What are the benefits of the clearing center for the Italian auto maker? "We've gained substantial savings," replied the CFO. "The center provides good discipline and gives us overall control of our foreign exchange exposure and management. It's working very well."

But clearing centers have one major flaw. Companies need large intracompany cash flows to justify their personnel and administrative costs.

Improved Information Through Netting

While netting can save a company substantial transaction costs, it can also help firms improve their reporting systems. A leading high-technology MNC found that its reporting system was greatly improved by its multilateral netting system. Prior to netting, the company had an antiquated and inefficient intracompany reporting system. This was the impetus for a better reporting system. Because the individual business units were not consistent in their reporting, the company developed a comprehensive computer system to consolidate the intracompany accounts. It also standardized intracompany invoicing. For all intracompany transactions, each unit of the company is now required to complete a form the company calls a "transfer advice." This details current intracompany sales and the corresponding currencies of transaction. The transfer advices are then fed into a data base designed specifically for this purpose, which provides a detailed "map" of the intracompany cash flows.

The system allows the company to retrieve and classify collective information on

Third-Party Netting

While multilateral netting is generally associated with intracompany cash flows, some firms include third parties in netting when not prohibited by exchange controls. It is much easier to include third-party payables, rather than receivables, in the netting system because companies cannot control the timing of payment from suppliers. "You can't make them pay on a specific day. So you can't include third-party receivables in a netting system," said a cash management consultant for a major multinational bank.

Companies can include third-party payables to the extent that currency is needed to make a payment. A bank expert gave an example: "Let's say Germany has to make a third-party payment in French francs. Normally, they would get the foreign exchange themselves if they didn't have a netting system or do it through the netting center if one existed. If France is in the netting system, the netting center would send French francs into France and France would send out the gross amount of their payables to the netting center. If France were to receive Ffr5 but pay Ffr10, the netting center would be long Ffr5. If Germany is a net recipient of funds and needs Ffr5, it can tell the netting center to send it the French francs it needs and send the remainder in deutsche marks, instead of having it send the entire amount due in deutsche marks. This will save Germany the forex costs. In this case the subsidiary received the French francs and paid the third party. It could also have instructed the netting center to pay

---

the basis of business unit, country, and transaction type (e.g., technical fees or trade accounts). It permits identification of account discrepancies between business units and provides help in promptly resolving the unmatched items among subsidiaries.

Establishing a standardized global reporting system was not something that was undertaken for its own sake; uniformity of information was developed to save money. Whether through improved exposure management, reduced clerical costs, or fewer currency conversions, the multilateral netting system acts as a mechanism for achieving that goal.

A CFO for a major MNC feels that the netting function takes a back seat to the advantages offered by a solid, efficient information system. "Frankly, I think that a netting system saves much less than active treasurers at work," he commented. "But it's the control I'm after."

The executive also likes the discipline that the system introduces. "This has a direct impact on the accounting staff. Without a netting system, the reconciliation work is awful. You usually reconcile your accounts just once a year, and then you run into huge difficulties. With netting, everything is done once a month," and as a result, the information fed into the reporting system is more accurate.

One of the major benefits of a multilateral netting system is that the reporting system can be extended to provide the information needed not only on trade and cash management but also for exposure management. A netting system captures the impact of intracompany cross-border transactions and provides much of the data needed

the French franc invoice on its behalf." This third-party netting system may require changing the timing of suppliers' payments. Moreover, good coordination is needed in order to remit foreign currency to suppliers without breaching constraints on holding foreign exchange in certain countries.

One company that provides a good example of third-party netting modified its basic system to accommodate the settlement of large foreign currency payables to third-party suppliers. The netting cycle for these obligations involves two settlement dates, on the tenth and the twenty-fifth of the month, so that suppliers do not have to wait more than a month for payment. All foreign exchange purchases and funds transfers for supplier payments are centralized in Switzerland, where the center has established special bank accounts for the currencies involved.

Netting participants simply telex the center before either of the two dates and inform it of all third-party accounts payable to be satisfied. The center then nets the payables by determining the method of payment that will cause the fewest foreign exchange transactions. It then buys and sells the required currencies on a spot basis. On settlement dates, the paying subsidiaries make payments in their local currencies to the center's accounts, where they are converted into the appropriate currencies purchased by the clearing center and paid out on the same day to the suppliers. This can cut the costs of foreign exchange transactions in half while reducing the total amount of funds involved. In addition, a participant can take advantage of supplier discounts by instructing the center to make advances.

by a corporate treasurer to assess his company's exposure. Fundamental to the operation of a netting system is a manager who can coordinate information, foreign exchange, and cash flows among the participating subsidiaries. The expansion of this function to include the active management of transaction exposure requires supplementing the basic netting data captured at the clearing center with additional information from the subsidiaries. Firms can add third-party transactions and other transactions not included in the netting system, tax-affect the entire amount, and use that information for making decisions on exposure management. In addition, the data base serves as the basis for operating analytical models used to test and measure various hedging options.

Cost Benefits of a Netting System

While it is difficult to do a precise analysis of the cost benefits of netting, the following method provides a good approximation.

First, add up the **start-up expenses**, including preparation costs—such as treasury, tax, and legal department support—administrative expenditures, bank advisory services, and instruction outlays to subsidiaries and centers responsible for operations. The experience of some companies indicates that these costs can range from $20,000 to $50,000.

Nine Advantages of Netting

MNCs can gain numerous quantitative and qualitative benefits by implementing a netting system—whether it be bilateral, multilateral, or domestic. It is critical to keep these advantages in mind when designing your own or purchasing a bank netting system. The major benefits of netting can be seen in nine areas:

(1) **Reduced currency-conversion costs because of fewer forex transactions.** One U.S. computer company slashed the number of currency deals from approximately seventy-five a month to fewer than thirty. As the firm's treasurer boasted, "We have generated $500,000 in annual savings by more than halving the number of forex transactions."

(2) **Finer forex spreads thanks to centralized foreign exchange trading.** As the treasury manager of a German regional office of a U.S. company put it, "We get an enormous amount of efficiency and savings because of the more competitive bidding."

(3) **Lower funds-transfer costs because of fewer transactions.** "What's the advantage? Fewer funds transfers and therefore lower costs," said one finance director.

(4) **Minimal float due to same-day value of transfers.** "A vital part of the system is the fact that all funds are transferred with same-day value, eliminating float," commented one company's assistant treasurer.

(5) **More effective planning/forecasting of cash flows.** "The biggest advantages are qualitative," in the view of one Swiss corporate executive. "It has allowed everybody to plan much better on transfers and therefore on needs. If you know on a certain

---

Next, compute the **savings** expected from the system by determining what the group's intracorporate transaction costs are without netting. To come up with this figure, three items are typically taken into consideration:

(1) **Commissions and spreads on foreign exchange.** Every time a nonlocal currency transaction is conducted, a cost is incurred for foreign exchange purchases. This cost can be determined by the following calculation:

$$\text{Commissions and spreads (in \%)} \times \text{amount of funds in transactions} = \text{amount spent on commissions.}$$

Some firms also calculate the opportunity costs on those spreads and commissions, e.g., what they could expect to earn if those funds were invested in thirty-day commercial paper. Company H, for example, calculated the value of forex transfers eliminated in this way. This was determined by comparing intracompany payables and receivables before and after netting, as follows:

day of the month that you're going to pay out francs, you can take advantage of the short-term money markets by investing until exactly that date."

(6) **Greater discipline over group settlement and reconciliation.** This benefit was best described by the treasurer of a Swiss electronics firm: "Prior to implementing the system, the companies dealt with one another. We would hear funny stories, claims from one company saying, 'This company has not paid us,' to which the other company would reply, 'We're not paying until they pay us for some other invoice,' and so on down the line. The netting system put a stop to the whole thing by saying, 'Everybody pays on one date, and what's due is due.'"

(7) **Smaller administrative work load for subsidiary managers.** "Netting allows my subsidiaries to refine and streamline their operations and reduce their overall burden," reported the treasurer of the U.K. regional office of a U.S. automotive company.

(8) **Better control over cash and exposure management.** The group treasurer of a Swiss MNC expounded on this point: "Before our netting system, it was an incredible situation, because one day we are receiving a currency, and the next day we are needing that currency. We were selling it one day, only having to buy it back the next. Netting has allowed for a very rational system of exposure management." A financial manager at a French firm agreed: "What you can calculate in forex savings of netting pales in comparison to the savings through good liquidity management through the system."

(9) **Better and more consistent banking transfer channels.** One U.S. MNC interviewed has established a worldwide netting program that channels all funds transfers through the global branch network of one bank. "We find the transfers go easier by having each subsidiary transfer or receive its funds at a branch of Bank X or one of its correspondent banks," said the firm's treasurer.

Unit	Gross Payables*	Gross Receivables*	Net Payables*	Net Receivables*
United Kingdom	9.83	1.35	8.48	
Germany Div. A	10.07	13.32		3.25
Netherlands	4.33		4.33	
Belgium	3.81	10.64		6.83
Germany Div. B	1.24	3.97		2.73
	29.28	29.28	12.81	12.81

*In $ millions.

The netting system eliminates $16.47 million in currency conversions (29.28 − 12.81 = 16.47). The company determined that an average foreign exchange transaction costs between 0.05 and 0.15 percent. Therefore, reduced forex × (0.05 − 0.15%) = cost/savings.

So the savings on currency conversions under the present system range from $8,235 to $24,705, depending on the cost figure selected.

(2) **Funds lost in float.** Every time funds are transferred from one location to another, money in the system is temporarily inaccessible to the company. To determine the cost of this float, the following equation is used:

$$\text{Eliminated payments} \times \frac{\text{days float saved}}{365 \text{ days}} \times \text{interest cost} = \text{cost of float.}$$

For example, Company H calculated the savings realized by eliminating one day's cross-border float as follows:

$$\text{Eliminated payments} \times 1 \div 365 \times 10\% = \text{savings.}$$

The 10 percent represents an estimate for the cost of capital. The company also considered a 15 percent cost of capital in order to obtain a range. For this firm, the savings on one day's float range from $4,512 to $6,768.

(3) **Transfer fees.** Banking costs are charged on transfers. This amount is determined by the following formula:

$$\text{Average transfer fees} \times \text{number of transfers} = \text{cost.}$$

In conducting this analysis, the company used a cost factor of 0.015 percent, which it derived from a study of worldwide transfer costs. Therefore, the calculation of savings in this area was quantified as eliminated payments $\times$ 0.015 percent. This results in a savings for Company H of $2,471.

Therefore, the total savings from Company H's current netting system can be calculated as follows:

	Low Estimate	High Estimate
Foreign exchange	$ 8,235	$24,705
One day's float	4,512	6,768
Transfer charges	2,471	2,471
	$15,218	$33,944

Start-up expenses divided by the amount of money saved determines the time required to realize the benefits of netting (i.e., the payback period).

Firms that are not natural candidates for netting are now finding that, although the savings may not be in six figures, justification of netting can be based on more qualitative benefits such as improved control. One U.S. food company, for example, has not found a cost justification for netting. As the treasurer of the company explained, "Each of our subsidiaries is responsible for its own exposure. When they participate in netting they run a currency exposure risk until settlement unless they cover. They take out forward contracts on the entire amount, not just on the expected net position. If the United Kingdom owes Germany Dm100, it will take a forward contract on the entire amount. They don't know what the company's net exposure is and they are only responsible for managing their exposure. Thus, we do not save on forex costs by netting. On top of that we have many small transactions, and our banks charge a transaction fee to handle these small amounts of foreign exchange. However, we still find the netting system valuable. Its great advantage is the discipline it imposes on each of our twenty subsidiaries. We feel that this advantage outweighs the cost of netting."

Computerizing the Netting Process

Local-currency settlement is a basic component of a netting system. For a system with a very limited number of participants, each participant's position may be settled manually. But as netting systems routinely have 20 to 30 participants—and some may have more than 100—the calculations required to put together a sizable netting operation are an ideal job for a computer.

Major international cash management banks and corporations have developed software for this purpose. But the programs vary considerably in their flexibility and optional applications. Some are written to calculate the current period's netting and nothing else. Most programs began in this simplest form, but many have expanded to include some or all of the following features:

- Remote input capability, allowing subsidiaries to report payables directly into the netting system;
- Reconciliation of intracompany accounts;
- Aging of payables/receivables over user-specific time periods (past and future);
- Automatic generation of telexes to participants informing them of their positions and giving remittance instructions to net payers;
- Simulation of lead/lag strategies;
- Inclusion of forward foreign exchange contracts, bank loans and deposits, and third-party obligations; and
- Calculation of foreign exchange gains and losses, pretax or aftertax, for an individual subsidiary or on a consolidated basis.

Banks' software programs are undergoing continuous enhancement. The rule in working with a bank seems to be, "If you don't see what you're looking for, ask."

Deciding Whether to Net

To decide if netting can benefit your company, four key factors should be looked at: sales and foreign exchange volume, intracompany trade flows, industry, and location of parent and subsidiaries.

(1) **Sales and forex volume.** This is a good indicator of whether netting will benefit your firm. Clearly, companies with large annual sales and forex positions are far more likely to net than their smaller counterparts. For example, a French manufacturer of consumer goods finds a netting system essential because it has over $1 billion in

annual turnover and nearly sixty subsidiaries spread throughout Europe, each generating large amounts of intragroup trade flows. On the other hand, the Swiss regional office of a well-known Japanese firm with only $200 million in sales simply found that "revenues did not justify or require netting. Almost all our products are produced in Japan, and the portion available for netting is very small."

(2) **Intracompany trade flows.** While the company's size is a good indicator that netting may be beneficial, the size of intracompany trade flows is a more precise measure. Since intracompany trade flows and possibly some third-party trade flows (but not the company's total sales) are the amounts to be netted, this figure is more telling of the benefits a firm can derive from netting. A large firm with little intracompany trade, for example, would have little use for netting. More accurately, companies must determine the extent to which their intracompany trade flows can be offset. According to an experienced cash management consultant, "The rule of thumb is that companies with at least $50 million in multilateral trade flows with a 50 percent offset ratio are likely to benefit from netting."

(3) **Industry.** Certain industries are ideally suited to use netting systems. Manufacturing firms, thanks to their complex cross-border trade flows, are the most likely candidates for netting. On the other hand, service companies show little interest in netting. The reason? Service companies tend to trade less than manufacturing firms and have less complicated cross-border cash flows.

Certain types of service firms have, however, found netting beneficial. For example, a major U.S. accounting firm manages a worldwide netting system out of Europe that includes fifty-six offices. Participants send full details of their credits and debits to the netting center in Switzerland—including work performed for clients of other offices—and they settle up on a monthly basis.

(4) **Location.** Companies with parent headquarters or subsidiaries located in countries with tight exchange controls may find it difficult to set up a netting system—or that the cost benefits are not worth the hassle of setting one up.

Dealing with Restrictions

While some countries may have strict rules on netting, it is often possible for a company to negotiate government approval if it knows how to go about it. "Be fair and candid about your netting proposal," a knowledgeable financial executive advised. "Make sure they understand how it works. Show them that their country will not be hurt and may even benefit by allowing you to net. Have a local who understands the system handle the negotiation."

Even in countries that restrict—or even technically prohibit—netting, such as Korea, Japan, and the Philippines, companies have been able to negotiate arrangements with the monetary authorities. For example, a French consumer goods company interested in a multilateral netting center was confronted with the difficulty of getting permission to net in France before that country liberalized its financial regulations. The company struck a deal with the French authorities to include France in their system. "We explained that the only things we were saving on were the bank rates, and we were not at all avoiding bringing money into France. The system would be limited strictly to commercial transactions. Other companies are trying to put too much into a netting system, and that gets them into problems. If other companies are as open with the authorities as we are, they too could operate netting."

One company was able to get its subsidiary in Spain into its netting system by having the subsidiary set up an offshore account in the United Kingdom to receive payment instructions for the netting center, also located in the United Kingdom. The payments went to this account. However, the Spanish subsidiary and the local bank were instructed to show gross receipts and payments on paper, thereby eluding the scrutiny of the local authorities. The legality of this tactic has not been tested in court, however. One consultant cautioned that "the government may frown on this approach if they find out. It appears to violate the spirit if not the letter of the law."

"If you use the right terminology in some countries," one experienced cash management expert commented, "you stand a chance of getting tacit approval. For example, if you tell the Spanish authorities that you want to 'rationalize' or 'consolidate' your funds, they may let you do it. They know the buzzwords—netting and pooling—but not the procedure. If you tell them you need to send $1,000 that is made up of receivables less payables, they may not realize you're netting. But you're taking a big chance that you'll get caught."

Company vs. Bank Systems

After deciding to institute a netting system, a corporate cash manager is faced with a vital question: Should the system be developed in-house or should a bank be consulted to conduct all or part of the operation? A company is faced with three basic options when selecting a system: (1) the nonbank programs, which are company designed and operated; (2) bank-designed but company-operated systems; and (3) bank-designed and -operated packages. As if these choices were not enough, there is a new arrival on the netting scene that is giving the bank systems some competition: netting software programs innovated by other companies. The options are spelled out below.

Company-Designed and -Operated Systems. Many netting users have designed their own systems, which operate without bank assistance. Typically, a company develops the necessary software to calculate net intragroup trade positions, sometimes with the help of outside consultants. Under these arrangements, all funds transfers and foreign exchange activities are handled directly by corporate cash managers.

There are many reasons for the popularity of company-designed and -operated netting systems:

- Company-designed systems make a firm less reliant on banks.
- Picking one bank's netting system may hurt the company's relationships with other banks.
- Bank programs may be incompatible with a company's internal organization and cash management system.

- Bank systems are not fully integrated to include accounting, accounts receivable, cash reporting, and other critical financial functions.
- Bank netting systems hinder the ability of companies to shop around for the best foreign exchange rates.

Bank-Designed and Company-Operated Systems. Cash managers may opt for a bank-designed software package operated directly by the corporation.

The group treasurer of a Swiss consumer goods company summed up the advantages in a metaphor: "By using a bank's software, the bank gave us a car with the keys in it and said, 'You drive it.' "

Bank-designed, company-operated netting systems offer companies two key benefits.

(1) **Reduced managerial time.** When a company leases or buys a bank's netting program, it can either run it or let the bank run it. If the latter course is chosen, the bank can take on the added function of centrally coordinating the information flow among subsidiaries, setting the foreign exchange rates used for settlement and conducting other related tasks.

(2) **Less resistance from local finance managers.** Bank cash management experts are often more successful than corporate treasury staff in selling the concept of netting to subsidiaries. Bank officers are usually seen as objective third parties with no intention of limiting the autonomy of local financial managers.

Bank-Designed and -Operated Systems. Once popular among MNCs, bank-designed and -operated netting systems—which give ultimate control of the netting operations and cash management support functions to a bank—are now used by only a small minority of companies.

Bank-designed and -operated systems are best suited to firms seeking to minimize the time spent on international cash management by relegating authority to experienced bank specialists. As one French treasurer explained, "We prefer to leave cash management to the experts."

Which to Choose? In the final analysis, the decision to use a bank or a nonbank system rests on a complex set of considerations unique to each company. Worries over control of forex trading, the level of business with one bank, decentralized organizational structures, and a host of other concerns all shape a company's choice.

No matter which netting method is selected, banks can provide a full range of support services. Even companies that design and operate their own systems are not eliminated from the bank netting market. They still need assistance in developing the system and taking care of special administrative and coordinative functions.

A Sophisticated Netting System

A $1.5 billion Italian multinational manufacturing company with a high proportion of cross-border and foreign currency flows has saved $550,000 per year by implementing a netting system it bought from a major U.S. bank.

The system saved the company about $300,000 a year in forex transaction costs and

$250,000 in transfer costs. It also provided four qualitative benefits: simplified administrative procedures for intracompany settlements, improved credit control on accounts receivable, better liquidity management by both subsidiaries and the parent company, and an organized way to collect information for an exposure management data base.

"It's working very well," reported a senior financial executive with the company. "We're gaining substantial savings. It's given us good discipline."

How the System Works.   The company began exploring netting at a time when it had a total of $600 million in intracompany and third-party trade flows and settled accounts in thirteen currencies. The company also had miscellaneous cash flows in countries where it had no subsidiaries but sold products directly from the Italian manufacturing operations.

The bank started by centralizing intracompany trade in a multilateral clearing center. Including Italy, twelve countries participate in the system. Miscellaneous sales to countries where the firm has no subsidiaries are not included; however, third-party foreign suppliers are.

Non-Italian subsidiaries are net payers, while the Italian group is a net receiver. This is because the subsidiaries are sales subsidiaries for products manufactured by the Italian group.

The subsidiaries are organized under an Italian holding company. The holding company also controls a finance subsidiary, which manages the netting system. The holding company decides on cash management strategies and uses the finance company to implement its strategies.

All payments are made through the finance company's accounts. The participants pay in local currency, except for South Africa, which pays in U.S. dollars or Italian lire because the rand is not readily convertible. The clearing center then converts the local currency in which it is long into the currency in which it is short. The net payment is sent in lire to the parent company in Italy.

Benefits of the System.   The company turned to netting for the usual reasons: to save costs by reducing the volume of cross-border transfers and the number of forex transactions.

Before implementing the netting system, intracompany settlements were made manually. There were no predefined remittance channels, and the methods and currencies of payment varied. The company lacked an automatic system to monitor and assess leading and lagging possibilities and exposure management strategies. Moreover, the firm had not negotiated special conditions to eliminate float on cross-border transfers.

The system was first run from London because that was where the bank that sold the system managed its European netting systems. At the end of 1984, when the company bought the bank's system, the finance company took control and moved the clearing center to Zurich, a location more convenient to the Italian headquarters. "The system was running smoothly and there was no longer any reason to let the bank run it," commented a finance executive with the company. "It's also costly. They were charging us $3,000 per month."

Netting Cycle

Date	Paying Subsidiary (Payer)	Netting Center	Receiving Subsidiary (Beneficiary)	Holding Company
Notification day (calendar day one)	Telex to clearing center	Receipt of telexes from subsidiaries before 1 P.M. Milan time		
	Advise payments to be settled through the clearing center			
	Preparation of forex control documentation	Input data received into netting system		
		Production of first summary of transaction per subsidiary and first center's position report		
		Telex holding company re completion of first round of data processing		
Review day (calendar day two)				Receipt of telex advice from netting center
				Remote retrieval and review of center's currency position and individual subsidiary positions
				Occasional changes by holding company

In the beginning, "we had all our accounts with [the bank] in London," he explained. "Now the accounts are with a branch of [the bank] in Zurich, but we are free to have accounts with as many banks as we want. We maintained accounts with a branch of [the bank] because it provides us with good collaboration and we had to repay them for it in some way. They supplied us with a good electronic banking system that replaced our manual system for giving payment instructions to the bank."

Supporting Roles. The clearing center is managed by the company's finance company, which in turn is controlled by the holding company. The clearing center

Date	Paying Subsidiary (Payer)	Netting Center	Receiving Subsidiary (Beneficiary)	Holding Company
	Receive confirmation telex of changes made by holding company			Telex advice to center and relevant subsidiary confirming the changes made; authorize center to begin netting
Review day plus one (calendar day three)		Receipt of modifications from holding company and input into netting system		Receipt of telex advice from center and review of data
		Production of second report re center's currency position and individual subsidiary positions		
		Telex holding company advising completion of second data processing		
Advice day (calendar day four)	Receive approximate net payer telex	Telex subsidiaries of their approximate net positions		Receipt of approximate net receiver telex
	Telex advising beneficiaries of settlement details		Receive advice telexes from paying subsidiaries	
			Prepare forex control documentation	▶

computes and advises the participating affiliates of their approximate net positions. It books exchange contracts on the spot market and calculates the participants' final exact net position.

In addition, it issues payment instructions for settling net receivables and checks on ZBAs. To juggle these accounts, a company spokesman explained, "the clearing center, which receives payments from the debtors and pays creditors, has to be at a zero balance at the end of the cycle. If it is not, it means that there is a mistake."

But the system remains flexible. In special situations, the finance company can

Netting Cycle (Continued)

Date	Paying Subsidiary (Payer)	Netting Center	Receiving Subsidiary (Beneficiary)	Holding Company
Transaction day (calendar day eight)	Receive final net payer telex	Book spot forex deals	Receive final net receiver telex	Receipt of telex advice from netting center; review final position
	Give instructions to remit funds to clearing center on value settlement date	Telex subsidiaries of their final net positions	Where required by exchange control regulations, forex rate to be advised to bank	
	Where required by exchange control regulations, forex rate to be advised to bank	Telex to holding company advising completion of processing by the netting center		
		Telex bank to confirm forex deals, advise of incoming funds, and instruct funds to be paid to net receivers on value settlement date; (mail confirmation of telex to bank); mail printouts to subsidiaries		
Settlement day (calendar day 10) Control day (calendar day eleven)	No action	No action

Clearing center accounts verified for zero balances; corrective action taken where required | No action | No action |

instruct a subsidiary (after consulting the holding company) to make payments outside the clearing system. For instance, said a spokesman, "a subsidiary may be late in payment because it could not collect from its customers. We have the flexibility to instruct it not to wait for the next netting cycle [there are two cycles of thirty days each] but to transfer it to Italy as soon as it has funds available."

Global Cash Management

The participating subsidiaries must advise the clearing center and all beneficiaries of the obligations to be settled through the clearing system. The subsidiaries must also verify their approximate net and final net positions. In addition, they instruct the bank to remit the net amount (value shipment date) to the clearing center and to prepare foreign exchange documentation where required.

The Netting Cycle. The netting cycle starts every fifteen business days. It does not fall consistently on a particular day because the dates are set to avoid problems with holidays in the different countries involved. "We only look at working days," a spokesman explained, "and we have to verify that all the days when someone has to do something are working days in all the other countries."

The cycle begins on calendar day one, the notification date. On that day all the participants notify the clearing center by telex as to the amounts they will pay. The center must be notified by 1 P.M. Milan time. (If necessary, they can send the information the previous day.) Participants also prepare any necessary foreign exchange notification required by local governments. The netting center receives the telexes and enters them into the netting system. It produces a summary of transactions per subsidiary and the center's position report. It then telexes the finance company advising that the first day's data processing has been completed.

On day two, the review day, the finance company receives another telex from the clearing center, summarizing in local currencies and dollars the transactions expected to take place in the netting center for that cycle. The finance company can also access the center's long and short currency positions, as well as the currency positions of individual subsidiaries (their receivables and payables by currency and their net position), directly on a computer terminal.

After reviewing this data, the finance company decides whether it should intervene and modify the instructions given to the participants. After checking for conformity with the procedures spelled out in the netting system, it may order the subsidiaries to lead or lag payments. "For instance," a spokesman elaborated, "if we expect a currency to devalue, we can order the subsidiary to accelerate payments. On the other hand, if we expect a currency to increase in value, we can have the subsidiary lag its payments. We also check to ensure that the date the payments are to be transferred to Italy does not exceed the maximum payment terms allowed by Italian regulations."

The company may also lead or lag for hedging purposes. "We also manage the foreign exchange risk of the group," said the spokesman. "We may see that this month we will be long in a currency and next month we will be short in that currency. After considering the interest rate of the lira vs. that currency, we may decide to instruct the participants to lead or lag to hedge our positions each month."

The finance company instructs the clearing center by telex of any changes needed. The center, in turn, forwards the instructions by telex to the subsidiaries.

Day three is review day plus one. On this day the netting center inputs the changes into its system and produces a second report showing the center's currency position and that of the individual subsidiaries. It telexes the information to the holding company.

Day four is advice day. On this day the center informs the subsidiaries of their net positions by telex. They are advised of the amount they must pay or can expect to

The Mechanics of Reinvoicing

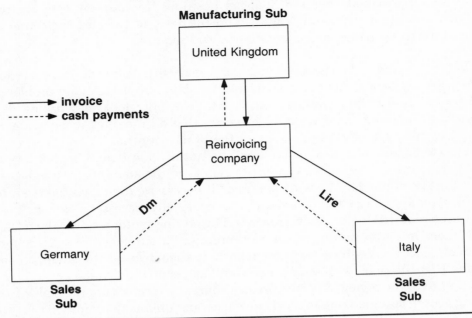

receive on the settlement date. The paying subsidiaries send the settlement details by telex to the receiving subsidiaries. Normally, the Italian group is a net receiver, while the non-Italian subsidiaries are all net payers. The Italian manufacturing subsidiary prepares any exchange control documentation needed by the Italian authorities.

Nothing occurs on days five, six, and seven. Day eight is the transaction day. On this day the netting center books the foreign exchange on the spot market for value dating two days later. The reason, explained the company spokesman, is "because they have to give the banks instructions two days before the settlement day to change the currencies in which it is long to the currencies in which it is short, in order to pay the net creditors of the center. For example, if the U.S. subsidiary were to pay $200 and the French subsidiary were to receive Ffr1,000, we have to change dollars into French francs." The netting center confirms the foreign exchange deal by telex with the banks.

The netting center sends a final telex to the paying subsidiaries confirming the net payment they must make. They then give instructions to their local banks to remit funds to the clearing center and ensure that no payment charges are deducted from the amount remitted to the center. Also, where required by exchange control regulations, the subsidiaries advise the bank of the foreign exchange rate.

The procedure is similar for the receiving participants, who also receive a final telex showing their net positions. Where required by exchange control regulations, they advise the bank of the exchange rate used. The finance company also receives and reviews a telex of the final positions from the netting center.

Global Cash Management

Nothing occurs on day nine. Day ten is the settlement day. All payments must be made and all collections received on that day.

Day eleven is the control day. On this day the clearing center verifies that all accounts in all the currencies are zero-balanced. There is a clearing account for each currency in the netting system, and if the accounts are not zero-balanced at the end of the cycle, a mistake has been made somewhere. A spokesman for the company gave an illustration: "If the U.S. subsidiary had to pay $200 and the French subsidiary received Ffr1,000, and the exchange rate were Ffr1:$1, the clearing center would convert the $200 into French francs and pay the French subsidiary. If at the end of the cycle the dollar account at the center shows $50 because the center only exchanged $150, it means that the French participant received a smaller amount than expected. The center has to correct this mistake."

Reinvoicing: A Flexible Cash and Exposure Management Tool

One of the original cash management vehicles, reinvoicing centers were developed in the 1950s by a number of innovative U.S. and European MNCs. They were created to improve the management of treasury operations, credit and collection, and purchasing by handling these functions from one central point.

Reinvoicing centers are normally located in countries with liberal exchange controls, a good banking system, and favorable tax rates and regulations. They can be set up independently as part of an offshore finance company or can be run out of the treasury department from corporate headquarters, regional headquarters, or a large subsidiary.

A reinvoicing center serves as an intermediary between a company's worldwide manufacturing units and the points of sale in different countries. Specifically, the reinvoicing company buy goods or raw materials from the parent company, manufacturing subsidiaries, or third parties and rebills the product to other subsidiaries (often sales units) or directly to third-party customers.

The Mechanics of Reinvoicing

A typical reinvoicing company works in the following way.

· **Takes title and reinvoices to the purchaser.** A reinvoicing company will purchase and take title to goods or raw materials produced by the parent company, subsidiaries, or third parties. The center does not usually take possession of the goods; they are generally shipped directly to the end buyer. However, some reinvoicing companies hold inventory; for example, one photocopying company has its European reinvoicing center stock expensive office machines and send them to European subsidiaries when they make a sale to third-party customers. With this method, a customer located in Europe can normally receive a $100,000 piece of equipment in a few days. It would not be practical for each subsidiary to keep these items in inventory; ordering and shipping them from the manufacturing subsidiary would take too long.

After the center takes title to the goods, it reinvoices them either to other subsidiaries or directly to third-party customers. A duplicate invoice can be generated by the reinvoicing company or by the subsidiary that generates the initial invoice. "It is generally more efficient to have the subsidiary generate both invoices," advised a cash management expert. Firms may want to draw up service contracts that compensate operating units for this support.

- **Changes the billings currency.** The reinvoicing company is usually billed in the currency of the selling company and, in turn, reinvoices in the local currency of the purchasing company. In this way, foreign exchange exposure is centralized at the reinvoicing center and removed from the selling and purchasing companies.
- **Sets transfer prices.** Setting an appropriate transfer price is one of the most delicate tasks faced by companies with a reinvoicing center. Tax authorities are always suspicious that the reinvoicing center is shifting profits to avoid taxes. As one treasury manager commented, "This is the touchiest of issues. I can guarantee you the local tax authorities will scrutinize this area." Therefore, companies must come up with a transfer price that is acceptable to tax authorities.

There are essentially three methods of determining a transfer price. Under the **cost-plus formula,** which is preferred by manufacturing-oriented companies, the firm adds a profit margin to the costs of producing the item. According to the financial director of a leading capital goods company, "All intracompany sales are cost plus 4 percent." Under the **resale-minus method,** the company takes a preset discount from its local selling price. This approach is frequently used by a marketing-driven company where local market conditions determine the price. The third alternative, setting a **free market price,** is generally chosen by companies selling commodities with a known market value.

No matter which formula is chosen, it should be applied uniformly. As one cash management consultant cautioned, "European countries have freedom of information for tax purposes. So if you're charging a 20 percent margin in Italy and 25 percent in Germany, sooner or later they'll find out."

The key question is how much leeway companies have in setting transfer prices to minimize taxes. Very little, in the view of one knowledgeable treasury consultant. "No one should use transfer pricing to accumulate profits in a country where they would not otherwise be accumulated," he stressed. "Tax authorities have become very sophisticated, and you will probably get caught." But another consultant noted one exception: "If you are small and aggressive, you have more flexibility than a highly visible, big, ponderous, bureaucratic organization. It also depends on your product and your relationship with the authorities. I've developed recommendations for small companies that the big guys wouldn't touch. A small company might get its wrist slapped, while a big one has much more to lose."

Although reinvoicing often gets the attention of tax authorities, it may actually result in fewer tax problems for some companies. A financial specialist elaborated: "If the German or French tax authorities have questions about a shipment from the United Kingdom, you can give them the reinvoicing center's books showing that you're charging the same formula to everyone in the system. You don't have to show them the books of the U.K. company. It's easier to deal with transfer pricing issues because everything is in one place. You can give them the comparisons they want without involving every subsidiary in Europe."

Nevertheless, some firms find reinvoicing taboo because they do not want their transfer-pricing system examined by tax authorities. Explained a treasury consultant: "We tell them that when we set up a reinvoicing center, we will visit the government authorities in the countries involved and explain how the transfer prices are set. They don't want to do that because they have been shifting profits out of the United States for twenty-five years and fear that the tax authorities will spot this when they have to explain their formula."

- **Sets the exchange rate.** To avoid accusations of profit shifting, reinvoicing centers must develop a method for setting the rate of exchange that is acceptable to tax authorities. Some companies use the spot rate, others the forward rate. The choice depends on how the company operates, as a cash management expert elaborated: "The forward rate is more consistent for a company that bases its transfer pricing on the cost-plus rather than the resale-minus method. It reflects the cost of covering the exchange rate. It is in line with the cost-plus method because what you are saying is that the selling price in, say, Italy is the cost of manufacturing in another country, plus a profit plus the cost of cover. So you're adding the costs that arise to come up with a transfer price. The spot rate is more consistent for companies that base their transfer price on the resale-minus method. You set a local currency selling price at a point in time and take the spot rate at that time. It's easy to justify to the authorities."

Some financial executives argue that the forward rate is conceptually more sound than the spot rate. However, one experienced cash management consultant disagreed: "Forward rates make sense if you feel they are unbiased indicators of what will happen when the invoice matures. But so few reinvoicing centers actually work on a transaction-by-transaction basis that it's less important than it might first seem. There are so many transactions maturing at so many different times that the reinvoicing center does not cover. The spot rate is fine in the real world because over time the gains and losses on the spot rate will offset."

However exchange rates are set, it is important that the method be used consistently. Tax authorities want to ensure that the reinvoicing center does not manipulate profits by "playing" with exchange rates.

Another key issue is how often the exchange rate should be changed by the reinvoicing center. The exchange rate policy reflects management's pricing strategy and the role of the reinvoicing center: How long should treasury cover exposure, and when should operating units change prices? Most reinvoicing companies change the exchange rate frequently; once a month is very common. However, some companies may hold a price fixed to meet foreign competition or for some other business reason.

sure for a long term," remarked a cash management consultant. Still other firms set a fixed rate, with the provision that if the currency moves over a certain percentage (say, 2 percent), the rate will be revised.

Whatever approach is taken, there is no such thing as a free lunch. One way or another, the reinvoicing center will pass on the cost of hedging to the exporting and importing subsidiaries. But who should bear the cost—the manufacturer or the importer? A cash management expert provides the answer: "You may have situations when it takes the manufacturer three months to make and ship the product requested by the sales subsidiary and it takes the sales subsidiary three months to sell the product and pay the reinvoicing center. We advise that the manufacturer pay for the exposure risk for the first three months and the subsidiary for the last three months. It's fair and objective. The important thing is to maintain everyone's confidence."

· **Charges a commission.** Most reinvoicing centers charge a commission for the service they perform. "This commission should be relatively small to avoid charges of profit shifting," a knowledgeable financial executive commented. The relationship between the reinvoicing center and the subsidiaries must be at arm's length.

Benefits of Reinvoicing

By concentrating cross-border trade flows in one entity, a reinvoicing company is well positioned to exercise direct control over a broad range of treasury functions, including cash management, overseeing bank relations, tax planning, and forex trading and hedging. Reinvoicing offers companies ten key advantages:

(1) **Centralizes currency exposure and removes risks from subsidiaries.** Typically, the reinvoicing center is billed in the exporter's local currency and reinvoices in the importer's local currency, thereby assuming the exposure risk. As the treasurer of a U.S. electronics MNC said, "The driving force behind the development of our reinvoicing company was the need to protect our subsidiaries from being billed in a currency other than their local currency and having to manage that exposure. We knew we could do it better from a reinvoicing company."

If the reinvoicing center is staffed with experienced currency specialists, it is well equipped to manage a company's exposure through advanced techniques such as leading or lagging, forward contracts, currency options, and swaps. "The main benefit for most reinvoicing companies is that it improves exposure management by centralizing expertise in one place," said the treasurer. "The experts can use hedging techniques, such as currency options, which would be beyond the skills of the financial staff of most subsidiaries."

Equally important, since it is generally located in a major money center with a few exchange restrictions, a reinvoicing company may have more flexibility than a local subsidiary in hedging currency risks. For example, an Australian MNC developed a Hong Kong reinvoicing company that acts as an intermediary for all the parent company's imports and exports. The Hong Kong center serves as a purchasing agent on behalf of the parent, importing capital goods and natural resources from nonrelated firms in the United States, Europe, and Africa. The reinvoicing company takes title to the goods, rebills the parent, and pays the exporter in U.S. dollars. The parent uses these imports to manufacture a diversified line of finished products both for domestic consumption and for export. The parent sells the manufacturers to the center, which takes title to them and resells them to the United States, Europe, New Zealand, and the Philippines. This arrangement offers a variety of cash and exposure management benefits. The parent can manipulate the currency of billing between itself and the center, choosing either U.S. or Australian dollars, depending on its currency outlook.

(2) **Upgrades monitoring and control of cash and trade flows.** Because they handle billing centrally, reinvoicing companies can simplify the tracking and analysis of intracompany payables and receivables. Just as important, they impose discipline on intracompany billing practices and observance of credit terms. "Our trade flows were very complex," remarked a senior financial executive of a U.S. manufacturing company. "We didn't have a good handle on them. The reinvoicing center gave us the systems we needed to control our trade flows."

But better control over trade flows is only part of the picture. Reinvoicing centers encourage subsidiaries to provide more thorough and timely reports on a variety of financial areas. For example, reinvoicing centers generally receive updated information on the expected currency positions of subsidiaries, enabling them to make better and quicker hedging decisions. "It's getting timely and useful information back to headquarters on a daily basis" that makes reinvoicing attractive to one company's treasurer. "There are certain things such as 'What's the volume, who's exposed, when will we need what currencies?' that management needs to know now, rather than in some lagged, decentralized reporting structure." Reinvoicing centers can also act as a repository of credit information and policies.

(3) **Centralizes cash and exposure management expertise.** "This [treasury management] is an area that is best handled on a consistent and efficient basis," said the financial manager of a U.S. food and beverage firm. "When you have a decentralized system with lots of people coming in and out—and they're handling foreign exchange—the philosophy becomes inconsistent. Things are tried, mistakes are made; sometimes mistakes must be made in order to learn. But the point is, you don't want to see those same learning mistakes made year after year. Therefore, having one center where that expertise is concentrated, with continuity of expertise and management philosophy, is a big plus. With foreign exchange, one mistake can wipe out the value of a million cases of milk."

(4) **Facilitates liquidity management.** Reinvoicing gives a company greater flexibility in shifting liquidity between subsidiaries by leading and lagging intracompany payments. For example, if both the exporting and importing subsidiaries need funds, leading and lagging would only work if done through a reinvoicing center. Without a reinvoicing center, the sales subsidiary would need to borrow funds to lead export payments and the manufacturing unit would have to borrow funds if the sales subsidiary lags payment. But with a reinvoicing center, the sales subsidiary can lag payments while the center leads payments to the manufacturer, thereby funding both

subsidiaries. "One of the nice things we do extensively is act as a central banker," the treasurer of a food conglomerate explained. "We can lead to the exporter and at the same time allow the importer to lag." The center can also shift liquidity between subsidiaries that are not trading with each other in the same fashion by having one lead to the reinvoicing company and the other lag.

(5) **Cuts borrowing costs and increases investment yields.** By handling bank borrowings through a reinvoicing center, a company has more clout than it would if each subsidiary financed on its own. For instance, banks are more willing to provide inexpensive export financing—and extend credit for exports to risky countries—when the entity they are dealing with does a large amount of borrowing with them. The savings from lower-cost financing generated by the reinvoicing operations often translate into reduced prices and easier credit terms for importers.

Similarly, by pooling cash resources at the reinvoicing center, a company may be able to maximize its investment yields. According to the finance executive of a high-technology U.S. firm, "We pool cash through our intracompany trade accounts via our reinvoicing center and invest it at a higher rate."

(6) **Opens arbitrage opportunities.** One MNC started using a reinvoicing company outside Germany to take advantage of arbitrage opportunities created in 1973 by that government's *bardepot* regulations, which were imposed to curb inflows of foreign funds. Because of the heavy penalty charged against capital inflows, German companies cut back drastically on borrowing from the Euro-deutsche mark market. As a result, a wide interest rate gap emerged between Euro-deutsche mark rates, which fell with the drop in demand, and domestic interest rates, which were as high as 13 percent. By setting up a reinvoicing company outside the country, the MNC was able to profit from this discrepancy.

Similarly, Asian reinvoicing offers an opportunity for firms to exploit interest rate differentials. A spokesman for a large Japanese firm that reinforces out of Hong Kong gave the following example.

Suppose the company wants to import logs from Indonesia, for which it will be billed in dollars. To finance the purchase, the Tokyo office would need to borrow dollars on the local market. This can be a costly proposition in Japan, according to the spokesman: "A foreign currency loan in Japan is rather expensive. The Japanese banks have a sort of cartel in dollars."

To avoid the high cost of borrowing dollars in Japan, the company reinvoices out of Hong Kong. Under this arrangement, the Indonesian subsidiary sells the logs to the Hong Kong company rather than to Tokyo. The sale is invoiced in dollars under a sight LC. In turn, the Hong Kong reinvoicing center sells the goods to the Tokyo office under a 180-day usance bill (also denominated in dollars). The goods are shipped directly from Indonesia to Japan, although title to the goods passes through Hong Kong.

By taking this reinvoicing route, the company can finance the purchase of logs by discounting the 180-day usance bill in Hong King at inexpensive dollar rates, rather than borrowing expensive dollars in Japan. Thus the firm is able to reduce its overall cost of financing.

(7) **Improves export trading, financing, and collection.** A major benefit of reinvoicing is that it enables firms to concentrate the needed expertise to trade successfully with low-volume, highly complex countries. "It's better to have one organization that deals with these exotic countries—one credit and collection department that knows the procedures on how to sell to Eastern Europe or to Poland or Nigeria," reasoned the treasurer of a well-known chemicals firm. The complicated task of trade financing and protecting against commercial risk is not handled by local financial managers but by a team of trained professionals at the reinvoicing center.

Reinvoicing centers also give exporters a marketing edge since importers are billed in their local currencies. "One reason Japanese trading companies have been so successful is their ability to bill in local currency," a financial executive remarked.

(8) **Acts as a central purchasing agent on behalf of a company's subsidiaries.** The financial manager of a U.K. company explained how purchasing is improved through reinvoicing: "Our reinvoicing center buys commodities needed by the subsidiaries to manufacture their products. By centralizing the purchasing at the center, we have more clout because we purchase large quantities and we have the expertise to determine when to enter the market and how to hedge our exposure."

(9) **Slashes bank transaction costs.** By handling banking transactions from a central point, the reinvoicing center may be able to negotiate same-day value on funds transfers, obtain preferential forex rates, and reduce other banking fees. In addition, since the reinvoicing operation can serve as a clearing center for multilateral netting, it reduces the number of funds transfers and currency conversions.

(10) **Provides tax advantages.** Tax reduction was the principal reason for the early popularity of reinvoicing. "Twenty-five years ago," the treasurer of a large computer and electronics firm recalled, "when we decided to set this thing up, there was an underlying assumption that we would save a lot of money in taxes." But, according to the spokesman, this is no longer the case. "The benefit has gone away; there is now very little tax advantage to having the center."

Indeed, some companies have become leery of reinvoicing centers because they have come under heavy scrutiny by tax authorities. Over the years, a number of countries have introduced legislation to reduce the tax benefits of reinvoicing and have cracked down on this method of sheltering profits in low-tax areas. Under Subpart F in the United States, for instance, profits generated by reinvoicing are taxable at the U.S. tax rate whether they are remitted or retained.

However, some companies are still able to gain tax benefits through transfer pricing as long as they do not go too far. An official at the Australian Reserve Bank spoke of an Australian firm that established a Hong Kong reinvoicing center. Through transfer pricing, the firm accumulated $7 million in profits offshore in the center. The official said, "Well, the tax commissioner said, 'You can't do that.' So it went to the high court of Australia, and the court decided the Hong Kong body was a completely

Why Reinvoicing Is Less Common in Asia and Latin America

Although used in North America and Europe, reinvoicing is less common in Asia and Latin America for the following reasons:

(1) **Limited foreign exchange availability and absence of forward markets.** Because such currencies as the Thai baht, the Philippine peso, and the Brazilian cruzeiro are hard to obtain outside those countries, companies feel they cannot take full advantage of the exposure management benefits of reinvoicing trade flows from these Asian and Latin American countries. As the Hong Kong-based regional treasurer of a U.S. firm explained, "If you look at our worldwide exposure system, you'll see that in Europe, the reinvoicing system is very good and gives you financing flexibility as well as good currency management. You see, in Europe you can trade all those currencies very easily on the Euromarket. But here, in the Asia/Pacific [area], we have a decentralized approach. The way we manage exposures is that all our intracompany invoicing is in U.S. dollars, which puts all the currency exposures out in the countries, where they manage it. If we changed our policies to have it where people were invoiced in different currencies, we'd have a hell of a problem. You just can't get the baht or the won too easily here in Hong Kong, and that obviously takes out some of the attractiveness of a reinvoicing center."

(2) **High start-up and maintenance costs.** Typically, Latin American or Asian operations are relatively low in volume. Since establishing and maintaining a reinvoicing center involves considerable up-front expenses, many firms simply do not feel the benefits justify the costs. This is especially true for firms whose sales represent only a small part of their worldwide operations. A spokesman for a U.S. firm's European reinvoicing center made this comment: "We've given a lot of thought to including Asia in the system or setting up a separate center, but we just can't justify it. Asia accounts for maybe 10 percent of our annual sales, and the volume isn't high enough to offset all the expenses of changing our invoicing procedures or putting up some people in a place like Hong Kong."

---

separate body under the same management and had nothing to do with the Australian parent company. As such, it was quite entitled to its income, and the tax commissioner couldn't have his tax."

Companies with excess tax credits may also get a tax break from reinvoicing.

One Company's State-of-the-Art Reinvoicing System

Experience speaks for itself, and Company I, a well-known U.S. chemicals firm, has plenty of it. "We've been reinvoicing for at least twenty years," the firm's regional treasurer reported. Run from European headquarters in Geneva, Company I's reinvoicing center handles an annual sales volume of $1.2 billion. Of this, $700 million

(3) **Disruption of current organizational structure.** A centralized cash and exposure management vehicle leads to redistribution of responsibilities among different corporate levels. Most companies are highly decentralized for Asian or Latin American operations and are therefore reluctant to adopt the centralized exposure and cash management decision-making structure of reinvoicing. Moreover, a reinvoicing center has a major impact on performance evaluation systems: It forces companies to modify evaluation criteria to take into account profit adjustments and to make certain that gains or losses in the center do not conceal poor performance at the subsidiary level.

(4) **Prohibitive government regulations.** Some vehicles are more at risk than others. Unlike netting or factoring, for instance, reinvoicing entails an actual transfer of ownership, debt, and cash to an intermediate party. Thus, it may be impeded by customs controls, foreign exchange rules, tax regulations, and other laws of the countries involved in the system. Companies note, for example, that reinvoicing authorities in many nations are extremely suspicious, believing that firms use the vehicle to shift profits from the home country to a low-tax area through transfer pricing. In Japan, for instance, monetary authorities frown upon reinvoicing for precisely this reason.

(5) **Corporate oversight.** Perhaps the main reason companies do not reinvoice in Asia and Latin America is that they have not looked closely enough at the opportunities for applying the strategy there. "When we established our center in the early 1970s," the treasurer of a large U.S. chemicals firm commented, "we didn't really sit down and review the possibility of a system for Asia. It was a question of priorities. The Asia/Pacific area is a smaller part of the business for most companies. We wanted to emphasize cash management where we had the most cash, and that was basically in Europe. That was over ten years ago, when Europe accounted for over two-thirds of our overseas activities." But since then, the Asia region has grown faster than Europe, "and it looks like exchange controls have eased. We're beginning to think again about doing an internal analysis on Asia/Pacific. My philosophy is, start it up now before we've got a huge organization out there. Let's do it while it's still manageable."

---

stems from intracompany sales; the other half billion represents direct sales from Geneva to third-party customers. A versatile system, Company I's reinvoicing center performs an assortment of cash management functions, including multilateral netting, centralized credit and collections, and—a sometimes overlooked benefit of reinvoicing—the coordination of all trade financing for export sales from Europe.

The Geneva office was originally set up to be a marketing coordination center, and that remains its primary function today. However, Company I began reinvoicing to cover the costs of its European headquarters operation. "What you have to think about is that this center has costs. And you have to cover that with something. The reinvoicing was developed to cover those costs." The Geneva regional office employs 1,200 people, about 15 of whom are involved in the reinvoicing system.

Since implementing this vehicle, Company I has realized tremendous cost benefits. Although the firm has never quantified the savings ("we have never even tried; it would be a monstrous experience"), the center does provide the following benefits to the company:

- Centralized exposure management and cheaper hedging costs;
- Reduced trade financing costs and risks;
- Greater leverage with banks and thus better service;
- Lower funds-transfer expenditures and currency conversion costs through netting;
- Specialized sales support for Eastern Europe, Africa, and the Middle East; and
- Reduced credit risk and collection delays.

How the System Works. "We are a reinvoicing company, so we have a lot of business flows from the parent company," the regional headquarters' treasurer revealed. "We buy the U.S.-sourced material [accounting for 50 percent of the center's volume] and then sell it to our sister companies in Europe, or we sell directly to countries where we maintain no company presence. And we buy European-sourced material—whatever production they don't sell domestically. Then we sell it again, either to sister companies or to outside customers."

Company I has operating units in Belgium, France, Germany, Ireland, Luxembourg, the Netherlands, the Scandinavian countries, and Spain, all of which produce and sell chemical products. The marketing arms sell products manufactured domestically as well as products from other European operations and the United States. But Company I does not channel all sales through the subsidiaries. The Geneva regional headquarters maintains its own sales staff and, in particular, sells to nations where subsidiaries do not exist, such as Austria and a number of countries in the Middle East and Africa. The regional headquarters and the Europe subsidiaries are all connected by electronic terminals, which greatly facilitate the process of sales and reinvoicing for the chemicals company.

To illustrate the mechanics of the company's reinvoicing system, the corporate spokesman cited an example involving an exporting subsidiary in Luxembourg and an importing subsidiary in Italy. Assume the Italian subsidiary's marketing staff receives an order from a domestic customer for Product P, which is produced in Europe by a sister subsidiary in Luxembourg. Italy then notifies Luxembourg via electronic message of the order, which Luxembourg, in turn, arranges to ship directly to the customer. The Luxembourg subsidiary automatically cuts two invoices, which are created by the supplying unit in Luxembourg. The company feels that having the manufacturer cut the invoices—one billing Italy in lire from Geneva and one billing Geneva in Luxembourg francs from Luxembourg—is the most efficient method. A third invoice is created by the Italian subsidiary and sent to the customer, billing it in lire. The trade is settled when the center receives Italy's lire payment and pays out Luxembourg francs to the manufacturing unit in Luxembourg.

The center conducts this settlement monthly through a multilateral netting system. In this way, neither subsidiary faces any exchange risk but transfers the exposure to

Geneva, where it can be dealt with by specialists. Company I's reinvoicing center handles about 4,000 such transactions monthly, ranging from a few thousand dollars in value to multi-million-dollar shipments.

Managing Currency Risks from Geneva. For Company I, the chief benefit of its reinvoicing system is that it removes the exposure burden from European sales subsidiaries and places it at regional headquarters. Thus, local managers are able to concentrate on what they do best—production and marketing.

Managing currency risk at the reinvoicing center is relatively simple, according to the spokesman: "There is no decision to be made here because company policy says we are to be fully covered on a worldwide basis. We define the exposure and then cover." The treasurer added: "We monitor currency by currency and send information to the states on a monthly basis. The United States arranges cover on their exposure, and we arrange the cover for our own."

Short- or long-term exposures are usually covered on the forward market. Company I is currently studying the use of options as an alternative technique, but the treasurer noted that "this is still in the early stages."

By managing exposure centrally, the reinvoicing center eliminates unnecessary hedging. For example, if one subsidiary is short in a currency while another is long in the same currency, the reinvoicing center will simply offset the exposed positions, rather than have each subsidiary execute a hedge on its own position (which occurs frequently in decentralized firms). And by centralizing foreign exchange trading activities, transaction costs are minimized.

Netting, Leading, and Lagging Capabilities. Company I has run an intracompany netting system for years. Until two years ago, netting was performed manually. But the company now uses a bank-designed multilateral system, which saves the company "several hundred thousand dollars a year," according to a company executive. The company also uses the netting center to manage intracompany liquidity. The system "gives you flexibility—up to a certain point," the treasurer said. "You cannot infringe on exchange regulations, but within these we can decide whether to finance one subsidiary or another simply by extending intracompany terms."

Tax Hurdles. Although Company I's reinvoicing center is located in Switzerland, it does not benefit from that country's liberal income tax rates. "I don't think there is any special tax benefit," asserted the treasury manager. The reason: Company I's operation in Switzerland is considered Subpart F and thus is subject to taxation by U.S. authorities whether profits are remitted or retained. The only tax advantage, according to the spokesman, is a short lag between the time the cash arrives and the time the U.S. Treasury department sends its bill.

To avoid hassles with tax authorities, the regional treasurer is careful when billing the parent for expenses incurred in running the European sales and treasury operations. In the view of Company I's spokesman, the practice of expense billing is "certainly if not more dangerous, then more criticized" than transfer pricing. "Some companies are more aggressive than us. I know companies that just bill to the United States the whole cost of their European headquarters." The treasury manager believes that European tax authorities are very suspicious of expense billings, and that one day the practice will come back to haunt companies using it in the form of a tax audit. According to Company I's spokesman, billings for such regional headquarters services as "guidance," "supervision," and "general coordination" are particularly vague and are likely stumbling blocks in the event of a serious audit. "This headquarters has costs," he said. "Either you cover them through a volume of business, and that means transfer pricing, or you have to initiate billings to the parent, and some of these billings will probably be disallowed." According to the spokesman, if a German auditor, for example, notices a bill for one-quarter the salary of the Geneva manager on the books of the German subsidiary, the officials will simply declare, "We assume that a German company can live without a European director."

Coping with Transfer Pricing.   One of the trickiest tasks facing companies that reinvoice is how to set prices without raising the hackles of local tax authorities. While there are several means of determining a transfer price, Company I opted for the resale method. Under this formula, a price is calculated by determining the ultimate selling price, and then working in reverse by subtracting a margin for the sales subsidiary and reinvoicing center. Thus, every link in the sales chain is given a "reasonable distributor's profit (RDP)." The RDP should be an arm's-length amount—i.e., a profit that would be earned by a nonrelated firm performing a similar service. Company I applies the RDP to the price charged by the sales subsidiary and the reinvoicing center.

To determine a transfer price through the resale method, Company I calculates the expenses incurred by each unit in the chain, adds a margin of RDP, and converts the figure to a percentage. For example, in the sale to Italy from Luxembourg, assume Italy will pay the equivalent of 100 Luxembourg francs to the reinvoicing center. Italy's average costs per sale are 20 percent, and 10 percent is considered RDP. Therefore, Italy will purchase from the reinvoicing center at Lfr70, or the ultimate sale price minus 30 percent. In turn, the Geneva headquarters has costs on average of 7 percent per transaction. To this is added 3 percent for RDP, so Geneva takes an additional 10 percent from the ultimate selling price. So Luxembourg sells to Geneva for Lfr60. With the ultimate selling price already determined by the market, the transfer pricing becomes mechanical.

Since prices are normally set in the local currency of the manufacturing plant, Company I must establish an intracompany exchange rate to calculate the transfer price. The company uses market rates, which are adjusted on a monthly basis. If a currency fluctuates more than 1 percent in a given month, the rate is adjusted to reflect the market rate. "This doesn't serve any other purpose than bookkeeping," the treasurer said. "It's purely an internal rate, with no bearing on the outside world."

Eventually, the treasurer cautions, you will be audited. He explained that one of the auditor's favorite questions is "Why do you sell to your domestic company at Dm1 and transfer to your Swiss headquarters at 70 pfennigs?" At this point, it's up to a company to justify the transfer-price spread. The treasurer explained that his transfer spread is based on several points. One is volume discounts. The center frequently deals in high volume, so it is entitled not only to buy at a low price but to sell at an increased profit. According to the manager, the headquarters profit is also justified by its expertise, which is necessary to sell to Eastern Europe, Turkey, and

Global Cash Management

Africa. The local subsidiaries should be expected to pay for this service, and in fact they do—through the RDP.

Improved Trade Financing. Company I's reinvoicing center provides another big advantage: It enables the firm to manage its own worldwide credit risks and trade financing centrally. In the words of the Geneva treasury manager, "We take the credit risk; the risk is here." The company's policy is to pass these risks on to banks, which are eager to build relations with the regional headquarters because of its sizable financial activities. "They come to visit us," the treasury manager explains with satisfaction. "I mean, we are the headquarters, and banks would love to open a relationship with us."

The firm now tries to capitalize on the banks' willingness to please whenever possible. "Five years ago, we would have received them with courtesy but would have ended the meeting with 'Sorry, chaps, let's keep in touch.' " Today, however, the center is using its clout with banks to make sales in tough world markets like Poland, Czechoslovakia, and Turkey. The manager tells the banks that if they arrange trade financings in these difficult nations, he will sweeten the deal by throwing forex their way. And for those banks that refuse to help, the manager has these ominous words: "Be careful, I have other banks knocking on the door."

Credit terms are set by the reinvoicing center in conjunction with parent headquarters. The terms are set by the reinvoicing center in conjunction with parent headquarters. The terms range from liberal to restrictive. In Switzerland, the terms can be as much as ninety days net on open account. The same applies to Italy, Germany, France, and other industrialized countries. The most restrictive is the confirmed LC, required on all deals to nations such as Poland, Romania, Turkey, and Nigeria.

Trade financing "is not free of charge," cautioned the regional treasurer, and the Geneva regional headquarters must pay flat fees, spreads over London Interbank Offered Rate (LIBOR), and commitment fees, depending on the type of trade credit. The reinvoicing center factors these costs into the transfer price it charges to importing subsidiaries. Although trade-financing costs vary with the creditworthiness of the country, Company I does not set an individual financing expense for each sales transaction. Instead, it applies an average cost of trade financing to all transactions, which is factored into the RDP. Trade financing for sales to German customers, for example, is cheaper than trade financing for exports to Nigeria. Nevertheless, the same expense-factor percentage is used to calculate both transfer prices. The net effect of the system is that exports to low-risk countries tend to subsidize those to high-risk markets.

Dealing with Exchange Controls. Company I's reinvoicing center has had few run-ins with exchange controls. According to the treasurer, "You may have occasional problems when a country is under heavy pressure, but it's more troublesome for your subsidiary, generally speaking." One of the biggest headaches for Company I, especially in France, is the paperwork. Before being able to pay a due invoice, the customs documents must be mated—meaning that every shred of documentation must be produced. In the event of a lost document, the regional treasurer believes it is usually better to just say, "Okay, we cancel the invoice—forget it!"

How In-House Factoring Works

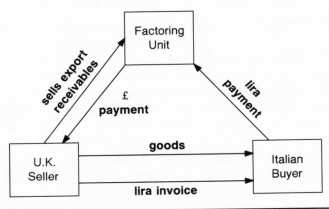

In some countries with liquidity problems, governments require import deposits. As Company I's manager put it: "This is where the Italians are specialists." The Italian government sometimes requires an importer to maintain a deposit of 50 percent of the imported value for a period of six months in a non-interest-bearing account.

The Company I treasury executive also has an appreciation for the "funny gimmicks" the French concoct from time to time, like the stipulation that exporters must receive foreign currency payments within thirty days. In this case, a subsidiary must buy the currency on the forward market. "These are the types of difficulties they give us," the treasurer complained. "It doesn't really hit the reinvoicing center, but it creates a problem for the local subsidiary."

In-House Factoring: An Alternative to Reinvoicing

Although the U.S. Tax Act of 1984 diminished many of its tax advantages, an in-house factoring company can still be a valuable cash management tool. The technique is appealing because it facilitates intracompany financing and achieves all the cash and exposure management benefits of reinvoicing without the problem of transfer pricing. In the words of one veteran cash manager, "Factoring has got to be easier than reinvoicing; there's nothing more difficult than reinvoicing."

With in-house factoring, a company's subsidiaries sell their intracompany or third-party export receivables at a discount to a related central factoring unit. The factoring unit normally pays the related exporter in its local currency and, in turn, receives payment in the importer's currency. Thus, foreign exchange risk and liquidity management can be centralized at the factoring center, creating an effect similar to reinvoicing. (See the diagram above for an illustration of the mechanics of in-house factoring.)

Most companies factor through an independent finance or factoring company incorporated in a country with low taxes, liberal exchange controls, or access to

352

capital markets. In Europe the favored site is Switzerland, followed by the United Kingdom and Belgium. The United Kingdom is popular among those companies more concerned about administrative costs than lower taxes. As the treasurer of one U.K. firm with a factoring operation commented, "Since our largest unit was located in the United Kingdom, and it would be the heaviest user of the system, it was decided to run it from the United Kingdom."

The Mechanics of In-House Factoring

In-house factoring can be complicated, but it typically involves eight key elements:

· **The exporter invoices the importer directly and then sells the receivables to the in-house factoring unit.** Unlike reinvoicing, the exporting subsidiary sells its products directly to the importer, not through a rebilling center; thus, only one invoice is issued. These invoices, which represent accounts receivable, are then sold to the factoring unit.

To free importing subsidiaries from forex risks, invoices are usually denominated in the importer's currency. Companies factoring export sales to third parties also bill in the importer's currency as a marketing technique. A spokesman for a U.S. capital goods manufacturer with an in-house factoring company elaborated: "The strength of the dollar has put more pressure on us to bill in the weaker currency of the importer. We have to do this to match our competition."

· **The factoring unit normally pays the exporter in its local currency and receives payment in the importer's currency.** This can be accomplished in various ways, depending on the currency of invoice. The financial manager of a large company manufacturing primarily from a U.K. plant described his firm's approach: "The invoice is stated in the currency of the importer—the marketing division. Invoices, or rather receivables, are sold to the factoring company, which converts the price to pounds and pays the United Kingdom." Through this simple operation, the foreign exchange exposures are centralized in the Netherlands-based factoring operation, including the cash management function.

The same thing can be accomplished, however, if the invoice is denominated in the manufacturer's currency. The manager of a Geneva-based factoring company explained the operation: "The German manufacturing company bills a French importer in deutsche marks. We will discount the receivable and pay the German his deutsche marks, but we will set a deutsche mark-to-French-franc exchange rate and receive francs from the French importer."

· **The exporting subsidiary can receive payment for discounted receivables right away or upon maturity.** Depending on the liquidity needs of the exporting subsidiary, the factoring unit may extend "maturity factoring," under which payment is not made until after the invoice matures, or "conventional factoring," with cash advanced prior to maturity. But factoring companies should be careful when delaying payment on discounted receivables in certain nations. A cash management expert offered this tip: "In countries like France and Italy you may have a problem because they'll ask you, 'If you don't factor immediately, why did you enter into the transaction?'"

- **The factoring unit sets a discount rate reflecting the prevailing interest rate and invoice term.** Companies should not attempt to set a discount rate too high or it will be disputed by tax authorities. "It must be an arm's-length rate and should be based on the rate for the currency in which the factoring company is financing itself," advised one cash management expert. The financial manager of a Geneva-based factoring company concurred: "We present-value or discount the receivable based on the Euromarket interest rate for that currency."

- **The factoring unit normally includes the cost of covering exposure in the discount.** A cash management expert gave an example: "A U.S. company will set a U.S. dollar price list and terms. If the terms are sixty days they will use the U.S. interest rate for sixty days as the discount rate because they are typically financed by the U.S. parent. Then they add on the cost of covering the exchange exposure. For example, if Germany is selling to Italy they will look at the deutsche mark and lira to get the premium or discount. Then they look at the U.S. dollar against the lira to get the premium or discount. What they are doing is getting the deutsche mark-to-lira cross rate but doing each piece against the dollar. Then they will determine how much it would cost to cover the exposure on that date. They will throw that into the discount rate when factoring the receivable."

- **The factoring unit usually charges a fee for the services it performs.** This can normally range from 0.1 percent to over 2 percent, calculated on the face value, depending on the collection risks assumed by the factoring center and the services it provides. "These can include collections, keeping accounting records, checking the importer's credit, and even completing the necessary export forms," remarked one financial executive. The more the factoring company does for the exporter, the more it can charge, but the fee must be justified to local authorities. Companies may be able to justify substantial fees and reap tax benefits. According to a leading cash management consultant, "A number of companies have been able to get away with a flat fee of 1 percent. And a 1 percent fee on thirty-day terms can be a lot of money."

- **Factoring systems sometimes include third-party export receivables.** Companies with high-value, low-volume sales are in the best position to factor sales to third parties, since they need to handle only a small number of transactions. On the other hand, firms with high-volume, low-value sales, such as producers of consumer goods, may find factoring third-party receivables an impossible task. As one cash manager commented, "I can't imagine why anyone would want to set up a system that would factor sales to as many people as we sell to. That would be a real nightmare; the system wouldn't be manageable."

However, a financial manager from another firm with high-volume, low-value sales was more optimistic. "You know, that would certainly be interesting," he responded. "We'd have to get involved with the credit and collections aspects, but that's not what we're presently doing. For now it's all intracompany. The manufacturing units invoice in the currency of the importer, and if that subsidiary then wants to sell across borders, that's for them to manage."

Of course, there are many benefits to be gained by centralizing intracompany and third-party credit and collections, not the least being the creation of a sophisticated marketing data base. But the increased volume is harder to handle, so companies should be careful in deciding whether the added benefits are worth the costs.

· **Factoring may be with or without recourse to the exporter.** Although a factoring unit may require recourse if it does not want to take on the credit risk of a third-party importer, it almost always factors intracompany sales without recourse. "Why would you factor intracompany sales with recourse, given that they are part of the same organization?" asked a financial executive in a leading transportation company. "You might want to factor sales to risky third parties with recourse if the selling subsidiary wants to take the risk to make the sale." One cash management consultant advised against any use of "with recourse" factoring: "Companies should factor without recourse so that the underlying transaction is seen as a true factoring transaction. Once you start fooling around with 'with recourse,' you run the risk that either the tax authorities, the exchange authorities, or both will start to look very closely at the transaction to see if risk has really passed. The whole underlying concept is that you are passing risk, and that's why you can charge a fee and load up the discount rate. We advise companies that they factor without recourse and make up any losses on the next batch of transactions that go through."

Benefits of In-house Factoring

In-house factoring systems are becoming popular because they provide numerous financial advantages. While they may be set up as simple discounters of intracompany receivables, factoring centers can also be developed into full-fledged treasury vehicles offering many of the capabilities of reinvoicing. "We looked into reinvoicing and we looked into factoring," said the financial manager of one Geneva-based factoring company. "We determined that we could set up a factoring company to be as useful for treasury management as a reinvoicing center."

In-house factoring offers companies ten major advantages:

(1) **They are usually simpler and less expensive to establish and operate than reinvoicing centers.** Since only one invoice is needed for factoring, rather than the two generated by reinvoicing, administrative work and costs are reduced. "Right off the bat a reinvoicing center doubles the paperwork," said one treasury manager.

(2) **Factoring avoids transfer-pricing problems and other tax and legal hurdles.** Because factoring involves the discounting of trade receivables, not the transfer of title from subsidiaries, it avoids the tax and legal problems associated with transfer pricing. The assistant treasurer of a pharmaceuticals firm explained: "We looked at reinvoicing. But since transfer pricing is such a touchy issue in our industry, we encountered a great deal of reluctance on the part of our divisional people. We look at factoring as something that can be accomplished much more easily." A financial executive for another firm concurred: "Factoring companies do not have the stigma

In-House Factoring

In 1984, the U.S. Treasury Department closed many of the tax loopholes of in-house factoring by imposing a number of tax rules under the Tax Reform Act of 1984. Before the act was passed, a company could use factoring to repatriate foreign-earned cash without paying the normal dividend tax. The factoring company, an overseas entity usually set up in a low-tax country, would earn profits by discounting the receivables of worldwide subsidiaries. In this way, the center would eventually accumulate sizable profits. To bring the profits back to the United States without getting hit by high taxes, the parent could simply sell its receivables to the factoring company, receiving the funds in return.

Companies also used factoring to shift profits from a high-tax jurisdiction to a tax-haven country. A factoring company in a low-tax country, like Switzerland or the Netherlands Antilles, would accumulate profits equal to the discount on the receivable. The money would stay in the low-tax country until remitted as a dividend or would be used to factor increasingly large receivables, as in the scenario above.

Finally, under the old rules, a factoring company could benefit firms with excess foreign tax credits. Factoring a receivable through an offshore center, a U.S. company could shift U.S.-sourced income to a foreign source, thereby increasing the allowable foreign tax credit and decreasing the overall corporate tax burden.

---

of transfer pricing, of shifting profits. Therefore, factoring companies undergo less government scrutiny than reinvoicing companies."

However, in-house factoring systems are not without their tax problems. The tax consequences of charging intracompany interest rates, services fees, etc., should be considered when establishing a factoring company.

(3) **In-house factoring centralizes currency exposure.** By paying an exporting subsidiary in its own currency and receiving payment in the currency of the importing subsidiary, the factoring unit assumes and can therefore centrally hedge foreign exchange risks.

(4) **Factoring reduces funds-transfer and currency-conversion costs.** Because factoring units handle financial transactions centrally, they have increased leverage with their banks and can negotiate low funds-transfer costs and narrow forex spreads.

(5) **Factoring companies can shift liquidity through a variety of techniques.** The most common methods are providing discount payments immediately or at maturity, leading and lagging import payments, and altering credit terms on exports. A cash management expert clarified a factoring company's options: "If the United Kingdom is selling to Germany in deutsche marks on sixty-day terms, the factoring company can tell the United Kingdom it will pay the exporter in sixty days and all it will do

A Frontal Assault

The Treasury Department moved to eliminate the tax advantages of factoring in three ways:

- It ruled that the acquisition of a U.S. receivable from a related U.S. person was actually an investment in U.S. property, which is tantamount to a dividend and taxable as such. This effectively negates the benefits of factoring U.S. receivables.

  Curiously, this rule does not apply to foreign receivables of foreign subsidiaries. For instance, a German subsidiary of a U.S. parent may sell its receivables to the factoring company without being subject to the dividend tax. The reason for the exemption is that the factoring company would be investing in German, not U.S., property.

  Further, the rule applies only to the receivables of related parties. A U.S. manufacturer selling to a third-party importer can sell the receivable to an offshore factoring center without having the payment for the receivable classified as a dividend.

- The law treats the discount earned by a factoring subsidiary as Subpart F income— and therefore as taxable in the United States, regardless of whether the cash is actually remitted. This applies to all factoring transactions in which receivables are acquired from related parties. As a result, most profits in the factoring company will

  ▶

---

now is take the exposure risk by locking in an exchange rate. The factoring company will guarantee them the sixty-day forward rate regardless of what happens to the currency. The factoring company can postpone paying a cash-rich exporter but immediately discount the invoices of a cash-poor exporter. The terms have to be set when the discount is locked in; they cannot be changed each day. They can also have the importer lead or lag payment. In this way, it is often possible to reduce the overall cost of borrowing for the company."

(6) **Factoring cuts borrowing costs and increases investment yields.** One factoring company estimates that it saves about $1.75 million in borrowing costs thanks to its presence in the marketplace and improved handling of internal funds. The treasurer elaborated: "If you know what you have to borrow, and you know a little bit in advance, and you know the duration you're going to have to borrow it for, then you're in a better position to go and negotiate terms."

Similarly, factoring companies can obtain the best returns on short-term investments since they are investing larger amounts than any single subsidiary and are able to control and forecast corporate liquidity more effectively.

(7) **Factoring can be done from a manufacturing unit or regional headquarters, thus avoiding the legal costs and hassles of incorporating a new corporate entity.**

In-House Factoring (Continued)

be taxable in the fiscal year they are earned. This rule prevents MNCs from accumulating profits in a tax-haven country.

· The tax rules, in effect, classify the discount earned on items produced in the United States as U.S.-sourced income, thereby eliminating the factoring company's ability to increase the allowable foreign tax credit.

The Corporate Reaction

Companies have had various reactions to the changes in the law, including the following typical responses:

(1) **Keep factoring because it makes business sense despite the tougher tax treatment.** Many companies set up factoring units to improve their treasury management function, not just to get tax breaks. The loss of tax benefits to such a firm does not negate the key advantages of factoring.

Some companies were not significantly affected by the tax changes. A prominent consumer-services corporation operating a factoring company in the Channel Islands provides an example. A company spokesman revealed that "we're carrying on business as usual. The new regulations really don't affect us." The spokesman explained that his factoring operation deals exclusively with foreign receivables. Thus, only the

---

For instance, one consumer goods company interviewed by BI merely added factoring to its existing operations in the Netherlands. "If you can avoid it, there's no point creating a whole new company," a spokesman for the firm commented. "We just felt it was easier to do it this way. We think it's much less expensive and certainly less cumbersome than setting up a separate company." By factoring from the Dutch subsidiary, the company gains all the benefits of centralized cash and exposure management while keeping a cap on administrative costs.

(8) **Companies may be able to gain tax advantages by setting up offshore factoring operations.** Although the U.S. Tax Reform Act of 1984 eliminated many of the tax benefits for U.S. MNCs, some still exist. As one treasurer put it: "We have a permanent tax deferral in the sense that our fiscal year and the fiscal year of the corporation are not the same. The profits of the factoring company are deferred in this way." When pressed further for details on the magnitude of the tax benefit, the treasurer responded, "That's worth a million dollars a year!"

Because of looser tax regulations in some countries, many non-U.S. MNCs may be able to gain significant tax advantages from factoring.

(9) **A principal benefit of factoring is its ability to provide export financing by discounting receivables.** "If your primary reason for setting up a cross-border vehicle

Global Cash Management

discount on the receivables, rather than the entire amount, is considered Subpart F income.

(2) **Stop factoring because of lost advantages.** Some MNCs decided that without the former tax advantages, factoring no longer made sense. "We've totally eliminated the factoring of U.S. receivables," a treasury executive remarked. He explained that his company chose to operate a Brussels factoring center "mainly to take advantage of the tax benefits."

(3) **Keep factoring to prove a point.** One MNC interviewed is continuing its factoring activities serving the United States and reevaluating those serving Europe.

"We had two types of factoring operations: one for U.S. receivables and one for European receivables," said the company's treasurer. "Concerning the U.S. factoring, we continue for a political reason. Before the new law came out, we did a great deal of lobbying, claiming it wasn't a fictitious operation just for tax purposes but a real one. After arguing so long, we have to give substance to that."

What about the unit's factoring of European receivables? "Because the European unit's earnings on the discount have been classified Subpart F, and also because we have found that the tax position of the affiliates has changed, we have stopped factoring there," said the treasurer.

The change in the affiliates' tax position refers to the fact that "affiliates for which we were factoring are now in a loss position," the treasurer explained, "so it is no longer worthwhile to add on to them charges that in any case became taxable for the factoring company."

is export financing, you would probably choose an in-house factoring company," advised a treasury consultant.

(10) **Factoring companies can deliver important services to exporters.** For example, they can conduct credit investigations of the importer. "If we find that the importer is not creditworthy, we will not factor his receivables," remarked a spokesman for a factoring company. Factoring companies take over the collection of the obligation. They can also provide bookkeeping services to the exporting subsidiaries, including reports on the monthly aging of accounts receivable, a statement of sales assigned to the factor and commissions paid, and a report covering invoices paid.

A Sophisticated Factoring Company

Company J, a leading U.S. firm, has developed one of the most sophisticated treasury vehicles in Europe today. The export factoring company established by the firm trades over $1 billion in foreign exchange annually and provides about $7 million a month in financing to affiliates. What started as a simple financial operation to facilitate exposure management has evolved into a major cash management facility, contributing over $700,000 in annual net earnings and saving the firm about $1.5 million in reduced currency losses, funds-transfer costs, and tax payments.

Even before setting up its factoring company in the early 1980s, the firm was no novice in cross-border cash management. It ran a reinvoicing center ten years ago but gave it up because of operational and tax hassles. "It was too hard to administer, and in fixing a transfer price from one location to another we had to be extremely careful that the pricing was at arm's length," noted the financial director. "So we closed it down and switched to direct billing."

But closing the reinvoicing center exposed the company to other financial headaches. "We had enormous difficulties in netting our affiliates' positions and managing exposure because of divisional barriers and country barriers that existed under a very decentralized system," recalled the director of finance. Because of these difficulties, what the company wanted was a treasury vehicle that would allow the firm to manage cash from a central location and protect the European affiliates from foreign exchange exposure, but without the administrative burden of reinvoicing.

In 1979, the company found the answer. That year the firm undertook a feasibility study to determine the advantages of setting up a factoring company. When the study indicated major cost savings, the company decided to establish a factoring company.

Organizational Twists: Dutch Address with Geneva Staff.

The factoring company began operating in 1980 and was registered on the Amsterdam Trade Register in 1981. Company J set up the factoring center as a limited-liability company registered as a private limited company (BV) under Dutch law, with two legal representatives and one address. It was capitalized with G3 million in 100 shares. The firm selected the Netherlands as a location because of that country's beneficial tax treaties with other European countries.

Although the factoring company is legally based in the Netherlands, it is run out of Geneva, where the firm's European regional headquarters is located. By organizing the factoring company in this way, the company can take advantage of existing administrative facilities and staff support at regional headquarters, thereby reducing operational costs. "We needed someone to take care of salaries and things like that. We have a service contract with them for these expenses," said the financial director. The factoring company also has its own staff of five people in Geneva: a foreign exchange dealer, a manager of cash and banking, an administrator, an accountant, and a secretary.

The factoring company typically discounts about $7 million a month. The company was originally set up to handle only European sales but has expanded to include Australia and a few United States divisions. The sales come from eight manufacturing sites: two in Belgium, two in the United States, and one each in Germany, the United Kingdom, France, and Italy. The manufacturing units sell to many other countries in Europe; however, Spain, Portugal, and Greece do not participate in the in-house factoring operation. A spokesman gave the reason: "In Spain, for example, we would have a lot of problems getting funds out on the due date. You can't have that kind of certainty in Spain. It's a problem with their banks, so they're not part of the system."

The factoring company sometimes buys third-party receivables of unrelated importers, provided they stem from sales of a manufacturing affiliate. This is done

Company J's In-House Factoring Operation

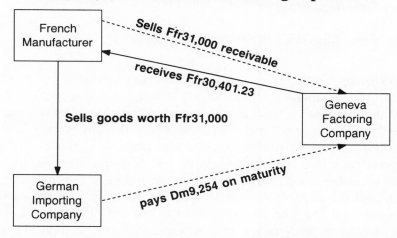

"whenever it is interesting in terms of volume and credit risk; they have to be first-class customers," said a financial manager. But third-party factoring currently accounts for less than 5 percent of the receivables.

How the System Operates.   The factoring company assumes the exchange risks stemming from intracompany sales transactions. Specifically, the factoring company pays the exporter in the currency of its choice, generally the local currency, with the discount rate based on the cost of borrowing in that currency. Likewise, the importer is invoiced in the currency of its choice, typically the local currency. "In purchasing the receivables," the financial director explained, "we changed the currency of the manufacturing company into the currency of the paying company. Neither has any exposure. We take the exposure here because we have experts such as a trader who can manage the exposures."

As an illustration of how the system works, assume that a French manufacturer sells a shipment of goods valued at Ffr31,000 to a German affiliate on sixty-day terms. The factoring company buys the receivable from the exporter and immediately discounts it. The discount rate is based on the French franc interest rate prevailing on the Euromarket, which, for the sake of assumption, was 11.75 percent at the time. The factoring company makes a cash payment to the French manufacturer of Ffr30,401.23, which is the invoice price less the discount. It notifies the German subsidiary to pay the equivalent in deutsche marks based on that week's prevailing spot rate of Ffr3.35:Dm1. The German subsidiary pays Dm9,254 at the date of redemption sixty days later.

Briefly, the essentials of the transaction are as follows:

Invoice of	Ffr31,000
Payment terms	60 days
Weekly spot rate	Ffr3.35:Dm1

Interest rate	11.75%
Paid to French affiliate	Ffr30,401.23
Interest for factoring company	Ffr598.77

The diagram above illustrates the transactions involved.

Weekly Factoring Cycle. Company J's factoring operation is conducted on a weekly cycle, as a financial spokesman explained: "All week, the manufacturing affiliates sell the invoices by telex to the factoring company, mentioning the invoice number, the date, the amount, and the equivalent in foreign currency. At the end of the week we put all the information into the computer, and on Monday we issue the discounting contracts that have been printed by computer. That is, we send confirmation to the manufacturing locations showing the name of the customer, the receivable amount, and the payable amount—which is made up of three parts: the gross amount, the discount fee, and the net payable. We send the receivable part of the form to the importing affiliate showing what they have to pay. We pay the net payable the next Wednesday, because on Monday we have all the figures and it takes two days to get the foreign exchange." Terms are set at sixty days, and leading and lagging are not permitted.

The exchange rate is based on the Amsterdam fixing on Friday afternoon; it is valid for the following week unless there are very large fluctuations in the amounts involved. The manager of cash and banking cited a case in point: "We don't give these rates to the operation in Italy, for example, because the amounts are large and the currency depreciates too much. We give them the rates on the day they sell the invoices."

Benefits of the System. In-house factoring has given the company the following benefits:

- **Sophisticated currency management.** By centralizing forex exposure at the factoring company and staffing up with a former chief trader from a European bank, Company J has turned currency management into a profit maker.
- **Competitive financing rates.** To encourage exporting subsidiaries to participate in the system, the factoring company charges a discount rate equal to or lower than their local cost of borrowing. This rule applies even when exporting subsidiaries have access to subsidized financing; for example, if the supplier is a French company eligible for preferential government export credits, the factoring company will provide a discount rate equal to or lower than the subsidized French rate.
- **Inexpensive funds mobilization.** The factoring company nets the discount receipts and import payments of subsidiaries, thereby reducing funds-transfer costs as well as currency-conversion costs. Because of its substantial banking business, the factoring company has also arranged for free money transfers with most of its lead banks.
- **Exposure coverage of cash flows outside the factoring center.** The center is also

responsible for protecting importers, both subsidiaries and third-party customers, from currency risks stemming from trade payments on invoices not factored. The spokesman explained how this is done: "They pay to our bank account in their country in their own currency."

· **Improved investment yields for subsidiaries.** The factoring company also takes short-term deposits from affiliates for any amount (but preferably over $50,000). The center offers investment rates as good as the best offered on the market.
· **Long-term loans and leasing.** The factoring company finances working capital and fixed assets of affiliates with loans at competitive rates. It also provides leasing and forfait packages to service a customer's special requirements.

A Successful Profit Center. To measure its success in managing cash and currency risks, the factoring company needed a way to analyze and control its various financial activities. To accomplish this, the factoring company was divided into three profit centers. Profit center one takes in all operations strictly related to the company's factoring activities, including exposure management and netting. Profit center two covers short-term borrowings and investments. Profit center three handles long-term financing and financial packages tailored to an importer's needs.

In a typical year, the company can earn almost $8 million in revenues from interest on bonds, discounting receivables, forex trading, and dealing in financial futures and bonds. Its annual net income may approach $500,000.

In addition, the factoring company has prevented expenses and losses from appearing on the books. According to a financial executive at the firm, this is "more than we show in profits. In fact we circulated a memo showing additional savings that it generated for the affiliates. They are not all aware of it. Some of them think that they are losing money by going to the factoring company." The factoring company estimated that it saved the subsidiaries about $1.5 million in currency losses, funds-transfer costs, and deferred income tax. These savings, some of which are difficult to quantify, are not reflected on the books of the finance company but ultimately appear as higher profits or lower costs for the subsidiaries.

Benefiting from an Offshore Finance Company

In its simplest form, a finance company is created by an MNC to minimize the cost of overall financing. It achieves this by tapping international markets and optimizing the company's borrowing portfolio. But a growing number of MNCs are establishing finance companies capable of doing more than floating bonds and equity issues. These sophisticated vehicles serve as one-step treasury centers and perform a number of cross-border cash management functions, ranging from cash pooling and leading and lagging to netting and in-house factoring. Some of the more sophisticated finance companies are even equipped to extend financing to third-party dealers and distributors. This section examines one of the most advanced, well-run finance companies operating in Europe today.

A State-of-the-Art Finance Company

Company K is a diversified U.S. food and beverage company. The firm maintains extensive overseas operations, with over ninety-five foreign subsidiaries. In Europe alone, the company has close to thirty affiliates, not counting franchises and licenses. This results in a flood of cross-border trade among European operations, subsidiaries on other continents, and the U.S. parent.

To help cope with the torrential cross-border flows, Company K established a finance company in 1982. Through its centralized treasury system, the finance company has been able to minimize forex exposure, and its improved liquidity management has reduced the firm's need for bank borrowings. Operating from Geneva, the finance company draws excess local currency from all units throughout the world (except where there are exchange controls) and pools the funds into what the company spokesman termed a "central bank." In turn, this "bank" is able to finance any cash-needy subsidiaries in the appropriate local currency. The subsidiaries are not permitted to borrow from local banks; instead they must go to the finance company.

The finance company pays interest on deposits and charges interest on subsidiary borrowings. "We borrow or lend at a fixed maturity," explained a spokesman for the company. "It can be one week or one year. At maturity date the subsidiaries pay the full amount or a partial amount or roll it over. We manage the mismatching of maturities. It's just like dealing with a bank." The finance company currently has over $100 million in assets.

"The main purpose of the finance company is not to make a big profit," said the spokesman. "We are not a profit center. The main purpose is to reduce the need for bank borrowings. We're not paying the banks. Depending on the country, the banks are charging a one- to three-percentage-point spread on the loan because of central bank requirements. We charge a very small spread."

Besides cutting financing costs, the finance company saves on the costs of exposure management. A spokesman explained: "A majority of the effort of the finance company is to cover the exposure of the subsidiaries. All these companies buy and sell currencies only through the finance company. Thus, we are able to net a lot of our exposure and cover mismatches."

As a consequence, the finance company is a major money saver for the subsidiaries. The spokesman estimates that savings on bank and foreign exchange spreads and through netting exposures are over $2 million per year.

Aside from the need to cover transaction exposure, the finance company has to deal with the impact of FAS No. 52 on intracompany loans. "A key impetus for creating the finance company was the adoption of accounting standard FAS No. 52," said a company spokesman. FAS No. 52 caused the company to change its financing and hedging strategy. Prior to the new standard, foreign operations were financed with low-cost dollars out of the United States. Dollar borrowings were not considered exposed under FAS No. 8, which preceded FAS No. 52. Under FAS No. 52, however, dollar borrowings became exposed. The redefinition of exposure under FAS No. 52 made local borrowing in local currency a more sensible option. The role of the finance company was to replace dollar financing with local-currency financing.

The finance company does not direct exposure management. That is the function of corporate treasury in the United States. "The finance company is the tool for executing the strategy," a spokesman explained. "The policy is established by our currency committee in the United States. Regional treasurers as well as the director of the finance company provide input and then it's a mutual decision. U.S. headquarters doesn't give all the details on exposure management. They just tell us that for the next month we must cover a certain percentage of different affiliates. They don't tell us item by item. We have to establish the specific requirements of the affiliates. The United States may say the dollar is getting stronger against a certain currency and a certain percentage of our exposures should be covered. We have to look at the invoices, work out all the details, and issue the contracts to the affiliates."

Operating from Two Locations. The finance company is unique in the way it is organized: "We are pioneers, and so a lot of other companies are looking at our structure," the company spokesman explained. Operations are split between two entities—the Geneva finance company and a London subsidiary. The foreign exchange and money market dealing room is in the London subsidiary. The London company has a service agreement with the finance company; it's an agent. London "deals with the banks, buys and sells currencies, and borrows and lends funds on our behalf. They also take care of our accounting via a data processing link."

The London unit was established at the same time as the Geneva finance company, and it performs its functions on a fee-paying basis. The company took this approach to be close to the U.K. market, where operating costs are lower than in Switzerland.

The finance company, in concert with London, acts as treasury consultant for the entire subsidiary network. "Instead of having treasurers in each entity, we have one here," the company spokesman remarked, adding, "this arrangement yields obvious economies of scale. We consolidate our position and, both for liquidity and exposure management, pass it on to our sister company in England, which has a window to the banks." Financing and exposure management decisions are made at U.S. headquarters, but London, acting under the direction of the finance company, executes the decisions. "We work very closely," said a company spokesman. The finance company has a staff of five: a finance director, an operations manager, two analysts, and a clerk.

Pooling. Beyond its financing of subsidiaries, the finance company boasts a vast repertoire of financial capabilities. One is cash pooling. The subsidiaries transfer their excess cash once a week to the finance company. A spokesman for the firm elaborated: "We don't want our subsidiaries to have excess cash. We lead or lag to pool this cash. Subsidiaries in countries without exchange controls deposit directly with the finance company. It's an investment, and we pay them an arm's-length interest rate—the interest rate of their currency on the Euromarket. If you pay them a different rate you can get in trouble. We may convert the funds to another currency and lend them to a subsidiary that needs that currency. We might also convert the funds of a subsidiary that invests its local currency with us but will need dollars in, say, three months."

Currency Management. A primary purpose of setting up the finance company was to eliminate currency risk for the operating companies. The finance company nets exposures and hedges. Because of the volume, the finance company gets pretty close to interbank rates when it buys and sells currencies.

The company also uses leading and lagging for liquidity and exposure management. As the spokesman explained, "If a subsidiary tells us it needs to buy dollars based on the decisions at U.S. headquarters, we cover their projected flows up to one year. They take out a foreign exchange contract with the finance company at arm's length. Then, when they need the dollars to pay for the goods, they tell us two days before and we either pay the supplier or send them dollars to make the payment themselves."

How to Implement a Cross-Border Treasury Vehicle

The previous sections described the functions, advantages, and disadvantages of the various cross-border treasury vehicles, with examples of each type. This section outlines the steps companies must take in order to successfully implement a cross-border vehicle, including measuring the need for a sophisticated treasury vehicle; selling the concept to top management and subsidiaries; conducting a cost/benefit analysis; and deciding where to locate the vehicle.

Do You Really Need a Treasury Vehicle?

While reinvoicing centers, export factoring companies, and finance companies are powerful tools for improving treasury management, they are not suitable for every firm. Before rushing into expensive feasibility studies, a company should first determine whether it is a good candidate for a cross-border cash management vehicle. For managers wondering whether a treasury vehicle is right for them, ten pivotal questions should be answered:

(1) **Do you want to centralize control over cash and exposure management?** Treasury vehicles can be a major benefit to decentralized companies wishing to centralize only specific financial activities of their subsidiaries without making radical changes in organization.

"We wanted to centralize treasury functions," one treasurer commented. "While we could have centralized control at our U.S. headquarters, it was less threatening to our managers to do it out of a reinvoicing center in Europe. The subsidiaries felt that a European reinvoicing center would be more evenhanded than the parent company."

"Sometimes dealing with the parent isn't easy," a cash management expert added. "It makes sense to have someone on-site in a region in the same time zone to answer questions. Many times the subsidiary is uncomfortable dealing with someone in the home office who they feel is trying to maximize the parent's figures and not the subsidiary's."

As a U.S.-based food company discovered, management styles in some firms make it "politically sensitive" to introduce a cross-border cash management center. A spokesman for the firm remarked, "What we had was little fiefdoms throughout Europe doing whatever they wanted to do, whenever they liked. We knew there was a lot of inefficiency, redundancy, and a lack of expertise in certain areas. We knew we had to overcome their resistance, but it took a lot of pressure from headquarters along with an active selling effort."

(2) **Do you want to protect your subsidiaries from foreign exchange exposure?** By billing and paying subsidiaries in their local currencies, the cash management center bears the full foreign exchange risk for the corporate group. Thus, management of both transactional and economic exposure can be centralized at the treasury center, where it can be handled more effectively by a team of well-trained currency specialists. "We needed a factoring company to deal with the currency exposure of the subsidiaries," the treasurer of a leading consumer goods producer observed. "The factoring company solved this problem in addition to improving our ability to manage exposure."

Cross-border treasury vehicles are particularly useful under the U.S. FAS No. 52, as a cash management expert pointed out: "A U.S. MNC could make the dollar the functional currency of the factoring or reinvoicing company and capture exposure in that vehicle. This would allow the company to centralize expertise and improve currency management."

(3) **Do you have substantial and complex cross-border trade flows?** The larger and more complex the intracompany trade flows, the greater the potential benefit of a cash management vehicle. While there is no magic number, some cash management experts believe that companies able to justify a netting center should explore more sophisticated vehicles. As one cash management consultant asserted, "$50 million in intracompany flows is a minimum threshold."

BI's research shows that the use of cross-border cash management vehicles is most prevalent among companies with over $2 billion in worldwide sales; these systems have limited applications for firms with less than $500 million in global revenue. However, a number of cash managers shared this philosophy: If your organization is growing in a region, it may pay to put a treasury vehicle in place before everything gets out of hand.

(4) **Do you have subsidiaries with excess cash and others with borrowing needs?** If the answer is yes, then you may well need a treasury vehicle to facilitate the pooling and shifting of cash. As one treasury executive explained, "We use our finance company to move cash from cash-rich subsidiaries to cash-poor subsidiaries. We couldn't do it nearly as easily without the finance company."

According to BI's survey, companies with over $100 million in cash and marketable securities are about twice as likely to use a specialized cash management vehicle as a firm with a cash position of under $100 million.

(5) **Do the tax positions of your subsidiaries vary considerably?** A treasury vehicle may also help you benefit through tax arbitrage. For example, your firm may

be able to shift funds through the center, so that interest income is earned in the country not paying tax and interest expenses are paid by the tax-paying subsidiary.

(6) **Can you benefit from economies of scale in financing and investing?** Companies may have several subsidiaries, each needing millions of dollars in financing. A treasury vehicle allows the company to make a single borrowing, rather than having individual subsidiaries obtain the smaller amounts on their own.

This enables the company to gain optimal financing rates. "By combining all our finance and forex functions into one entity," the treasurer of a U.S. consumer services corporation said, "we've created a creditworthy unit for borrowing—especially long-term borrowing—and we get the best rates." The same holds true for investing excess cash. Treasury vehicles allow a company to pool excess cash and invest it at a higher rate of return.

(7) **Is your company in an industry that will benefit from using a cross-border cash management system?** In general, treasury vehicles are most valuable to firms heavily involved in exporting and importing goods and raw materials. Indeed, BI's research shows that service companies have little need for treasury vehicles.

Not unexpectedly, certain types of treasury vehicles are better suited to particular industries. For instance, reinvoicing centers are favored by producers of intermediate goods—particularly chemicals companies—because of the heavy purchasing and re-selling of products involved in the business.

(8) **Do you have a manager capable of running a treasury vehicle?** A cash management consultant offered this advice to firms: "The person has to know his company. He has to know what's in the pipeline, what's being shipped, what's in inventory. Can he believe in the forecasts he gets from the subsidiaries, because they will cause him to cover himself? He has to understand and be able to work with the subsidiary sales managers. It's very hard to just bring someone in from the outside who can do an effective job."

(9) **Can setting up an offshore treasury vehicle give your company more flexibility in dealing with exchange controls and tax regulations?** While some U.S. MNCs originally set up treasury vehicles to reap tax benefits or get around exchange controls, these reasons carry much less weight today. Tight controls on transfer pricing and revisions in tax regulations have diminished many of the benefits for U.S. MNCs. However, a cash management expert commented, "A number of companies use factoring and finance companies to get around domestic exchange controls and gain substantial tax advantages."

(10) **Is the treasurer looking for a pulpit?** Some companies have set up treasury centers to give the treasurer greater visibility, not because the centers were necessary. "Treasurers can have a hard time showing that they contribute to the company's bottom line," the consultant remarked. "They feel that operating executives get all the glory. By setting up a captive bank, finance company, or factoring company, they can point to profits they are generating. You have to examine all the motivations of all the players before establishing these vehicles."

Company L first became interested in treasury vehicles aftre finding out that its chief competitor, a manufacturer of business machines, installed a sophisticated rein-voicing center. But on closer inspection, the company's treasury manager found that his organization did not need the same capabilities that a treasury vehicle offered his competitor. "How could we possibly look at the same issue and come up with opposite conclusions?" he asked. "There's a whole series of facts that led us to our decision not to run a treasury vehicle." The treasury manager cited four of them:

(1) **Because of its unique worldwide cash position, Company L has little need to shift funds among subsidiaries.** "Having an entity in place that can shift liquidity becomes beneficial to a company that has enormous and possibly seasonal changes in their cash position—from country to country and even from division to division," the treasurer explained. "Most of the companies we have are in a continuous excess-cash position. When subsidiaries need funding, it is generally for the long term—and this is infrequent."

In contrast, Company L's competitor is in constant need of funds. It uses a reinvoic-ing center to pool the funds of European operations and funnel cash home as quickly as possible. "If you look at the competitor, you'll find they're into almost weekly transfers of funds," said the financial executive. "Without the reinvoicing center, they'd lose the ability, simply because administration would become too great."

(2) **Company L has modest borrowing requirements, since it is not growing as fast as other makers of business machines.** The competitor must minimize borrow-ing because it relies heavily on debt in order to finance a growth rate two to three times that of Company L. By consolidating its intracompany cash position through a reinvoicing center, the competitor cut its funding needs.

For Company L, however, the need to slash borrowing is far less urgent. "They consume their annual income every year in the business; we don't," explained the treasurer. "They're heavily leveraged; our borrowing will soon be under 10 percent of our equity."

Because of stable sales, Company L is able to maintain much lower inventory levels than other growing firms. "Some companies in our industry consume their entire net income on financing huge inventories and growth," remarked the executive. "We don't have to do that."

(3) **Company L does not believe that its subsidiaries are exposed, so it is not necessary to centrally manage currency risk.** The firm generally uses the local currencies as the functional currencies under FAS No. 52, and intracompany trade transactions are normally billed in dollars. Although some companies might expect this to lead to currency exposure, Company L is not among them. "This is a philo-sophical argument as to whether a consolidated corporation that is U.S. based is exposed to dollar intracompany payables/receivables," explained the treasurer. "Our CFO feels there is no exposure except for the tax effect. Exchange exposure is really

the subsidiaries' ability to convert their local-currency revenue streams to pay dollars."

(4) **Company L's tax situation does not lend itself to setting up an offshore finance company.** Because the company has more foreign-sourced income than tax credits, it could not gain any tax advantages from setting up an offshore finance company. "If you're in an excess-credit position," the treasurer explained, "you would want to create a subsidiary, because you want its income to flow through a low-tax market. It's important to realize that an excess limitation does not imply that you shouldn't operate a vehicle such as reinvoicing or a factoring finance company. The tax status simply says it's not a requirement that a company go to a corporate structure. It doesn't say not to develop and improve cash management; the needs still exist to improve cash flow, borrowings, and lendings management. In fact, all of the facts we looked at said go ahead and develop an offshore treasury management group. The only thing you don't need to do is put the shell of a corporation over it."

Cash Management Without a Vehicle. While Company L ruled out a formal treasury vehicle, it still needed a way to improve its cash management in Europe. Since subsidiaries generally have excess cash and thus do not need to borrow funds, the company is establishing a system to maximize returns on its idle funds. To manage short-term investments in Europe, the firm is organizing a special cash management division at its U.K. regional headquarters.

"An individual here in London, an investment specialist, can manage the excess cash for the subsidiaries without actually removing it from their statutory books," the treasury manager explained. "So, for example, if we have millions of dollars located in Germany, we'll direct him from London on where to put it—whether it be in deutsche marks, dollars, or any other currency we choose."

The company chose its U.K. regional headquarters as the site rather than corporate headquarters in the United States because of its proximity to European subsidiaries and its knowledge of local market conditions. "From the United States, we don't have the same feel for the London interbank market and the London rates. In the United States, they're better equipped to deal with the New York and Chicago banks."

But the arrangement is not without its drawbacks. In countries with stringent exchange controls, for example, the London office is not able to move funds cross-border for investment purposes. "For instance," the treasurer explained, "the restriction on Italy will be that we have to deposit lire locally. It doesn't mean that our guy in London can't scope out the lira marketplace. He's still the guy who knows what the banks are offering, what the yield curves are doing, and what the projected interest rates are. So we can still let him make the arrangements, only within Italy."

Selling the Cross-Border Vehicle to Management

As Machiavelli said, "There is nothing more difficult than to take the lead in the introduction of a new order of things." These words aptly describe what many parent companies go through when educating subsidiaries about centralized cash management. Indeed, subsidiaries' first reaction to centralization is usually aversion, since it threatens to take away their most precious assets: control and independence. "The problem is that you're taking power out of local management's hands and putting it in the treasury vehicle," explained one treasury manager. "We met with a lot of resistance initially, and the fact that headquarters wanted it only went so far."

Hence, when designing a centralized cash management system, parent companies, as well as providers of cash management services, cannot lose sight of subsidiaries' basic concerns: They should strive for a system that takes advantage of corporate financial synergies without sacrificing a subsidiary's sense of self-determination. Thus, a centralized system cannot simply be thrust upon subsidiaries; they must embrace it.

To help convince local managers and senior corporate executives to accept a treasury vehicle, companies should pay special attention to the following points:

(1) **Stress the inefficiencies of the current system and the benefits of the new system.** As the assistant treasurer of a U.S. consumer goods firm commented, "You've got to make them see how inefficient it is to have one division selling lire forward while its neighbor has lira payables. It makes no sense from a corporate perspective." Pointing this out to each local manager is the first step in persuading the subsidiaries to accept the concept of centralization.

"We were able to sell the system by showing them how they would be getting better service in the areas of foreign exchange, credit and collections, and in general giving them more flexibility," a second manager added.

"The way to sell it is to simply point out anywhere you can find inefficiency, which in most companies is everywhere," said a cash management consultant. "Make a comparison of what is happening today with all the inefficiencies and then show how a future system could improve the picture. If you can show reasonably and objectively that things could be done more efficiently, people are willing to hear about it."

A strong though often overlooked argument for establishing a factoring company or reinvoicing center is the collection of treasury-related information at a central point on a timely basis. This can be used to aid management decisions in a way that may not have been possible in a decentralized operation.

The treasurer of a consumer products manufacturer was able to sell his idea for a reinvoicing center because "it would not only help us with our liquidity and currency management, but would solve some other problems we had making timely hedging decisions. When you have information sooner, you have more time to work out your strategies. And you can move money around faster since you know where you stand from a financial viewpoint much sooner than before."

(2) **Appeal to their self-interest.** A U.K. treasurer described how his firm appealed to the self-interest of local financial managers to obtain their support: "One of the ways we felt we could centralize—instead of just saying to the subsidiaries, which are very powerful, 'You will be centralized because we say so, we can do it better than you, etc., etc.'—was to offer them something. So we say, 'You come to us and we'll give you a good rate, and if you find your bank is not giving as good a deal you'll come to us more often.' That's a much better approach."

Dublin Dock Companies: A Valuable Tool in Managing the Global Treasury

Conduit financing isn't what it used to be. In the wake of the U.S. Tax Reform Act of 1986, clear-cut tax incentives have become muddled by myriad income baskets and excess foreign tax credits. Thus, both for U.S.-based MNCs and other multinationals (similar tax codes are in effect in the United Kingdom and Japan), navigating the treacherous waters of global taxation has become increasingly difficult. Dublin dock companies (DDCs), situated in the International Financial Services Center (IFSC) of Ireland, provide much needed ammunition in the fight against the global tax network.

Not Just a Tax Haven

A lower global tax bill is on the mind of almost every international corporate treasury manager. Yet taxes alone cannot and should not be the sole motivating factor behind any treasury management decision. Lower taxes must fit into the context of all other treasury decisions, such as whether the creation of a treasury vehicle to handle European treasury functions is necessary. If the answer is yes, then a DDC allows for the full range of treasury management functions. Even so, the Irish government has been avoiding the "tax haven" label like the plague. "We're not interested in treaty shopping," stresses John O'Brien, vice president of research and information at the Industrial Development Authority (IDA) of Ireland.

What are the advantages of a DDC over other European locations? Essentially, a company established as a DDC is immediately eligible for a package of tax-related and other incentives. Highlights include the following:

- A 10 percent corporate tax rate;
- No withholding taxes on dividends and interest;
- Low-cost cross-border financing techniques;
- Low overhead and cheap local financing;
- A European Community (EC) location; and
- Exemption from municipal taxes.

A firm that put these words into action is a well-known U.S. electronics company with manufacturing units in Belgium, Germany, the United Kingdom, France, and Italy, and sales offices throughout Europe. Until recently, the firm had worked under a decentralized structure. "Our operating units have a lot of autonomy," said the regional manager of cash and banking. "If they have a good position in a foreign currency, they do not want to give it up just for the sake of the group." In fact, the firm was forced to abandon its attempts to establish a reinvoicing center over a decade ago, partly because of its decentralized organizational style, which made the center "too hard to administer."

In addition, while DDCs can work to reduce excess foreign tax credits (and, under special circumstances, can generate non-Subpart F income), they also provide a viable alternative for treasurers in search of an offshore financing center to support such treasury functions as risk management, investment management, and cash management for their European operations.

The doors of the IFSC are open to companies of all shapes and sizes. The flexible requirements allow both MNCs and start-up ventures easy access to the incentives offered by the government. As long as the firm is not a postbox operation, a license is likely to be granted.

"There are a lot of names in the pipelines," says an official at Ulster Investment Bank, a licensed DDC and a member of the National Westminster Group. NatWest closely monitors the applicants in search of business opportunities and clients for the basic banking services it offers at the IFSC.

The center is best suited for new international players, notes the Ulster director. "It's more difficult to justify transfer from [elsewhere] to Dublin if you're already based in Europe," he states. But for those planning their first foray into Europe and hoping to get it right from the start, the IFSC is a definite possibility.

That Perfect EC Location

With the impending integration of the European market, many treasurers may find that it is more cost-effective to have a centralized European treasury management operation, rather than a mix of local operations, and that it looks better if that center is located within the EC. The rationale is that decentralized operations tend to bury natural hedges and arbitrage possibilities created by the spectrum of currencies and interest rates.

Until now, companies have chosen to take advantage of low withholding taxes in Switzerland, for example; but as 1992 nears, observers familiar with EC thinking say the Commission will not view favorably those MNCs that choose a non-EC country to coordinate their EC operations. If this is true, several tax havens lose their appeal. Exotic locations may be tax paradises, but they provide no European market penetration.

▶

To reap the benefits of centralized cash management without raising local manager's hackles, the company turned to in-house factoring. It set up a company in Geneva through which the firm purchases all of its subsidiaries' foreign currency receivables and assumes their foreign currency payables. On all intracompany transactions, manufacturing units bill in their local currencies, and importing units pay the factoring operation in their own currencies. "We have taken the currency risk here in the center and manage the positions," said the cash manager.

Of course, the most effective way a parent can induce its subsidiaries to participate in a centralized cash management system is to give them a piece of the profits. For

Dublin Dock Companies: A Valuable Tool in Managing the Global Treasury (Continued)

There are also the drawbacks of not being set up in a host country that immediately enables the MNC to perform similar operations EC-wide. Under the EC's second banking directive, most financial operations will be "grandfathered in" if they are established before 1992. After that, new ventures will have to be approved by the EC itself and by its twelve member states separately.

BCCs vs. DDCs

Some 150 MNCs have already used a similar vehicle, the Belgium coordination center (BCC), to take care of their European treasury management needs. However, firms now contemplating such a move should perhaps look at DDCs first.

BCCs and DDCs enjoy the same types of tax advantages. DDCs, however, boast a couple of extra benefits that make them better suited to treasury management. This is especially true for the smaller players that consider the EC a future market and would like to avoid future relocation by setting it up properly from the beginning. A number of factors come into play here:

· **Flexible licensing.** To qualify for a BCC, a company must be a member of a multinational group, defined as an enterprise having a combined group equity of at least Bfr1 billion and yearly turnover of Bfr10 billion. The company must also hire ten full-time employees within the first two years of operation.

The qualifications for a DDC, however, are much less restrictive. Even though five employees are expected to be hired, for example, the government will allow companies to share in the facility through joint ventures, effectively eliminating employment as a factor. With a DDC, it is possible to have a licensed company that has a management contract with another licensed company.

· **Convenience.** Ireland is simply a more comfortable location for an MNC's treasury management. The common language is English, the time zone is similar to London's, and it is easier to commute to London. There is also a highly skilled local work force waiting to be tapped. The government also makes it very easy to bring in foreign executives, as nonresident employees are exempt from local income taxes on income earned overseas.

· **Section 84 loans.** Dublin also offers more financial flexibility, such as low financing costs through Section 84 loans. These can also work to reduce significantly the cost of intercompany borrowing and aid in the channeling of income throughout Europe.

---

example, a U.K. manufacturer has implemented a system under which operating units send excess cash to the parent. "Any surpluses automatically come to us through the pooling system," according to the firm's assistant treasurer, "so that no operating companies invest funds." He described how subsidiaries are rewarded: "We give them interest on their funds in cash. We don't have intracompany bookkeeping or notional rates; everything is settled quarterly in hard cash."

An innovative Italian corporation adopted a similar approach to establish its multilateral netting system. According to the company's CFO, "The biggest problem we faced was selling the idea to subsidiaries. We put on big slide shows for them showing the benefits." But even more effective was the company's promise to share the system's savings with its subsidiaries. "The savings go back to the subsidiary in actual cash, so they can see how they benefit. This is the most important thing."

(3) **Demonstrate how the impact on local operations will be minimal.** Most subsidiary managers will not mind having some functions, such as exposure management, handled at a central location; it will allow them to devote more time to operational issues. Financial executives who wish to implement a treasury vehicle should explain to operational management that the vehicle will not affect the way they manage operations but will improve control over certain financial functions.

(4) **Avoid a biased location.** A potential problem arises when subsidiaries perceive the vehicle as a biased organization. Locating the vehicle in the same region as the participating subsidiaries can give comfort to many subsidiary managers who fear greater direct control from the parent. This technique does not always work, however. One company initially located its reinvoicing center in the same building as an existing operation in France. "That's why we later moved the operation to corporate headquarters in Los Angeles," explained the company's assistant treasurer. "When it was in Paris, it was perceived as an arm of the French company, which resulted in considerable resentment from the other subsidiaries. Moving to Los Angeles, we became associated with headquarters, and that added the legitimacy we needed."

(5) **Offer subsidiaries autonomy in dealing with outside banks.** Treasury vehicles that act as in-group banks reduce the business that subsidiaries give to third-party banks. However, a local manager who has a solid relationship with local banks may not want to cut back on the business he gives his bankers. One way to deal with this resistance is to offer a subsidiary the choice of dealing with its local bankers or the finance company. If the banks offer better rates, then the subsidiary is free to trade outside of the group. If the treasury vehicle offers comparable or better rates, subsidiaries must invest with or borrow from the in-house unit.

This was the key to the success of one company's treasury vehicle. "We do not force anyone," a spokesman said. "They do not have to discount, they do not have to place funds with us. If they have a working capital need, whatever it is, we say, 'You go to your own banks and get a quotation from them, and then you ask us. Maybe we can outbid the bank.'"

But implementing the system was not that easy. "Some of the subsidiaries were trying to cheat by quoting better rates than their banks were actually offering," said the company's spokesman. These wrinkles were ironed out eventually, however. "The rates are no longer contested by the operating companies. Now it's all peace and happiness."

Corporate staff should also examine the motives behind a local manager's attitude. Some managers may wish to maintain a relationship with their bankers for reasons unrelated to financial benefits. "Some just don't want to give up a free lunch with their local banker," remarked an executive at a finance company.

(6) **Involve local managers in the development of the system.** One way to overcome resistance is to confer often with subsidiary management in the early stages and to include their senior staff as directors and members of the vehicle's board. If they are involved in the decision- and policymaking processes, their objections will be voiced with less enthusiasm.

(7) **Visit companies that have already established vehicles.** Some companies adopt this approach, combined with meetings with firms that have reviewed and discarded the relevant treasury vehicle. A related technique is to have one of these companies make a presentation to subsidiary representatives (and senior management) on the advantages and disadvantages of that company's system.

(8) **Bring in an outside consultant.** A treasury manager for a U.S. firm with a newly functioning reinvoicing center noted, "It's a good idea to bring in an outside consultant to help develop the sales pitch. Both the headquarters and subsidiary people are more likely to put faith in an outsider's objectivity."

(9) **Explore the cost benefit.** Perhaps the most important issue for senior management is the net cost benefit. The quantification of the cost benefit of an initial setup and ongoing operation can be used to gain management's attention. To succeed, the expected savings or profit should be substantial. As one cash management expert noted, "Companies have a silver bullet: When does it make sense for management to get involved in setting up something that will save money? It may be $50,000, $500,000, or $1 million, depending on the size of the company. If the project can't save at least that much, it isn't worth the effort. They have more pressing things to look at."

Establishment of the net cost benefit should include the effect of any tax implications—often viewed as the critical element for the successful acceptance of the project. For this reason, tax experts should be involved in the initial phases of the project, because their concurrence will be a driving force in getting the project accepted.

But not all companies conduct cost/benefit analyses. As the treasurer of one firm with a sophisticated factoring operation said, "We did not do a cost/benefit analysis because the benefits were so obvious and the costs so minuscule in comparison."

Overcoming Resistance to a Treasury Vehicle

One of the concerns decentralized companies face is the imposition of centralized control and structured discipline on their subsidiaries. "Our subsidiary managers are very independent and resist any intrusion from corporate headquarters," said a spokesman for one highly decentralized U.S. high-technology firm. "When we asked that they participate in a netting system they raised dozens of objections. But their real concern was that they would lose an element of control over their operations and damage their reputations with local banks." In order for a treasury vehicle to operate successfully, all levels of management must be sold on the concept. The following two cases illustrate how two companies overcame these problems.

Global Cash Management

Selling Headquarters and Local Management.   The assistant treasurer of Company M, a consumer products firm, faced the problem of convincing his company that netting was a valuable cash management tool.

"Going to a bank and getting a netting system, which is only a program, is simple," he remarked. "The difficult part is convincing senior headquarters management and subsidiary managers that they need the system and then implementing the system." The company's four Asian manufacturing sites—Malaysia, the Philippines, Taiwan, and Hong Kong—export their production to six sales subsidiaries in the United Kingdom, France, Italy, Germany, Canada, and Australia. The resulting intracompany transfers are considerable. In addition to sales, the Italian subsidiary manufactures some of the company's larger products and supplies them to the other selling subsidiaries, creating yet another channel of interdivisional cash flow.

"When I joined the company three years ago, I saw that this maze of intracompany transactions was just like a cobweb," commented the assistant treasurer. "We had massive cash flows that were global in nature and not simply concentrated in Europe or Asia or South America, as with many other MNCs. We needed a netting system that could hook these countries together." He soon found that persuading headquarters and foreign management was going to be a long and difficult task. It took a year to design the system, convince management that it was worthwhile, and educate foreign controllers before the system could finally be implemented.

"The first person I had to sell on the system was myself," remarked the assistant treasurer. "I had to run the numbers to be sure that there would be substantial savings and advantages to the system." This took almost six months and required several trips to the foreign subsidiaries to gather the necessary information—information that is generally not readily available. Research was conducted to compile data on which subsidiaries were importing and which exporting; the amount of cash involved; the currency of invoice; the terms of payment; the use of LCs; and the speed at which cash was moving.

With the research figures in hand, the assistant treasurer was ready to confer with the company's bank, a major New York money center bank that was also a leader in supplying cross-border netting systems for MNCs. After reviewing the data provided by the treasurer, the bank was able to confirm that the savings from netting would be substantial.

Convinced of the merits of the system, the assistant treasurer submitted a formal proposal to be reviewed by senior company officials. "Everyone in management had different concerns about the system," said the assistant treasurer. Three were immediately voiced by the corporate treasurer. First of all, what would be the effect on the subsidiaries' borrowing requirements? he wondered. This proved to be a difficult question to answer because the company was changing its product lines and the year-old data he was equipped with would not necessarily apply. "I had to make a lot of assumptions to answer him," the assistant treasurer explained, "but eventually he was convinced that any problems could be handled."

The treasurer's second concern was with the difficulty of imposing a rigid procedure on the subsidiaries' controllers. The assistant treasurer convinced the treasurer that once the advantages they would gain from the system were explained to the controllers, they would gladly go along. He pointed out how the controllers' jobs would be

The Implementation Seminar

After selling the system successfully to fellow managers, the assistant treasurer at Company M had to face the arduous task of implementation. To train local controllers of subsidiaries participating in the netting system, the company held a seminar in London for European controllers and another in Hong Kong for those in Asia. A representative from the coordinating bank ran the London seminar, and the assistant controller moderated the seminar in Hong Kong.

The sessions covered the specifics of the system: the timing, the calendar, the roles of each participant, the information needed. The assistant treasurer was quick to point out that the company needed more information to manage itself than was strictly required for the netting system. "We went way beyond the netting system requirements of the bank, which only concerned itself with cash movements and with communications in a gross sense, e.g., France owes Hong Kong $500,000. We needed a lot more information. France cannot pay Hong Kong unless they have all the proper invoices. We needed a system of communication that went from one participant to the other, identifying the details. They have to identify by invoice exactly what they are paying. We had to decide other issues, such as which currencies would be used for invoicing and what selling terms could be used."

The company nets once a month on a prescribed calendar, with gross cash movement per month of about $15–20 million. Netting reduces cash movement by 50 percent, generating savings to the company estimated at over $100,000 a year.

---

made easier by the netting operation: The system would facilitate cash planning and forecasting, reduce the amount of paperwork involved in paying and receiving invoices, and produce a consistent set of records that would identify all important exports and imports.

The third problem that bothered the treasurer was the effect of government restrictions. The assistant treasurer turned to experts at the bank to resolve this concern. "We went country by country, and they [bank representatives] told us the difficulties involved with each and how they could help us gain government permission to net." For example, the bank's cash management experts pointed out that Italy at that time allowed netting only with special permission, and they knew how to meet the country's requirements. "All I had to do was send our controller to the bank," said a very pleased assistant treasurer. "They showed him the forms and how he could fill them out. It took three months to get permission from the central bank in Italy."

Once the treasurer was sold on netting, the next step was convincing his boss, the CFO. In the words of the assistant treasurer, "We knew what he wanted. It wasn't the savings—it was control. So we just hit on the control issues, showing him how netting would improve his control of global cash movements, invoicing, and shipping." The CFO was delighted and gave his approval.

Next, treasury had to present the arrangement to operating management at corporate headquarters. The biggest issue plaguing this group was transfer pricing. The operations people were concerned that transfer prices might be used to alter and shift profits. The netting system would have no effect on transfer pricing, the assistant treasurer explained, and there were no significant tax considerations. The main selling points for the operating managers was the same as for the foreign controllers: ease of planning and predictability of cash flow.

The CEO also had to sign off on the new system. He turned out to be the easiest to win over. "He just wanted to be sure that other respected companies were using this system," said the assistant treasurer. "The bank gave him a list of their clients and he was sold."

Getting the support of the foreign subsidiary managers turned out to be a considerably longer process, however. Aware of the potential difficulties from the beginning, the assistant treasurer started the ball rolling early. "When I first visited the subsidiaries to gather information, I started a one-on-one relationship with them. I threw the system at them the first time I met them and kept them updated. I asked for their advice and support so that by the time I got the approval from U.S. headquarters I had them pretty much sold on the system." The European managers loved it because they felt that it would ease their borrowing requirements. They would pay only once a month and have to borrow less.

The Asian subsidiaries liked the system because it promised to cut down on the extensive time they had to devote to tracking payments. The assistant treasurer provided an illustration: "Payments going from Italy to Malaysia at times had taken twelve to fifteen weeks and had been known to become lost, requiring numerous man-hours to track down. They were going through so many channels, with instructions that were sometimes less than specific. The idea that they would get in one lump sum everything that was due to them with same-day value was wonderful."

How Company N Sold Centralized Cash Management.   Company N, a U.K. tobacco manufacturer, also had to take an arduous course to gain management support for a new cash management system. The company is set up as a holding company in the United Kingdom, with major subsidiaries in the United Kingdom, Germany, Belgium, and the Netherlands, plus smaller ones in Fiji, Malta, and Cyprus. It imports raw materials from the United States, Latin America, and the Far East. "It's a 365-day market in this industry," the treasurer remarked. "It all depends on where the sun is shining." The corporation was built up through acquisitions in the early 1970s, resulting in what the spokesman called "a loosely formed group of four or five large, independent European manufacturers under the umbrella of a holding company in the United Kingdom." Given its far-flung operations and the subsidiaries' desire for autonomy, the firm, not surprisingly, adopted a decentralized policy for cash management.

But in the late 1970s, the treasurer, who was at the time working in the finance department of the U.K. subsidiary, began experimenting with centralization. "We made sure that our local operations here were pooling funds and matching their currency needs." When the test succeeded, the treasurer took the notion of centralized cash management to the finance staff of the holding company. The treasurer recalled his argument: "We could do this as an international rather than just a U.K.

domestic function. You know: 'What are we doing in the Netherlands, with their forex exposure and liquidity, and what about Germany?' "

But his idea was shot down by the holding company's board of directors, which is made up of the CEOs of each of the companies in the conglomerate. "We ran up against this philosophy, or idea, of an autonomous unit. Each chief executive had a profit center and was responsible for everything. The feeling was, they knew their markets a lot better than we ever would, and what right did we have to delve into their management structure and actually start to wrest decisions away from them?"

There was a ray of hope, however. The board agreed to fund a study by a large U.S. money center bank to determine the potential benefits of a centralized cash management system. After months of research, the bank's consultants found that "each of the operating companies was acting as its own autonomous unit, both importing and exporting and therefore dealing in foreign currencies. And these flows could be matched if they were all pulled together into a central function to alleviate paying grand sums of money to the banking community. What they learned was that the company as a whole was going into the market on the same day on different sides, one company buying dollars and the other selling dollars." Based on an in-depth analysis of the firm's trade flows, the bank estimated that Company N could match 70 percent of its foreign currency inflows and outflows.

Armed with this conclusive information, the spokesman and the bank consultants made a convincing presentation to the board of directors in 1979. "We showed them such a tremendous amount of potential savings and gave them facts that they really couldn't dismiss. In their role as directors, they had to say it was a benefit, it was for the good of the group." Nonetheless, the approval process dragged on for nearly two more years, leaving the treasurer in corporate limbo. "I moved over to the holding company in 1980, and it was a very tough time for me personally, because I wasn't really sure that there would be a job at the end. No one would make the decision to have a centralized treasury function."

The sticking point was the degree of control the directors were willing to concede to the central department. "Some of the directors wanted to reduce us to some kind of advisory council," said the treasurer. As a compromise, the finance staff proposed creating a separate entity for treasury with a board that included each company's finance director, "who reports to the chief executives on the board of the holding company." In addition, they suggested setting up a treasury review committee, made up of the companies' treasurers, which would monitor the operations of the central department. According to the spokesman, "This was the line of least resistance within a structure that philosophically and organizationally just couldn't cope with a central treasury function."

But still the negotiations dragged on. In 1981, the proponents of the plan found a champion in the newly appointed CEO of the holding company. "He came in and needed something to hang his hat on, to make his mark," the treasurer explained, "and this looked like a really good thing to him." Finally, in July 1981, the board gave its approval.

Upon receiving the green light, the finance department quickly proceeded to install

Global Cash Management

an advanced internal reporting system and set up a hybrid reinvoicing/in-house factoring vehicle in the United Kingdom. The savings from this centralized cash management approach have been impressive. Last year, each subsidiary's treasurer was asked to report what he would have done to handle his currency transactions and risks over a six-month period if the centralized treasury system were not in operation. According to the corporate spokesman, "We compared their ideas with what we actually did and figured out that we saved the company about £7 million." As the icing on the cake, the department reduced the annual borrowing costs of the U.K. subsidiary alone by £750,000. "Everyone's happy now. I mean, you can't quibble with the fact that it's saving us a lot of money, can you?"

Cost/Benefit Analysis at Company O

The following is a synopsis of an actual audit and feasibility study conducted for a U.S. MNC. While Company O already operates a multilateral netting system, the study was commissioned to show where additional improvements in cash management could be made. To perform financial functions for its European and North American operations, Company O wanted to establish an international finance company in the United Kingdom—Company O Management Company (MC).

One of the functions of MC would be to act as a collecting and paying agent for its Division A exporters dealing with third parties. A cash management system would be established whereby all receivables could be collected in the accounts of Bank X in the country of the currency being collected. Bank X maintains an extensive global network, with branches in every country of operation. These bank accounts would be monitored by both MC and the exporter, using the bank's electronic banking facility.

Intracompany payments, together with third-party collection payments from MC to each exporter, would be included in the existing multilateral netting system, which would be administered by MC. Payments for imports from third-party suppliers would also be included. Finally, the netting system would be expanded to include intracompany payments from operations in the United States, Canada, and France.

The feasibility study examined six basic savings components and two cost components. The realizable, annualized savings are summarized below:

Component	Savings
(1) Optimized multilateral netting system	$ 29,000
(2) Reduced remittance-processing time by customer and remitting bank	26,000
(3) Reduction in cross-border transfer float by collecting in the country of the currency being collected	46,000
(4) Reduction in cross-border transfer commissions and charges by collecting in the country of the currency being collected	41,000
(5) Use of incoming foreign currencies to source outgoing foreign payments in the same currencies	16,000
(6) Use of interest-bearing collection accounts	8,000
Total estimated annual savings	$166,000

Annualized costs associated with the proposed cash management system are estimated as follows:

Component	Savings
(1) Computer time-sharing charges for accessing Bank X system	$ 17,000
(2) Communication charges (telex, SWIFT) for additional cross-border funds transfers	13,000
Total estimated annual costs	$ 30,000
Total system savings	$136,000

Analyzing the Savings

· **Optimized system savings.** The company's first consideration was to quantify the savings to be gained from expanding the netting system to include the United States, Canada, and France.

There were substantial gains to be made in decreased float and commissions. If these transfers were included in the netting system and made out of Bank X's account, the bank could waive the commissions, generating a savings of $12,330.

The company would also realize a savings on the eliminated float. For example, on payments from France to Germany, the float savings are

$$Ffr52 \text{ million} \times 9\% \times 3 \div 365 = Ffr38,466.$$

At an exchange rate of Ffr5.70:$1, this amounts to roughly $6,750.

The total savings to be realized by the inclusion of these countries was determined to be $17,100. The inclusion of all three countries reflects the incremental savings from the optimized multilateral netting system—savings component 1—of $29,430, rounded to $29,000.

· **Reduced remittance processing.** The value of reducing DSOs is represented as

$$\text{Gross sales} \times 9\% \text{ (cost of funds)} \times 1 \div 365.$$

With sales of $98.25 million, one day's reduction saves approximately $24,000. On average, it was estimated that one half day would be eliminated from the remitter's processing time, based on the bank's experience with other companies. Therefore,

$$\text{Savings} = \$98.25 \text{ million} \times 9\% \times 0.5 \div 365 = \text{approximately } \$12,000.$$

The experience of Bank X has shown that another half day could be eliminated from the remitting bank's processing time. In other words,

$$\text{Savings} = \$98.25 \text{ million} \times 9\% \times 0.5 \div 365 = \text{approximately } \$12,000.$$

So the total savings on remittance-processing time, savings component 2, comes to $24,000.

- **Reduced cross-border float time.** The total cost of float time on cross-border transfers was calculated as

$$\text{Cost} = \text{transfer amount} \times \text{days' float} \times 9\% \times 1 \div 365 \text{ (where the cost of funds is assumed to be 9\%).}$$

Third-party sales in currencies other than the exporter's were determined to be $83 million. Therefore, savings from the elimination of two days' float, savings component 3, amounts to

$$\$83 \text{ million} \times 9\% \times 2 \div 365 = \text{approximately } \$41,000.$$

- **Reduced cross-border transfer charges.** For the German subsidiary, open-account sales transfers ($25.61 million) are received at a branch of a major German bank, where the bank charges a cross-border transfer commission of 0.1 percent. Charges of 0.05 percent at a second bank, Bank Y in Dusseldorf, were eliminated. Therefore,

German bank commission	$ 25,610
Bank Y commission	−12,810
Savings	$ 12,800

The Belgian unit also incurs cross-border transfer commissions. The unit has approximately 720 open-account cross-border sales receivables every year. Each transfer attracts an average commission of Bfr1,000. By receiving collections from the MC unit denominated in Belgian francs once a week, the total number of transfers would be reduced to fifty-two. These fewer, larger collections would be charged an average weekly commission of Bfr8,300. The reduced commissions resulting from fewer transfers was calculated as approximately $8,000 a year.

Under the present system, incoming foreign currency-denominated transfers also attract a foreign exchange commission of Bfr500. Using the same assumptions as above, this commission presently amounts to 720 × Bfr500 = Bfr360,000, or, in U.S. dollars, $10,285 a year. Under the proposed system, payments would be received from MC once a week in Belgian francs, thus eliminating the commissions altogether. Savings: $10,285.

For the German unit, the bank can also halve commissions on drafts and LC collections. With present commissions at $32,220, the Bank Y commission would be $16,110, for a savings of $16,110.

If LCs were collected in Bank Y accounts outside of Belgium, the savings would be as follows:

Eliminated incoming transfer commissions	100 × Bfr300 = $ 860
Eliminated forex commissions	100 × Bfr300 = 860
Savings	$1,720

This brings the total savings for component 4, eliminated transfer charges, to

$$\$48{,}915\ (12{,}800\ +\ 8{,}000\ +\ 10{,}285\ +\ 16{,}110\ +\ 1{,}720).$$

· **Eliminated currency-conversion costs.** By having MC collect receivables and make payments on behalf of the exporters, the expense of converting incoming funds to local currencies and local funds to outgoing currencies would be eliminated. Assuming a .05 percent spread for both buying and selling, savings from eliminated forex charges on incoming-funds conversion (currently $8 million) amounts to

$$\$8\ \text{million}\ \times\ .05\%\ \times\ 2\ =\ \$8{,}000.$$

Eliminated outgoing commissions ($15.39 million at present) amount to

$$\$15.39\ \text{million}\ \times\ .05\%\ =\ \$7{,}700.$$

This brings the total for component five, eliminated forex costs, to $15,700 (8,000 + 7,700).

· **Increased interest on idle funds.** In most locations, the nonresident collection account with Bank X would be interest-bearing. Third-party receivables denominated in foreign currencies to the exporter (currently $57.32 million) would earn interest at an average rate of 8 percent. This brings savings component 6, overnight interest earned, to a total of

$$\$57.32\ \text{million}\ \times\ 8\%\ \times\ 1\ \div\ 365\ =\ \text{approximately}\ \$12{,}563.$$

Incremental Costs.   The bank estimates its costs in two parts. One is an estimated annual time-sharing cost of $17,000, based on $350 per location per month. Four sites are necessary for the system ($350 × 4 sites × 12 months = approximately $17,000).

The other cost increment relates to the increased volume of telex or SWIFT communiques, which the remitting bank must send to carry out the transfer instructions for the netting system. These are around $10 per transfer. Assuming twenty-five bank accounts and one transfer each week from each account, then annual communication costs amount to

$$25\ \times\ \$10\ \times\ 52\ \text{weeks}\ =\ \$13{,}000.$$

This brings the total estimated costs of Company O's communications systems to $30,000 (17,000 + 13,000).

Where to Locate the Vehicle

Choosing the best place to locate a treasury vehicle has been the thorn in more than one treasurer's side. The right location can yield savings on forex and borrowing costs and strengthen the company's negotiating position with banks. But companies that choose the wrong location risk bureaucratic hassles with the central bank, burdensome taxes, and exchange controls. To pick the best location, companies should answer the eight questions in the following checklist.

(1) **Is a subsidiary already operating in the country?** Tapping people and facilities at an existing subsidiary can help reduce start-up and operating costs. "We set up our reinvoicing company in Geneva because we already had a subsidiary in that city serving as our regional headquarters," said the treasurer of a U.S. manufacturing MNC. "Sharing facilities saves us a lot."

(2) **Are labor costs reasonable?** Skilled clerical and financial employees cost more in Switzerland than in most other European countries. Some companies split their operations, maintaining a small staff in Switzerland and a larger staff in another country. However, residence requirements may restrict this strategy: To qualify for resident status, some countries require that more of the management and operational functions be performed in the country of incorporation than in other countries.

(3) **Are banking costs reasonable?** The cost of foreign exchange contracts, funds transfers, borrowing, and maintaining accounts differs by country. For example, banking costs in London are reputed to be lower than those in Switzerland. "We get better rates in the United Kingdom than in Switzerland because there's more competition," noted one financial executive.

(4) **Is the location convenient to a money center?** The vehicle must be either in a major money center country, such as the United Kingdom, or in a country that has good communications with—and is in the same or similar time zone as—a major money center.

This point is especially important to U.S. MNCs. In general, from a U.S. tax viewpoint, such a vehicle could well be located in the United States. But from the perspective of day-to-day operations, obtaining and acting on information for Europe on a timely basis with only a two- or three-hour communications window is extremely difficult.

Compounding this difficulty is the fact that the window opens late in the operating day of the financial markets in Europe. Thus, practical requirements usually lead to the establishment of a vehicle in the same time zone in which it is going to operate, unless a company intends to establish a twenty-four-hour treasury function.

(5) **Is the country's financial infrastructure adequate?** The country should have a financial infrastructure capable of absorbing big transactions and providing good communication. The banks must be able to offer accounts denominated in a number of different currencies for the collection of third-party receivables, payments to third

Performance-Evaluation Implications

A key to successful implementation of a treasury vehicle is making sure that the system used to evaluate performance fairly reflects the activity and the vehicle. The performance of both the participating subsidiaries and the vehicle itself must be evaluated.

Evaluating Subsidiaries

Generally, MNCs with decentralized financial decision making evaluate subsidiary performance, including interest expense and foreign exchange gains or losses. Progress toward a centralized treasury function inevitably involves revising the criteria for evaluating subsidiaries.

One step in this direction is to monitor local-currency profitability before interest expense and foreign exchange gains or losses. This simple approach, however, can lead to problems in ensuring efficient use of capital. For example, working capital requirements often increase as subsidiaries come to see extension of credit terms to third parties as a costless marketing tool.

To minimize these problems, many centralized MNCs impose direct quantitative controls on working capital. Less frequently, MNCs develop a "notional" capital charge based on the corporation's consolidated cost of capital. This charge is then applied to the subsidiary's total capital assets, regardless of the actual capital structure of the legal entity, and performance is evaluated net of notional interest expense.

A common problem encountered when MNCs centralize treasury functions is the resistance of subsidiaries to the loss of perceived profitable activities. One way of overcoming this resistance is by using the actual or notional distribution of profits accruing to the centralized treasury vehicle. "We charge [subsidiaries] less than the market cost of borrowings for funds we send them and give them part of the profits of the center," remarked a financial director of a Geneva reinvoicing center.

Performance evaluation must be tailored to the way a company operates and according to how responsibility is allocated. As one financial executive said, "You have to look at what the subsidiary is doing and what the treasury vehicle is doing and whether the performance-evaluation system correctly delineates their responsibilities. If it doesn't, you have a problem. You need consistency."

Some subsidiary managers are very pleased that the treasury vehicle has removed exchange exposure from their books. "Our subsidiary managers were delighted with the reinvoicing center," said the assistant treasurer of a U.S. manufacturing company. "The picture for the local managers has actually improved. I mean, their foreign

---

parties, and intracompany movement of funds. These accounts will be required to support foreign exchange transactions.

Most companies choose to locate these multiple-currency operating accounts in a major money center, usually London, even though the vehicle may be incorporated

currency payables and receivables could move any number of cents in a day, and your poor subsidiary manager would show up with a loss or a profit—all depending on the rate. Now he doesn't have this headache. It's the reinvoicing center's problem."

But the issue is not that simple. Many executives do not realize that the treasury vehicle does not remove exchange exposure from the subsidiary; it simply shifts it to operating exposure. That is, the subsidiary may not show transaction exchange gains and losses, but the costs of these movements will be reflected in selling prices and costs. A treasury vehicle will pass on the cost of hedging to the subsidiary in the local-currency price of the goods. According to a cash management consultant, "Ninety-nine times out of 100, the reinvoicing center does not absorb the risk. It reprices the risk out and sends it back to the marketing or manufacturing company.

"If a company used to treat exchange gains and losses as below-the-line items when evaluating a subsidiary's performance," he added, "the subsidiary will in fact be more accountable for currency movements because it will be in the operating margin. Before, an Italian manager might say that he has no control over his deutsche mark imports because he sells in lire. Now, his life can become more complicated because he will have less control over his gross margin." Subsidiary managers have to make sure that the use of transfer pricing is not distorting their performance.

Evaluating the Vehicle

Along with adjusting their system of evaluating subsidiary performance, companies must evaluate the performance of the treasury vehicle itself, given that it has centralized certain financial functions. Firms should determine whether the vehicle has brought about the benefits the initial studies indicated. In assessing its performance, all the benefits that arose during the cost/benefit analysis should be examined. A key measure is the firm's gains resulting from having the reinvoicing center manage investments and borrowings, as opposed to having the subsidiaries handle these functions. The vehicle's performance in exposure management can be measured against a fully hedged position, an unhedged position, and a best rate.

A related issue concerns operating the treasury vehicle as a profit center. The choice depends largely on where the company wants its profits. "Do you want to make a profit in a vehicle or profit by having a vehicle?" is how one cash management expert explained it. "Setting up a vehicle may save the company $2 million a year, but most companies would not want to keep $2 million in a Swiss reinvoicing center. They set it up so that the money is passed back to benefit the company. Under Subpart F, you'll get taxed on the profits at the center. Frequently, in order to sell the operating units on the treasury vehicle, you have to give them part of the benefit."

---

in another country. The vehicle's ability to use offshore bank accounts will be one of the considerations in choosing its country of incorporation.

(6) **What tax rate will apply to the vehicle?** A key factor influencing the location of a company's treasury vehicle is the local corporate tax rate. Belgium, for example,

has attracted companies wishing to establish finance and factoring companies by allowing ten-year tax holidays for such firms. Various cantons in Switzerland have low corporate tax rates, which remain attractive even when combined with the federal tax.

Tax considerations may also depend on the tax status of existing subsidiaries in that country. For example, a company might want to set up a highly profitable treasury vehicle in a country where a subsidiary is losing money so that the profits of the vehicle offset the losses of the subsidiary, thus minimizing local taxes. On the other hand, if the treasury vehicle suffers losses, they could be offset against the profits of the operating company.

(7) **How will the tax-treaty network affect withholding taxes?** More important than the local tax rate is the network of tax treaties in a country. According to a financial executive of one reinvoicing company, "Our goal is to make sure there are tax treaties that will reduce withholding taxes on payments of interest, royalties, and license fees."

Traditionally, a number of countries with low or nonexistent corporate tax rates have been used to site financial vehicles. "Brass plate" companies with no actual substance can be established in these tax havens, with all management and operational functions performed offshore. Certain governments, however—notably those of the United States and the United Kingdom—are looking closely at companies, headquartered in their countries, that shelter taxes in this way. For this reason—and to a lesser extent because of the negative publicity that surrounds the issue—many companies are looking to establish finance vehicles in countries such as Switzerland or Belgium, whose tax authorities tend to scrutinize less closely.

(8) **Are exchange controls flexible?** Forex regulations should be flexible at the least and nonexistent if possible. "Since the reason for establishing our vehicle was to increase our options and flexibility, it was important that we locate in a country with few restrictions," said a financial executive of a manufacturing firm that uses a reinvoicing center.

Using a local tax or legal expert will improve the chances for a quick resolution to any problems with the central bank. One alert firm looking to set up a treasury vehicle in Belgium used the same Belgian tax firm that was currently drafting the country's new laws governing coordination centers.

Another problem many MNCs face once the treasury vehicle is set up is restrictions on moving payments across national boundaries. If a manufacturing company's plant is located in a country other than the treasury vehicle's country, these movements can be blocked by exchange controls. However, even countries with relatively tight exchange controls can be flexible when dealing with companies that generate exports and employ many nationals. "Rules are meant to be bent on a case-by-case basis," counseled one cash management consultant.

Global Cash Management

A good way to get around this problem, according to one treasurer, is to use your leverage with local labor unions. Employing nationals in manufacturing means that the unions will be willing to go to bat for you with local officials to get the restrictions eased, especially if you make clear to the government that maintaining the operation (and local employment) depends on having access to the treasury vehicle.

Appendix

Cash Management Regulations in Twenty Key Countries

Argentina

Hold Accounts

- Foreign currency held locally by residents.
- Residents may hold forex time deposit accounts in the form of negotiable CDs for a minimum period of sixty days.
- Foreign currency held abroad by residents. Residents may hold forex time and demand deposit accounts abroad.
- Local currency held domestically by nonresidents. Interest-bearing time deposit and non-interest-bearing demand deposit accounts are allowed.
- Foreign currency held domestically by nonresidents. Interest-bearing time deposit and non-interest-bearing demand deposit accounts are permitted.

Leading, Lagging, and Netting

- Advance payments for exports may be received up to 360 days prior to shipment. But for exports stipulated in Law 21453, advance payment may be received only 180 days before shipment.
- Advance payments may be made for up to 5 percent of the free on board (f.o.b.) value of a list of capital goods imports costing between $50,000 and $2 million. Leading of larger amounts requires prior approval by the Central Bank.
- The Central Bank does not approve netting operations. Payments for traditional exports (e.g., grains) must be made either in advance or upon shipment when they are covered by irrevocable LCs. However, payments for priority exports may be lagged for up to 180 days from the shipment date unless longer terms are allowed under government financing arrangements.
- Import payments for noncapital goods must be made no more than 120 days after

delivery, with the exception of those originating in countries belonging to the Latin America Integration Association (LAIA). Imports from these countries must be paid in ninety days unless the product is on a list of LAIA-negotiated goods (which consists of several thousand items). In the latter case, the settlement is immediate. The central banks of the LAIA countries settle these payments quarterly. LCs, previously hard to obtain, are now available.

Australia

Hold Accounts

· Foreign currency held locally by residents. No restrictions.
· Foreign currency held abroad by residents. Funding of foreign currency accounts must comply with tax-screening requirements where there are prescribed transactions with residents of designated tax havens.
· Local currency held in Australia by nonresidents. A$ accounts may be held locally by nonresidents, overseas incorporated companies, foreign banks, and foreign governments, and by overseas offices of Australian incorporated companies and overseas offices and agencies of Australian banks.
· Foreign currency held in Australia by nonresidents. No restrictions.

Leading, Lagging, and Netting

· Leading and lagging of payments are permitted for export purposes, as well as for capital transactions. No exchange formalities apply. Netting is also freely permitted.

Belgium

Hold Accounts

· Foreign currency held locally by residents. Export proceeds and invisible receipts convertible at the official rate can only be used for similarly convertible import or other payments. Interest-bearing fixed deposits can be neither withdrawn nor rolled over and have a maximum term of thirty days. However, interest-bearing demand and time deposits convertible at the financial rate may be held freely.
· Foreign currency held abroad by residents. Residents may hold funds eligible for the financial rate in demand and time deposits abroad, but not funds convertible at the official rate, such as export proceeds or related receipts.
· Local currency held locally by nonresidents. Nonresidents may hold funds convertible at the official rate in interest-bearing demand and time deposits.
· Overdraft accounts are not permitted.

- Foreign currency held locally by nonresidents. Nonresidents can hold interest-bearing demand or time deposits convertible at the financial rate for use in remittances abroad.

Leading, Lagging, and Netting

- Export proceeds must be surrendered within eight days of receipt, or deposited in a controlled foreign currency account.
- Import lags are possible for unlimited periods. However, to change the lagging period, special permission from the Belgo-Luxembourg Exchange Institute (BLEI) is necessary and may be withheld.
- The bilateral netting of financial transactions is freely allowed.
- Netting of trade transactions, however, requires BLEI approval.
- No netting of trade against financial transactions is permitted.

Brazil

Hold Accounts

- Foreign currency held in Brazil by residents.
- Borrowers with outstanding foreign loans may hold interest-bearing dollar accounts indefinitely in the Central Bank. Interest equivalent to the LIBOR rate is paid monthly.
- Foreign currency held abroad by residents. Residents are permitted to hold bank accounts abroad with prior authorization and must declare these on yearly income tax returns.
- Local currency held in Brazil by nonresidents. Nonresidents may open a bank account in Brazil if the funds result from local remuneration or a transfer from abroad made via a bank.
- Foreign currency held in Brazil by nonresidents. Nonresidents may not hold foreign currency in a Brazilian bank.

Leading, Lagging, and Netting

- Payment delays of 180 days to eight years are allowed in Brazil for foreign durable goods, raw materials, and capital equipment.
- Prepayment of imports is not generally allowed.
- Export lags require official permission. The Central Bank requires that market interest rates be paid.
- Prepayment of exports is permitted with no limits in Brazil.
- Prepayment of at least 15 percent of the value of goods is required when the credit terms of a transaction exceed two years.
- Bilateral netting is forbidden.

Canada

Hold Accounts

· Foreign currency held locally by residents. No restrictions apply.
· Foreign currency held abroad by residents. No restrictions apply.
· Local currency held in Canada by nonresidents. No restrictions apply.
· Foreign currency held in Canada by nonresidents. No restrictions apply.

Leading, Lagging, and Netting

· Leading and lagging of export and import payments are allowed.
· Bilateral and multilateral netting are permitted.

France

Hold Accounts

· Foreign currency held locally by residents.
· Exporters, importers, or traders operating in France may keep unlimited forex balances but must notify the Banque de France of annual transactions with foreigners exceeding Ffr5 billion.
· Residents must prove that total cash and forward purchases are less than or equal to their future currency spending.
· Foreign currency held abroad by residents. Exporters, importers, and traders may hold forex abroad freely but must notify the Banque de France if the amount exceeds Ffr5 billion.
· Local currency held locally by nonresidents. Nonresidents may hold francs in interest-bearing demand and time deposit accounts in France.
· Foreign currency held locally by nonresidents. No restrictions.

Leading, Lagging, and Netting

· Export leads face no restrictions, while imports can be covered forward for three, six, or twelve months, depending on the currency. Exporters, importers, and traders face no restrictions on lags. For others, nonallocated foreign currency over Ffr 50,000 (except ECUs) held abroad must be repatriated and converted in three months.
· Bilateral netting is allowed for residents who regularly hold forex abroad.

Germany

Hold Accounts

· Foreign currency held locally by residents.
· Residents may hold foreign currency in Germany in interest-bearing demand and time deposits, inclusive of ECU deposits.
· Foreign currency held locally by nonresidents. Nonresidents may hold deutsche marks in interest-bearing and time deposit accounts.
· Local currency held locally by nonresidents.
· Nonresidents may hold Dm in interest-bearing and time deposit accounts.
· Foreign currency held locally by nonresidents. Interest-bearing time and demand deposits are allowed for all foreign currencies, including ECUs.

Leading, Lagging, and Netting

· No restrictions.

Hong Kong

Hold Accounts

· Foreign currency held locally by residents. No limitations.
· Foreign currency held abroad by residents. No limitations.
· Local currency held in Hong Kong by nonresidents. No limitations (nor is authorization to remit principal or interest abroad required).
· Foreign currency held in Hong Kong by nonresidents. No limitations (nor is authorization to remit principal or interest abroad required).

Leading, Lagging, and Netting

· Leading and lagging of export and import payments are allowed without restrictions. Both bilateral and multilateral netting are freely permitted.

Italy

Hold Accounts

· Foreign currency held locally by residents. Only certain types of forex accounts may be held by residents, basically for commercial purposes in itemized cases. Interest-bearing demand and time deposit accounts are also allowed.

- Local currency held locally by nonresidents. Nonresidents may hold lira. Interest-bearing demand and time deposits are allowed.
- Foreign currency held abroad by residents. Residents are permitted to hold forex abroad only for commercial purposes in itemized cases. Interest-bearing demand and time deposit accounts are also allowed.
- Foreign currency held locally by nonresidents. Nonresidents may hold forex in Italy. Interest-bearing demand and time deposits are allowed.

Leading, Lagging, and Netting

- No restrictions apply to import leading or lagging. Bilateral netting is allowed for any type of transaction.

Japan

Hold Accounts

- Foreign currency held locally by residents. Approval for these accounts is automatic if they are held in authorized forex banks. Interest-bearing demand and time deposit accounts are allowed.
- Foreign currency held abroad by residents. Authorization is necessary, but all types of accounts are allowed.
- Local currency held domestically by nonresidents. Approval is automatic if the accounts are held in authorized forex banks.
- Foreign currency held domestically by nonresidents. Approval is automatic if the accounts are held in authorized foreign exchange banks. Interest-bearing time deposit and non-interest-bearing demand deposit accounts are allowed.

Leading, Lagging, and Netting

- Export and import leads and lags are allowed for up to 360 days. Prepayments of plant equipment, however, can be made up to three years in advance. Longer credit terms require prior approval. Bilateral netting requires prior authorization from the Ministry of Finance (MOF) and the Ministry of International Trade and Industry (MITI); multilateral netting is not permitted.

Korea

Hold Accounts

- Foreign currency held locally by residents. Both individuals and corporate residents can hold unlimited amounts of foreign currency.

- Foreign currency held abroad by residents. Korean firms and private citizens may maintain foreign currency accounts abroad through their overseas branches.
- Local currency held domestically by nonresidents. Nonresidents may hold checking and demand deposit accounts.
- Foreign currency held domestically by nonresidents. Nonresidents may freely withdraw money from their foreign currency accounts. They may not deposit foreign currency from "unclear domestic sources" and withdraw it later.

Leading, Lagging, and Netting

- Export leads are limited to 120 days. In addition, leading of export payments into Korea is limited to 1 percent of total annual exports for large companies and 6 percent for small and medium-sized companies.
- Import leads of up to 360 days are allowed.
- A lag period of 360 days is allowed for exports. Longer periods of up to three years have been allowed when finance is provided by a reputable bank.
- A sixty-day lag period is generally allowed for imports. Lags are limited to thirty days for imports from Japan, Taiwan, the Philippines, and Hong Kong.
- Netting is allowed between local foreign-invested firms and their parents, between overseas branches of Korean firms and their head offices, and between foreign firms located in Korea's free-export zones and their home offices.

Mexico

Hold Accounts

- Foreign currency held locally by residents. Resident companies may hold forex. The minimum deposit is $5,000, and the dollars must come from abroad. Payments from these accounts can only be made abroad.
- Foreign currency held abroad by residents. Residents may open forex accounts abroad.
- Local currency held locally by nonresidents. Nonresidents may hold local currency accounts in time deposit and non-interest-bearing demand deposit accounts. The minimum time deposit is P100,000.
- Foreign currency held locally by nonresidents.
- Nonresidents, except for diplomatic missions and foreign correspondents, cannot hold forex locally.

Leading, Lagging, and Netting

- A 10 percent advance payment at the controlled rate is allowed on imports. A 20 percent advance payment is permitted on long-term import credits. Advance payment for exports is allowed without limits. Bilateral or multilateral netting between companies is not permitted.

Netherlands

Hold Accounts

· Foreign currency held locally by residents. No restrictions. Interest-bearing demand and time deposit accounts are available.
· Foreign currency held abroad by residents. No restrictions. The central bank must be notified.
· Local currency held domestically by nonresidents. Nonresidents may hold guilders in interest-bearing time and demand deposit accounts.
· Foreign currency held domestically by nonresidents. No restrictions. Interest-bearing demand and time deposit accounts are available.

Leading, Lagging, and Netting

· No restrictions. Bilateral and multilateral netting is permitted, although all netting transactions must be reported to the central bank.

Spain

Hold Accounts

· Foreign currency held locally by residents. Residents are not allowed to keep forex locally worth more than P50,000 unless authorized. Spanish exporters are allowed to hold bank accounts in forex.

Leading, Lagging, and Netting

· The lagging of export payments in Spain is limited to thirty days from the agreed-upon payment date. Proceeds must be converted into pesetas with fifteen days of receipt.
· Import leads and lags are restricted to thirty days from the agreed-upon payment date. If payments are delayed beyond invoice terms, the subsidiary cannot pay interest unless it received authorization.
· Permission is needed for bilateral and multilateral netting.

Sweden

Hold Accounts

- Foreign currency held locally by residents. While resident companies may hold foreign currency accounts without authorization, interest is paid without limit only on accounts held by shipping and insurance companies. For other companies, interest is payable for a maximum of sixty days.
- Foreign currency held abroad by residents. Sveriges Riksbank (Bank of Sweden) approval is needed before companies—other than shipping or insurance companies—can hold foreign currency abroad.
- Local currency held locally by nonresidents. Non-interest-bearing deposit accounts are allowed without authorization.
- Foreign currency held locally by nonresidents. Interest-bearing deposit accounts are permitted without authorization.

Leading, Lagging, and Netting

- Leading and lagging of payments are permitted for export and import purposes within customary terms of trade. Otherwise, permission is required. Bank of Sweden approval is required for bilateral and multilateral netting of financial transactions and multilateral netting of trade transactions. Bilateral netting of trade transactions does not need prior authorization.

Switzerland

Hold Accounts

- Foreign currency held locally by residents. Interest-bearing demand and time deposit accounts require no authorization.
- Foreign currency held abroad by residents. No limitations.
- Local currency held by nonresidents. Interest-bearing demand and time deposit accounts need no authorization.
- Foreign currency held locally by nonresidents. Interest-bearing demand and time deposits are allowed without permission.

Leading, Lagging, and Netting

- Leading, lagging, and bilateral and multilateral netting are freely permitted and widely practiced by Swiss-owned and foreign firms.

Taiwan

Hold Accounts

- Companies may hold interest-bearing foreign currency demand and time deposit accounts without authorization. No foreign currency checking accounts are available.
- Foreign currency held domestically by nonresidents. Nonresidents may hold foreign currency bank accounts in Taiwan.
- Foreign currency held abroad by residents. Residents are allowed to hold foreign currency bank accounts abroad.
- Foreign currency held domestically by residents. Residents are permitted to hold foreign currency bank accounts in Taiwan.
- Local currency held domestically by nonresidents. No limitations.

Leading, Lagging, and Netting

- Payments for both imports and exports may be led or lagged by 360 days. No prior approval is required. Netting has been allowed since the removal of exchange controls in 1987.

United Kingdom

Hold Accounts

- Foreign currency held locally by residents. Residents may hold foreign currency in the United Kingdom in interest-bearing demand and time deposit accounts.
- Foreign currency held abroad by residents. No limitations.
- Local currency held domestically by nonresidents. Sterling interest-bearing demand and time deposit accounts are allowed.
- Foreign currency held domestically by nonresidents. Interest-bearing time and demand deposits are allowed.

Leading, Lagging, and Netting

- No restrictions.

United States

Hold Accounts

· Foreign currency held locally by residents. No restrictions.
· Foreign currency held abroad by residents. No restrictions.
· Local currency held locally by nonresidents. Nonresidents may hold U.S. dollars in interest-bearing time deposit and non-interest-bearing demand deposit accounts.
· Foreign currency held locally by nonresidents. Nonresidents are not permitted to hold foreign currency in the United States.

Leading, Lagging, and Netting

· Freely permitted.

Venezuela

Hold Accounts

· Foreign currency held locally by residents. Local bank accounts may not be denominated in foreign currency. However, some Venezuelan banks have offshore affiliates that permit companies to maintain foreign currency accounts abroad and manage them directly from Venezuela.
· Foreign currency held abroad by residents. Residents may hold foreign currency abroad.
· Local currency held domestically by nonresidents. Interest-bearing time deposit and non-interest-bearing demand deposit accounts are allowed.
· Foreign currency held domestically by nonresidents. Interest-bearing time deposits and non-interest-bearing demand deposit accounts in foreign currencies are not allowed.

Leading, Lagging, and Netting

· Exporters are allowed to sell their export dollars on the free market for exports that occurred after March 13, 1989. Multilateral and bilateral netting are permitted.